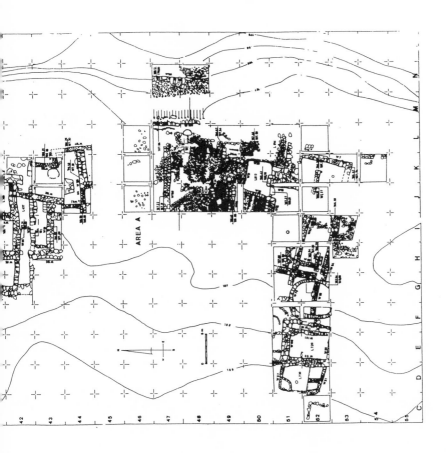

Bethsaida

THE BETHSAIDA EXCAVATIONS PROJECT
REPORTS & CONTEXTUAL STUDIES
GENERAL EDITORS
RAMI ARAV AND RICHARD A. FREUND

THE BETHSAIDA EXCAVATIONS PROJECT (BEP)
is a consortium of faculty, staff, and students from
The University of Nebraska at Omaha, USA
Truman State University, USA
Michigan State University, USA
The University of Munich, Germany
Wartburg College, USA
Dana College, USA
The Graduate Theological Union, USA
Rocky Mountain College, USA
The Jerusalem Center for Biblical Studies, USA

ASSOCIATED FACULTY
Director of Excavations · Rami Arav
Chief Geologist · John F. Shroder
Chief Geographer · Michael Bishop
Project Coordinator · Richard A. Freund
Mark Appold · John T. Greene · Jeffrey Kuan
Heinz-Wolfgang Kuhn · John J. Rousseau · Fred Strickert

ASSOCIATED STAFF
Sandra Fortner · Delvin Hutton · John Mark Nielsen
Elizabeth McNamer · Toni Tessaro
Monica Blizek · Teresa Castellhano

BETHSAIDA

A CITY BY THE NORTH SHORE OF THE SEA OF GALILEE

Edited By
Rami Arav and
Richard A. Freund

VOLUME ONE
Bethsaida Excavations Project

Thomas Jefferson University Press
Kirksville, Missouri
1995

Copyright ©1995
The Thomas Jefferson University Press
at Truman State University
Kirksville, Missouri, 63501-4221 USA

Library of Congress Cataloging-in-Publication Data
Bethsaida Excavations Project Reports and Contextual Studies.
    p.   cm.
    Includes bibliographical references and indexes.
    Contents: v. 1. Bethsaida : a city by the north shore of the Sea of Ga-
lilee / edited by Rami Arav and Richard A.Freund
    ISBN 943549-30-2 (casebound) ISBN 943549-37-X (paperback)
    1. Bethsaida (Extinct city) 2. Excavations (Archaeology)—Israel—
Bethsaida (Extinct city) 3. Bible—Antiquities. 4. Rabbinical literature—
History and criticism. I. Arav, Rami. II. Freund, Richard A. III. Bethsaida Excavations Project Reports and Contextual Studies.
    DS110.B476B48   1993
    933—dc20   94-41015
                                                     CIP

Contents

PART I

ARCHAEOLOGY AND GEOLOGY OF BETHSAIDA

PART 2

LITERATURE OF BETHSAIDA

Figures, Plates, and Tables

Abbreviations

AJBA	*The Australian Journal of Biblical Archaeology*
AJSL	*The American Journal of Semitic Languages*
ANEP	*The Ancient Near East in Pictures Relating to the New Testament.* Ed. James Bennett Pritchard, 2d ed. Princeton, N.J.: Princeton University Press, 1969
AS	*Anatolian Studies*
AW	*Antike Welt*
BA	*Biblical Archaeologist*
BAR	*Biblical Archaeology Review*
BASOR	*Bulletin of the American Schools for Oriental Research*
BCE	Years before Common Era. Equivalent to BC dates of modern Western convention. Add 2,000 years for BP or CE date equivalency.
BJPES	*Bulletin of the Jewish Palestine Exploration Society*
BiMes	*Bibliotheca Mesopotamica*
BM	*Beth Mikra*
BP	[Years] Before the Present
CE	Common Era. Equivalent to AD dates of modern Western convention
EI	*Eretz-Israel*
EKKNT	Evangelisch-Katholischer Kommentar zum Neuen Testament
ESI	*Excavations and Surveys in Israel*
FRLANT	Forschungen zur Religion und Literatur des Alten u. Neuen Testaments
HA	*Hadashot Arkheologiyot [Archaeological Newsletter]*
HNT	*Handbuch zum Neuen Testament*
HTKNT	Herder's theololgischer Kommentar zum Neuen Testament
IEJ	*Israel Exploration Journal*
JAOS	*Journal of the American Oriental Society*
JEA	*The Journal of Egyptian Archaeology*
JNES	*Journal of Near Eastern Studies*
LA	*Liber Annos*
LÄ	*Lexikon der Ägyptologie*
MDAIR	*Mitteilungen des Deutschen Archaeologischen Instituts, Römische Abteilung*
MeyerK	H. A. W. Meyer, Kritisch-exegetischer Kommentar über das Neue Testament
NEAEHL	*The New Encyclopedia of Archaeological Excavations in the Holy Land.*
MT	Masoretic Text

NT	New Testament
NTD	Das Neue Testament Deutsch
OA	*Oriens Antiquus.*
OBO	*Orbis Biblicus et Orientalis*
OIC	*Oriental Institute Communications*
OIP	*Oriental Institute Publications*
OT	Old Testament
PEFQSt	*Palestine Exploration Fund, Quarterly Statement*
PEQ	*Palestine Exploration Quarterly*
QDAP	*The Quarterly of the Department of Antiquities in Palestine*
RB	*Revue Biblique*
RLA	*Reallexikon der Assyriologie*
RSF	*Rivista di Studi Fenici*
RSO	*Rivista degli Studi Orientali*
SBS	*Stuttgarter Bibelstudien*
THKNT	Theologischer Handkommentar zum Neuen Testament
VT	*Vetus Testamentum*
WMANT	Wissenschaftliche Monographien zum Alten und Neuen Testament
ZDPV	*Zeitschrift des Deutschen Palästina-Vereins*

BETHSAIDA: A City by the North Shore of the Sea of Galilee

ERRATA AND CORRIGENDA, VOLUME I

The following errata/corrigenda either were missed in proofreading or resulted from emendations by the editors or contributors after printing.

Page no.	For	Read
Chapter by Rami Arav		
7, line 14	bounders	boulders
19, line 2	(II-VIII)	(III-VIII)
19, line 14	(pl. II.1, p. 37)	(pl. III.1, p. 37)
22-23 *Add:* Fig. 14. Hellenistic-Early Roman Courtyard		House at Area B,
the so-called "Fisherman House"		
25, line 28	(pl. X.3)	(pl. IX.3)
26, line 2	X.4	X.1
26, line 19	70.1	LXX.1
28, caption	*omit* "an anchor"	
33, line 3	sickles	pruning hooks
33, fig. 21	sickles	pruning hooks
33, line 8	*Please omit reference to fig. 22*	
34, Fig. 22	Strigilis	Weaving Shuttle
35, No. I.4	Mouth Jar	Bowl
43,	*Legends IX.2 and IX.3 should be reversed*	
44, table	nos. X.4, X.5, X.6, X.7	nos. X.1, X.2, X.3, X.4
47, table	XII.1 *and* XII.2	XIII.1 *and* XIII.2
62, n. 2	A. Major	A. Mazar
63, line 18	Major, A.	Mazar, A.
Chapter by John F. Shroder Jr. and Moshe Inbar		
85, line 32	optile	apatite
86, table	Geganya	Deganya
Chapter by Sandra Fortner		
100, line 12	(pl. IX.2)	(pl. X.2)
100, line 13	(see no. 6)	(pl. IX.36)
100, line 23	(pl. IX.1)	(pl. X.1)
101, line 14	(pls. II.1)	(pls. I.1)
101, line 17	(pls. 1.3-4 and IX.1-2)	(pls 1.3-4 and X.1-2)
101, line 24	(pls. I.3, IX.1-2)	(pls. I.3, X.1-2)
102, line 31	(pls. IV.15-16; X.2)	(pls. IV.15-16; XI.2)
102, line 32	(on Eastern Sigillata A)	(no Eastern Sigillata A)
104, line 14	(pls. VII.30-34)	(pls. VIII.30-34)
104, line 16	(pl. VII.31)	(pl. VIII.32)

Continued

Page no.	For	Read

Chapter by Sandra Fortner *continued*

Page no.	For	Read
104, line 17	(pl. VII.30) & (pl. VII.33)	(pl. VIII.30) & (pl. VIII.33)
104, line 19	(pl. VII.31)	(pl. VIII.31)
104, line 20	(pl. VII.30)	(pl. VIII.30)
104, line 20	(pl. VII.33)	(pl. VIII.33)
105, line 11	(pl. VIII.35)	(pl. IX.35)
105, line 19	(pls. VIII.37, ix 3)	(pl. IX.37.xii.3)
105, line 35	(pls. VIII.38, xi.4)	(pls. IX.38.xiii.4)
108. illus.	I.3.ix.I.3	I.3.x.1.2
111, illus	IV.15.x.2	IV.15.xi.2
115, illus. VIII.32	dar red	dark red
115, illus	VIII34.xi.1	VIII.34.xii.1
116, illus.	IX.37.xi.3	IX.37.xii.3
116, illus.	IX.38.xi.4	IX.38.xiii.4
121, line 3	IX	XIII
126, line 45	Dr. Monika Burnett	Dr. Monika Bernett

Chapter by Toni Tessaro

135 & 136, figs. 7 and 8 *Please reverse the drawings*

Chapter by Baruch Brandl

Page no.	For	Read
142, line 32	υραευσ	υραευς
148, line 19	*Kingdoms Samal*	*Kingdoms. The Aramaic Kingdoms Samal*
148, line 38	Tarsus.	The Kingdom of Que.
149, line 25	el-Biyaza	el-Biyara
149, line 27	*lqyhw*	*hlqyhw*
149, line 28	*lmbthyhw*	*lmbthyhw*
154, n. 71	Herbordt 1991	Herbordt 1992
155, n. 105	*Add before* Yeivin 1978:	Mazar and Cornfeld 1975: 179.
156, no. 107	Mazar and Cornfeld 1975: 179	Rabin 1982. col. 387
161, line 49	_____, and C.H.B. Altman	Loud, G., and C.H.B. Altman
164, line 23	*Orient 29*	*Orient 27*
165, line 46	Khorsahad	Khorsabad

Chapter by Rami Arav

Page no.	For	Read
200, n. 2	[page no.] 55	[page no.] 60
201, n. 17	[page nos.] 1–49	[page nos.] 27–29

Page no.	For	Read

Chapter by John T. Greene

Page no.	For	Read
226, nn. 24, 26	1979-1981	1983
226, n. 26	197	1981
226, line 32	1892	1982
226, lines 34, 36	1892	1983
227, line 11	1987	1981
227, lines 31, 32	JSP	The Jewish Spectator

Chapter by Heinz-Wolfgang Kuhn

Page no.	For	Read
246, line 15	εἰς τὸ πέραν προς	εἰς τὸ πέραν πρὸς
247, line 15	θαλάσσηs	θαλάσσης
254, n. 15	ἔσται ἤ	ἔσται ... ἤ
255, nn. 20, 21	1921	1968
255, n. 24	Ibid., 78	Kuhn and Arav 1991, 78
255, n. 25	Ibid., 53-54	Theissen 1992, 53-54
255, n. 30	Grundmann 1896	Grundmann 1986
	Schweizer 1898	Schweizer 1986
256, line 4	des Johannes	nach Johannes
256, line 10	omit "reprinted 1972"	

Chapter by Mark Appold

Page no.	For	Read
242, line 11	21: 99-121.21	21: 99-121

Chapter by John J. Rousseau

Page no.	For	Read
266, line 33	Navich	Naveh

Chapter by Richard A. Freund

Page no.	For	Read
274, lines 14, 17, 18, 20	ציידו	ציידן
274, line 21	צידו	צידון
274, line 22	ביציידו and ציידו	ביציידן and ציידן
274, line 30	בציידו	בציידן
274, line 35	בציידו	בציידן
275, line 10	ר 'יוסי בר 'ציידין	ר' יוסי בר' ציידין
275, line 11	ר 'יוסי ברבי בצידן	ר' יוסי ברבי בצידן
275, line 12	רבי יוסי בביציידן	רבי יוסי בביציידן
275, line 13	ר 'יוסי בר 'ציידין	ר' יוסי בר' ציידין
283, line 21	בצידן מעשה	מעשה בצידן
303, map caption	Cities	Roads
304, line 35	sometimes	Sometimes
305, line 48	sandran	sadran
305, line 49	נאלפלף	פלפלן
307, nn. 35, 36	These footnotes are reversed	

Continued

Page no.	For	Read

Chapter by Richard A. Freund *continued*

309, n. 64	Actgs	Acts
310, line 21	Ziv	Zvi
311, line 33	Rabbinowitz	Rabbinovicz

Bibliography

315, lines 27-30	ירושלמי: שקליס ו'ב'.	ירושלמי: שקלים ו'ב'.
	קוהלת רבה : ב' ,יא'.	
	משנה, עבוה זררה : נ'ז'.	משנה, עבורה זרה: נ'ז'.
	ש'ר חש'ר'ס רבה : א'.	שיר חשירים רבה: א'.

316, line 10 *The correct title of Bargil Pixner's article is:* "Searching for the New Testament Site of Bethsaida"

Indexes

323, col. 2	EXTRA-CANONICAL	RELATED MATERIAL
	Pseudepigrapha	Related Material

324 *Please ignore Index of Rabbinical Writings; it is flawed.*

328, col. 2	צ[יידין, 275-277	[ב]צ[יידין, 275-277
329, col. 2	בצידון	בציידן
334, col. 2	*Omit:* paralells: Tel Anafa, 101	
334, col. 2	*Please combine* Kefar Hananya *references*	
335, col. 1	(מאסה) בסידנ	Maaseh Bethsaida

Foreword

B ETHSAIDA HOLDS THE DUBIOUS DISTINCTION of being one of three towns targeted by Jesus for ultimate divine condemnation, and for being compared unfavorably with those notorious pagan cities of Tyre and Sidon (in a Q saying preserved in Matt. 11:20-24 and Luke 10:13–15). While the demise of Bethsaida was not as dramatic as the prophetic pronouncement, the life of that city nevertheless came to an end in 67 CE when it was besieged and captured by the Roman armies under the command of Vespasian and Titus after being attacked earlier by rebel Jewish forces under the command of Josephus and his subordinate Jeremiah. It was the curious fate of this strategically located and amply populated town of the first century CE to be lost, not only in time but also in space.

Most of the places mentioned in the Gospels and early Christian literature have been tracked down, identified, memorialized, and monumentalized with churches and other commemorative structures by indefatigable pilgrims and travelers—whether correctly or mistakenly—especially after the Roman Empire adopted Christianity, but Bethsaida is barely mentioned by any of them, and then is lost to view once more. It was not until the nineteenth century that serious efforts were made to locate this important site. After all, Bethsaida is mentioned in all four Gospels and must have played a significant role in the earliest traditions of the ministry of Jesus and his disciples. Most if not all of the disciples came from the area, and some of them were natives and citizens of Bethsaida itself (Peter, Andrew, and Philip at least). The general location around the Sea of Galilee was known, and the eminent Biblical scholar and explorer Edward Robinson identified the site with reasonable accuracy. Nevertheless, it is only in the last few years and as a result of the current excavations at et-Tell and exploratory probes at two neighboring sites that a true picture has emerged and the city of Bethsaida has been restored to reality, if not to an actual and active existence.

Any tell or artificial mound is an acceptable objective for serious archaeological research, but the value of the undertaking is enhanced if the place can be named and identified with a real city known from ancient records. Careful digging and appropriate assembly and analysis of the recovered material objects—from common pottery shards to exquisite works of art, from ordinary dwellings to great public buildings (including temples and palaces), from simple tools and weapons to inscribed coins and written documents—can supply significant background information about such places during the time of their occupation, supplementing and filling in the picture described and reflected in extant records.

The current enterprise is a worthy attempt to restore to its rightful place in the long story of the Holy Land an important town of the Galilee or the Golan (the exact extent of each district remains in dispute), and more particularly to the time when the movement—later to be known as Christianity—began in a restricted area around the Sea of Galilee. In spite of voluminous written sources about the Holy Land of the Greco-Roman period and the extensive excavations of numerous sites in the region of the Galilee–Golan, little is known of the ordinary life of the small and midsized Jewish communities in the first century CE. More information is always welcome. It is the Jewish life of these villages and towns, some of which had mixed populations, that needs to be recovered as well as that of the more distant and cosmopolitan centers. Of all the towns and villages mentioned in contemporary sources, Bethsaida offers exceptional opportunities for exploration and excavation because it was depopulated later in the first century and then abandoned entirely and forever by the time of the late Roman period—a boon and a blessing for archaeologists.

Already numerous gains can be reported from the ordinary results of excavation; the normal and typical activities of the town can be recovered. The reconstruction of the life of the Jewish community is an achievable objective, and with it a clearer understanding of the Judaism proclaimed and practiced in Bethsaida and other towns in the vicinity. It was in this area that Jesus began his public ministry and gathered his disciples, who came from and belonged to the same villages and towns. It was in Bethsaida that "mighty works" were initiated, and where immediate controversy followed, leading to the ominous pronouncement cited above. The more we learn and know about life in the Galilee–Golan and its towns and villages in the first century CE, the better we will understand the Judaism of that time and place as well as the elements that produced and increased the tensions between one group of Jews and another, ultimately leading to the historic breach between persons and communities.

The nexus in the first century that makes Bethsaida a place of abiding and absorbing interest to the people of the Book is, however, not the only significant moment in the life of the different cities that occupied the site. Bethsaida was settled long before the Greco–Roman period, all the way back to the Bronze Age. This is hardly surprising because Bethsaida is located strategically near both the Sea of Galilee and the famous Via Maris. During the Iron Age, Bethsaida served as a trading post in the Northern Kingdom of Israel. We can presume that the settlement was a victim of the Assyrian conquest in the latter part of the eighth century BCE. The period of greatest population and activity was the Greco–Roman, stretching from the third and second centuries BCE until the latter part of the fourth century CE. Only when all the life stories of these cities are told, when all the pieces of the jigsaw puzzle for each of them are assembled, or—to use a more appropriate image—when all the tiles and tesserae of the mosaic have been put in their proper places, will the task of exploration, excavation, and examination be completed.

A word about the organization and personnel of the Bethsaida Excavations Project is also in order. A rich opportunity to practice the new archaeology has presented itself, and the leadership of the Bethsaida Excavations Project has taken full advantage of it. We are a long way from the days of Sir Flinders Petrie and one-man archaeology, and even the best and most brilliant archaeologists now operate in teams. The team assembled for this expedition includes experts from the United States, Europe, and Israel; it is impressive for its breadth and depth and it ensures that every stone and pebble and clump of dirt as well as every artifact will receive a full measure of attention and be recorded in exhaustive catalogs. Coordinate and ancillary disciplines are fully represented in the staff, and they will wring all available information out of the mound and its remains. When they are finished with their labors we will know more about the city that disappeared from time and space than we know about many cities that have been with us all the time.

David Noel Freedman

University of California, San Diego
Summer 1994

Preface

I N 1838, the prominent American Edward Robinson explored the northern shores of the Sea of Galilee with only a compass, for there were no scientific maps of the area except those of Napoleon on which the Sea of Galilee was represented in quite an imaginary state. Robinson climbed the largest mound there, which was nameless and called simply et–Tell ("the mound"). After a thorough exploration of the site, he suggested that this was perhaps Bethsaida. Fifty years later, the German scholar Gottlieb Schumacher conducted a survey in the same region. Schumacher doubted that an area located two kilometers from the seashore could have been the site of the fishing village mentioned in the New Testament, and he suggested alternatively two other ruins on the shoreline, el–Araj and Ma-sudiyeh, as possible sites for Bethsaida. Thus the question remained unsettled until our excavations were begun in 1987.

On top of the complication created by et–Tell being far from the shoreline, literary evidence is none too helpful for defining the precise location of the city. While Josephus states in *Wars* 2.9:1 that Bethsaida is located in the lower Golan near the estuary of the Jordan River, the writer of John 12:21 claims that Bethsaida is situated in Galilee. From this confusion arose a long subsidiary debate of whether there are two Bethsaidas or only one. Many compromises were offered, the latest one presented by Bargil Pixner, "Searching for the New Testament Site of Bethsaida," *Biblical Archaeologist* 48 (December 1985), who suggests two Bethsaidas, one at et–Tell and the other at el–Araj, while the Jordan River was shifted to a course between the two sites. In fact, none of the scholars tried to solve the problem by archaeological methods, perhaps because the area was inaccessible to them .

THE BETHSAIDA EXCAVATIONS

The Bethsaida Excavations project was launched in 1987 on behalf of the Golan Research Institute as a probe into the two main contenders for the site of Bethsaida: et-Tell and el-Araj. The probes made it clear that et-Tell is a mound that contains a settlement which dates to the first century CE. The probes made it equally clear that El-Araj and Masudiyeh date only from the Byzantine period, with nothing underneath. Apparently Robinson was correct in 1838!

Since 1988 the site has been excavated extensively, first under the sponsorship of the University of Haifa, and from 1991 under the Bethsaida Excavations Project (BEP), a consortium administered by the University of Nebraska at Omaha, whose membership is listed on page ii of this volume.

DEVELOPMENT OF THE PRELIMINARY REPORTS

This volume is the result of a group of scholars invited to participate in a symposium on Bethsaida at a conference of the International Society of Biblical Literature in Münster, Germany, 28 July 1993. Issues raised in the symposium helped to shape the material presented here and also led us to invite contributors who were not at the conference to submit their research results.

In this volume the evidences of antiquity are divided into two major parts: Archaeology and Geology of Bethsaida and Literature of Bethsaida. Because of the great link between the spiritual and intellectual achievements of humankind and the material culture in which those developments took place we trust that each part will inform and elucidate the other. When we go to the writings of the Hebrew Bible, the New Testament, and Rabbinic literature we can get certain pictures of the literary and religious communities at the northern shores of the Sea of Galilee. The spiritual leaders whom we know from the texts were well rooted in their own society and in the material culture of their environment. We do not expect to discover the history of the literary texts as we uncover Bethsaida, but we do uncover some of the story of daily life, of insignificant things of the times when great spiritual ideas were shaped and these ideas were preserved in writing.

The silent evidence uncovered at Bethsaida may lead us in new directions and help us to read the texts anew. For example, we learn that Bethsaida is much older than we thought. What we know about Bethsaida from history and literature is only about half of the story of that site. We now know from the large amount of material finds that et-Tell was inhabited during the Iron Age. The presence of a large, thick wall and a large public complex from this period leads us to assume that it may have been a major Iron Age city. Bethsaida seems to confirm the thesis of Rami Arav that most of the Hellenization of this region came by way of the Romans.

In Part 1, Archaeology and Geology of Bethsaida, Arav presents a brief preliminary report on the Bethsaida excavations through 1993. This report renders a glimpse of the finds of the dig and offers a general notion of the physical remains of the site. Five additional reports offer more details of the project. The geological and geographical work of John F. Shroder Jr. and Moshe Inbar provides an important step in establishing the parameters of the archaeological research and continues a long geomorphological research on this area done by Inbar. Shroder and Inbar offer hypotheses for the regular fluctuations in the level of the Sea of Galilee and its relation to the et-Tell site. Sandra Fortner and Toni Tessaro help to fix the variety of vessels and the chronology of the Bethsaida site by providing details of the Hellenistic and Roman fineware and cooking pots that were found during early stages of the excavation and by comparing them with finds from other sites.

Several unique finds were made in the early stages of the Bethsaida excavation. Baruch Brandl reports on the unusual Israelite bulla (clay seal) discovered in 1989; Fred Strickert discusses the importance to Bethsaida's history of the unique coins minted by Philip, son of Herod the Great, which were discovered in 1992 (and which have been discovered at only three other sites).

In Part 2, Literature of Bethsaida, six scholars demonstrate how the evidence found thus far at Bethsaida can modify our understanding of the texts and offer strong arguments for the authenticity of Bethsaida references in the New Testament and Rabbinic literature. Rami Arav uses the archaeological evidence from et-Tell together with the rendering of place-names around the Sea of Galilee as they appear in the Masoretic Text, in two versions of the Septuagint, and in the Vulgate to offer a suggestion for a new reading of those place-names and suggests what the nature of this place was during the Iron Age. John Greene uses the archaeological and geographical evidence from Bethsaida together with that from Gamla to discuss the military significance of et-Tell and the way Bethsaida has been regarded by Josephus and others.

Heinz–Wolfgang Kuhn reviews the archaeology of et-Tell together with modern exegesis of New Testament references to Bethsaida in a discussion of the story of Jesus' feeding of the multitude and the extent of Jesus' activity at Bethsaida. Mark Appold discusses the mighty works of Jesus that are associated with Bethsaida by the New Testament and other traditions and the likelihood of Bethsaida's being a site of early Christian activity. John Rousseau provides insights into the New Testament story of the healing of the blind man at Bethsaida and the story's authenticity. Finally, Richard A. Freund offers a rich study and analysis of the changes in names for the site, the forms of New Testamentt and Rabbinic archaeology and literature, and some Rabbinic descriptions of Bethsaida.

To correlate Biblical and ancient literary accounts with archaeological and geological information is not easy. To be sure, earlier in this century Biblical archaeology of ancient sites was sometimes done with certain theological agendas. In this volume care has been take to employ a text–critical approach to literary and religious texts related to the Galilee and Golan, an approach clearly informed by analysis of shards and other physical data.

Despite the obvious importance of the site, little systematic literature has been written about Bethsaida. A bibliography of early and late literature related to Bethsaida is included in this volume. The reader needs to be reminded that much information in encyclopedias and atlases comes from popular and religious speculation or nonsystematic studies.

We trust this volume will find wide acceptance by archaeologists, Biblical scholars, historians, and others interested in the Bethsaida site. We look forward to compiling other preliminary findings and studies in future volumes.

Acknowledgments

S INCE 1989, THE STATE OF ISRAEL officially has recognized et-Tell as Bethsaida on maps of the area, and excavations have continued since then. The Golan Research Institute and the University of Haifa sponsored the first four seasons of probes and excavations. In 1989, university students and faculty from the Omaha, Nebraska, area became involved in the probes. In 1991, a group of international faculty met at Kibbutz Gadot in the Galilee and formed the Bethsaida Excavations Project. Since 1991 the project has been sponsored by the international consortium of university faculty known as the Bethsaida Excavations Project (BEP). This consortium is administered by the University of Nebraska at Omaha (UNO), and presently includes Dana College, The Graduate Theological Union, Jerusalem Center for Biblical Studies, Michigan State University, Northeast Missouri State University (now Truman State University), Rocky Mountain College, The University of Munich, and Wartburg College. Other institutions including Albertson College, Doane College, St. John's University, and the United Theological Seminary have participated in the excavations. Rami Arav is the director of excavations and a member of the International Studies faculty at UNO. The BEP consortium had its Israeli base of operations for the excavations at Kibbutz Gadot in the Galilee until 1995. BEP teams and subgroups are headed by faculty from associated universities; designated faculty are directors, supervisors, and summer excavation staff. Students of BEP institutions and unaffiliated individuals represent the major financial and year-round support and coordination of the project. The Israel Tourism Corporation (starting in 1994) contributes significantly to our excavation budget. Major fund-raising and grant writing responsibility as well as academic supervision of the project rests with UNO, the associated universities, and the BEP directors and supervisors.

The present excavations are a five-year project (1992 to 1996) at Bethsaida that was developed under the auspices and with the support of UNO's Departments of International Studies, Philosophy and Religion, and Geology and Geography. It is funded by private and public sources and was undertaken in conjunction with other university faculty worldwide; it is licensed by the Antiquities Authority of Israel. In 1994, the Israel Tourism Corporation awarded $300,000 (approximately 1 million New

Israeli Sheqels) to the project to help ensure that the site could be excavated in a timely manner and to help the project prepare the site for visitors.

We express our gratitude to the Jewish National Fund and in particular to Mr. Amos Harpaz for their enthusiastic and generous support of the dig. We thank the Golan Regional Council and especially the vice chairman, Mr. Itzhaq Wiseman, for their support and confidence in the project from its start.

A laboratory for processing pottery and restoring finds by students and staff was established at Kibbutz Gadot after the summer of 1991 and was staffed year-round in three-month and six-month shifts by university students. Prior to 1991, trained individuals such as artist Tom Goeke of Chicago, Illinois, and John Mark Nielsen of Dana College donated their time on behalf of the project to help with the drawing of maps and pottery and other tasks associated with data collection. From 1991 onward, students and staff usually apprenticed first in Israel and then continued to process and restore finds and make drawings of them at Kibbutz Gadot. The work of some dedicated individuals is worthy of mention: UNO students Mike and Therese Homan first set up the laboratory with Toni Tessaro in 1992 and were followed by Bruno and Teresa Castellhano, Rick and Denise Baesler, Sandra Fortner of the University of Munich, and Beth Seldin Dotan, a graduate student at the University of Nebraska at Lincoln, who began in the fall of 1994. At the present time, the finds of the dig are housed at Beit Yigal Allon in Kibbutz Ginnosar. We thank the museum staff for their kind hospitality, and in particular Mrs. Nitza Kaplan

The Bethsaida Excavations Project (BEP) extends special thanks to the Dean of International Studies and Projects Thomas Goutierre, who has supported the BEP from its inception in 1990 and has provided support—both financial and moral—and staff for the project. Grant money, which was crucial in the initial stages of the project's development, was provided for some of the staff and faculty through the UNO Committee on Research.

Monica Blizek, departmental secretary of the Department of Philosophy and Religion at UNO, who served from 1991 to 1994 as the U.S.A. administrative assistant to the project, has ensured that the thousands of letters received in connection with the excavations were answered in a timely fashion and was responsible for the word processing of the manuscript of this volume. The chairman of the Department of Philosophy and Religion, Professor William Blizek, did yeoman's duty over the past five years in the areas of fund-raising, scheduling, and staffing. He was instrumental in the creation of the Bethsaida Exhibition of Antiquities at the UNO Fine Arts Building gallery. The exhibition was the culmination of the first five years of our association with the Bethsaida excavations. A committee which includes Jeanette Bauer, Robert Bodnar, Rami Arav, William Blizek, John Shroder, and Richard A. Freund was formed to present the first exhibition of Bethsaida antiquities for the public; Robert Bodnar was commissioned to design and develop the display. Funding for the exhibition was provided by longtime supporters of Bethsaida-related activities in Nebraska, including the University of Nebraska Foundation, Nebraska Humanities Council, the Henry Monsky Lodge of B'nai B'rith of Omaha, the regional office of B'nai Brith, local service clubs, and private individuals. In particular, the BEP thanks the chancellor of UNO, Dr. Del Weber, for supporting the excavations, the exhibition, and its gala opening hosted by Nebraska's Governor E. Benjamin Nelson, Omaha's Mayor P. J. Morgan, and UNO's Chancellor Weber.

The BEP officially acknowledges the State of Israel and especially the Antiquities Authority of Israel, directed by Amir Drori, for help and insight during the past five years of excavation and for facilitating the 1994 Bethsaida exhibition of antiquities.

The project was housed at Kibbutz Gadot in the Galilee between 1991 and 1994. This kibbutz helped immeasurably in the progress of our excavations through their goodwill and assistance in setting up laboratories and helping to acquire equipment necessary for the excavations. The project thanks the people of Kibbutz Gadot and especially Tuvia Urbach, the bed and breakfast coordinator at the kibbutz; Ruchi Milrad, the kibbutz bed and breakfast daily director; Victor Freedman, the gardener and unofficial historian at Kibbutz Gadot, who introduced students and faculty to kibbutz life; and Arnon Yaari, the BEP administrator in Israel through December 1994. We owe a debt of thanks to Father Bargil Pixner, whom we lovingly call "the [spiritual] father of Bethsaida," for his personal support and attention. His yearly visits to the site and his continued interest in the excavations at Bethsaida have provided our students with reading material and insights.

Some of the maps in this volume were produced by Marvin Barton, staff cartographer in the Department of Geology and Geography at UNO. Laurel Mannen, Judaic Studies Administrator at the University of California, San Diego, and Risa Levitt Kohn, a Ph.D. candidate in Biblical studies at the University of California, San Diego, organized manuscript materials and provided important insights. Shamim Khan Nielsen, the present coordinator of the project at UNO also helped shepherd the book through the computer.

David Noel Freedman, Professor of Biblical and Judaic studies at the University of California, San Diego, first heard some of our research papers at conferences of the Society of Biblical Literature and graciously consented to write the foreword to this volume. We thank Dr. Robert V. Schnucker, director of The Thomas Jefferson University Press at Truman State University, for guidance in the publication process, and the TJUP associate editor, Paula Presley, who edited the volume for publication and wrote the indexes.

Part I

Archaeology and Geology of Bethsaida

Rami Arav

Bethsaida Excavations: Preliminary Report, 1987–1993

T HE MOUND OF BETHSAIDA is situated north of the Sea of Galilee, at the northern center of an alluvial plain known as Beteiha (see facing page and endpapers).[1] The oval-shaped mound, one of the largest sites near the Sea of Galilee, is an extension of the lava flow that formed the Golan Heights (see fig. 1). The mound is 400 meters long by 200 meters wide; its highest point is 165.91 meters below sea level; it rises approximately 30 meters above its surroundings and is approximately 45 meters above the Sea of Galilee. On a clear day, there is an excellent view of the entire sea from atop the mound.

The mound is divided into two distinct areas, presumably into a lower city, which constitutes most of the site, and an upper city, which is at the northeastern edge. Excavations have been made at the site of the upper city only. The eastern slope of the mound descends steeply into a short ravine that separates the mound from a natural hill of boulders and large rocks. The southern and the western sides of the mound slope gradually to the Beteiha (Bethsaida) plain. Access to the mound is easiest from the north, where it extends from the basalt plateau that forms the Golan Heights. Although the Jordan River runs only 250 meters west of the mound, the inhabitants of Bethsaida used water from two springs in the foothills at the sides of the mound. The larger spring is in a southwest foothill, and the smaller is in the southeast.

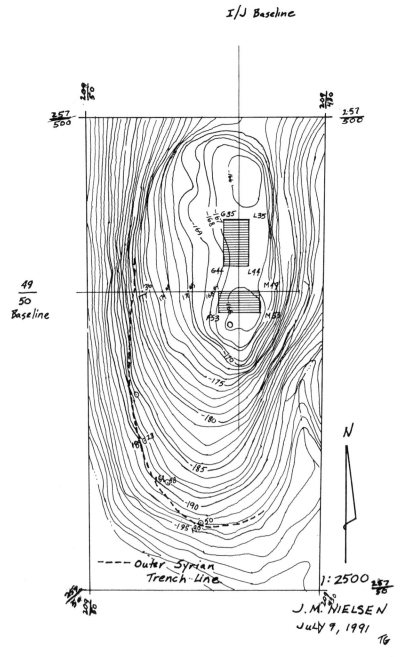

Fig. 1. Topographical plan of Bethsaida, showing the upper city at the northeast of the mound and the surveyors' baselines

EXCAVATIONS IN AREAS A, B, AND C, 1987 TO 1993

Three areas were designated for the excavations. Area A, at the south, was designed to contain two sections, one on the eastern steep slope extending to the western moderate slope, and the other in a north–south direction extending to the southern edge of the upper city. North of Area A are Areas B and C, which were planned to be large-area excavations to obtain insight into the settlement patterns and city planning of the site.

Before the results of the excavations are discussed, it is important to describe the difficulties of digging in a site such as this. Settlers on the basalt terrain usually made extensive use of the abundant basalt stones and boulders. While basalt provided strong and durable buildings, it creates great difficulties for the archaeologists who excavate them. Not only are basalt construction blocks heavier than equivalent limestone blocks, but basalt can be used over and over again for centuries without any obvious erosion and without losing its maximal construction qualities. So it happens that basalt architectural elements or even entire structures may exist and be reused for a millennium or longer. This creates difficulties in establishing the stratigraphy of a site. Sometimes it may happen that structures which were built centuries apart are found almost at the same elevation.

Other difficulties at Bethsaida involve the state of preservation of level number 2, the Hellenistic–Early Roman level. Level 1, on top of it, represents primarily a destruction level. Bethsaida's proximity to the main roads makes the site accessible to stone looters. Beginning already with the Late Roman period, houses at the site were dismantled and carted off to other sites. The outer face of wall number 62 in Area A was peeled off and its stones taken away. Elaborate stones that were found scattered in small numbers far outside any known architectural context are testimony of this phenomenon. Excavation provides archaeological evidence that points to the existence, during the Middle Ages, of large pits that presumably served as limestone kilns for burning the limestone of the site into plaster. Large pieces of limestone which had apparently been fired in a kiln are at the site.

From the seventeenth to the twentieth centuries, the mound served as the home of the Bedouin tribe of El-Talawiyeh. Tribe members built humble structures and buried their dead around their sheik's tomb on the slope of the hill. Dozens of tombs were discovered during the excavation seasons. They did not, however, create any major stratigraphic problems. They were excavated only superficially; outside of the damage caused by the graves themselves, the remaining area was unharmed. However, many of the remains at the site had been destroyed by Syrian military installations which were constructed there from the 1950s to 1967. These installations contain underground bunkers, military mortar positions, zigzagging trenches across and along the edges of the mound, and major earthworks made by the leveling and sloping of large areas. Considering all this, it is easy to understand why the upper level at the site would not yield optimal remains, and why any substantial retrieval should almost be considered another miracle of Bethsaida. Seven levels of occupation have been discerned thus far:[2]

Level 1   All material discovered from the Middle Ages (ca. 500–1500 CE) to the present.

Level 2   Four phases of occupation between the Early Hellenistic period and the Early Roman period (333 BCE–67 CE).

Level 3   Remains of the Babylonian and Persian periods (586–333 BCE).

Level 4   Iron Age IIC (III; 720–586 BCE).

Level 5   Iron Age IIB (925–720 BCE).

Level 6   Iron Age IIA (1000–925 BCE).

Level 7   Early Bronze Age (3050–2700 BCE).

Selected finds from Areas A, B, and C are discussed in the following sections.

Area A

The upper ridge of the mound is built upon two peaks, with a saddle in between. Area A (fig. 2) is on the southern peak. We suspect that the saddle is a result of major leveling that took place during the Middle Ages.

The Iron Age in Area A

The excavations revealed, in levels 4 through 6, partial remains of a massive structure. The structure was built in level 6 and has undergone alternations during the subsequent levels. It is noteworthy that during the Hellenistic period in level 2 there were still a few walls of the building in use. During the lifespan of level 6, the structure contained a single large room that measures 21.2 by 11.5 meters. A large segment of the northern wall was excavated, and it includes an elaborate entrance to the structure (in square J51). This entrance is 1.65 meters wide and is flanked by two heavy jambs built by large bounders (fig. 3, W10, W25). In this section it is preserved to a height of 1.5 meters. An enormous threshold measuring 1.3 by 1 meter was discovered at the entrance. Heavy slabs inside the structure suggest remains of a floor. The eastern side of the wall next to the entrance contains a series of offsets. The first offset is 1.2 meters east of the entrance, where the wall is recessed 0.4 meter; the second is 3.15 meters from the entrance where the wall is recessed 1.7 meters. The corner of the building is 8.1 meters away from the entrance. The entire northeastern wing of the building was of substantial construction, 2.85 meters thick and built from large boulders.Thickening in this wing may be evidence of a tower location. The east wall (W7) is poorly preserved and the entire width has yet to be ascertained. The west wall (W68) is in much better condition; it measures 1.10 meters wide. The south wall (W64) was found in fair condition. In squares H–I 53 the wall was covered by a Hellenistic floor, which indicates that it went out of use during that period. A pit in square G52 near the corner of W68 and W64, dug in the Hellenistic period, supports this conclusion. The northwest corner has not been excavated, but its location is quite clear. The southwest and the southeast corners are obvious. However, further excavations at this area will be made to determine the entire size of this building. Two column parts, probably belonging to this structure, were discovered near and inside the building. One is a column base of a nonclassical order that was found in a secondary use (in square I51; fig. 4) It measures 0.53 meter in diameter and 0.4 meter high. The other is a column end that was discovered in a Hellenistic pit inside the building (in square I52) which measures 0.6 meter in diameter and

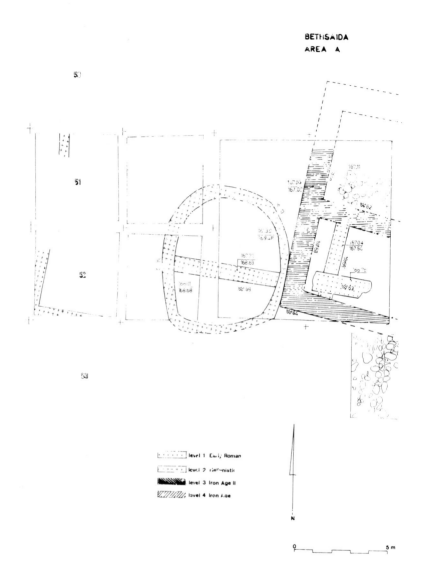

Fig. 2. Plan of Area A (1993)

Rami Arav

Fig. 3. Area A, showing the facade (J50) of the public building and entrance

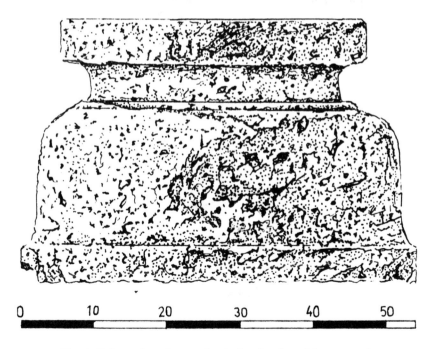

0　　　10　　　20　　　30　　　40　　　50

Fig. 4. Column base in nonclassical order, found in a secondary use.
BEP photo by Anne Lynan; drawing by Dawn Tipka

0.5 meter high. Based on the architectural finds discovered thus far, the monumental appearance of the building, the column base, and the column end, together with a figurine wearing the *atef* crown and the stelae in front of the entrance (see below), we propose that the building could have been a temple or perhaps another *Bit Hilani* structure

A few alterations were made in the building in level 4. A partition wall (W62) divided the main room of the building in to two sections. This wall is 0.95 meter wide, and except for a section in the axis of the entrance that was destroyed by a Syrian military trench, it was preserved almost to its entire size. Stones from the wall were looted in antiquity, and only the lower course is preserved to the entire width. It is assumed that this wall may have changed the function of the structure, although the original function of the structure is uncertain.

In front of the structure there is a large plaza, paved with good masonry, which extends toward Area B at the north (fig. 5). The plaza, which was discovered only a few inches below the surface, reaches the level of the threshold of the main building and belongs to level 5 or 6. The later upper layers were presumably removed in the modern period. A wall (W150) was discovered at a distance of 17 meters north of the entrance. The top of the wall is in the same level as the plaza; it seems to have gone out of use when the plaza was paved, and belongs to level 6. The pavement of the plaza near this wall was preserved to two layers, indicating long usage and a repair.

A short distance from the gate of the monumental building, in front of the tower and on the plaza pavement, there was a row of basalt stones in vertical position, resembling the Biblical *Matzevot* (מצבות) stelae (fig. 6). Next to it was a thick layer of a burned wooden beam, suggesting the presence of an *Asherah*. During the 1993 excavation season, a canal was discovered under the pavement of the plaza. The canal started at a wall running in the plaza and ended at the *Matzevot* area (fig. 7).

The eastern side of the plaza ended near a thick wall interpreted to be the city wall (W160 and W161). The wall was built of large boulders and measures, at squares M47–48 and N47–48, some 8 meters (fig. 8). It is possible, however, that this wide wall was a tower. Further excavations should make this point clear. The area in front of the monumental building (squares J50–K50) was altered during the late phase of Iron Age II. A large, shallow pit had been excavated into the plaza and was supported by revetment walls (W20, W21, W22). It measures approximately 4.5 meters square. The floor of the pit is paved with plaster and was found filled with pottery shards.

Fig. 5. Large paved plaza of good masonry in front of the structure, extending towards Area B at the north

Fig. 6. A row of basalt stones in vertical position in the plaza

Fig. 7. A canal under the Iron Age pavement, starting at a wall that runs in the plaza and ends at the *Matzevot* area

Fig. 8. Eastern face of city wall, formed of large boulders, at square N47

The Hellenistic and Early Roman Periods in Area A

As a rule, the Iron Age remains were covered with a red material made of burned clays and ashes. This material was discovered in all areas and presumably functioned as filling and leveling for the terrain so that an even infrastructure could be laid at the Hellenistic level. Presumably segments of the Iron Age structure were left above the red filling and reused during the late Hellenistic period. Wall 65 (in square H52), which measures 0.70 meters wide, and the remains of a floor (at square H51) dating from this period, discovered near its west end, indicate longtime usage of this part of the Iron Age building. Most of the Hellenistic walls were 0.70 meters wide. A small structure measuring 3 meters by 4 meters (perhaps a small tower) that was built over the plaza (W98) and a wall (W95) that runs to the building were among the finds from this period. During the Roman period few modifications were made to this wall.

West of the main building, the Iron Age remains descend abruptly, perhaps because of the Iron Age retaining wall that supported the upper structures. At this point an oval structure built with massive boulders was discovered (W70). It measures 6.8 meters by 5.5 meters. This structure had a partition wall 0.90 meter wide in the center. The oval house, dating from the Hellenistic period, was perhaps used as a granary. Only a few structures were discovered west of the granary. Whatever is still there was once composed of thick walls built from large boulders. An opening in one wall (W90) led to a room that was perhaps roofed. The purpose of these structures is not yet clear. In addition, many pits were dug into the Iron Age levels (levels 5 and 6) during the Hellenistic period. The pits contained discarded pottery, bones, and architectural elements. Among the most interesting finds in the pit was a shard of pottery of a Red Figure style vase. The shard is so fragmentary that it is impossible to decipher the painting (fig. 9).

Iron Age Finds in Area A

The following is a description of selected items that were discovered through the years.

Pottery. The pottery from Area A (pls. I and II) includes vessels from Iron Ages IIA and IIB. Because of stratigraphic disturbances, it was not possible to obtain clear and clean loci of either Iron Age IIA or IIB. The Hellenistic-Early Roman loci were easier to observe; even so, many of the loci produced significant amounts of mixed pottery. Plates I and II presents the varieties of Iron Age pottery that were discovered.

Fig. 9. Shard of pottery showing a fragment of Red Figure style vase
found in a Hellenistic pit

FIGURINE. A clay figurine with *atef* headgear (fig. 10) was discovered in
locus 588, which is within the public building. The clay figurine is reddish
and contains basalt grits. It measures 6 centimeters in length, 3.2 centimeters in width, and is 2.5 centimeters thick. The figurine is a mold cast, and
presents the head of a male wearing a tall crown with a thick knob at the
end, perhaps representing a precious stone. The situation of the neck
shows that the head was attached to an entire figure, which is lost. The
crown, adorned with two feathers, is a type that was known in the Ammonite kingdom during the ninth to seventh centuries BCE. and may represent a god or a king.[3] This identification is based on the interpretation of
2 Sam. 12:30, "The crown, which weighed a talent of gold and was set with
a precious stone, was taken from the head of [the Ammonite god, or
Malkam, their king], and placed on David's head."

OSTRAKON. An Aramaic ostrakon (fig. 11) was discovered west of the massive structure. The locus where it was discovered is not fully excavated and
the precise purpose and date of this locus are still uncertain. The ostrakon
bears four letters in an Aramaic script, incised on a large part of an Iron
Age vessel. The reading of the inscription is: עקבא, meaning Aqiba. Professor Y. Naveh proposed that this is a proper name.[4] The Aramaic name for
the root עקב is the root for the proper name יעקב (Jacob). It should be

18   *Rami Arav*

remembered, though, that in the north Sea of Galilee there is a place
known as *Aqabiya*, which is mentioned in a Byzantine inscription from
the synagogue of Hamat Gader and is identified with Kefer Aqeb, about
seven kilometers southeast of Bethsaida.[5]

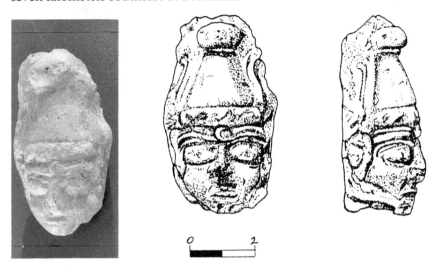

Fig. 10. Clay figurine with *atef* headgear

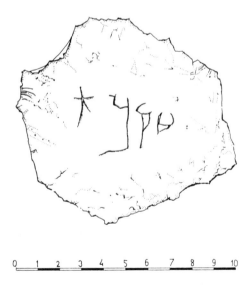

Fig. 11. Ostrakon bearing the name *Akiba*

Hellenistic and Early Roman Finds in Area A

Pottery. Late Hellenistic and early Roman pottery (pls. II–VIII) is divided into common ware and fineware (pls. VI.2,3 and VII.4). In many excavations common ware is considered to be local, and fineware is frequently considered to be imported. Recent research suggests, however, that this is not always the case. Fineware was often produced locally or within a periphery of 100 kilometers, and common ware may have been carried with travelers. Plates III–VIII presents only a small number of selected finds from Area A. The entire range of the discovery will be presented in the final report. The earliest Hellenistic finds are black Athenian pottery and oil lamps which date to the mid-fourth century BCE. The latest finds are from the Early Roman period and are the so-called Herodian oil lamps. Among the pottery presented in pl. III.1 notice the large Late Hellenistic pilgrim flask (pl. II.1, p. 37), which is made of very fine clay. Similar vessels were discovered in a Late Hellenistic tomb in Hagoshrim (northeast upper Galilee; unpublished) and in Hazor (vol. 1, pl. LXXIX.13), and ascribed to level I, Hellenistic period. Noteworthy also is a well-fired gray ware juglet with a spout, perhaps an oil lamp filler (pl. VII.4, p. 41).

Clay Seal. The seal (fig. 12) measures 2 centimeters by 2 centimeters. It is made of clay and has a truncated pyramidal handle. A hole is pierced at the handle. The bottom of the seal is incised to be pressed against clay. The incisions do not render a clear picture. If our interpretation is correct, it shows two figures standing on a boat. The boat, which is depicted clearly, is similar to the type known by the Greeks as a Phoenician *hippos* boat, which is a Phoenician work boat for shallow water or coastal sailing.[6] In front of the boat there is a reed, perhaps symbolizing the swamps around Bethsaida. Above the men on the boat is a round object and at the left is a semiround object. These objects may represent casting of a ring net. Although this seal is presented among the Hellenistic–Roman finds, there is no certainty that it indeed belongs to this period since the locus did not yield clear and undisturbed finds and the depiction has, to the best of our knowledge, no parallel. The type of the seal may indicate Iron Age manufacture; this type of boat was produced already during the Iron Age.[7]

Rami Arav

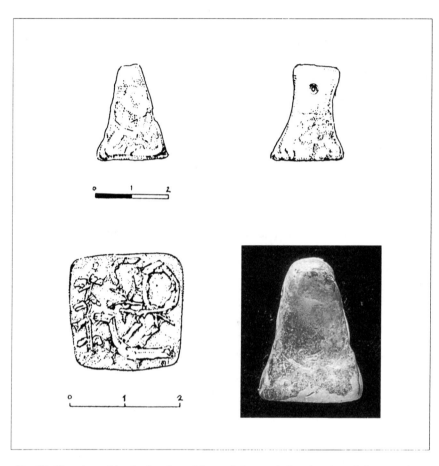

Fig. 12. Drawing of back, front, and face of clay seal showing two fishermen in a
hippos boat; photo,front of seal.

CLAY FEMALE FIGURINE. A small fragment (fig. 13), measuring 2 centimeters by 4 centimeters, of the head of a female figure was discovered in Area A. It was made on a mold and depicts a woman with curled hair covered with a veil. Remains of red color are seen on her hair. Identification of this figurine is uncertain. It is perhaps a likeness of Livia–Julia, wife of Augustus and mother of the Emperor Tiberius in this case, then depicted in one of her characteristic poses as priestess of Augustus. The special hairstyle (*Melonenfrisur*) would fit for the way of depicting Livia-Julia since the reign of Tiberius.[8] Bethsaida–Julias was named for Livia-Julia, probably to promote the Roman imperial cult in Palestine.

Fig. 13. Clay female figurine

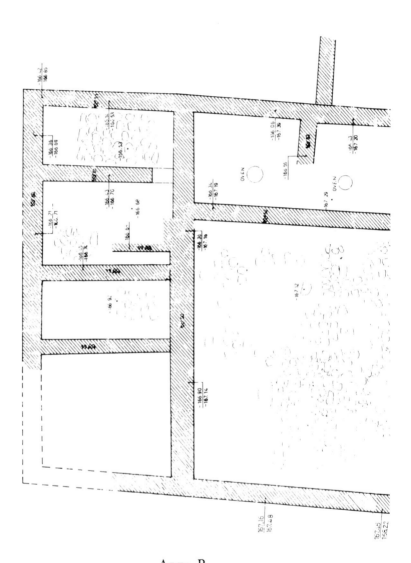

Area B

Area B (fig. 14) extends north of Area A and was found damaged by heavy destructions as noted above. The western sections of the structures were destroyed and disturbed to such an extent that little was found from the Hellenistic–Early Roman levels.

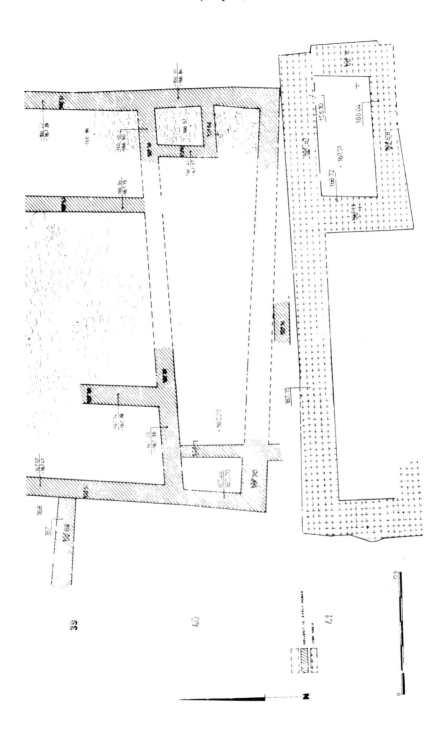

THE IRON AGE IN AREA B

A palace in the Assyrian–Aramean style known as *Bit Hilani* was discovered in levels 5 and 6 in Area B (squares G 42–44, K42–44). The palace is built very massively of large boulders and thick walls. Some of the boulders weigh over one ton, and the average width of the walls is 1.4 meters. The palace is not yet fully excavated; so far an area measuring 27.5 by 25 meters has been unearthed. The palace consists of four rooms along the northern wall (W67), other rooms along the eastern and western walls, and a throne room at the center. The latter has not yet been excavated. The northern rooms may have served as storage rooms; they measure 5 by 2.5 meters. One of the rooms (L365) yielded rich finds that contained jars, jugs, cooking pots, vessels imported from Phoenicia, and basalt vessels. Particularly interesting was a stamped handle showing a dancer. Slightly north of W67, a Phoenician-style bulla was discovered. (See other chapters of this volume for descriptions of some of these items.) The facade of the palace has not been fully excavated; however, it seems to be facing the plaza at the south. The ground plan of the structure, including the storage rooms and the throne room, looks similar to south Anatolian buildings.[9]

Level 4 represents significant changes in the ground plan and function of the palace. A long partition wall (W191) was built along the throne room and it perhaps ceased to function as such. The entrances to the storage rooms were blocked and the finds there were sealed. Two corridors had been created on top of the throne room as a result of the construction of the partition wall; these corridors perhaps served for weaving; the probable existence of a loom was indicated by the collection of loom weights that were found there (fig. 15).

Fig. 15. Group of loom weights found in locus 427. The weights were arranged in a few lines that may represent their original location on the loom.

IRON AGE FINDS FROM AREA B

A large number of pottery vessels were discovered in Area B. Most of the intact jars were found Locus 365. A few others were found in adjacent rooms. A following report surveys thoroughly the finds from this room. This locus represents the final stage of the existence of the palace, level 5. Finds from the other loci and levels will be considered in detail in subsequent volumes of the Bethsaida Excavations Project.

POTTERY. Iron Age pottery from this area includes jars, jugs, cooking pots, oil lamps, vessels imported from Phoenicia, and basalt vessels (pls. IX–XIV). Most of the vessels have parallels in other Iron Age sites such as Hazor and Megiddo. However, there are few vessels that differ in texture and the treatment of the clay. They are not as fine as those known from Hazor. The clay is darker than usual and has a large amount of basalt grits. As mentioned, a significant number of loom weights was found in a corridor next to the northeastern room. The loom weights were arranged in few lines that perhaps represent their original position on the loom (fig. 15) and belongs to the third phase of the building when it ceased to function as a palace

COOKING POT. One complete cooking pot was discovered at L365 (pl. IX.1). It is a closed type, with thick walls and a ridge under the rim. This cooking pot has parallels at Hazor Area A, level VI (*Hazor,* vol. 1, pl. LXXII.4 and vol. 2, pl. LXIX.11) and is dated to the first half of the eighth century BCE.[10]

CRATER. Hazor Area A produced a crater similar to one discovered in L365 (pl. IX.2). The Bethsaida crater is darker in color, has four handles from the neck to the shoulder, and a groove below the rim. The date of the Hazor crater is the ninth century BCE.

LARGE JAR. One example of this jug was found in L365 (pl. X.3). The rim of the jug is missing. Similar jugs were found at Hazor Area A, level VIII, that date to the ninth century BCE, and at Tel Qiri,[11] where it is named a cooking jar group IV and dated from Iron Age II.

BOWLS AND PLATES. Four large bowls were discovered in this area (pl. X.4–7). Three are distinguished by thick walls and a groove below the rim.

There is no exact parallel to these bowls at Hazor. The fourth bowl (pl. X.4), made of rich clay, has a slip, and is burnished inside and outside. The Hazor parallel is sometimes known as a Samarian Bowl, and dates from the ninth century BCE.

JUGS. Three types of jugs have been discovered in this locus. One type has a threefold rim, and the handle connects the rim to the shoulder (pl. XI.1) In two of these jugs there is a ridge below the rim (pl. XI.2). This type has parallels at Hazor level VIII.[12]

The second type of jug found in this locus is slightly more globular in shape, and has a long, thin neck with a ridge over it (pl. XI.3). The handle connects the ridge to the shoulder. This type was reported at Hazor level VIII (*Hazor*, vol. 2, pl. LVIII.21, 29).

The third type consists of a red slip and a burnished jug with a long, conical neck and plastic decoration on the shoulder (pl. XII.1). This type is known at Hazor level VIII as a Cypro-Phoenician type (*Hazor*, vol. 2, pl. LVIII.25, 27).

The fourth type is a cylinder juglet with a threefold rim (pl. XII.2). This type has parallels at Hazor level VI dating from the first half of the eighth century BC. (*Hazor*, vol. 2, pl. 70.1, 2, 8).

JARS. These jars have plain, ridged, or folded rims. Some have stress shoulders (Pls. XIII.1, 2; XIV.1). Parallels are at Hazor level VIII–VI (*Hazor*, vol. 2, pls. LX.9; LXXI.5,6; LX.1-6).

OIL LAMPS. Oil lamps (pls. XIV.2–3) typical to Iron Age II and are found also at Hazor level VIII (*Hazor*, vol. 2, pls. LXI.17–20).

BASALT FOOTED BOWL. A basalt footed bowl of outstanding shape and craftsmanship was found in L365 (pl. XIV.4).

HELLENISTIC–EARLY ROMAN FINDS FROM AREA B

The eastern side of the public house is preserved to a higher level than the western, where modern destruction has taken place. On the eastern side a few Late Hellenistic–Early Roman walls were unearthed on top of the Iron Age walls (W192, W82, W193, W196, W197). The Hellenistic walls are by and large 70 centimeters wide and run in a northeasterly direction.

North of the massive Iron Age building, an entire spacious courtyard house which dates from the Late Hellenistic–Early Roman period was excavated. It measures 18 meters by 27 meters and is built with small field-stones in walls of 0.7 meter (fig. 16).The house was found in a much destroyed state. At the west it was preserved to a level of one course only and at the east it was preserved to a level of 1.3 meters. The house has a central court that is surrounded by rooms. Three rooms at the north were excavated thus far. The northeast was paved and a nice threshold was found. Two parallel walls next to each other in the next west room may indicate a staircase. A spacious kitchen was excavated at the east in which two ovens were discovered together with kitchenware.

A large amount of Late Hellenistic–Early Roman pottery was discovered in the house, among which was a significant amount of fineware. Among the coins that were discovered in the house are two silver didrachmae of Demetrius II. A report on the coins is appended to this chapter.

This house contained many fishing implements such as lead net weights in two types, a round lead weight of the so-called musket type,[13] and a long, crooked needle (fig. 17). It is reasonable to assume that the house was owned by a fisherman's family. A detailed report of the fishing finds of this house will be presented in a subsequent volume.

Fig. 16. Aerial view of Late Hellenistic–Early Roman "fisherman" house in Area B

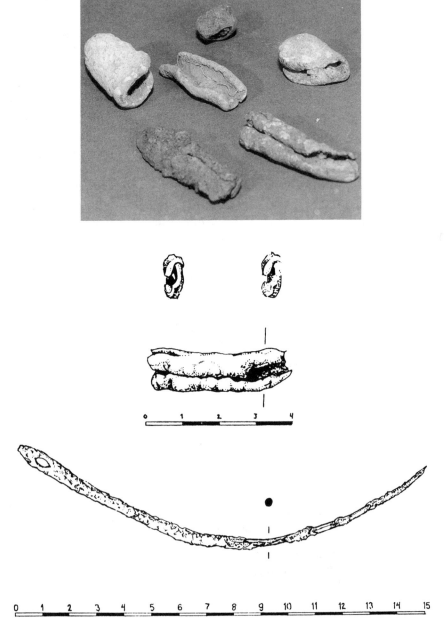

Fig. 17. Fishing implements, net lead weights, a needle, and an anchor

AREA C

Area C (fig. 18), north of Area B, was first excavated during the 1992 season.The excavations reveal thus far a single large room at L900 that measures 11.3 by 4.5 meters (fig. 19) adjacent to an almost quadrate courtyard 12 meters by 12.80 meters (L911). An entrance to this courtyard was discovered at the south (W203). The walls are of fine masonry, 0.7 meter thick. An entrance measuring 1.10 meters wide at the west wall of the room leads to the courtyard. Long nails found next to the entrance indicate that the entrance had a wooden frame. Large basalt beams discovered near the southeast corner presumably came from a fallen corbeled roof (fig. 20). An oven near the entrance, a complete set of grinding stones near W200, and remains of cooking pots suggest that L900 was the kitchen of the house. The beginning of a wall (W206) shows that the house extended to the north. Pavement remnants were found at the west side of the courtyard. Debris from the corbeling was discovered on the floor of the east section of the courtyard.

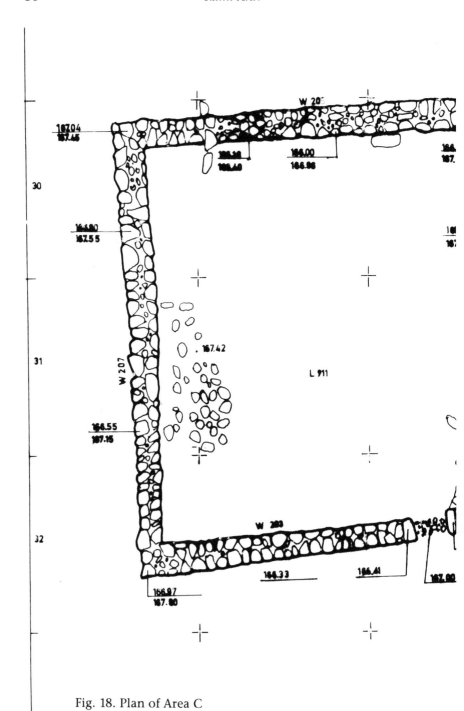

Fig. 18. Plan of Area C

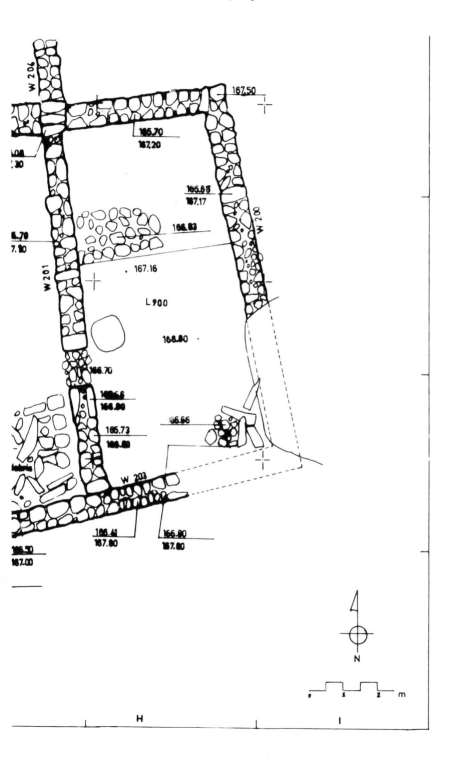

Fig. 19. A Hellenistic–Early Roman house in Area C

Fig. 20. Large basalt beams, near southeast corner, presumably from a fallen roof

THE FINDS OF AREA C

The house at Area C contained pottery vessels dating from the Hellenistic and Iron Age periods (see pls. XVII–XVIII). Three iron sickles with short bent blades were found near the northern section of L900 (fig. 21). These types of sickles are sometimes depicted on mosaic pavement as being used in vineyards.

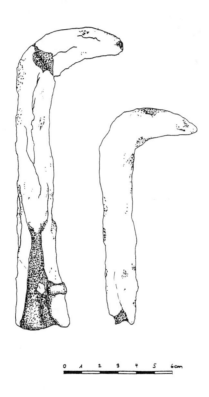

Fig. 21. Iron sickles, found near the northern section of L900

An unusual find discovered in the courtyard next to W201 is a *strigilis* (skin scraper), normally used at athletic exercise centers (fig. 22).

Among the coins is a silver tetradrachme minted at Tyre by Demetrius II in 129/8 BCE and a Tyrian silver coin dating from the late fifth or early fourth century BCE.

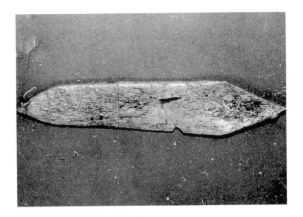

Fig. 22. Strigilis found in courtyard next to W201

A gold earring (fig. 23) was discovered on a balk at Area C. It was made of two pieces soldered together with a strap. The first piece is a pin, sharp at one end and thick at the other; the second piece is smashed and shows the head of an unidentified animal, made of gold and decorated leaf. The head is decorated with small gold balls in the granulations technique, and has gold and silver twisted strings in the filigree technique.

Fig. 23. Gold earring from Area C
BEP photo, H.-W. Kuhn

PLATE I
IRON AGE POTTERY FROM AREA A

No.	Object	Locus	Basket	Description
I.1	Jar	730	2194	Brownish ware / gray core
I.2	Jar	712	2216	
I.3	Jar	736	2224	Reddish ware / gray core/few small white grits
I.4	Mouth Jar	717	2096	Reddish ware / gray core / white and gray grits

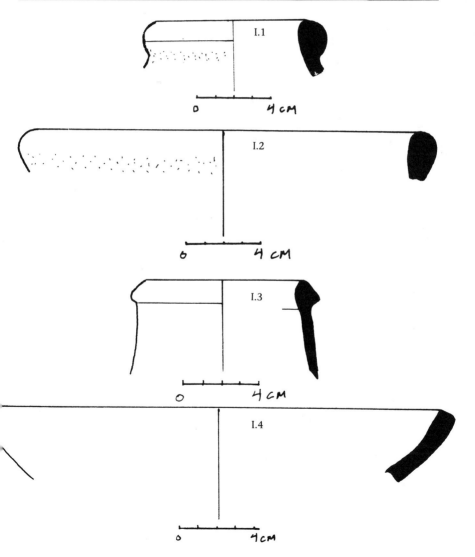

PLATE II
IRON AGE POTTERY FROM AREA A (CONTINUED)

No.	Object	Locus	Basket	Description
II.1	Jar	730	2194	
II.2	Cooking Pot	730	2194	Reddish brown ware / gray core / many white grits
II.3	Crater	730	2194	Red ware / small white grits/few large red grits
II.4	Bowl	730	2218	Light brown ware / gray core / small white grits

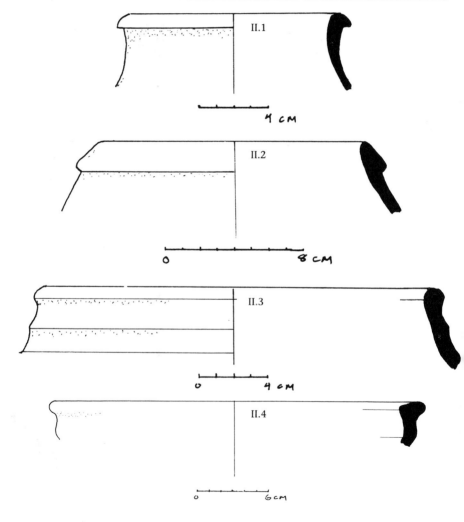

PLATE III
HELLENISTIC & EARLY ROMAN POTTERY FROM AREA A

No.	Object	Locus	Basket	Description
III.1	Pilgrim's Flask	311	1303	Reddish ware / good gray core
III.2	Cooking pot	502	1505	Brownish ware / fine / well-fired pot / intact / tall neck

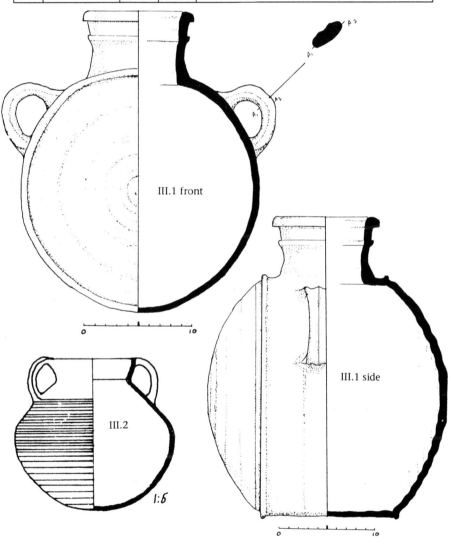

III.1 front

III.1 side

III.2

1:6

PLATE IV
HELLENISTIC & EARLY ROMAN POTTERY FROM AREA A (CONT'D.)

No.	Object	Locus	Basket	Description
IV.1	Cooking pot	712	2116	Reddish ware / fine / few grits
IV.2	Cooking pot		2001	Reddish ware / few grits
IV.3	Cooking pot	735	2238	Reddish ware / fine / well fired / few gray grits
IV.4	Cooking pot	712	2116	Reddish ware / few grits

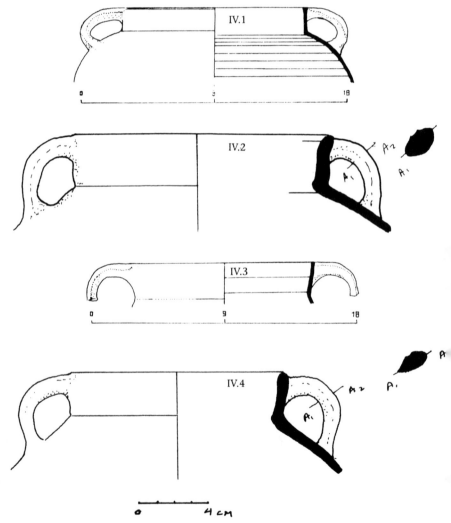

PLATE V
HELLENISTIC & EARLY ROMAN POTTERY FROM AREA A (CONT'D.)

No.	Object	Locus	Basket	Description
V.1	Cooking pot	717	2096	Reddish ware / few grits
V.2	Cooking pot	712	2116	Reddish brown ware
V.3	Cooking pot	431	5234	Brown clay / secondarily burnt

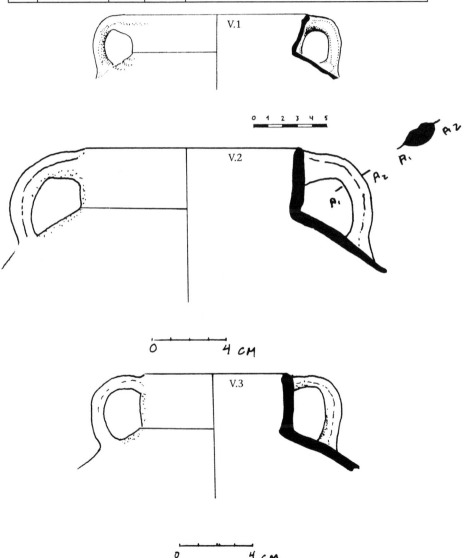

PLATE VI
HELLENISTIC & EARLY ROMAN POTTERY FROM AREA A (CONT'D.)

No.	Object	Locus	Basket	Description
VI.1	Jug	566	1842	Yellowish ware / fine with very few grits
VI.2	Jug	L52	1432	Orangish ware / fair, no grits
VI.3	Jug	560	1869	Yellowish ware / fine

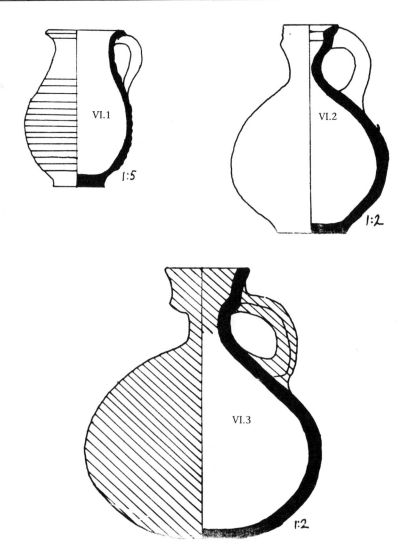

PLATE VII
HELLENISTIC & EARLY ROMAN POTTERY FROM AREA A (CONT'D.)

No.	Object	Locus	Basket	Description
VII.1	Jug	559	1838	Orange-pinkish ware / few grits
VII.2	Jug	559	1846	Yellowish ware / fine / very few grits
VII.3	Juglet	559	1838	Orange ware / good, some grits
VII.4	Juglet with spout	570	1868	Gray ware / fair, well-fired juglet

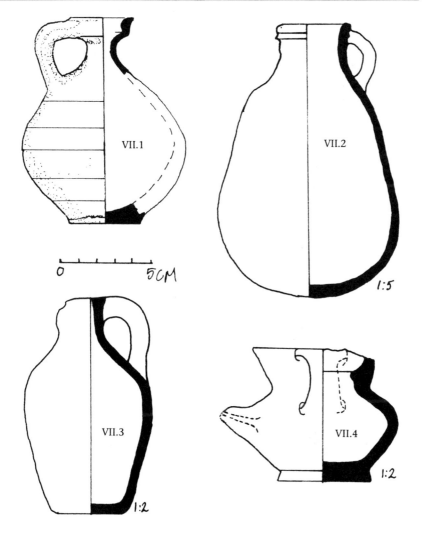

Plate VIII
Hellenistic & Early Roman Pottery from Area A (cont'd.)

No.	Object	Locus	Basket	Description
VIII.1	Amphorisk	717	2080	Orangish ware / fine, no grits
VIII.2	Small amphora	568	1853	Orange-yellowish ware / few grits
VIII.3	Fish plate	365	4149	Light-brown reddish ware / gray core with fine grits
VIII.4	Galilean bowl		1003	Reddish ware / fine, very few grits
VIII.5	Crater	734	2208	Orange ware / many grits

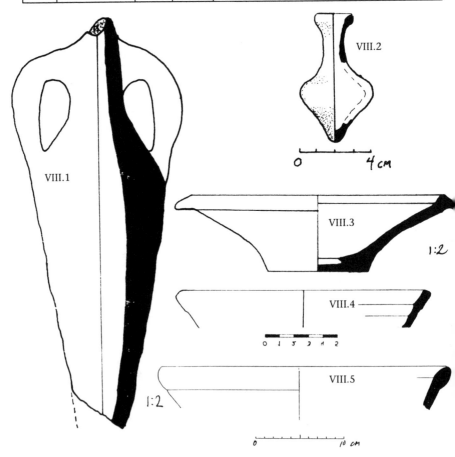

PLATE IX
IRON AGE POTTERY FROM LOCUS 365, AREA B

No.	Object	Locus	Basket	Description
IX.1	Cooking pot	365	4201	Reddish-brown ware / gray core / many grits
IX.2	Crater	365	4129	Gray ware / fair amount of grits
IX.3	Jar	365	4171	Red ware / good firing / many grits

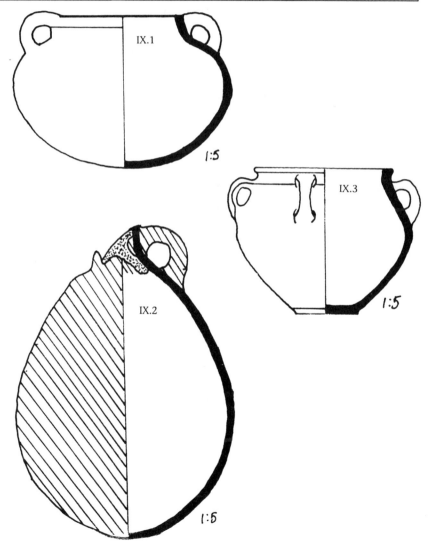

PLATE X
IRON AGE POTTERY FROM LOCUS 365, AREA B (CONT'D.)

No.	Object	Locus	Basket	Description
X.4	Bowl	365	4185	Red slip, inside and outside
X.5	Bowl	365	4156	Brownish ware
X.6	Bowl	365	4149	Light brown ware / fair, with many white grits
X.7	Bowl	365	4149	Light brown ware / fair to good / many white and black grits

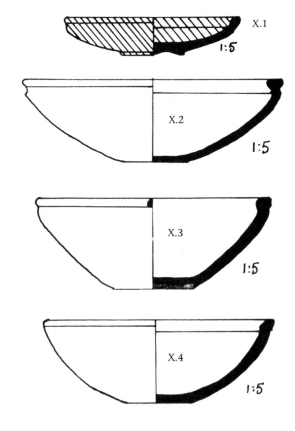

X.1
1:5

X.2
1:5

X.3
1:5

X.4
1:5

Plate XI
Iron Age Pottery from Locus 365, Area B (cont'd.)

No.	Object	Locus	Basket	Description
XI.1	Jug	365	4149	Reddish-pink ware / fair-to-good
XI.2	Jug	365	4185	Orange ware / poor, with many white and black grits
XI.3	Jug	365	4158	Orange ware / good-to-excellent / well-fired

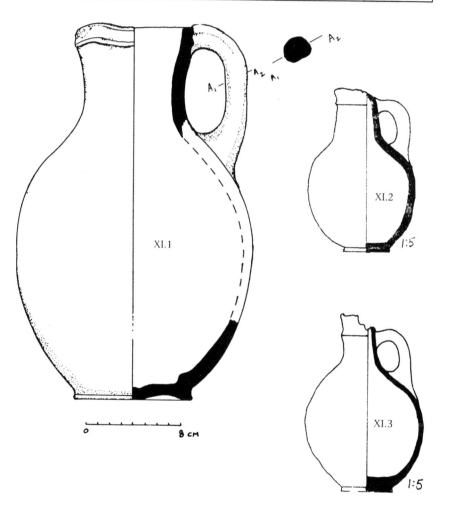

PLATE XII
IRON AGE POTTERY FROM LOCUS 365, AREA B (CONT'D.)

No.	Object	Locus	Basket	Description
XII.1	Jug	365	4201	Reddish ware / coarse with black and white grits / burnished red slip / lump beneath bottom of handle
XII.2	Juglet	365	4202	Brownish ware / poor, few grits

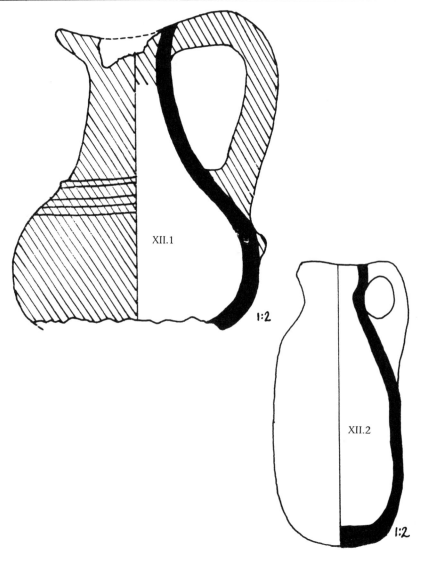

XII.1

1:2

XII.2

1:2

PLATE XIII
IRON AGE POTTERY FROM LOCUS 365, AREA B (CONT'D.)

No.	Object	Locus	Basket	Description
XII.1	Jar	365	4173	Light-brown ware / fair-to-good, with many white grits
XII.2	Jar	365	4153	Pink ware / poor-to-fair / many grits

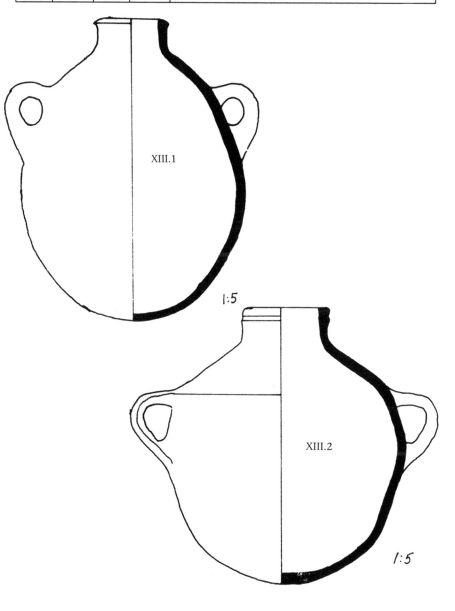

XIII.1

1:5

XIII.2

1:5

PLATE XIV
IRON AGE POTTERY FROM LOCUS 365, AREA B (CONT'D.)

No.	Object	Locus	Basket	Description
XIV.1	Jar	365	4164	Beige ware / fair / many white grits
XIV.2	Oil lamp	365	4185	Brownish ware / gray core / many grits
XIV.3	Oil lamp	365	4185	Brownish ware / gray core / many grits
XIV.4	Basalt footed bowl	365	4184	Gray basalt

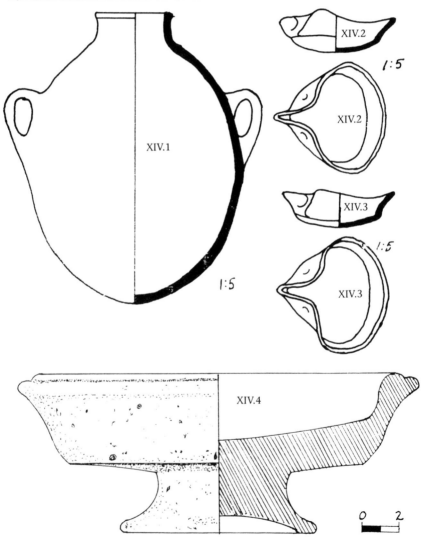

PLATE XV
HELLENISTIC POTTERY FROM AREA B (CONT'D.)

No.	Object	Locus	Basket	Description
XV.1	Pilgrim's flask	—	1001	Spattered wash ware
XV.2	Fish bowl	312	3098	Spattered wash ware
XV.3	Fish bowl	314	3052	Red slip inside
XV.4	Oil lamp	429	5230	Gray ware / eggs and dark plastic decorations
XV.5	Potter's mark	360	5001	Brownish-gray / few grits

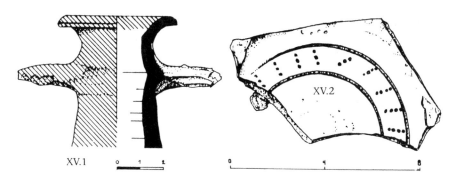

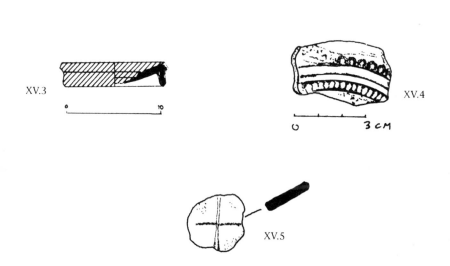

PLATE XVI
HELLENISTIC POTTERY FROM AREA B (CONT'D.)

No.	Object	Locus	Basket	Description
XVI.1	Jar	402	5016	Yellowish ware / few grits
XVI.2	Jar	302	3021	Yellowish ware / few grits
XVI.3	Cooking pot	314	3020	Reddish ware / few white grits
XVI.4	Cooking pot	314	3020	Reddish ware / few white grits
XVI.5	Cooking pot	360	5012	Orange ware / small white grits
XVI.6	Cooking pot	302	3025	Reddish ware / few white grits
XVI.7	Jar	302	3025	Reddish ware / few grits

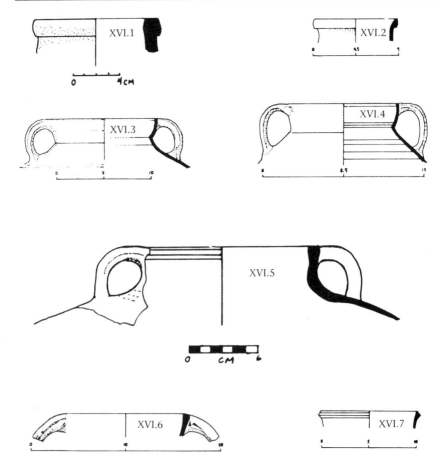

Plate XVII
Pottery finds from Area C

No.	Object	Locus	Basket	Description
XVII.1	Jar (Hellenistic)	907	9031	Orange white ware /few grits
XVII.2	Jar (Hellenistic)	907	9032	Yellowish ware / few grits
XVII.3	Jar (Hellenistic)	901	9020	Red-orange ware / few grits
XVII.4	Jug (Hellenistic)	900	9004	Red-brownish / many grits
XVII.5	Cooking pot (Hellenistic)	909	9037	Reddish ware / many gray grits

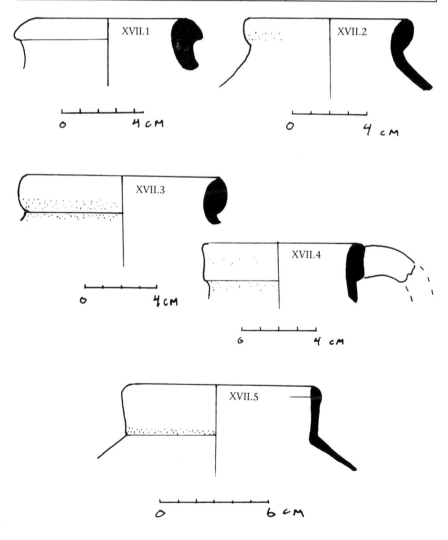

Plate XVIII
Pottery finds from Area C (cont'd.)

No.	Object	Locus	Basket	Description
XVIII.1	Jug IA	919	4163	Brown ware / many white grits
XVIII.2	Jug IA	919	4196	Brown-pink ware / some grits
XVIII.3	Crater IA	919	4175	Reddish-brown ware / white grits

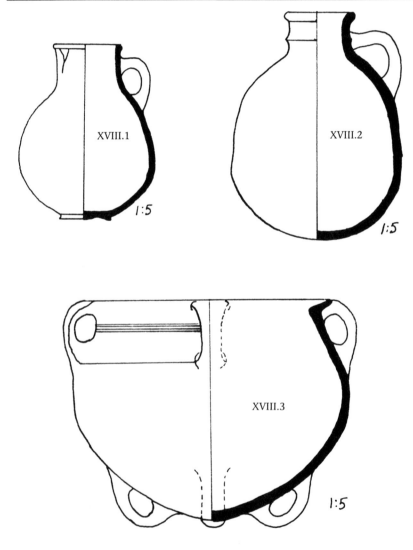

APPENDIX TO CHAPTER 1
by *Cecilia Meier, Eretz Israel Museum*

BREAKDOWN OF COINS BY PERIOD (UNTIL 1993 SEASON)

Period	No. of Coins	Percentage
PERSIAN		2.6%
Fifth Century BCE	1	
Fourth Century BCE	1	
PTOLEMAIC		
285–221 BCE	11	14.5%
SELEUCID		27.8%
222–139 BCE	21	
HASMONEAN		9.2%
136–63 BCE	7	
HERODIAN		5.2%
4 BCE–96 (100) CE	4	
ROMAN PROVINCIAL		6.6%
235–260 CE	5	
LATE ROMAN		1.3%
307–337 CE	1	
BYZANTINE		2.6%
565–576 CE	2	
ISLAMIC EMPIRE		11.8%
Zandjids (12th century CE)	2	
Mamluk (14th century CE)	5	
Mamluk (15th century CE)	1	
Persian (18th–19th? centuries CE)	1	
OTTOMAN EMPIRE		14.5%
Turkey (19th century)	11	
MODERN		2.6%
Syria	1	
Medal	1	
ANCIENT TOKEN? (unidentified)	1	1.3%
Totals	76	100.0%

CATALOG OF SELECTED COINS FROM ALL AREAS
compiled by *Cecilia Meier, Eretz Israel Museum*

CAT. NO.	SIZE (MM)	Metal	DESCRIPTION	LEGEND	COIN
			FIFTH CENTURY B.C.E		
1	8	AR	*Obv.* Dolphin *Rev.* Owl standing *r.*, head facing over its *l.* shoulder, with crook and flail		[Photo not available]
			FOURTH CENTURY B.C.E		
2	26–29	AR	*Obv.* Melquart, bearded, riding, right, on hippocamp with curled wing *Rev.* Owl standing *r.*, head facing over *l.* shoulder, with crook and flail; cable border all in shallow incise circle		
			PTOLEMY		
3	24–26	Copper core, plated	*Obv.* Head of Ptolemy I [?], to *r*, with diadem *Rev.* Eagle, *l.*, on thunderbolt Ancient forgery?	[ΠΤΟΛΕΜΑΙΟΥ Β]ΑΣΙΛΕΩΣ	

CAT. NO.	SIZE (MM)	Metal	DESCRIPTION	LEGEND	COIN
4	27.5–29	AR, on copper core?	*Obv.* Head of Ptolemy I (?) to r. *Rev.* Eagle standing *l.*, on thunderbolt	[ΠΤΟΛΕΜΑΙΟΥ] ΒΑΣΙ[ΛΕΩΣ]	
6	28.3–28.5	Æ	*Obv.* Head of Zeus to r., diademed, borders of dots *Rev.* Eagle standing *l.*, on thunderbolt, wings open In field *l.*: Σ	ΠΤΟΛΕΜΑΙΟΥ ΒΑΣΙΛΕΩΣ	
8	23–23.5	Æ	*Obv.* Bust of Zeus Ammon, r. diademed *Rev.* Eagle standing *l.*, on thunderbolt, wings closed; to *l.*, club.	ΠΤΟΛΕΜΑΙΟΥ ΒΑΣΙΛΕΩΣ	
12	37–38.5	Æ	*Obv.* Head of Zeus Ammon, diademed, r. *Rev.* Eagle standing *l.* on thunderbolt, wings open; to *l.*, cornucopiae bound with fillet	[ΠΤΟΛΕΜΑΙΟΥ ΒΑΣΙ]ΛΕΩΣ	

CAT. NO.	SIZE (MM)	Metal	DESCRIPTION	LEGEND	COIN
			SELEUCID		
16	20.5–22	Æ	*Obv.* Head of Antiochus III r., diademed *Rev.* Hinder part of galley *l.*, with rudder Date: PKΔ =124 = 189/8 BCE	ΒΑΣΙΛΕΩΣ ΑΝΤΙΟΧΟΥ	
21	21–22	AR	*Obv.* Head of Demetrius II, 1st reign; diademed and draped border of dots *Rev.* Eagle *l.* on prow; wings closed; in field *l.*, club with monogram of Tyre; border of dots	ΒΑΣΙΛΕΩΣ ΔΗΜΗΤΡΙΟΥ Date: HΞP (?) = 167 = 145/4 BCE	
22	20–21	AR	*Obv.* Bust of Demetrius II r., diademed *Rev.* Eagle *l.* on prow; wings closed; in field *l.*, club with monogram of Tyre; border of dots Date: not clear (CP?)	ΒΑΣΙΛΕ[ΩΣ] ΔΗΜΗΤΡΙΟΥ	

CAT. NO.	SIZE (MM)	Metal	DESCRIPTION	LEGEND	COIN
27	28–29.5	AR	*Obv.* Head of Demetrius II r., diademed *Rev.* Eagle standing *l.*, on beak of galley, wings closed, palm over shoulder; to *l.*, club with monogram of Tyre	ΔΗΜΗΤΡΙΟΥ ΒΑΣΙΛΕΩΣ Date: ΔΠΡ 184: 129/8 BCE	
			HASMONEAN		
37	12.7–14.5	Æ	*Obv.* Legend within wreath *Rev.* Double cornucopiae in center pomegranate, border of dots	[י]הוחנן[·] [ר]בח לדהי רבח [כ] רבחהו	
38	14–15.5	Æ	*Obv.* Anchor surrounded by circle *Rev.* Star with 8 rays, surrounded by diadem	[ΑΛΕΞΑΝΔΡΟΥ ΒΑ]ΣΙΛΕΩΣ [ךלמה] ןתנוהי	

CAT. NO.	SIZE (MM)	Metal	DESCRIPTION	LEGEND	COIN
39	13.5–15.5	AE	*Obv.* Legend within wreath *Rev.* Double cornucopiae field below; in center pomegranate; border of dots	יהו הכהן הג גדל חבר [ה]י[ה]ד[י]ה ־	
HERODIAN					
43	17.5–18	Æ	*Obv.* Head of Tiberius to r.; laureated and draped *Rev.* Facade of temple with four columns	[KAICAPOC CEBACTOY] [ΦΙΛΙΠΠΟΥ ΤΕΤΡΑΡΧΟΥ] Between columns: [L]ΔΓ = 33 = 29/30 CE	
44	17.5–19	Æ	*Obv.* Head of Tiberius to r. *Rev.* Facade of tetrastyle temple Date effaced	[effaced] [effaced]	

CAT. NO.	SIZE (MM)	Metal	DESCRIPTION	LEGEND	COIN
45	18.5–19	Æ	*Obv.* Head of Domitian r. *Rev.* Nike standing r., resting l. foot on crested helmet, and writing on shield which rests on l. knee Date effaced (year 24 = 84/85 CE?)	ΔO[MET KAI] ΓEPMA[NI]	
46	25.3–27	Æ	*Obv.* Bust of Salonina r., wearing crescent; hair braided with plait carried up the back of head to the crown *Rev.* Nike standing to front, head to l.; raising r. hand & holding wreath below it; murex-shell. Date 253–268 CE	COPNE ΣAΛ[ONINAAVG] COLTY [RO METRO]	
			ROMAN PERIOD		
47	27–28.7	Æ	*Obv.* Bust of Julia Mamaea to r., hair tied at back in chignon, and draped *Rev.* Ovoid baetyl (sacred stone), encircled by serpent on r., palm tree on l.; murex shell. Date 235 CE	...MAE... T[VPI]OPVM	

CAT. NO.	SIZE (MM)	Metal	DESCRIPTION	LEGEND	COIN
48	26–27.5	Æ	*Obv.* Bust of Valerianus r., laureated *Rev.* Athena seated on Roma, *l.* with back; in *r.* hand, pair of statuettes on prow(?), with left she leans on spear at foot of which is her shield; in field *l.*, murex shell; border of dots	IMPC[RLICVALE]RIANVSAVG COLT V ROMET (Col[onia] Tyro Met[ropolis])	
49	28–30	Æ	*Obv.* Bust of Otacilia to r., traces of double struck under chin, hair up in chignon and waves, draped; border of dots *Rev.* She wolf, standing *r.*, looking down to suckling Romulus and Remus	M[OT]ACIΣEVHPA[AVT] COΛ ΔAMA [METP] *In vexillum:* LEG VIR	
50	28–30	Æ	*Obv.* Bust of Otacilia Severa to r., diademed and draped *Rev.* Scene "Sacrifice of Astarte"	MO[]TA[C SEVERA] COL DAM [AMETR]	

APPENDIX CONCLUSIONS
by Cecilia Meier

Based on the numismatic evidence of the seventy-six coins excavated at Bethsaida, the earliest occupations seem to have been around the first half of the third century BCE. There is one Phoenician coin from the fifth century BCE and another Phoenician coin from the fourth century BCE. There are nine coins (including two ancient forgeries) of Ptolemy II (285–246 BCE), two of them from Alexandria and three from Tyre.

The largest collection of coins—twenty-one—are from the Seleucid period. Five of them are from Antiochus III (222–187 BCE), one is from Antiochus IV, and one from Antiochus V; there is a gap of twenty years until Demetrius II. Fifteen of these twenty-one coins were minted in the Phoenician city of Tyre.

There are seven Jewish coins, all from the Hasmonean period. Two are from John Hyrcanus I (Yehohanan), two from Alexander Jannaeus (Yehonatan), and two from Judas Aristobolus II (Yehudah) from 136–63 BCE. It is probable that the Hasmoneans came right after the Seleucids left, because there are no coins after Demetrius II.

The most important coins of the find are no doubt the two from Philip (son of Herod the Great), since one of the major cities located within his jurisdiction was Bethsaida. One of the coins is dated year 33 (= 29/30 CE), during the same year that the procurator Pontius Pilate struck his first coins in Judea.

No coins from the procurators were found.

One coin from Agrippa II dated 84/5 CE was found. Since then, the site seems to have been abandoned until the second half of the third century, but reoccupied for only for a short period (235–260 CE) and then completely abandoned during the Late Roman and Byzantine periods (only three coins were found from these periods). Until the Islamic period with the Zandjids of the twelfth century and the Mamluks of the fourteenth century, and much later during the Ottoman Empire, Bethsaida seems to have been resettled and then abandoned again.

CHAPTER NOTES

1. According to Jastrow 1976, 156, the root *Betah* can indicate a hollow, column-like receptacle for collecting rainwater, which was kept near the house; that may indicate the swampy nature of the plain.
2. The subdivision of Iron Age preferred here is in accordance with A. Major 1990, 296–297.
3. A variant of this crown is known from Canaanite deities, but the feathers are not obvious there. See an example of a god covered with silver and gold from Minet el-Beida, a Syrian god in bronze covered with gold and silver, and the god and goddess from the Balua'h stela, in ANEP, figs. 481, 484, 488. Closer parallels were found in Ammonite tombs in Amman; see *The New Encyclopedia of Archaeological Excavations in the Holy Land*, 1445. There are several differences in the depiction, however. The Ammonite figures are all bearded and the knob is not so prominent as it is in the Bethsaida statuette.
4. Naveh 1978. 58–59.
5. This proposal was made in a letter to me by Prof. J. Naveh, and I thank him for it.
6. Raban and Stieglitz 1991, 36.
7. For truncated pyramidal Iron Age seals see Dothan 1993, fig. 36:9. For Iron Age "Hippos" boats, see ANEP, fig. 107.
8. See Fittschen 1983.
9. Frankfort 1954.
10. Amiran 1969, pls. 71:5 and 9; 75:17; Yadin 1960, vol. 2, pl. LXIX:11.
11. See Ben Tor, et al. 1987, fig. 34.3.
12. See Yadin, et al. 1958, 1960,1961. *Hazor*, vol. 2, pls. 58.25,27.
13. A similar type was discovered in the ancient boat of Ginosar; see S. Wachsman 1990.

LITERATURE CITED

Amiran, R. 1969. *Ancient Pottery of the Holy Land.* Ramat Gan, Israel: Massada Press.

ANEP = Pritchard, James Bennett. 1954. *The Ancient Near East in Pictures Relating to the Old Testament.* Princeton, N.J., Princeton University Press, 1954.

Ben Tor, Amnon, et al. 1987. *Tell Qiri, A Village in the Jezreel Valley, Qedem,* Monograph 24, Institute of Archaeology. Jerusalem: Hebrew University.

Dothan, M., and Y. Porath. 1968–1970. *Ashdod.* Vol. 5, *Excavation of Area G: The Fourth-Sixth Seasons of Excavations.* ATIQOT, 23. Jerusalem: Dept. of Antiquities and Museums, Ministry of Education and Culture.

Fittschen, Klaus, and Paul Zanker. 1983– . *Katalog der römischen Porträts in den capitolinischen Museen und den anderen kommunalen Sammlungen der Stadt Rom.* Beiträge zur Erschliessung hellenistischer und kaiserzeitlicher Skulptur und Architektur, Bd. 3, 5. Mainz am Rhein: von Zabern.

Frankfort, Henri. 1954. *The Art and Architecture of the Ancient Orient.* The Pelican History of Art, Z7. Harmondsworth, Middlesex: Penguin Books.

Jastrow, Marcus. 1975. *A Dictionary of the Targumim, the Talmud Babli and Yerushalmi, and the Midrashic Literature.* Philadelphia: Traditional Press.

Major, A., *Archaeology of the Land of the Bible,* New York: Doubleday, 1990.

Naveh, M. J. 1978. *On Stone and Mosaic: The Aramean and Hebrew Inscriptions from Ancient Synagogues.* [Hebrew.] Jerusalem.

The New Encyclopedia of Archaeological Excavations in the Holy Land. 1993. Jerusalem: Israel Exploration Society.

Qedem 24 = A. Ben Tor, et al. 1987. *Tel Qiri: A Village in the Jezreel Valley, Qedem* 24. Monographs of the Institute for the Institute of Archaeology. Jerusalem: Hebrew University of Jerusalem.

Raban, A., and R. R. Stieglitz. 1991. The Sea Peoples and Their Contributions to Civilization, *Biblical Archaeology Review* 17 no. 6: 36.

Wachsmann, Shelley. 1990. *The Excavations of an Ancient Boat in the Sea of Galilee (Lake Kinneret).* Atiqot: English series, no. 9. Jerusalem: Israel Antiquities Authority, 1990.

Yadin, Y., et al. 1958, 1960, 1961. *Hazor,* 4 vols. Jerusalem: Magnes Press and Jerusalem Exploration Society.

John F. Shroder Jr. and Moshe Inbar

Geologic and Geographic Background to the Bethsaida Excavations

THE GEOGRAPHIC AND GEOLOGIC NATURE of the Bethsaida archaeological site at et-Tell on the northeast side of the Sea of Galilee first contributed to its prehistoric development as a city and then ultimately to its abandonment. The purposes of this chapter are threefold: (1) to characterize the processes and chronology of landform development near Bethsaida in the northern Jordan Valley–Sea of Galilee and the southwestern Golan Heights, (2) to establish the mechanics and timing of shoreline changes that removed easily navigable waters from their original position, directly adjacent to Bethsaida, to a point now some two kilometers farther away, and (3) to establish, insofar as possible with an ancient city whose location has long been disputed, that et-Tell is geologically and geographically the only logical site in the region to be considered as the lost city of Bethsaida.

El-Araj, directly at the north edge of the Sea of Galilee, has long been suggested as the site of Bethsaida, apparently because it is a coastal location. People are generally unsophisticated about long-term geologic change common to areas with active tectonism, delta growth, and changing water levels, so that a site no longer on the coast would not be recognized as a former port. The result has been undue attention to a site such as El-Araj. In fact, the small size of El-Araj, lack of built harbor facilities,[1] periodic seasonal flooding, and occasional catastrophic inundation from seismic *tsunami* waves probably would have rendered it unsuitable for long-term development as much more than a fishing outpost. Nevertheless, Mendel Nun felt that El-Araj was the true Bethsaida, but that the city had been destroyed by rising water levels.[2]

Emil Gottleib Kraeling discussed the enigmatic "two-Bethsaidas" approach to the classic problem, in which et-Tell is referred to by others as Bethsaida-Julias, having been renamed by the Tetrach Philip.[3] El-Araj was then thought to be another Bethsaida. Karl Eric Wilken is supposed to have found two-thousand-year-old pottery and coins in "alluvial sand" only one meter below the surface at El-Araj, which he equated to Bethsaida-Julius.[4] "Alluvial sand" implies river, wave, or *tsunami* transportation of artifacts as float from somewhere else, which is useless in archaeological determination. Both C. Serruya and Nun have also maintained that El-Araj is the true site of Bethsaida and that rising water levels have covered or washed away the ancient site.[5] On the other hand, Rami Arav reported only Byzantine archaeology *in situ* in his recent probes at El-Araj.[6] In addition, the geological instability discussed in detail below makes El-Araj an unlikely site to equate with Bethsaida.

Field and library work in 1992 and 1993 have now established that the et-Tell site has the necessary strategic, logistical, agricultural, fishing, water, and anchorage characteristics that would have attracted early settlers to establish a city of the importance that Bethsaida clearly had. In this chapter, therefore, the et-Tell site will be referred to as Bethsaida as proofs of that fact are further developed. For example, an Early Bronze Age (5,200 to 4,000 BP) to first-century CE habitation span of the city has been established. Moreover, the landform processes that can be observed at present have allowed formulation of hypotheses that this former fishing village of Bethsaida is now some two kilometers from the highly unstable water's edge of the Sea of Galilee through some combination of (1) uplift of the site away from the lakeshore by rift faulting (shore-up hypothesis), (2) building out of the shoreline around the site by flash flooding of the Jordan and other nearby rivers (shore-out hypothesis), and (3) drop in water level of the Sea of Galilee away from the site by climate-controlled reduced inflow, or by downcutting or downfaulting of its upper Jordan inlet and lower Jordan outlet (water-down hypothesis). The following is background to the development of these three hypotheses as well as a guide to further work in progress.

The Geology and Regional Geomorphology

The Dead Sea–Jordan Rift system has been proposed to be a tensional graben between two faults,[7] but actually seems to be a sinistral transform fault connecting an incipient ocean ridge—the Red Sea—with an upthrusted collision zone, the Taurus Range in southern Turkey.[8] The shear is caused by the opening of the Red Sea and the motion of the Arabian sub-plate away from the African plate (fig. 1).

Shearing occurs along a largely south-north trending, slightly arcuate line, consisting of a series of en echelon left-stepping left lateral strike-slip master faults of varying lengths. These faults characteristically die out to the north by bending outward (northeast), and the movement is taken up by the strike-slip faults to the left (to the west). Movement on this rift system began sometime before the middle Miocene (about 20 million years ago) and has continued intermittently to the present. Instrumental and historic records indicate a short-term seismic slip rate of 0.15 to 0.35 centimeter per year during the last thousand to fifteen hundred years, while estimates of the average long-term Pliocene-Pleistocene rate are 0.7 to 1.0 centimeter per year. Either much creep along the fault takes place to explain this disparity between short-term and long-term slip rates, or the slip rate varies over periods of a few thousand years.[9] Magnetotelluric profiling across the rift and the Golan Heights indicates an upward throw of about 2,000 meters on the eastern rift fault in this region.[10]

Seismic activity is all too commonly cited as the probable cause of destruction of ancient cities, even when there is little unequivocal evidence of earthquake activity. Directional building collapses, rather than random orientations, are usually cited as evidence; indeed, a number of west-tilting walls at Bethsaida suggest some cause linked to seismicity. Still, such hypotheses must be treated with considerable caution in the absence of more detailed analyses by seismologists.

In addition, at least three *tsunamis* are known for the Sea of Galilee (749, 1759, and 1837 CE),[11] which indicate that a number of others should have occurred farther back in antiquity. Such catastrophic flood phenomena are the result of local earthquakes and achieve maximum height and destructiveness on gently sloping shallow coasts, such as that of the Beteiha Plain around Bethsaida. El-Araj would have been devastated by such phenomena, but et-Tell would have been left high and dry.

The upper part of the Jordan River crosses a rather complex region (fig. 2). In the north is the Hula depression *rhomb graben* or pull-apart

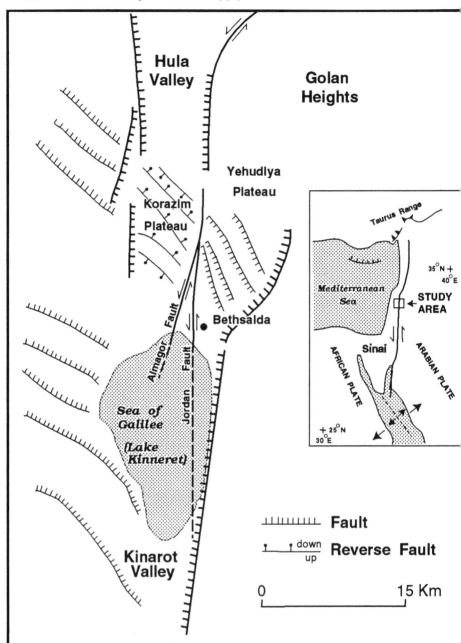

Fig. 1. Generalized fault and location map of the northern Dead Sea–Jordan transform fault system. Heavy lines denote major faults of the transform system; other
faults represent the plate margin internal deformation. Inset shows the tectonic setting of the Bethsaida study area (after Heimann and Ron 1993).

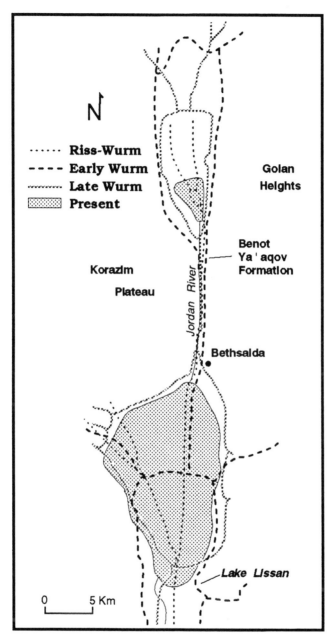

Fig. 2. Hydrography of the Kinneret and Hula regions during the late Pleistocene and Holocene showing the results of changing climates and tectonic movements (after Horowitz 1979). It is probable that Lake Lissan extended much farther north into the Jordan Valley well beyond where this map shows it to be.

basin,[12] underlain by Plio-Pleistocene and Holocene lake and marsh deposits and some volcanics, to a thickness of 2.8 kilometers or more.[13] The Sea of Galilee (Lake Kinneret, Lake Galilee), about 210 meters below sea level, occupies another probable *rhomb graben* controlled by the geometry of the strike-slip fault. The greatest depths, more than 40 meters, occur on its eastern side.

Between the Hula depression and the Sea of Galilee is the Rosh Pinna (Korazim plateau) saddle, in which several Plio-Pleistocene basalts are exposed. Pre-rift Cretaceous and Eocene rocks also occur at shallow depths below the basalt.[14] H. Heimann and H. Ron have reported that the Korazim block underwent intensive deformation after 1 million years ago.[15] The young deformation is expressed in a counterclockwise block rotation of about eleven degrees, a reverse faulting component, and a light folding of the whole structure. This intense deformation is probably a result of a transfer of the main tectonic activity and a horizontal slip from the north-south Jordan fault to the north-northeast to south-southwest Almagor fault. Field and seismic evidence indicates that the Almagor fault is young, and because it is not parallel to the main north-south plate motion, compression results. The result has also been faulting of the Yehudiya Plateau, upon the edge of which Bethsaida is located. A series of northwest-southeast trending *horsts, grabens,* and fault steps down to the southwest has resulted.

The Jordan River flows about 10 kilometers from Hula to the Sea of Galilee (Lake Kinneret) between the Korazim Plateau on the west and the Golan Heights on the east. The river is entrenched in a narrow and rubble-choked gorge, and probably is oriented along a splay of the rift fault. Slope failures are common in the basalt rocks of the Jordan canyon, and many occurred in the large flood of 1969.[16] In addition, other older landslides have choked the canyon, temporarily impounded the Jordan, and caused breakout floods. These landslides and floods have provided plentiful debris to the river, which has thereby extended its delta into Lake Kinneret more rapidly. The canyon represents a 270-meter drop from Hula to the Sea of Galilee.

Volcanism in the northern fifth of the rift is genetically associated with the seismically active tensional Golan–Hauran–Jebel Drouz–Wadi Sirhan tectonic trend, which has a northwest-southeast orientation, and not with the north-south trending Dead Sea–Jordan Rift.[17] The Golan Heights plateau, east of this segment of the rift, is mostly underlain by basalt units, including a number of cinder cones, which began extruding about 5 million years ago up to more recent times[18] (fig. 1).

The generally profuse jointing of the basalts produced plentiful construction stone for the builders of Bethsaida, although the greater density of basalts over most other rock types must have engendered a good deal more labor in lifting. Columnar jointing occurs in a number of the flows in both the Jordan and Meshoshim gorges only a few kilometers from Bethsaida; the basalt columns were used as roof construction materials in the ancient buildings at the site. Limestones from beneath the basalts in the region were also brought onto the site, presumably for carbonate plasters or other uses, but no *in situ* remnants of plaster floors or walls have yet been discovered.

The Hula Basin began to subside in the Neogene, and subsidence continues at present.[19] During the glacial part of the Pleistocene, the two troughs at the Hula Valley and the southern Dead Sea subsided at more or less the same rate—about 1 millimeter per year—with a lesser subsidence recorded for the central Jordan Valley.[20]

Streams, freshwater lakes, and marshes have existed more or less continuously in the Hula Basin, and their fluvial, lacustrine, and paludal sediments are interstratified with basalts from neighboring areas.[21] An older basalt in the immediate vicinity was extruded about 1,700,000 years ago and the younger Yarda basalt about 900,000 years ago. Above the Yarda basalt the fluviolacustrine sediments of the Benot Ya'aqov Formation (fig. 2) were deposited in the basin and subsequently deformed by tectonic activity associated with ongoing rifting. Rocks of the formation extend along both sides of the Jordan River drainage from the Hula Basin, and are below its water level as well. Biostratigraphy, magnetostratigraphy, and K-Ar dating constrain the age of the Benot Ya'aqov Formation to between 240,000 and 730,000 years BP. Acheulian artifacts found embedded in the formation have typical African characteristics,[22] and show one of the main routes of travel for early man of the time.

In the late Pleistocene, a late Wurmian pluvial phase lasted in northern Israel from about 18,000 to 11,000 years ago and the Ashmura Lake in the Hula Valley extended considerably to occupy a large part of the basin.[23] Considerable spring activity deposited travertine in the Hula area, but travertine deposition also followed fault lines farther south near Bethsaida and may have had no particular climate association. The Ashmura Lake shrank a bit during the early Holocene and then during the Atlantic substage (7,000 to 4,500 BP) it expanded again. At this same time, gravel and colluvium also began to accumulate in wadi valleys. During the past 4,500 years the preceding Atlantic colluvial sediments were cut by rather strong erosion, forming a Lower Terrace in parts of the Jordan Valley, while Ashmura Lake shrank to become widespread peat bogs and the smaller Hula Lake.[24]

The main tectonic phase which formed the present-day basin or *graben* of the Sea of Galilee took place during Early Pleistocene,[25] at which time the artifact-rich sediments of the Ubeidiya Formation were deposited in the south.[26] Following another short volcanic phase, in which the Yarmuk Basalt flowed down some river gorges, the salty Lisan Lake (fig. 2) occupied the rift valley 80,000 to 10,000 years ago from south of the Dead Sea at least to the southern part of the Sea of Galilee, and left its depositional record as the Lisan Formation.[27] It is possible that the lake waters extended several kilometers north from the Sea of Galilee into the Jordan River gorge upstream from Bethsaida, because fine-grained lacustrine clays have been discovered there recently beneath five meters of river gravel.

At the south end and in the center of the Galilee (Kinneret) basin the present en echelon main faults have been observed in seismic data as wide zones of deformation rather than as distinct fault planes. As a result of changes in the geometry of the fault system some compression and shortening of the basin sediments produced an uplifted anticline in the south starting about 2 million years ago and ending in the late Quaternary (fig. 3). At present, the south part of the basin is instead subsiding.[28] Other studies involving shallow seismic reflection and refraction data for the whole of the Sea of Galilee also indicate active tectonic processes in this area.[29] Folds and faults occur in the uppermost sediments of the Sea. The most deformed areas are along the margins, but some of the deformation also occurs at the center of the Sea in its deepest portion. The rocks below the basin are also seismically active, and a number of earthquakes have occurred around and beneath the Sea in historic time.

Subsidence began to become pronounced again some 18,000 years ago in the Sea of Galilee area when fresh water began to be established there.[30] The basin subsided some 40 to 50 meters from this time to the present. A. Heimann has noted that the average rate of subsidence of the Sea of Galilee basin has been 0.2 millimeter per year. Horowitz thought that the sedimentation rate was about 1 millimeter per year, and Nir concluded a sedimentation rate of 1 to 1.6 millimeters per year. On the other hand, Serruya and Stiller and Assaf noted rates of 2 to 7 millimeters per year. Clearly there is a diversity of opinion as well as variable rates at different places, but in any case the rates are fairly rapid.[31]

As a result of this sedimentation the Tabgha Formation was deposited in the Sea of Galilee basin from about 18,000 years ago up to the present.[32] A carbon-14 date was obtained from shells in sediment 4.5 meters below the lake bottom, which was itself 14.5 meters below the water surface on the west side of the lake. The date of 2,370 ± 90 years BP was judged anomalous by Horowitz because of suspected contamination,[33] but the reasoning behind this supposition is not clear. In any case, the Tabgha Formation is fairly young. It consists of more than 22 meters of dark brown to black clays, some of which show their origin from weathered basalt. Parts of it were deposited on the Beteiha Plain (fig. 3) during expansion phases of the Sea of Galilee. Bones of *Hippopotamus*, *Bos*, and other vertebrates have been found in it. Pollen spectra from boreholes show that the lower part of the unit was deposited during a wetter pluvial (glacial elsewhere) in the latest Pleistocene, and the upper part during a climate episode similar to that of the present.

SOILS

Only limited work on soils at a small-scale map level has been done in the region.[34] Four main types of soils exist there. Terra rossa soils have developed on limestones and dolomites and are most widespread in Upper Galilee and in the Hermon area. These are thought to have an eolian component and to have resulted mainly from periods of greater precipitation. Dark Rendzina soil has formed on Eocene carbonates and occurs in Lower Galilee, the southern Golan, and the northern and western slopes of the Irbid Plateau southeast of the Sea of Galilee. Light Rendzina soils have developed mainly upon marls of Lower Cretaceous and Senonian age, patches of which occur in Lower and Upper Galilee, and on top of the Irbid Plateau. Grumosols and brown Mediterranean soils have also developed on the basalts and are widespread in eastern Lower Galilee and in the Golan Heights.

Most of the terra rossa soils of the region are not actively forming in the drier climate of the present. Most are characterized by the absence of an A horizon, which, therefore, must have subsequently eroded away.[35] Such truncated soil profiles are common in the northern Galilee area where this research has been concentrated. Many truncated A-horizons are thought to be human-caused. Redeposition of the eroded A-horizons

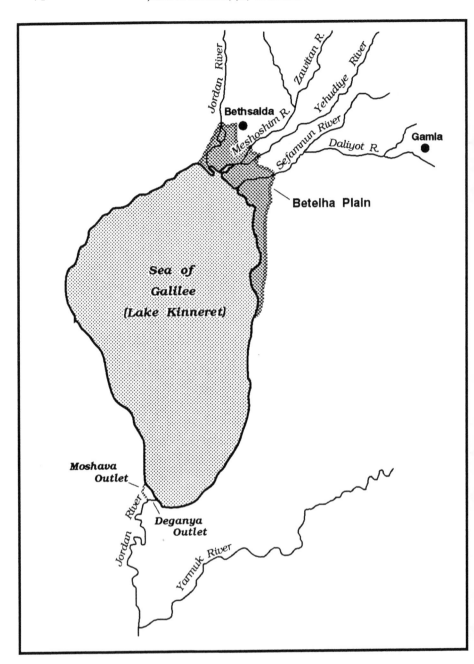

Fig. 3. Topographic map of Jordan River inlet and outlets from the Sea of Galilee, together with other features mentioned in the text.

probably occurred down wadis and into the Beteiha Plain and Sea of Galilee bottom throughout the course of human settlement in the region.

VEGETATION HISTORY

Pollen diagrams obtained from a number of boreholes in the rift valley sediments have enabled reconstruction of past vegetation history for much of the Cenozoic,[36] but only the Quaternary is considered here. Horowitz divided this period into ten palynozones. The lowermost two represented a pre-glacial Pleistocene,[37] the succeeding seven were considered of glacial–interglacial equivalence, and the uppermost are of Holocene age. Pollen spectra from the late Wurmian pluvial episode indicate spreading of the northern Mediterranean forest more or less to the middle of Israel, and the Mediterranean maquis south to the latitude of the southern Dead Sea. The pluvial climate was characterized by rather mild winter rains, some amount of summer rains, and generally higher rainfall than present. These conditions resulted in the spread of human settlements over the entire region, even south into the deserts. The areas around the Jordan Valley lakes supported several large Neolithic settlements, as at En Gev on the east shore of the Sea of Galilee and elsewhere.

In the Versilian substage (11,000 to 7,000 years BP) of the Early Holocene the pollen spectra show that the vegetation is more or less compatible to that of the present.[38] During the Atlantic substage (7,000 to 4,500 years BP) the regional pollen spectra indicate that the vegetation was considerably richer than at present and the northern Mediterranean forest penetrated the country far into the southern deserts.

Baruch studied cores from the bottom of the Sea of Galilee and concluded that the observed palynological changes there were caused by vegetation fluctuations in the past five thousand years which were essentially the outcome of human activities.[39] At the end of the fourth millennium BCE (about 5,000 years BP) the natural vegetation around the Sea apparently was still in an undisturbed state; its composition as revealed through the pollen record reflected climatic conditions not unlike those presently prevailing in the area. Increasing human interference with the natural vegetation in subsequent periods, however, would have masked any further climatic effects. The activities of humans responsible for the observed changes were interpreted to be of two kinds: cultivation and forest clearing activities. This lasted about 3,500 years, from about 5,000 BP to about 1,500 BP. Subsequently the easing of human pressure on the vegetation enabled the forest to regenerate until the beginning of the last century. The composition of the regenerated forest differed in certain respects from the primeval forest that had prevailed in the area 5,000 years earlier, thus reflecting the long-term effects that anthropogenic factors had on the natural vegetation. As a result of the renewal of forest clearing activities this forest was decimated heavily during the last two hundred years, but re-expanded slightly during the last several decades, mostly as a result of the steps taken toward its restoration.

Development of the Bethsaida City Site

The city site at et-Tell was established as a result of a number of geologic and geographic factors. The main causes for selecting the site as an ideal living place, and its ultimate development into the multimillennial habitation that it became, may be classed as strategic location, available water supply, throughfare access, and rich livelihood possiblities.[40]

Strategic Location

The earliest of the ancient settlements would have been primarily dependent upon its own arrangements for defense. The original peninsular ridge of basalt of et-Tell, jutting out above the lake plain and lake edge as it did, would have provided plentiful sources of rock for defensive walls, broad views of approaching hostile elements, and relatively impenetrable estuaries, swamps, and thorn thickets on three sides for defense. On the other hand, El-Araj would have been clearly defenseless in its low-lying position and therefore would not constitute a reasonable site for the location of Bethsaida.

Available Water Supply

The Bethsaida spring directly below the base of et-Tell would have provided the best of dependable water sources to the town. The Jordan River and the nearby estuary and lake sources would have been further reliable water sources for the animal flocks. El-Araj, however, would have been a malarial site, subject to periodic seasonal lake floods, *tsunami* waves, and Jordan River flood inundation then as now, inasmuch as Nun has noted that the water level of the Sea of Galilee does not seem to have been greatly different in Roman times than today.[41]

Throughfare Access

The Bethsaida tell is not directly located on any known main road of antiquity, but clearly it and nearby Gamla (fig. 3), also at the northeast end of the Sea of Galilee, were directly between the well-known north–south access routes, the Via Maris and the Kings Highway. Because of the dynamic nature of the lakeshore and the extensive flood sedimentation of the rivers along the northeast shore, the original travel routes along the east side of the Jordan valley and the Sea of Galilee are not apparent today. Nevertheless, the topography of the area would have allowed relative ease of access. The presence of other nearby settlements in antiquity argues strongly for interconnectivity between them. Below the canyon of the upper Jordan near Bethsaida the braiding of the river reduces velocity and depth, which in antiquity would have enabled ease of fording at this place (fording at the El-Araj site would have been impossible). Finally, the position of et-Tell close to the junction of the Jordan River mouth, the lakeshore, the lake plain, and the uplands indicates that this nodal location offered a variety of transport types and directions of access that would have made the site ideal for the formation of a settlement for the several millennial longevity that our archaeological excavation shows it to have had.

Rich Livelihood Possibilities

The presence of rich volcanic soils on the gentle uplands of the lower Golan Heights and the Beteiha Plain, coupled with diverse fishing in the Jordan River and the Sea of Galilee would have provided a reasonably rich livelihood in agricultural land as well as different fishing areas for the settlement. Plentiful trees on the uplands would have provided fruit, nuts, oil, and fuel. Dependable spring and river water sources would have also allowed irrigation.

The four main criteria for establishment and long continued maintenance of a settlement at et-Tell were clearly well met for this site. The tell is thus seen to have all the necessary requirements for an important and well-developed city that was reestablished and rebuilt at the same location over the millennia each time it was destroyed by war or other hazard. On these grounds alone the probability increases greatly that, compared to the other small and poorly developed ancient village sites in the region, et-Tell is indeed the only reasonable choice in size and location to be the lost city of Bethsaida.

Geomorphic Development in the Late Quaternary

Hula and Upper Jordan River Valley

In Israel, typical conditions of the Holocene epoch lasted from about eleven thousand years ago to the present.[42] In the Hula Valley the Ashmura Lake shrank considerably at the outset and travertine deposition ceased. Ever since the early prehistoric cultures of lower to middle Paleolithic in the region, humans have interfered in the water cycle of the Jordan River through deforestation and overgrazing of pastures. In the Hula, only civilizations that were masters in the use of irrigation endured from BCE into the Common Era.[43] From the Hellenistic period to the Byzantine and early Arabic times (fourth to eighth centuries CE), settlement in the Hula Valley was uninterrupted, and literary sources testify to dense and prosperous settlement there at the time of the Crusades. From the beginning of the fourteenth century to more than five hundred years afterwards, the Hula was uninhabited, shunned by settlers, and visited only by Bedouin shepherds. This occurred because of the Mongol invasion at the end of the thirteenth century and the building of the Benot Ya'aqov (Daughters of Jacob) bridge about 1260 CE.

The basalt arches of the bridge narrowed the bed of the Jordan so that the lake rose in the winter and the swamps extended northward almost to the edge of the valley.[44] Between 1887 and 1904 CE, drainage works included the widening and cleaning of the Jordan outlet. During the early years of the British Mandate the old bridge was replaced by a suspended bridge at the Benot Ya'aqov outlet. In addition, small irrigation projects included the diversion of water from the main channel by building local periodic dams which caused drainage problems in the upper parts of the valley.[45] With the establishment of the State of Israel in 1948 the Hula began to be drained. The main works affected an area of 60 square kilometers and were completed in 1958.

The drainage of Lake Hula and its peat-filled swamps, coupled with other human-induced changes in the Upper Jordan basin, have created a new hydrological and sedimentological regime in the Upper Jordan River. Annual mean maximum peak discharges have increased at the valley outlet from 57 cubic meters to 96 cubic meters per second. The flood routing index has been doubled and floods have been transmitted through the system in a much shorter time. Prior to drainage modification, most of the river's annual suspended sediment discharge, about 70,000 tons, was deposited in Lake Hula and its swamps. In the past forty years, however, water and sediment have moved more rapidly towards the Sea of Galilee.[46]

The Jordan River drains an area of 1,590 square kilometers and supplies 650 million cubic meters per year of discharge, or about 40 percent of the total water budget of Israel. The main Jordan sources are the Mount Hermon area karstic springs. Average annual rainfall varies from 400 millimeters in the southern area to 1,600 millimeters in the Mount Hermon area. Storm flow results from heavy rainfall in the northern part of the catchment and the Hula Valley, and starts in the north after an accumulative rainfall of 300 millimeters. Major floods from the Hula Valley occur after storms with precipitation intensities of 50 millimeters per day. The average flow rates range from 18 million cubic meters per year in August to 75 million cubic meters per year in February. The mean annual water yield has been about 521 million cubic meters per year.[47]

A rainstorm of an estimated hundred-year frequency generated a peak discharge of 214 cubic meters per second on the Upper Jordan during the flood of January 1969. The Jordan River canyon may have been scoured in part down to bedrock during the peak of this flood. About fifty-odd slope failures occurred in the gorge, which produced plentiful debris. A total amount of about 100,000 cubic meters was removed in the flood, whereas the average annual debris removal is an estimated 500 cubic meters per year.[48] Boulders up to two meters were moved, many new bars formed, and the channel completely reshaped. A new delta of the Jordan was produced in the Sea of Galilee and caused the shoreline to advance as much as 0.5 kilometer into the lake[49] (fig. 4). The lower course of the Jordan River past Bethsaida was not reoriented dramatically by the flood, however, and still retains its westward deflection. This deflection is apparently the result of flood sedimentation by the Meshoshim, as well perhaps as left–lateral motion along the rift fault. On the other hand, part of this westward deflection may also be due to the fact that erosion of the consolidated and sticky clays to the east would have been more difficult than erosion of the heavily jointed basalt interbedded with weak scoria layers on the west.

On the left (east) bank of the lower Jordan River a number of terraces occur that may also reflect uplift associated with rift tectonics. The T_0 terrace is up to 4 meters above the bed of the modern Jordan; it is hummocky and boulder strewn, and largely reflects the flood of 1969. The T_1 terracette occurs about 8 meters above the present river, is weakly developed across basalt bedrock, and is underlain by as much as 1 meter of

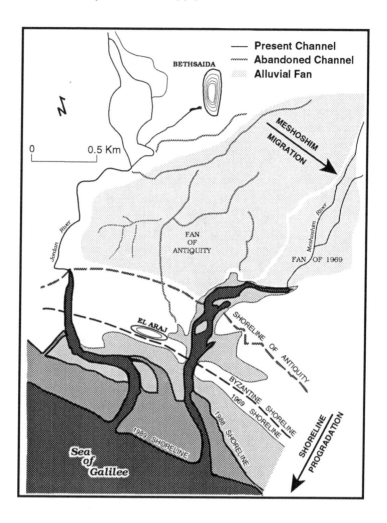

Fig. 4. Composite geomorphological map of the Bethsaida region taken from aerial photographs of 5 Sept. 1969, 23 Jan. 1988, and 21 Nov. 1989, showing landform changes through time. The shoreline of antiquity is marked by a slight change in slope, different vegetation, and slightly more irregular topography. It is undated. The fan of antiquity is mainly from Meshoshim deposition at an unknown time in the past. Abandoned channels occur over its surface. The fan of 1969 was produced by floods on the Meshoshim at that time. Also in 1969, after the flood the estuary to the east of el-Araj was much larger than at present. The 1988 and 1989 shoreline changes are the result of water-level fluctuations. The Bethsaida spring and pool are shown directly west of Bethsaida.

travertine, which is probably a spring deposit. The T_2 terrace is about 15 to 20 meters above the river and the T_3 about 50 meters above the river, but these may reflect only basalt flow surfaces, weathering surfaces, or fault blocks, and may not be fluvially eroded. The T_3 terrace has several meters of loose blocky basalt-derived soils on it, with as yet undated potsherds in it that may have resulted from downslope soil erosion transport, perhaps from Byzantine or other settlements uphill. These terraces may reflect greater uplift on the east side of the rift because they do not seem to appear on the west. Some of the lower terraces could relate to the level of Lake Lisan, at 108 meters below sea level, which probably covered the Beteiha Plain 10,000 to 12,000 years ago.

LOWER GOLAN HEIGHTS VALLEYS

The valleys of Daliyot (Gamla), Sefamnun, Yehudiye, and Meshoshim drain the southwest Golan (fig. 3). The Gamla archaeological site near the head of the Daliyot valley is situated on a basalt-capped knife-edged ridge directly between the two tributary canyons that form the Daliyot. This easily defensible site was produced geologically by fluvial incision of the 80 to 100 meters thick basalt caprock over the underlying Neogene carbonates and unstable fine clastics. These lithologies in combination are one of the most unstable of configurations known, and numerous slope failures result.[50]Collapse sinks and swallowholes in the basalt caprock have allowed plentiful water infiltration to aid in the collapse of the caprock. Landslide benches and knife-edged ridges by back-to-back failure commonly are produced in such situations as well, and plentiful slope-failure clastics choke associated stream valleys with debris that can be mobilized readily in torrential rainstorms. The Daliyot valley was set up, therefore, by geological conditions to provide an excellent defensible site at Gamla as well as to provide at the same time plentiful debris for deposition downstream across the Beteiha Plain to the shores of the Sea of Galilee.

   Only the Daliyot valley has the basalt overlying the unstable sedimentary units. The Yehudiye and Meshoshim flow only across basalt bedrock, which provides debris through its extensive network of cooling joints and interbedded scoria zones. In general these upper river valleys are not as choked with debris as are the Gamla valleys, and they tend to be vegetated extensively. Nevertheless, during the same 1969 event that produced the strong flood on the Jordan, a peak flow of 300 cubic meters per second occurred in the nearby Meshoshim, which drains 160 square kilometers of basaltic terrain in the Golan Heights into the Sea of Galilee just east of the Jordan outlet. Here boulders 1 meter and larger in size were transported about 3 kilometers downstream and many of the preflood landforms in and around the channel were reshaped.[51] A new alluvial fan was spread across the upper part of the Beteiha Plain, but the estuary into the Sea of Galilee was not entirely infilled (fig. 4).

BETEIHA PLAIN

This flat-lying-to-gently-sloping plain measures about 2 kilometers wide and about 5 kilometers in length alongshore (fig. 3). It is composed of Quaternary sediments overlying the edges of the Golan basalts and reflects long-term fluvial, estuarine-paludal, and lacustrine sedimentation at the edge of the Sea of Galilee to produce the underlying Tabgha Formation. The slopes of the lower floodplains of the Daliyot, Sefamnun, Yehudiye, and Meshoshim rivers across the Beteiha Plain are about 1.3 degrees down from an altitude of about 100 meters below the Sea of Galilee water level. This contrasts with the slope of the lower Jordan River across the plain where it has only about half the gradient of the others.

Thicknesses of sediment in the Beteiha Plain are largely unknown, but boreholes drilled for the bridge abutments across the Jordan River 1 kilometer north of the lakeshore were 26 meters to basalt on the right (west) bank of the Jordan and 40 meters to the bedrock on the left (east) bank (fig. 5). Two meters of fine-grained floodplain deposits over coarser, probable shoreline deposits occur in seven boreholes 1 kilometer north of the present shoreline. Analyses of aerial photographs of the plain reveal that the Meshoshim river, which now flows south-southwest, once flowed west. At this time gravelly alluvial fan sedimentation forced the Jordan River to the west about 1 kilometer in a loop around the distal end of the Meshoshim fan. Paleochannels on the Meshoshim fan not only reveal the westerly flow direction but also show channels to the south (fig. 4). It is possible that the main south-oriented channel is a remnant of a filled estuary to Bethsaida now buried beneath the alluvial fan gravels from Meshoshim.

Over 10 meters of basalt gravel capped by 1 meter of fine-grained soil are exposed in a large gravel quarry at the mouth of Daliyot stream below Gamla. The soils of the Beteiha Plain overall have the clayey, rich, and crumbly pedons characteristic of basalt-derived materials. Extensive cracking and some gilgai relief occur as well. Depths of 1 to 2 meters of this fine-grained soil type occur above basalt gravels. Flash flood

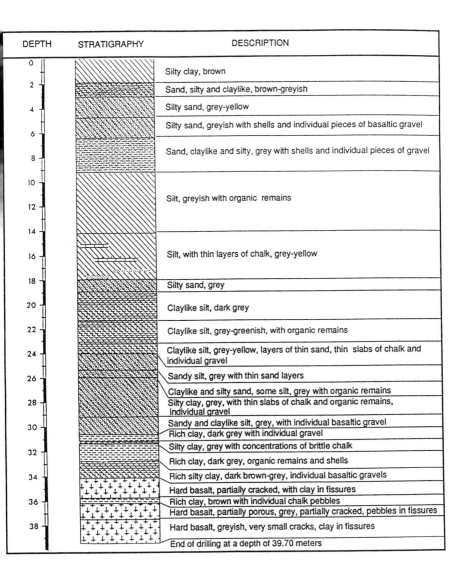

DEPTH	STRATIGRAPHY	DESCRIPTION

Silty clay, brown

Sand, silty and claylike, brown-greyish

Silty sand, grey-yellow

Silty sand, greyish with shells and individual pieces of basaltic gravel

Sand, claylike and silty, grey with shells and individual pieces of gravel

Silt, greyish with organic remains

Silt, with thin layers of chalk, grey-yellow

Silty sand, grey

Claylike silt, dark grey

Claylike silt, grey-greenish, with organic remains

Claylike silt, grey-yellow, layers of thin sand, thin slabs of chalk and individual gravel

Sandy silt, grey with thin sand layers

Claylike and silty sand, some silt, grey with organic remains

Silty clay, grey, with thin slabs of chalk and organic remains, individual gravel

Sandy and claylike silt, grey, with individual basaltic gravel

Rich clay, dark grey with individual gravel

Silty clay, grey with concentrations of brittle chalk

Rich clay, dark grey, organic remains and shells

Rich silty clay, dark brown-grey, individual basaltic gravels

Hard basalt, partially cracked, with clay in fissures

Rich clay, brown with individual chalk pebbles

Hard basalt, partially porous, grey, partially cracked, pebbles in fissures

Hard basalt, greyish, very small cracks, clay in fissures

End of drilling at a depth of 39.70 meters

Fig. 5. Core drill of sediments from Beteiha Plain at east edge of road bridge over Jordan River.

Fig. 6. Ancient wall of basalt boulders at the edge of the pool formed by the Bethsaida spring. The pool is artifically dammed at the present.

Fig. 7. Flood gravels of <1 meter overlying black, organic-rich muds near Bethsaida spring. These muds were deposited in a quiet-water environment such as that of a lake, swamp, lagoon, or estuary, which probably would have been suitable for navigation.

watercourses and gentle-sided dry washes 1 to 4 meters deep cross the plain and have basalt boulders scattered along them. Some hummocky piles of debris occur along the larger flash flood courses that are the result of boulder bedload transport. Ben-Avraham et al. noted that in their seismic reflection profiles from the northeast margins of the Sea of Galilee, certain reflections were produced from probable submerged and buried boulders resulting from such floods.[52]

Close to the edge of the Bethsaida archaeological site a large, deep spring flows west with a discharge of about 0.02 cubic meter per second into a pool and deep channel to the Jordan River. A few meters from the spring at the edge of the pool an ancient wall occurs that may be part of an old dock facility (fig. 6). Shallow drilling around this pool has shown a fine clay to 1.5 meters depth that turns into more silty sand at about 2 meters depth. The spring thus may once have connected to a backwater channel into a much shorter Jordan River and thence to the closer shores of the Sea of Galilee or to an estuarine channel directly into lake.

About 25 meters from the Bethsaida spring, a backhoe trench was cut 1.5 meters deep into fine-grained clay-rich sediment, presumably the same as that beneath the present Bethsaida pool. This deposit is a black, organic-rich mud with bones and shells only 50 to 70 centimeters beneath a fluvial gravel cover (fig. 7). Fine-grained deposits of this nature indicate a quiet or slack-water deposition mode as is characteristic of lagoons, estuaries, swamps, or backwater river areas. The mud passes laterally south within about 10 meters to a less organic, lighter colored lake mud characteristic of the Tabgha Formation. The top of the mud at the spring is 205 meters below sea level, which is about 5 meters above the modern mean level of the Sea of Galilee at -210.3 meters (see table).

Samples of the organic rich mud from just beneath the gravel cover and an apatite-bearing artiodactyl bone from the same horizon were recovered for radiocarbon dating and sent to the Krueger Laboratory in Cambridge, Massachusetts. The organic clay was dated at 2455±90 carbon-14 years BP and the bone optile at 2,035± 170 C-14 years BP. Radiocarbon dates are within ±100 years of calendrical dates for at least the past 2,500 years.[53] Therefore, starting with the standard calendrical value of the year 1950 for the BP date to begin the back calculation, together with the outside limits of the single standard deviation value in the carbon-14 data expressed by the ± symbol, and then rounding off the resulting values, these carbon-14 dates equate to mud and bone being deposited in open quiet waters close to the Bethsaida tell about 2,700 to 1,800 years ago.

Lake-Level Fluctuations of the Sea of Galilee in historical and
recent times (after Nir 1990)

Meters b.s.l.	Fluctuation
-201	Base of Bethsaida tell.
-203 -204	Bethsaida spring.
-204	Top of wall at pool below Bethsaida spring.
-205	Top of lagoonal black mud at Bethsaida spring.
-207	Highest ground at el-Araj.
-208	Approximate level of Jordan River at south end of Bethsaida tell. Historic high water mark of Kinneret (Sea of Galilee) in 1929.
-209	General level of el-Araj.
-210 -211	Lowest Kinneret level during Roman times (Nun estimate).
-211	Original natural Moshava Kinneret sill at Jordan River outlet. Harbor foundations of antiquity.
-212 -213	Historic Kinneret low water mark of 1934 and 1986.
-214	Sill at Geganya outlet since 1932.

We hypothesize that this mud represents a quiet water body suitable as an anchorage at the site through some combination of (1) lake sedimentation uplifted above modern mean lake level along the rift fault, (2) estuarine sedimentation terminated by overlying Meshoshim and Jordan flood gravels, (3) ponding of a channel of the Jordan as the delta extended lakeward and thereby caused channel aggradation, and (4) ponding of a channel of the Jordan by Meshoshim alluviation. As with the known downwarp rate of the Galilee basin of 1 millimeter per year, a postulated similar, and therefore reasonable, rate of uplift over the past two thousand years would uplift lake muds only about 2 meters from their present level at the lakeshore, instead of the approximately 5 meters observed at the Bethsaida spring. Therefore, we presume a water gradient to the lake which implies a riverine slope down the Jordan or down the Bethsaida spring stream and into an estuary. In the model, the large alluvial fan generated by the Meshoshim may have first deflected and ponded the Jordan

River to form part of a riverine anchorage, besides progressively over-whelming prior estuarine anchorages.

Some of the other nearby stream channels pass into a variety of es-tuarine complexes at the margins of the Sea of Galilee. The banks of these estuaries are in places 1 to 2 meters above the historic highwater mark of 208.7 meters below sea level (table). It is probable that these deeper water estuaries have been kept open and free of accumulated debris partly by fluctuations of the level of the Sea of Galilee. In this model, during low water-level stands the periodic stream floods and debris flows would have scoured the channel bottoms free of accumulated sediment and thereby entrenched the channels. During high stands of lake level the estuaries would maintain deep water. Such coastal configurations with deep estua-rine channels are characteristic of deltaic and estuarine marine coasts that have a strong tidal range. The Sea of Galilee does not have tides but its long period fluctuations of lake level at an average of 1.48 meters per year may crudely mimic tides that cause deep estuarine coasts. Strong currents induced by winds may also influence these features. Furthermore, the newly discovered information about catastrophic *tsunami* floods from the Sea of Galilee[54] indicates the likelihood of onshore erosion and sedimen-tation effects from that process as well.

Close to the shores of the lake some minor beach ridges of silt and sand occur, especially near the mouth of the Jordan River (fig. 4). These beach ridges are offset left laterally a few meters across the mouth of the Jordan, perhaps as a result of recurrent movement of the rift fault be-neath. None of these beach ridges were observed further inland close to Bethsaida. The small el-Araj archaeological site of probable Byzantine age (fourth to sixth century CE) is located on a beach ridge at the edge of the lake close to the Jordan River, which shows that at least part of the lake-shore was in place as an offshore bar or beach ridge about 1,500 years ago. Depth to bedrock at the el-Araj site has been shown by a borehole to be greater than 94 meters. The surface of el-Araj is littered with basalt cobbles and boulders about 1 meter in size, with most about 0.25 meter and a few about 0.5 meter. The area was probably originally emplaced as flash flood deposits that were subsequently reworked into an offshore bar or beach ridge parallel to the coast by the dominant general lake circulation coun-terclockwise (east to west) and the summer wind-driven clockwise (west to east) longshore drift in the area.

Sea of Galilee (Lake Kinneret)

The level of this freshwater lake was predominantly dependent in antiquity upon the rate of inflow of the Jordan River from the north, less the outflow of the lower Jordan, plus evapotranspiration from the lake surface and its margins. The outflow involved two outlets, the Moshava Kinneret sill at 211 meters below sea level (fig. 3) and the Deganya outlet, which since 1932, was reconstructed at 214 meters below sea level (table). The Deganya outlet is submodern, being reported first in 1106 CE. Nun felt that the two outlets served contemporaneously to drain the lake during high levels following peak midwinter runoff.[55]

The inability of the shallow and narrow outlets to drain the large volumes of winter flood water caused lake level fluctuations, then and now, with the result that deviations usually were between 0.8 to 1.2 meters with general extremes of about 2 meters.[56] Two years of drought in 1985 and 1986 allowed the lake level to drop several meters and exposed many ancient weirs, docks, and a wooden boat from about two thousand years ago (table).[57] Conversely, abnormally high runoff in 1991 and 1992 raised the level to about 208.9 meters below sea level. In the past sixty-seven years of record the all-time recorded high was 208.7 meters below sea level and the low was 212.9 meters below sea level, for a maximum range of 4.2 meters. The mean annual fluctuation for this period has been 1.48 meters.

Levels of the Sea of Galilee have fluctuated in the geologic past, as attested to by the extensive Lake Lisan sediments well outside the boundaries of the present shoreline. Thus we may postulate a long history of steady drawdown of lake level at the Bethsaida archaeological site. Moreover, no significant still stands at any one level can have occurred during this process because no raised beaches of wave erosion and deposition were ever produced, as is characteristic of so many former shorelines elsewhere.

Postulated fluctuations of the Sea of Galilee in the past six thousand years are controversial. D. Neev noted that the lake level should have dropped rather rapidly as a result of the quick channeling effect of the relatively steep course of the lower Jordan through soft, easily erodable Lisan sediments from the Sea of Galilee to the Dead Sea. He thought that between 4,000 and 2,500 years BP there was a drop rate of 10 to 15 millimeters per year, while since 2,500 years BP the rate has dropped to 2 millimeters per year.[58] If accurate—and the rate seems reasonable, particularly in light of the fact that Rotstein et al. noted present-day subsidence in the outlet area[59]—the total downcutting and consequent lake lowering would be 20 to 24 meters. This would be roughly equivalent to a total drop in lake level from about 190 meters below sea level to its present 211 meters below sea level, more than enough to dramatically alter the coastline of the Sea of Galilee and cause the shoreline to change in the Bethsaida area.

Temporary rises of the level of the Sea of Galilee due to outlet blockages are likely to have occurred in antiquity as well. The Jordan River is known to have been blocked many times in the past, and if the blockage was close enough to the Sea of Galilee outlet, the lake level would have been raised for a while until the blockage was overtopped and eroded away. For example, the Jordan was stopped at least once by unknown causes (Josh. 3:16) as well as from known earthquakes and landslides in 1267 CE and 1546 CE.[60] In addition, several slope failures into the lower Jordan in the nineteenth and early twentieth centuries are also known to have blocked the river,[61] with the most recent occurring in 1967. The active tectonism near the Jordan outlet of the Sea of Galilee[62] also indicates potential for blockage there.

In spite of the above observations and interpretations, Ben Arieh and Nun felt that the present lake level and its minor fluctuations under natural conditions up to 1932 were instead reflective of conditions throughout history.[63] No extreme level changes were thought by them to have occurred in the past. The lowest level during Roman times was thus estimated at 210.5 below sea level (table).[64]

Whether the Sea of Galilee fluctuated to a greater or lesser extent in the past 5 millennia or so is thus not entirely clear. But in any case it is probable that in antiquity the level of the Sea of Galilee fluctuated quite as much as it does now, and would therefore have had considerable control upon shoreline sedimentation processes. Estuarine mouths would have come and gone in response to riverine flood erosion and deposition; similarly, beaches, spits, offshore bars, and islands would have been but temporary features of an ever dynamic coastal landscape. At the present time, the Jordan delta and the Meshoshim estuary give the appearance of long-lived stability yet they were altered dramatically only twenty-five years ago. At the same time, the old offshore bar or beach ridge at el-Araj is almost awash. Such conditions are seen to be the norm on a coastline that is subject to rapid change.

CONCLUSION

The three hypotheses (shore-up, shore-out, water-down) posed to explain the isolation of the Bethsaida archaeological site from the shore of the Sea of Galilee require further detailed assessment and chronology construction in order to establish which mix of the three is the most appropriate to explain present relationships (figs. 8A, 8B, 8C). The following is a summary of what we know, coupled with a proposal of some needed research directions that can be pursued to accomplish a more complete understanding of the evolution of Bethsaida.

THE SHORE-UP MODEL

As noted, evidence of uplift in the region is presented by the gentle planar slope of the Beteiha Plain, which resembles an uplifted lacustrine bottom, as well as the presence at the base of the tell of the Tabgha formation clays well above present lake level. Nevertheless, such postulated uplift of 5 meters in only about two thousand years would require a rate of about 2.5 millimeters per year. Although certainly possible in active tectonic areas, this rate seems about two or three times too rapid for the region and therefore probably should not be used to account for the observed difference in altitude of lake muds above present water level. We can hypothesize reasonably only one-quarter to one-third of the difference in levels to be uplift related.

THE SHORE-OUT MODEL

Sediment in storage is plentiful in all the lower river valleys of the region and in some of the upper reaches as well. Flash floods are seen to have eroded much new sediment from along the Jordan and Meshoshim rivers in the 1960s. Extensive mounds of boulders and debris are spread throughout the upper Beteiha Plain from the Meshoshim to the Daliyot canyon mouths, and some of these features occur all the way to the lakeshore and offshore as well. The Jordan River flood gravels of 1969 were spread throughout a zone about 1 kilometer wide across the Beteiha Plain to the lakeshore. Gravels overlying estuarine muds at the Bethsaida spring appear to have been emplaced by a flood on the Jordan prior to the 1969 event.

The modern sedimentation patterns thus enable better understanding of the development of the Meshoshim fan of antiquity. This fan deflected the Jordan to the west, and probably ponded part of the river at

Bethsaida, perhaps covering a major estuary to Bethsaida, and forming a shoreline of antiquity farther north than at present.

It is clear, therefore, that modern and ancient flash floods have poured plentiful sediment across the Beteiha Plain and into the Sea of Galilee. Such events, occurring perhaps every century or few centuries, would not only have been capable of forming navigable ponded areas along the Jordan but also would have been sufficient to partially fill the estuarine bays close to Bethsaida and thereby destroy the town's harbor facilities. Building out of the shore by fluvial deposition, so characteristic of most ports of antiquity,[65] is thus seen as a partial explanation for the present location of Bethsaida 2 kilometers from the modern Sea of Galilee shoreline.

THE WATER-DOWN MODEL

Historical fluctuations of the level of the Sea of Galilee are seen to be high frequency (climate or about annual) and small magnitude, as well as low frequency (perhaps earthquake, landslide, and downcutting) and moderate magnitude. In addition, there are low frequency and high magnitude *tsunami* floods that would have periodically swept the Beteiha Plain from offshore. All these fluctuations apparently are responsible for maintaining the estuarine coast of the northern Sea of Galilee. Such drowned river valleys are one of the most likely sources of navigable waters during the time of Bethsaida, and were likely far closer to the city site then than they are now. Some downcutting of the lower Jordan also may have reduced the water level to a minor extent in the past two millennia, but it is likely not significant to the Bethsaida port, given the recent exposure of ancient weirs and docks[66] in the drought of 1985–1986 that show the water level of antiquity did greatly differ from that of the present.

The problem of navigation and harbor facilities of the presumed fishing village of Bethsaida in antiquity is thus seen as a complex combination of land-up, shore-out, and water-level fluctuations on this rather unstable coastline (fig. 8). Indeed, for ancient Bethsaida to have maintained even a marginally useful harbor for the length of time it did is somewhat surprising given the apparent level of coastal instability. It is possible that el-Araj served as a temporary anchorage at times, but for reasons outlined extensively above, it is unlikely to have been more than a fishing outpost. Whether or not et-Tell is in fact Bethsaida, at least in terms of its original proximity to navigable waters, is thus not seen as a problem of any greater relevance than the proper identification of most other cities of antiquity.

Attention to the factors listed above should enable formulation of a more precise chronology of isolation of the Bethsaida site from the shoreline of the Sea of Galilee. It is not a question of whether or not Bethsaida was once closer to the shoreline, but rather it is a question of how and when that change occurred. In fact, given the mix of strong geological controls operating at the site, shoreline changes are seen to be the norm and not some odd event. The only real problem remaining to be solved is the proper elucidation of the complex interrelationships between the three controls and the rate and exact type of change through time. Future research will solve this problem.

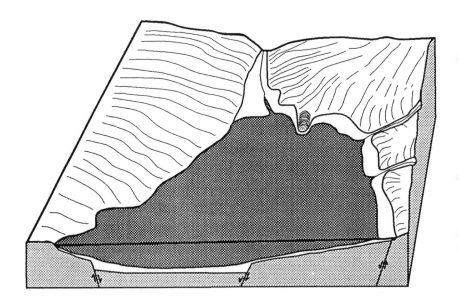

(A) ~5000 yr B.P.

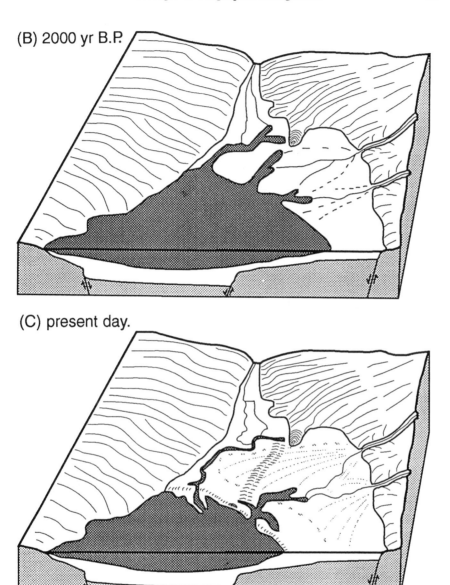

(B) 2000 yr B.P.

(C) present day.

Fig. 8. Block diagrams of hypothetical environmental changes near Bethsaida. View is looking north across the Sea of Galilee along the Jordan River with Bethsaida beginning as a peninsula on the north shore of the lake and gradually becoming isolated as the Beteiha Plain builds out, or as the north shore is raised, or as the water level declines somewhat. Fault blocks in the lake bottom are conjectural, as is the rate of sedimentation on the lake bottom as illustrated.

CHAPTER NOTES

1. Nun 1991.
2. Ibid.
3. Kraeling 1952.
4. Wilken 1953; Kraeling1952.
5. Serruya 1978.
6. Rami Arav 1988, 1989; oral communication, 1992.
7. Michelson, Flexer, and Erez 1987, 125–134.
8. Kashai and Croker 1987, 33–60.
9. Garfunkel, Zak, and Freund 1981, 1–26.
10. Rotstein and Goldberg 1981, 147–164.
11. Ben-Menahem 1991, 20:195, 216, n. B12
12. Heimann and Ron 1987, 117–124.
13. Picard 1965, 337–366; Yuval 1967, 55.
14. Fleischer, unpublished report.
15. Heimann 1990; Heimann and Ron 1987.
16. Inbar and Even-Nir 1989, 23-40.
17. Kashai and Croker 1987.
18. Michelson 1972; Mor 1973.
19. Horowitz and Horowitz 1985, 365–390.
20. Horowitz 1987, 107–115.
21. Goren-Inbar et al. 1992.
22. Goren-Inbar and Belitzky 1989, 371–376.
23. Horowitz 1979.
24. Karmon 1960, 169–193.
25. Michelson 1973, 15–19.
26. Bar-Yosef and Goren-Inbar 1993.
27. Freund and Saltzman 1966, 42–43.
28. Rotstein et al. 1992, 251–254.
29. Ben-Avraham et al. 1986, 175–189.
30. Horowitz 1987.
31. Heimann 1990; Horowitz 1968; Nir 1986; Serruya 1976, 48–56; Stiller and Assaf 1973, 397–403.
32. Horowitz 1979.
33. Horowitz 1979.
34. Ravikovich 1969; Dan and Raz 1970; Baruch 1983.
35. Horowitz 1979.
36. Horowitz 1987 Baruch 1983.
37. Horowitz 1987.
38. Horowitz 1979.
39. Baruch, 1983.
40. See Aharoni 1979.
41. Nun 1991.
42. Horowitz 1979.
43. Karmon 1960.
44. Ibid.
45. Inbar 1982a, 439-449; 1982b, 53-66.
46. Ibid.
47. Ibid.
48. Inbar 1977; Inbar and Schick 1979; Inbar and Even-Nir 1989, 23-40.

49. Inbar 1974, 197–207; Inbar 1987, 333–353.
50. Shroder 1971.
51. Inbar and Schick 1979.
52. Ben-Avraham 1981.
53. Bradley 1985, 472.
54. Ben-Menahem 1991.
55. See Bar-Adon 1956, 50–55; Nun 1991.
56. Nir 1986, 1990.
57. Wachsmann 1990.
58. Neev 1978.
59. Rotstein et al. 1992.
60. Watson 1895, 253–261; Braslavsky 1938, 323–336.
61. Glueck 1946, 268.
62. Ben-Avraham, Shaliv, and Nur 1986, 175–189.
63. Ben Arieh 1965, 307–312.
64. Nun 1991.
65. Eisma 1978, 67–81.
66. Nun 1992.

LITERATURE CITED

Aharoni, Y. 1979. *The Land of the Bible: A Historical Geography.* Philadelphia: Westminster Press.

Arav, R. 1988. Et-Tell and el-Araj. *IEJ* 38, 3:87–188.

_____. 1989. Et-Tell. 1988. *IEJ* 39. 1–2: 99–100.

Bar-Adon, P. 1956. Sinnabra and Beth Yerah in the Light of the Sources and Archaeological Finds. *Eretz Israel.* 4:50–55 (Hebrew).

Baruch, U. 1983, The Palynology of a Late Holocene Core from Lake Kinneret (Sea of Galilee). Unpublished M.A. thesis, The Hebrew University, Jerusalem (Hebrew).

Bar-Yosef, O., and N. Goren-Inbar. 1993. The Lithic Assemblages of 'Ubeidiya, a Lower Palaeolithic Site in the Jordan Valley. *Qedem,* Monograph 34, Institute of Archaeology. Jerusalem: Hebrew University of Jerusalem.

Ben Arieh, Y. 1965. Lake Kinneret Level Fluctuations. *Mada'* 9:307–312.

Ben-Avraham, Z., A. Ginzburg, and Z. Yuval. 1981. Seismic Reflection and Refraction Investigations of Lake Kinneret-Central Jordan Valley, Israel. *Tectonophysics,* 80:165–181.

_____, Z., G. Shaliv, and A. Nur. 1986. Acoustic Reflectivity and Shallow Sedimentary Structure in the Sea of Galilee. *Jordan Valley* 70:175–189.

Ben-Menahem, A. 1991. Four Thousand Years of Seismicity along the Dead Sea Rift. Journal of Geophysical Research, v. 96, n. B12, p. 20. 195–20, 216.

Bradley, R. S. 1985. *Quaternary Paleoclimatology.* Boston: Allen and Unwin.

Braslavsky, J. 1938. The Earthquake and Division of the Jordan in 1546. *Zion,* 6:323–336.

Dan, J., and Z. Raz. 1970. *The Soil Association Map of Israel.* Jerusalem: Ministry of Agriculture (Hebrew).

Eisma, D. 1978. Stream Deposition and Erosion by the Eastern Shore of the Aegean. *The Environmental History of the Near and Middle East since the Last Ice Age,* ed. W. C. Brice. London: Academic Press. 67–81.

Fleischer, E. 1968. The Subsurface Geology of the Hula Valley and Korazim Area. *Geological Survey of Israel.* Unpublished report, 8 pp.

Freund, R., and U. Saltzman. 1966. Notes on the Geology of Lake Kinneret Region. *Israel and its Inland Waters,* ed. D. Por. 17th SIL Congress. 42–43.

Garfunkel, Z., I. Zak, and R. Freund. 1981. Active Faulting in the Dead Sea Rift. *Tectonophysics* 80:1–26.

Glueck, N. 1946. *The River Jordan.* Philadelphia: Westminster Press.

Goren-Inbar, N., and S. Belitzky. 1989. Structural Position of the Pleistocene Gesher Benot Ya'aqov Site in the Dead Sea Rift Zone. *Quaternary Research* 31:371–376.

Goren-Inbar, N., S. Belitzky, K. Verosub, E. Werker, M. Kislev, A. Heimann, I. Carmi, and A. Rosenfeld. 1992. New Discoveries at the Middle Pleistocene Acheulian Site of Gesher Benot Ya'aqov, Israel. *Quaternary Research* 38:117–128.

Heimann, A. 1990. The Development of the Dead Sea Rift and its Margins in Northern Israel during the Pliocene and the Pleistocene. *Geological Survey of Israel.* Report GSI/28/90.

Heimann, A., and H. Ron. 1987. Young Faults in the Hula Pull-Apart Basin, Central Dead Sea Transform. *Tectonophysics* 141:117–124.

_____. 1993. Geometric Changes of Plate Boundaries along Part of the Northern Dead Sea Transform: Geochronologic and Paleomagnetic Evidence. *Tectonics* 12:477–491.

Horowitz, A. 1968. Upper Pleistocene-Holocene Climate and Vegetation of the Northern Jordan Valley, Israel. Geological Survey of Israel, Report No. P/2/68, Jerusalem (Hebrew).

_____. 1979, *The Quaternary of Israel.* New York: Academic Press.

_____, and M. Horowitz. 1985. Subsurface Late Cenozoic Palynostratigraphy of the Hula Basin, Israel. Pollen et Spores, v. 27 (3, 4), pp. 365–390.

_____. 1987. Palynological Evidence for the Age and Rate of Sedimentation along the Dead Sea Rift, and Structural Implications. *Tectonophysics* 141:107–115.

Inbar, M. 1974. River Delta on Lake Kinneret Caused by Recent Changes in the Drainage Basin. Geomorphologische Prozesse und Prozesskombinationen in der Gegenwart unter verserschiedenen Klimabedingungen. Report of the Commission on Present-day Geomorphological Processes (International Geographical Union). Abhandlungen der Akademie der Wissenschaften in Gottingen. 197–207.

_____. 1977. Bedload Movement and Channel Morphology in the Upper Jordan River. Unpublished Ph.D. thesis, The Hebrew University, Jerusalem.

_____. 1982a. Measurement of Fluvial Sediment Transport Compared with Lacustrine Sedimentation Rates: The Flow of the River Jordan into Lake Kinneret. *Hydrological Sciences Journal.* 4:439–449.

_____. 1982b. Spatial and Temporal Aspects of Man-induced Changes in the Hydrological and Sedimentological Regime of the Upper Jordan River. *Israel Journal of Earth Sciences.* 31:53–66.

_____. 1987. Effects of a High Magnitude Flood in a Mediterranean Climate: A Case Study in the Jordan River Basin. In *Catastrophic Flooding,* ed. L. Mayer and D. Nash. Boston: Allen and Unwin. 333–353.

_____, and M. Even-Nir. 1989. Landslides in the Upper Jordan Gorge. *Pirineos, Journal on Mountain Ecology.* 134:23–40.

_____, and A. P. Schick. 1979. Bedload Transport Associated with High Stream Power, Jordan River, Israel. Proceedings: National Academy of Science, USA, Geology, v. 76, p. 2525–2517.

Karmon, Y. 1960. The Drainage of the Huleh Swamps. *The Geographical Review* 50:169–193.

Kashai, E. L., and P. F. Croker. 1987. Structural Geometry and Evolution of the Dead Sea–Jordan Rift system as Deduced from New Subsurface Data. *Tectonophysics* 141:33–60.

Kraeling, E.G. 1952. *Bible Atlas.* New York: Rand McNally and Co.

Michelson, H. 1972. The Hydrogeology of the Southern Golan Heights. *Tahal Report* HR/72/037, Tel Aviv (Hebrew).

_____. 1973. Geology of the Kinneret Area. In *Lake Kinneret: General Background,* ed. T. Berman. Israel: National Council for Research and Development, report 12–73, pp. 15–19.

_____, A. Flexer, and Z. Erez. 1987. A Comparison of the Eastern and Western Sides of the Sea of Galilee and its Implications on the Tectonics of the Northern Jordan Rift Valley. *Tectonophysics.* 141:125–134.

Mor, D. 1973. The Volcanism in the Central Golan Heights. Unpublished M.Sc. thesis. The Hebrew University, Jerusalem (Hebrew).

Neev, D. 1978. The Geology of Lake Kinneret. *Kinneret Assemblage of Scientific Articles.* Tzemak, Israel: Publications Lake Kinneret Auto (Hebrew).

Nir, Y., 1986. Recent Sediments of Lake Kinneret (Tiberias), Israel. *Geological Survey of Israel,* report no. GS/18/86, Jerusalem.

_____. 1990. Sedimentation in Lake Kinneret and the Preservation of the Boat. In *The Excavations of an Ancient Boat in the Sea of Galilee (Lake Kinneret),* ed. Wachsmann, Shelly, 'Atiqot: Israeli Antiquities Authority. 23–28.

Nun, M. 1989. *The Sea of Galilee and its Fishermen in the New Testament.* Kibbutz Ein Gev, Israel.

_____. 1991. *The Sea of Galilee: Water Levels, Past and Present.* Kibbutz Ein Gev, Israel.

_____. 1992. *The Sea of Galilee: Newly Discovered Harbors from New Testament Days.* Kibbutz Ein Gev, Israel.

Picard, L. 1965. The Geological Evolution of the Quaternary in the Central-Northern Jordan Graben, Israel. Geological Society America Special Report 84: 337–366.

Ravikovich, S. 1969. *Manual and Map of Soils of Israel.* Jerusalem: Magnes Press (Hebrew).

Rotstein, Y., Y. Bartov, and U. Frieslander. 1992. Evidence for Local Shifting of the Main Fault and Changes in the Structural Setting, Kinarot Basin, Dead Sea Transform. *Geology.* 20:251–254.

Rotstein, Y., and S. Goldberg. 1981. Magnetotelluric Profile across the Dead Sea Rift in Northern Israel. *Tectonophysics.* 80:47–164.

Serruya, C. 1976. Rates of Sedimentation and Resuspension in Lake Kinneret. *Interactions between Sediments and Fresh Water,* ed. H. I. Golterman. The Hague: Dr. W. Junk Publishers. 48–56.

_____, ed. 1978, *Lake Kinneret.* The Hague: Dr. W. Junk Publishers.

Shroder, J. F., Jr. 1971. Landslides of Utah. *Utah Geological and Mineral Survey,* Bulletin 90.

Stiller, H., and Assaf, G. 1973. Sedimentation and Transport in Lake Kinneret Traced by 137Os. in Hydrology of Lakes. *Proceedings Helsinki Symposium,* July 1973. IAHS Pub. No. 109, p. 397–403.

Wachsmann, S. 1990. *The Excavations of an Ancient Boat in the Sea of Galilee (Lake Kinneret).* 'Atiqot: Israeli Antiquities Authority.

Watson, C. M. 1895. The Stoppage of the River Jordan in AD 1267. *Palestine Exploration Fund, Quarterly Studies.* 28:253–261.

Wilken, K. E. 1953. *Biblisches Erleben im Heiligen Land.* Baden: Verlag der St. Johannis Druckerei C. Scheweickhardt, Lahy Dinglingen.

Yuval, S. 1967. Gravimetric Survey in the Hula Valley. *Israel Journal of Earth Sciences* 16:55.

Sandra Fortner

Hellenistic and Roman Fineware from Bethsaida

D URING THE EXCAVATION SEASONS OF 1987 TO 1992, almost four
hundred fragments of Hellenistic and early Roman red and mixed-
slip fragments of fineware were found at Bethsaida (et-Tell). This preliminary report identifies and discusses a selection of different wares and
forms of tableware. In this early stage of excavation, without stratification,
proposals from other sites will be compared in relation to dating and origin.[1]

To avoid adding confusion to the mass of terminology for Hellenistic slipped fineware, this preliminary report creates no new nomenclature. Wares are separated by color and consistency of clay and slip, and
generally referred to as late Hellenistic and early Roman fineware. Relief-
decorated ware is specified under a separate heading.

HELLENISTIC SLIPPED FINEWARE

CONSISTENCY OF CLAY AND TYPES OF SLIP

The term fineware includes pottery in Bethsaida which has a generally
fine clay with a soft or slightly hard texture, and only a few grits (or
none), and a clean break. For the most part, the color is pale orange, pink-
ish, or slightly gray. The slip varies from orange-red to brown and black,
with a good deal of mixed red and brown-black, and it is glossy or dull,
thick or thin. Except for some elaborate examples with thick, glossy slip, a
considerable amount of degenerated manufacture appears. Despite the

presence of fine clay, the applied slip is thin, cracked, and dull, and usually peeling off. The impression is that of a "washed" paint.[2] Thick, black, glossy slip is rare, compared to the red and mixed slipped fragments.

MANUFACTURING TECHNIQUES[3]

All fragments of plain fineware of Bethsaida are wheel–made. Ringbases of plates, bowls, and other vessels are applied secondarily. Relief-decorated bowls are mold-made with an extra wheel-made rim. The soft-to-medium-hard break leads us to assume that medium firing temperatures were used. Before they were fired, the vessels were coated with slip. There are two major techniques of applying the slip to open forms: (1) the complete interior and the exterior rim areas are coated; often trickled drops are visible on the exterior lower half of the vessel (pl. IX.2); and (2) the complete vessel is coated (see no. 6). Fingerprints show that the vessels were held by hand at the ringbase while the slip was applied.

Many examples at Bethsaida have two-colored slip as a result of stacking in the oven. F. Follin Jones remarks that bowls were stacked in kilns and most of the chromatic irregularities occurred because there was not sufficient reduction to ensure complete blackening of the vases. On bowls with incurved rims this means, according to Follin Jones, that the exterior upper rim is black while the rest of the bowl is red.[4] If the kiln's atmosphere is, in contrast to reduction, oxidizing, then the results of the firing is expected to be red, and covered parts of vessels would be black or dark brown, like the inner circle of the interior bottom (pl. IX.1). Since correlation of fragments with the stratigraphy of Bethsaida is not yet possible, no statements about chronological associations of good glossy fragments and degenerated vessels will be made.

UNDECORATED VESSELS

The majority of forms in Bethsaida consists of bowls, dishes, and a few jugs. With the exception of two bowls, no complete profiles of vessels have yet been found. The only decorations are stamps on some plates and bowls. Predecessors of some forms, such as the bowls with incurved rim, appear in the late fifth century BCE in Greece and during the third century BCE in Syria, Palestine, and Egypt. The beginning of regional and local forms of these vessels in Palestine cannot yet be determined.[5] We cannot even restrict the terms "regional" or "local" to certain areas.

Open Forms

Plates with Incurved Rim. A common form in Hellenistic contexts is a broad plate with incurved rim, beveled on the inside and S-shaped on the outside, often with rouletted and stamped decoration at the center.[6] It should be noted that plates with incurved rim, though found throughout the Middle East, are never uniform. Each fragment seems to be individual, at Bethsaida as well as at other sites.[7] Arthur Cornell, Jr. divides the broad Tel Anafa plates with incurved rim and ringbase into three chronological variants, dating mainly from the shape of the bottom and ringbase area.[8]

Since no complete plates have been found at Bethsaida this method cannot be followed; only approximations may be made for dating. The plates with incurved rim are assumed to date from the middle of the second century BCE until the first quarter of the first century BCE.[9] Two examples (pls. II.1 and I.2) show the nonuniformity of shapes in Bethsaida. In fact, none of the plate and bowl fragments are identical to one another.

Bowls with Incurved Rim. The bowl equivalent to the broad plate described above is deep, with incurved rim and ringbase (pls. I.3–4 and IX.1–2). This form is common at sites with Hellenistic fineware.[10] The suggested dating by Paul W. Lapp ranges from 200 to 100 BCE and is strengthened by the evidence from Tel Anafa for this form.[11] At Bethsaida, 112 fragments with numerous nuances of rim profile, clay, and slip color appear. The dominant texture of fabric is a pale orange, fine clay, mostly without grits. The covering slip is red on ninety-six examples, black on only sixteen fragments. One complete profile (pls. I.3, IX.1–2) suggests the reconstructible shape of the other rim fragments. There is no uniformity in rim and lip shape.

Fishbowls/Plates. The characteristic features of this form are a rather shallow shape, broad everted rim, a ringbase, and a cuplike depression in the middle of the bottom. The depression has a raised edge and is always smaller in diameter than the ringbase.[12] The vessels are covered with either a black, black-brown, or red slip. Chronological evidence for fishbowls/plates derives from sites such as Beth-Zur, Tarsus, or Samaria.[13] This form was used between 200 BCE to 100 BCE.[14]

Thus far, twenty-eight rim and bottom fragments of fishbowls/plates can be identified at Bethsaida. The slip of fourteen fragments is red, twelve are black, and two fragments are secondarily burnt. The rim diameters vary from 8 to 23 centimeters.

CLOSED FORMS

JUGS. No complete jug could be identified at Bethsaida, but only some rim and handle fragments and one bottom fragment were found. Two types of jug rims are presented in this preliminary report. Although very different in shape and thickness, both types belong to the fineware categories defined in the introductory chapter. Similar in shape (but not ware) to the thin-walled rim fragment (pl. III.8) is Samaria form 25 (Eastern Sigillata A), which dates from the first century BCE to the first century CE. Parallel in shape to the fragment of a thick-walled, wide-mouthed jug (pl. III.9) is an amphora from Tarsus.[15]

Two shapes of handle fragments exist in Bethsaida. One is thin, almost angular, which seems similar to the handle of a *lagynos*-shaped jug (pl. III.11).[16] This differs completely from the other flat, almost broad type with slightly bent handles to which no exact parallel has yet been found (pl. III.12). The same may be said concerning a bottom fragment of a closed vessel, probably a jug (pl. III.10). No exact proposals for dating can be made for Bethsaida jugs and handles except that they are Late Hellenistic.

DECORATED BOTTOM FRAGMENTS

ROULETTED DECORATION. A common decoration on bowls and plates with incurved rim is roulette decoration. This usually consists of two preserved circles on the interior bottom of some vessels (pl. IV.13–14). Completely preserved patterns of decoration on plates from Tel Anafa and Samaria-Sebaste show two or three rows of rouletting.[17] No decoration or the omission of one of the mentioned schemes may also be observed on pottery in this category.[18]

PALMETTE STAMPS. Palmette-shaped stamps are a common decoration motif on Eastern Sigillata A from early Hellenistic to Roman times, as examples from Samaria-Sebaste, Tel Anafa, and other sites show.[19] They occur with rouletting.[20] The Bethsaida material has so far only produced two examples of different palmette decoration (pls. IV.15–16; X.2) on Late Hellenistic fineware (on Eastern Sigillata A).

MISCELLANEOUS FORMS

Compared to the vast number of bowls and plates with an incurved rim as well as fishbowls/plates, only a few examples of various rim shapes of plates and bowls occur at Bethsaida. Most of them have no parallels and so no final determinations have been made for dating. In some cases not even general proposals for reconstruction of the shapes can be made. One example is a single, almost complete bowl with an S-shaped rim and handle (pl. V.17), which is similar to a small deep bowl with pinched handle (*skyphos*),[21] a form that seems to have been widespread in Palestine during the third to second century BCE.[22] Five other singular examples of bowls (with no parallels so far) are (1) one with an S-shaped rim (pl. V.18), (2) one with a thin, straight rim (pl. V.19), (3) one cylindrical thick-walled bowl (pl. V.20), (4) one small, almost cylindrical bowl with a grooved neck (pl. V.21), and (5) another small bowl with everted rim (pl. V.22).

Representative of the plates found at Bethsaida is a shallow plate with a triangular lip (pl. VI.23) similar to the plate with thickened rim at Samaria, which derives from fifth to fourth century BCE Attic forms with rouletting and palmettes. Parallels to the Bethsaida fragment date to the second century BCE.[23]

A dish with an angular profile (pl. VI.24) has no exact parallels in Late Hellenistic contexts. Similar black-slipped examples from Samaria-Sebaste ("bowl with outcurved rim") date from the late third to the first century BCE.[24]

Two small body fragments of a bowl or a *krateriskos* (pl. VI.25–26) have fluted decoration that is similar to the decoration of bowls found at Tel Anafa. Chronological evidence yielded by Tel Anafa about this form suggests that it is a relatively late development in the repertoire of Late Hellenistic Red Tableware shapes that appeared late in the second phase, around 100 BCE, and continued into the first century BCE. Further parallels to bowls with fluted decoration starting below the rim area occur in different wares, such as the so-called Megarian bowls and the earliest forms of Eastern Sigillata A in Hama and Samaria.[25]

HELLENISTIC MOLDED RELIEF DECORATED BOWLS. A Hellenistic form that is widespread in the eastern Mediterranean region is a relief-decorated, moldmade bowl, generally known as a Megarian bowl.[26] The main features of this deep form, which has no ringbase, are: a half-round shape, a slightly everted or straight grooved rim, and relief decoration starting

below the rim area and including the bottom (fig. 1). The decoration consists mostly of floral motifs. Various examples of different buff clay and
slip show the lack of uniformity of this ware as well as indicate that different workshops produced it.[27] Relief-decorated bowls derive from early
Hellenistic silver bowls with similar shape and decoration.[28] This ware apparently was produced in the third century BCE and continued until the
first century BCE.[29] and probably later. Its origins are extremely difficult
to trace and have not yet been entirely determined.[30]

Fig. 1. Typical mold-made relief-decorated bowl, found in Turkey.
Courtesy Prähistorische Staatssammlung Munich. Used by permission.
(Not to scale)

Only three shapes of rim profiles from Bethsaida may be distinguished (pl. VII.27–29). A number of body fragments with various motifs
differ in slip and decoration. The color of clay is quite uniformly pale orange, but occasionally a creamy grayish; it is fine and contains no grits.
The color of the thin or thick slip varies, from shades of red to black,
glossy or dull (pl. VII. 30–34).

Decorations like *kymation* with a pearl row and flower buds beneath (pl. VII.31), heart-shaped leaves below the *kymation* (pl. VII.28),
acanthus leaves (pl. VII.30,) or overlapping scales (pl. VII.33) belong to the
general repertoire of relief-decorated bowls, as examples from Oboda, Tarsus, Antioch, and so forth suggest.[31]

Most of the fragments at Bethsaida are thin-walled, with elaborately molded decoration and a fine slip. These are probably imports, since they occur in major sites like Tarsus and Antioch. Some rather thick-walled fragments, with thin, peeling slip and slightly crude decoration tend to be from local workshops. Parallels to some Bethsaida fragments with rows of long buds are found in Tarsus and date to the Late Hellenistic period.[32]

Roman Red Slipped Ware

Barbotine Decorated Bowls. Only a few early Roman forms and fragments could be identified by date in the material of Bethsaida. One body fragment of a bowl with Barbotine decoration (ivy leaf) is known in Bethsaida (pl. VIII.35). Parallels from Oboda, Dura-Europos, and Hama come from Roman levels. The closest parallels seem to be hemispherical bowls from the potter's shop at Oboda. Bowls in Palestine with this decorative pattern are Augustan.[33] A rim fragment of a thin-walled bowl with heavily incurved rim is similar in shape to a Roman Barbotine decorated bowl from Oboda.[34]

Eastern Sigillata A

The bottom fragment of a bowl with a strong, slightly grooved ringbase (pls. VIII.37, ix.3) differs in thickness, quality, and consistency of slip from the other previously described ware. It reminds one of Western Terra Sigillata in shape and slip, but has no exact parallels. The origins of the Bethsaida fragment have not yet been determined, but similar ringbases occur in Hama. The Hama pieces belong to hemispherical bowls of the first century CE. Close parallels to the Bethsaida bottom fragment are hemispherical bowls with everted lip of Eastern Sigillata A of the first century BCE. Another close parallel comes from Jerusalem.[35] A bottom fragment of the same kind and a handle fragment of a juglet are the only other Eastern Sigillata A representatives found thus far at Bethsaida.

Late Roman Terra Sigillata

No complete Late Roman strata have yet been systematically identified or investigated at Bethsaida. Of the seventy-six coins identified to date, five are Roman Provincial (third century CE), one is Late Roman (fourth century CE) and two are Byzantine (sixth century CE). These coins and two joining bottom fragments of a Late Roman Terra Sigillata dish (pls. VIII.38, xi.4) are the only finds which indicate a Late Roman presence at

Bethsaida. It is important to note that all the coins and fragments were found in Area A, at a place where the uppermost layers sustained severe damage from modern disturbances.

The fragments are to be identified as Hayes Form 50 A, found over a wide geographic area, of the late third century CE (fig. 2). This large undecorated dish possesses a broad flat bottom and high straight walls that rise at an angle to a plain rim. The tiny beveled foot is under the edge of the bottom. These pure, hard dishes with clean breakage were manufactured in North Africa and imported by most of the provinces of the Roman Empire. The surface of this form is very smooth and is coated with a thin slip. J. W. Hayes suggests a dating from about 230/40–325 CE.[36]

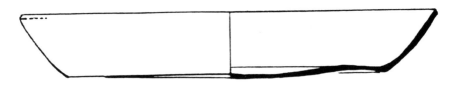

Fig. 2. Complete profile of Hayes 50A. Drawing after Hayes

SUMMARY

The fineware discovered at Bethsaida consists of about four hundred fragments of predominantly Hellenistic fineware of different forms, and some evidence of Roman fineware and Terra Sigillata. The Hellenistic ware is relatively homogeneous as regards clay and slip. The main forms are bowls and plates with incurved rim and fishbowls/plates. Only a few closed and miscellaneous forms could be identified so far. Decoration on bottom fragments is scanty and consists of palmettes or rouletting. The general time span for dating ranges from 200 BCE to 100 BCE, and rarely to the first century BCE.

Different from the Hellenistic undecorated plain ware are twenty-seven fragments of mold-made relief-decorated bowls—a style common in Hellenistic and sometimes Roman layers. The Bethsaida fragments compare favorably with parallels from Hellenistic and Roman layers at different sites.

Little evidence is available on early Roman fineware and Eastern Sigillata A pottery at the site. Two fragments of Barbotine decorated bowls that clearly date to the last decades of the first century BCE and the beginning of the first century CE have been found. Probably three to four fragments represent early Roman Eastern Sigillata A. No Western Terra

Sigillata (Italian Arretine Terra Sigillata or South Gaulish Terra Sigillata) have been found. A decline of the number of fineware from the first century CE is obvious. The main evidence for fineware dates from the second and beginning of the first centuries BCE.

One piece of Terra Sigillata pottery is exceptional because of its importance to dating the last period of occupation at the site. It is a fragment of a Terra Sigillata plate imported from North Africa which dates to the third or fourth century CE. The appearance of this piece and the few Late Roman coins at Bethsaida raises questions about whether there was a settlement at et-Tell in the third or fourth century CE. A number of coins dating from the middle of the third century CE also suggest this.[37]

Plate I. Hellenistic Fineware

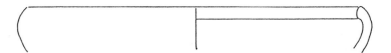

I.1. Rim fragment of broad plate with incurved rim and lip. Clay pale orange, fine, no grits. Slip red-brownish, glossy, exterior peeling off. Diameter 20 cm, preserved height, 2.6 cm.

I.2. Rim fragment of plate with slightly incurved rim, no clear lip. Clay creamy, fine, no grits. Slip black, glossy, peeling off. Diameter 18 cm, preserved height 1.8 cm.

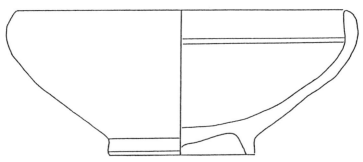

I.3.ix; I.3. One complete profile of bowl with incurved rim and ringbase. Clay pale orange, fine, some grits. Slip dark red-brownish, thick, dull, except interior of bottom and exterior rim area, where slip is brown black, thick, dull. The lower half of exterior surface is not covered with any slip. Rim diameter 16 cm, ringbase diameter 7.5 cm. Height 7 cm.

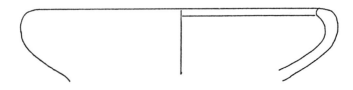

I.4. Rim fragment of bowl with strong incurved rim and lip. Clay pale orange, fine, no grits. slip dark red-brownish, thick, dull. Diameter 12 cm, preserved height 3.5 cm.

Plate II. Hellenistic Fineware

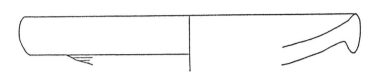

II.5. Rim fragment of fishplate with drooping rim. Clay light red greyish, hard, fine, some grits. Slip covers complete fragment, thick, black, dull. Rim diameter 14 cm, preserved height 3.6 cm.

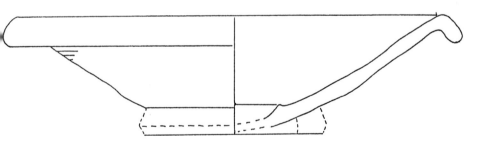

II.6.x.1. Almost-complete profile of fishbowl; missing ringbase. Clay pale orange, fine, no grits. Slip medium brown except on exterior bottom, red. Rim diameter 18 cm, preserved height 4.8 cm.

II.7. Three joining bottom fragments of a fishbowl with ringbase. Clay pale orange, fine, no grits. Slip covers the complete fragment, orange to dark orange and brown, dull. Ringbase diameter 5.4 cm, preserved height 2.2 cm.

PLATE III. HELLENISTIC FINEWARE

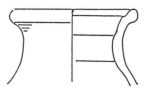

III.8. Rim fragment of thin-walled jug with part of the neck. Lip slightly everted with ridge inside. Clay pale orange creamy, fine, no grits. Slip covers exterior surface, interior in rim area only, red to dark red and brown, dull, peeling off. Dia. 5 cm, preserved height 3.1 cm.

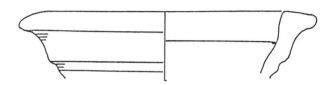

III.9. Rim fragment of thick-walled widemouthed jug with horizontal, slightly flaring lip, stepped neck. Clay light orange, fine, some grits. Slip covers fragment completely, dark red, brownish, dull, peeling off. Rim diameter 10 cm, preserved height 2.9 cm.

III.10. Bottom fragment of jug with ringbase. Clay pale orange, fine, no grits. Slip on exterior surface only, orange red, dull. Diameter of ringbase 8 cm, preserved height 1.4 cm.

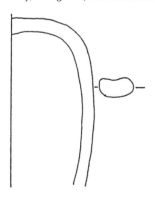

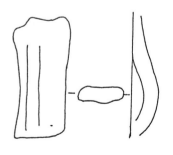

III.11. Almost-complete flat angular handle of jug. Clay light red, fine, no grits. Slip covers complete fragment, reddish brown, peeling off. Length 6.9 cm, width 1.5 cm.

III.12. Fragment of flat, broad, slightly bent handle of jug. Clay light orange, fine, no grits. Slip covers complete fragment, dark brown to black, patchy, dull, peeling off. Length 4.3 cm; width 1 cm.

PLATE IV. HELLENISTIC FINEWARE

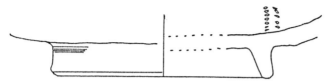

IV.13. Bottom fragment of plate/bowl with ringbase. Two preserved rouletted circles. Clay pale orange, fine, no grits. Slip covers complete fragment; patchy, red-brownish to brown, thick, glossy. Diameter of ringbase 6 cm, preserved height 1.8 cm.

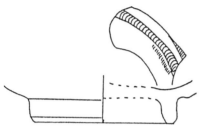

IV.15.x.2. Two joining bottom fragments of plate with ringbase. Interior bottom decorated with five radially stamped palmettes, enclosed by one preserved rouletted circle. Clay pale orange, fine, few red grits. Slip covers complete fragment including ringbase; orange brownish, peeling off. Ringbase diameter 9 cm, preserved height 2.1 cm.

IV.14. Bottom fragment of plate with ringbase. Two preserved rouletted circles. Clay pale orange, fine, no grits. Slip covers most of fragment; patchy, purple, red to black, thick, glossy. Diameter of ringbase 9 cm, preserved height 2.7 cm

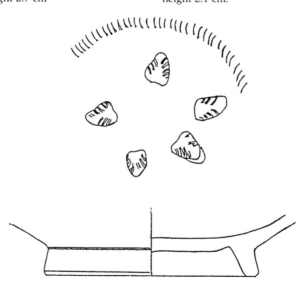

IV.16. Bottom fragment of bowl/plate(?); ringbase chipped off. One fragmentary palmette-shaped stamp. Clay pale orange, fine, no grits. Slip covers complete fragment; purple red, brownish, thick, dull. Length 4.3 cm; width 3.3 cm.

Plate V. Hellenistic Fineware

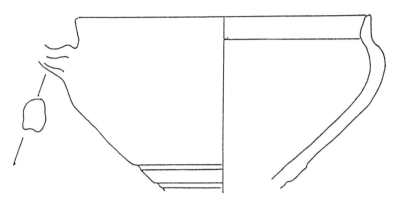

V.17. Almost-complete fragment of bowl with S-shaped profile; broken round handle. Two grooves on lower exterior half. Clay pale orange, a few grits. Slip covers most of upper half of bowl; red-brownish, dull, peeling off. Rim diameter 12 cm, preserved height 6.7 cm.

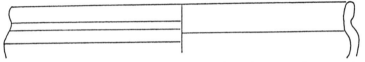

V.18. Rim fragment of S-shaped bowl with low neck. Clay pale orange, fine, no grits. Slip covers fragment completely; dark red-brownish, dull, peeling off. Rim diameter 14 cm, preserved height 2.4 cm.

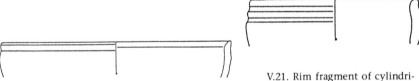

V.19. Rim fragment of thin-walled bowl with low neck and slightly inverted lip. Clay pale orange-creamy, fine, no grits. Slip covers fragment completely; black thick, glossy, peeling off. Rim dia. 13 cm, preserved height 2.0 cm.

V.21. Rim fragment of cylindrical bowl with double-grooved neck. Clay light orange, fine, no grits. Slip covers complete fragment; exterior red-brownish, dull, interior light brown, dull, peeling off both sides. Rim dia. 7 cm, preserved height 2.3 cm.

V.20. Two joining rim fragments of thick-walled cylindrical bowl. Clay pale pink, fine, no grits. Slip covers complete fragment; reddish brown, dull; interior, dark red, dull exterior, slip peeling off. Rim diameter 12 cm, preserved height 2.3 cm.

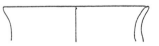

V.22. Rim fragment of straight bowl, everted rim. Clay light red, fine, no grits. Slip covers complete fragment, patchy, dark red, brown-black, thick, almost shiny. Rim dia. 8 cm, preserved height 1.9 cm.

Plate VI. Hellenistic Fineware

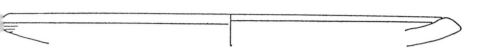

VI.23. Rim fragment of shallow plate, everted rim, "triangular" lip. Clay light orange, fine, some white grits. Slip covers complete fragment, dark red-brownish, dull. Rim diameter 18 cm, preserved height 1.3 cm.

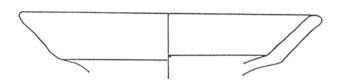

VI. 24. Two joining rim fragments of angular dish with everted sides. Break consists of grey and pink layers. Slip covers complete fragment; creamy; inside rim area red. Rim diameter 12 cm, preserved height 2.5 cm.

VI. 25. Body fragment of vertical fluted, molded bowl. No decoration in rim area. Clay pale orange, fine, some grits. Slip covers complete fragment, interior brownish, dull; exterior red-brownish, dull peeling off both sides. Length 2.4cm, width 2.1 cm.

VI. 26. Body fragment of vertical fluted, molded bowl. No decoration in rim area. Clay pale orange, some grits. Slip covers complete fragment; red purple, thick, dull, peeling off. Length 3.2 x width 2.9 cm.

Plate VII. Hellenistic Fineware

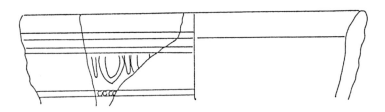

VII.27. Rim fragment of relief-decorated bowl with *kymation* and pearl row. Clay pale orange, fine, no grits. Slip dark brown reddish, glossy. Dia. 14 cm, preserved height 4.1 cm.

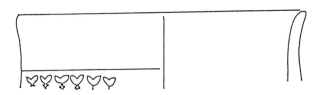

VII.28. Rim fragment of relief-decorated bowl with band of heart-shaped leaves. Clay pale orange, fine, few grits. Slip exterior surface brown to black, patchy; interior surface dark orange brown, patchy, dull. Diameter 12 cm, preserved height 3.1 cm.

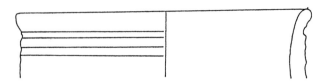

VII.29. Rim fragment of relief-decorated bowl; relief chipped off. Clay creamy, fine, no grits. Slip brown black, patchy, glossy. Diameter 12 cm, preserved height 3.1 cm.

PLATE VIII. HELLENISTIC FINEWARE

VIII.30. Thin-walled body fragment, relief-decorated bowl with elaborately shaped acanthus leaf. Clay pale orange, fine, no grits. Slip exterior surface red-brownish to dark brown, patchy, dull; interior surface dark brown-black, glossy. L. 3.8 x w. 0.9 cm.

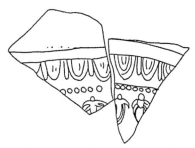

VIII.31. Two joining body fragments, relief-decorated bowl with *kymation*, band of pearls, flower buds beneath. Clay pale orange, very fine, no grits. Slip exterior surface black, glossy; interior surface red-brownish, glossy, peeling off both sides. L. 4.1 x w. 3.4 cm.

VIII.32. Body fragment, relief-decorated bowl with band of pearls, heart-shaped flowers below. Clay pale orange, fine, no grits. Slip interior dar red, dull, exterior black, dull, peeling. L. 2.1 x w. 1.5 cm.

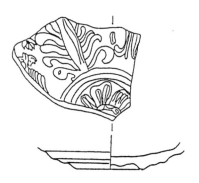

VIII.33. Body fragment of a bowl with overlapping scales. Clay orange-brownish-grayish, fine, no grits. Slip black, glossy. L. 2.1 x w. 1.8 cm.

VIII.34.xi.1. Thin-walled bottom fragment, relief-decorated bowl with palmette decoration, rosette in center of grooved bottom. Clay creamy gray, very fine, no grits. Slip on interior surface only, black, glossy. Bottom diameter 3 cm.

Plate IX. Mixed Pottery

IX.35. EARLY ROMAN FINEWARE. Body fragment of bowl with red barbotine decoration. One leaf and some fragments of other floral decoration are visible. Clay pale orange, fine, no grits. Slip covers complete fragment, dark red-brownish, dull, peeling off. Length 3.9, width 1.9 cm.

IX.36. EARLY ROMAN. Rim fragment of thin-walled bowl with heavily incurved rim. Clay pale creamy, fine, few grits. Slip covers complete fragment, dark brown, thick, dull. Rim diameter 10 cm, preserved height 1.3 cm.

IX.37.xi.3. EASTERN SIGILATTA A. Bottom fragment of bowl with slightly grooved ringbase. Clay pale orange, fine, no grits. Slip covers complete fragment including ringbase. Slip dark red-brownish, thick, glossy. Ringbase diameter 6.4 cm, preserved height 2.1 cm.

IX.38.xi.4. LATE ROMAN–NORTH AFRICAN SIGILATTA. Bottom fragment of a dish. Hayes 50A. Clay orange, hard, fine, no grits. Slip covers the interior surface only, dark orange, thick, smooth, glossy. Ringbase diameter 14 cm, preserved height 1 cm.

PLATE X. HELLENISTIC FINEWARE

X.1. Bowl with incurved rim, interior view (not to scale).
Photo, Heinz-Wolfgang Kuhn.

X.2.. Bowl with incurved rim, exterior view (not to scale).
Photo, Heinz-Wolfgang Kuhn.

Plate XI. Hellenistic Fineware

XI.1. Fishbowl (not to scale).
Photo by Sandra Fortner.

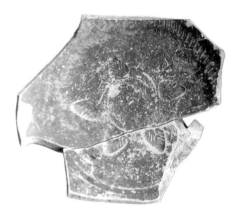

XI.2. Bowl with incised palmettes and rouletted circle (not to scale).
Photo by Sandra Fortner.

PLATE XII. MIXED POTTERY

XII.1. HELLENISTIC FINEWARE. Bottom fragment of relief-decorated bowl with rosette medallion and palmette (not to scale). Photo by Sandra Fortner.

XII. 2. HELLENISTIC FINEWARE. Body fragment, relief-decorated bowl with acanthus leaf (not to scale). Photo by Sandra Fortner.

XII.3. EARLY ROMAN EASTERN SIGILATTA A. Bottom fragment of bowl with ringbase, exterior (*l.*) and interior (*r.*) (not to scale). Photo by Sandra Fortner.

PLATE XIII. MIXED POTTERY (*continued*)

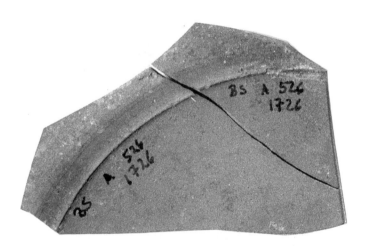

XIII.4. LATE ROMAN NORTH-AFRICAN TERRA SIGILLATA. Fragment of Hayes 50A, interior (*top*) and exterior (*bottom*) (not to scale). Photo by Sandra Fortner.

CATALOGUE NUMERS FOR PLATES

The follow chart provides catalog numbers for the fragments depicted in Plates I through IX. All of the fragments are stored at Beit Yigal Allon, Ginnosar, Israel.

Plate No.	Area	Date of Discovery	Basket No.	Drawing No.
I.1	A	26 July 1989	1678	92,380
I.2	A	02 June 1992	2144	92,209
I.3	B	03 May 1990	4081	92,455
I.4	A	10 April 1989	1535	92,389
II.5	A	05 July 1990	1828	92,489
II.6	B	03 July 1990	4124	92,356
II.7	B	11 July 1990	4166	92,354
III.8	A	29 June 1990	1781	92,229
III.9	B	21 June 1992	5199	92,311
III.10	B	25 June 1992	5217	92,310
III.11	A	02 July 1990	1792	92,219
III.12	B	17 June 1990	4095	92,321
IV.13	A	19 July 1989	1670	92,226
IV.14	A	29 June 1990	1781	92,396
IV.15	B	26 July 1990	4223	92,362
IV.16	A	11 July 1989	1632	92,333
V.17	A	04 July 1990	1810	92,270
V.18	A	03 July 1990	1800	92,239
V.19	A	30 April 1992	2068	92,213
V.20	A	02 July 1990	1795	92,216
V.21	B	27 July 1990	4099	92,350
V.22	B	28 June 1989	3030	92,471
VI.23	B	29 June 1992	52323	92,312
VI.24	A	04 May 1992	2088	92,207
VI.25	B	27 May 1992	5157	92,487
VI.26	A	10 July 1991	2035	92,302

Plate No.	Area	Date of Discovery	Basket No.	Drawing No.
VII.27	A	14 May 1989	1559	92,260
VII.28	B	07 July 1989	3075	92,472
VII.29	B	05 July 1989	3060	92,425
VIII.30	B	10 April 1989	2035	92,452
VIII.31	A	27 June 1990	1765	92,255
VIII.32	A	26 June 1990	1759	92,252
VIII.33	A	04 May 1989	1508	92,453
VIII.34	B	28 June 1990	4100	92,331
IX.35	B	25 July 1990	4216	92,332
IX.36	B	05 July 1990	4242	92,494
IX.37	B	06 July 1990	1832	92,246
IX.38	A	?	1726	92,518

CHAPTER NOTES

1. Parallels in shape and similar clay and slip, according to the description in excavation reports and studies about Hellenistic/early Roman pottery, occur in Tel Anafa, Samaria-Sebaste, Tarsus, Hama and other sites. Especially useful for the material of Bethsaida is the chapter "Hellenistische Glanztonwaren" in the Kuhnen 1989, 11–84. A helpful addition provided types 101–199 (Hellenistic decorated ware) in the corpus of Palestinian ceramic by P. Lapp, pp. 200–209. The study of J. Gunneweg attempts to collect differently named sigillata wares under the term "Eastern Terra Sigillata" and divides them into two groups according to the chemical data of a vast amount of analysis of fragments. The terms Eastern Terra Sigillata I and II refer to the different origins of the clay. However, until we can analyze the Bethsaida material (which will be the task of the following excavation seasons), no associations can be made. An appropriate term for thin-coated, red-slipped vessels in the Palestinian area seems to be "Palestinian red-slip ware." This term was created by J. W. Hayes for this kind of ware found in Jerusalem (Hayes 1985, 182–183).
2. Similar observations at Tarsus by Follin Jones for the Local Undecorated Glazed Ware. Follin Jones 1950, 153.
3. Detailed description in Cornell 1982, 44 – 46.
4. Follin Jones 1950, 154.
5. Kuhnen 1989, 15.
6. Cornell 1982, 52.
7. Cornell 1982, 53.
8. He gives a minute description of his form 1 and its variants, mainly separated by the shape and size of the bottom area. See Cornell 1982, 51–57. Unfortunately, it is not possible with the fragments from Bethsaida to distinguish chronological variants.
9. Cornell 1982, 57, observed that his first two variants, which are similar to plate nos. 1.1 and 1.2 in Bethsaida, coexist through the phases in which Late Hellenistic Red Slipped tableware occurs at Tel Anafa, from the first part of phase II, ca. 150 to 125 BCE, to phase III, ca. 100–80 BCE.
10. Kenyon describes this form thus: "The oldest of our Hellenistic bowl types . . . most popular and widely exported"; Crowfoot et al. 1957, 249, fig. 49. Kuhnen 1989, 75, cites this form under GT II "Schalen mit einbiegendem Rand" and mentions sure dated sites. Lapp 1961, type 151.1, "small deep bowls with incurved rim." Cornell 1982, pp. 151–153, describes this as an "Echinus Bowl" and writes, "It appeared in a great variety of sizes, ware types, finishes, and nuances of shape."
11. Lapp 1961, 200; Cornell 1982, 152. Kuhnen 1989, 76, places the black-slipped glossy fragments in the Early Hellenistic period, the other fragments in the Late Hellenistic period as well.
12. The erratic term fishbowls/plate derives from the cup–like depression and from the word ὀξύβαπηον scratched on the bottom of one preserved specimen from Olynthos. The food dipped in the depression may have been fish; Cornell 1982, 144–147.
13. Cornell 1982, 52, 145–146; Crowfoot et al. 1957, fig. 37, nos. 1–8, fig. 54, pp. 260–263.
14. Lapp 1961, 206–207. This type of plate appeared much earlier in Attic ware, which was actually made in Athens. The buff colored fragments at Ashdod were dated by accompanying Rhodian Amphora handles from the latter part of the third century BCE. Evidence from Samaria, Tel Anafa, and Tarsus suggest a use until approximately 100 BCE. See Gunneweg et al. 1983, 95. Kuhnen 1989, 75 esp. nn. 10–12, mentions dated sites for this form as well.
15. Crowfoot et al. 1957 states that those jugs are often referred to as Hellenistic, and the long-grooved neck with its acute handle certainly resembles that of late *lagynoi*. See

Crowfoot et al. 1957, 340, fig. 82.2. Nevertheless, the Bethsaida fragment is not to be listed under Eastern Sigillata A! The second rim shape is very similar to a vessel of another ware, described as decorated amphora. This Attic import dates to the Middle Hellenistic unit in Tarsus; see Goldman 1950, 219, pl. 125, no. 117.

16. Gunneweg et al. 1983, fig. 22.3.
17. Cornell 1982, pls. 3–9; Crowfoot et al. 1957, fig. 49.1, 3, 5 (bowls with incurved rim from the late fourth and third century BCE), fig. 51.3 (flat plate with thickened rim dating to the late fourth and early third century BCE).
18. Cornell 1982, 59.
19. Crowfoot et al. 1957, 253 ff. Kenyon also gives a short history of development of palmettes from the early fifth century in Greece onward in chronological order. See also Cornell 1982, 62–68, plates 11–15.
20. Cornell 1982, 62–68, plates 11–15.
21. Lapp 1961, type 151.4, "Small deep bowl with pinched handle." Christensen and Johansen 1971, 19–20, fig. 8.80. Crowfoot et al. 1957, fig. 39.5, "Skyphos with loop handles pinched back on the rim."
22. Lapp 1961, 204.
23. Crowfoot et al. 1957, 252–253, fig. 51; 5. 6, grey ware.
24. The black-glazed bowls with outcurved rim from Samaria originate from earlier Attic forms. See Crowfoot et al. 1957, 244–248, fig. 48. A parallel in shape from Antioch dates approximately to the second half of the early Hellenistic period there. Waagé 1948, 16, 43–44, plate II.
25. Cornell 1982, 181–182. Samaria form 19 belongs to the repertoire of Eastern Sigillata A and is described as a bowl with round base, fluted, with a molded rim. See Crowfoot et al. 1957, 342, fig. 82, 7. Hama also provides fragments of form 19. Parallels from Samaria belong to the earliest examples of this ware in the first century BCE. See Christensen and Johansen 1971, 120–124, fig. 46; 19, 5a. A red-glazed fragment of group VIII from Dura-Europos is very similar to the Bethsaida fragments. The dating of this group is based principally on comparison with evidence from Samaria and Tarsus. See Cox 1949, 7, 13, pl. IV, 77, cat. no. 77.
26. Essential reports are: Edwards 1986, 389ff.; Laumonier, 1977; Rotroff, 1982; Siebert 1978. Useful for comparison are the finds and the chapter about Megarian bowls in Crowfoot et al. 1957, 272–281.
27. The study of Rotroff 1982 is compulsory also for relief-decorated bowls in the Hellenistic Eastern Mediterranean world.
28. Hausmann 1959.
29. Lapp 1961, 209, lists examples of different sites in Palestine dating from 150 BCE to 20 CE. With regard to the material of Athens, Rotroff assumes the beginning of relief decorated bowls in the second half of the third century BCE. See Rotroff 1982, 6–13, 32–43.
30. Rotroff 1982, 42, concludes: "The great amount of trade carried on in the Hellenistic period makes it uncertain whether the bowls found on any site were produced there or elsewhere, unless a large number of molds are found on the site as well. It is impossible to locate the origins of most of the imports."
31. Plate VII; 31: see Negev 1986, no. 14. Plate VII, 28: see Goldmann 1950, fig. 129, no. 151. Plate VII, 33: See Waagé 1948, Antioch fig. 14, no. 1.
32. This pattern is also found on later Arretine Sigillata; see Goldman 1950, figure 129 no. 151, p. 222 (fragment of a Hellenistic relief-decorated bowl). Further parallels appear in Samaria. See Crowfoot et al. 1957, 5, 62, 276. A close parallel to the acanthus leaf (plate VII, 30) was found in Tarsus; see Goldman 1950, figure 129, B.

33. The potter's shop shows several bowls (but no complete profiles) with a simple ivy leaf pattern surrounding the bowl. The ware is predominantly buff-colored; the slip ranges from red to light brown, mostly dull, unevenly applied, and tends to peel off. All fragments of this kind of bowl are from the "Nabataean dump"; see Negev 1986, pp. xxi and 16, nos. 99–108. A close parallel to the pattern on a skyphos is among the Augustan grave goods of a tomb in Tel Abu-Shusha. The excavator dates the tomb to the first century CE. See Siegelman 1988, 13ff. A fragment of a red-coated barbotine cup in Dura Europos is undated and is listed under group VIII "Miscellaneous." Cox dates it according to the similar decoration after Knipowitsch as Augustan and later. However, Knipowitsch's evidence derives from stylistic comparison only; see Cox 1949, p. 7, pl. IV, 75, cat. no. 75. See Knipowitsch 1968, p. 27, fig. 5, pl. IV, 4. Some fragments from Hama with the same kind of decoration date to the Roman period. See Papanicolaou-Christensen et al. 1986, 20– 21, cat. no. 250, fig. 6f.
34. The rim fragment of Bethsaida is similar to the shape of the barbotine-decorated bowls from Oboda. Cf. note 33 above.
35. Johansen compares the Hama fragment to parallels from the Agora that date to the first century CE.; see Christensen and Johansen 1971, figs. 45: 17.1 and 45: 17.5. A similarly shaped base of an Eastern Sigillata A hemispherical bowl with everted rim (type 251.2a) mentioned by Lapp 1961, 37, 211, dates between 75 to 25 BCE. Compare also Hama form 27, fig. 72; 27B.16 (crater). Christensen and Johansen 1971, 188ff., list this form under early Eastern Terra Sigillata of the first century BCE. The general dating for this form is late Augustan; see Hayes 1985 189, nos. 1–5.6, plate 52.6.
36. For a detailed description of this form, dating evidence, and distribution; see Hayes 1972, esp. 69ff., and fig. 12.
37. According to coin analysis of Cecilia Meir, five coins found in Area A in different loci date to this period. See chapter 1 of this work for the coin analysis.

LITERATURE CITED

Cornell, L. A., Jr. 1982. *Late Hellenistic and Early Roman Red-Slipped Pottery from Tel-Anafa, 1968-1973*. Ann Arbor: University of Michigan Press.

Cox, D.H. 1949. The Greek and Roman Pottery. In Rostovtzeff et al. 1949 (q.v.), *The Excavations at Dura-Europos*.

Crowfoot, J. W., and G. M. Crowfoot, K. M. Kenyon. 1957. *The Objects from Samaria*. Samaria-Sebaste Series, 3. London: Palestine Exploration Fund.

Christensen, A. P., C. F. Johansen. 1971. *Hama: Fouilles et Recherches de la Fondation Carlsberg: 1931-1938*. Volume 3.2: *Les Potteries Hellénistiques et les Terres Sigillées Orientales*. Copenhagen: Nationalmuseets Skrifter.

Edwards, C. M. 1986. Corinthian Moldmade Bowls: The 1926 Reservoir. *Hesperia* 55:389 ff.

Follin Jones, F. 1950. The Pottery. In *Excavations at Gözlü Kule, Tarsus*, ed. H. Goldman. Volume 1: *The Hellenistic and Roman Periods*. Princeton: University Press.

Goldman, Hetty, ed. 1950. *Excavations at Gözlü Kule, Tarsus*. Volume 1: *The Hellenistic and Roman Periods*. Princeton: Princeton University Press.

Gunneweg, J., I. Perlman, J. Yellin. 1983. *The Provenience, Typology and Chronology of Eastern Terra Sigillata*. Quedem 17. Monographs of the Institute of Archaeology, The Hebrew University of Jerusalem. Jerusalem: Ahva Press.

Hausmann Ulrich. 1959. *Hellenistische Reliefbecher aus attischen und boötischen Werkstätten. Untersuchungen zur Zeitstellung und Bildüberlieferung*. Deutsches Archäologisches Institut Abteilung Athen. Stuttgart: Kohlhammer.

Hayes, J. W. 1985. Hellenistic to Byzantine Fine Wares and Derivatives in the Jerusalem Corpus. In *Excavations in Jerusalem 1961-1967*, ed. A. D. Tushingham. Volume 1. Toronto: Royal Ontario Museum. 181-194.

_____. 1972. *Late Roman Pottery*. London: Heffer and Sons. 1.

Knipowitsch, T. 1968. *Untersuchungen zur Keramik Römischer Zeit aus den Griechenstädten an der Nordküste des Schwarzen Meeres*. I. *Die Keramik Römischer Zeit aus Olbia in der Sammlung der Erimitage*, Materialien zur Römisch-Germanischen Keramik 4. 1929; reprinted Bonn: Habelt.

Kuhnen, H.-P. 1989. *Studien zur Chronologie und Siedlungsarchäologie des Karmel (Israel) zwischen Hellenismus und Spätantike*. Beihefte zum Tübinger Atlas des Vorderen Orients Reihe B (Geisteswissenschaften), 72. Wiesbaden: Reichert.

Lapp, P.W. 1961. *Palestinian Ceramic Chronology 200 B.C.-A. D. 70*. Publications of the Jerusalem School, Archaeology 3. New Haven: American Schools of Oriental Research (ASOR).

Laumonier, A. 1977. *La céramique hellenistique à reliefs: Ateliers ioniens*, Exploration Archéologique de Délos Faitie par L'École Française D'Athenes, 31. Paris: Boccard.

Negev, A. 1986. *The Late Hellenistic and Early Roman Pottery of Nabataean Oboda, Final Report*, Quedem, 22, no. 14. Jerusalem: Hebrew University Institute of Archaeology.

Papanicolaou-Christensen, Aristea, R. Thomsen, G. Ploug. 1986. The Graeco-Roman Objects of Clay: The Coins and the Necropolis. In Hama: *Fouilles et Recherches de la Fondation Carlsberg. 1931-1938*. Vol. 3.2, *Les Potteries Hellénistiques et les Terres Sigillées Orientales*. Copenhagen: Nationalmuseets Skrifter.

Rotroff, Susan I. 1982. *Hellenistic Pottery: Athenian and Imported Moldmade Bowls*, The Agora, 22. Princeton, N.J.: American School of Classical Studies at Athens.

Rostovtzeff, M., A. R. Bellinger, F. E. Brown, N. P. Toll, C. B. Wells, editors. 1949. *The Excavations at Dura-Europos*. Final Report IV, Part 1, Fascicle 2. New Haven: Yale University Press, London: Humphrey Milford and Oxford University Press.

Siebert, Gerard. 1978. *Recherches sur les ateliers de bols à reliefs du Péloponnèse à l'époque hellénistique*. Bibliothèque des Écoles Francaises d'Athènes et de Rome, 233. Paris, Boccard.

Siegelman, A.. 1988. Archaeological Discoveries at Tell Abu-Shusha, Mishmar Ha-Emeq (Hebrew). In *A Herodian Tomb near Tell Abu-Shusha*, ed. B. Mazar. Jerusalem: Israel Exploration Society.

Waagé, F. O. 1948. *Antioch on the Orontes*. Volume 4.1: *Ceramic and Islamic Coins*. Princeton: University Press, London: Oxford University Press, and The Hague: Martinus Nijhoff.

ACKNOWLEDGMENTS

During the preparation of this article questions arose regarding the correct identification of different wares. I am especially grateful to Dr. Renate Rosenthal-Heginbottom (University of Göttingen) for listening to my proposals of identification and confirming them, and for pointing out some useful parallels to me. I also thank Prof. Dr. Michael Mackensen (University of Munich) for confirming my suggestions about the Late Roman fragments and for showing me some Eastern Sigillata fragments for comparison. I am indebted to Prof. Dr. Rami Arav (UNO), who gave me the opportunity to research Hellenistic and Roman fineware in Bethsaida. I thank also Prof. Dr. Heinz-Wolfgang Kuhn (University of Munich), who supported the research through financial aid, and I especially thank Dr. Monika Burnett (University of Munich).

Toni Tessaro

Hellenistic and Roman Ceramic Cooking Ware from Bethsaida

COOKING WARE SHARDS AND COMPLETE VESSELS that date from the Iron Age to the Hellenistic–Roman Period have been found in large quantities over the past five years at the Bethsaida excavation site. Intact cooking pots were surprisingly rare.

This chapter is a preliminary report on the Hellenistic and Roman cooking ware found during the 1992 excavation in Areas A and C (see table on p. 128). The main purpose of this report is to establish a preliminary typology of cooking pots according to the length of the rims, and to attempt to see whether there was development from one form to the other and to attempt to provide dates to this classification. It is assumed, however, that the overall picture of the relation between the types would be representative and further analysis would not change the basic concepts. We do not attempt to uncover the production center of this manufacture. Parallels to the Bethsaida cooking pots are taken from sites such as Kefar Hananya, Capernaum, and Khirbet Shema'.

Cooking ware is separated into two broad classifications: globular cooking pots and shallow casseroles. The globular cooking pot classification is based on the various shapes and sizes of rims; texture plays no role in these types. The average size of the fragments studied is 2 centimeters. Six types of Late Hellenistic–Early Roman cooking ware were found at Bethsaida.

HELLENISTIC-ROMAN COOKING WARE FROM BETHSAIDA 1988–1991			
DESCRIPTION	NO.	PERCENTAGE OF TYPE	PERCENTAGE OF TOTAL
GLOBULAR COOKING POTS			
Short neck with lid device	27	36.5%	20.0%
Tall neck straight	21	28.4%	15.4%
Short neck plain	7	9.4%	5.1%
Triple ridge	19	25.7%	14.0%
TOTAL COOKING POTS	74	100.0%	54.5%
CASSEROLES			
Flat shelf rim	12	19.4%	8.9%
Everted rim, red clay	11	17.7%	8.0%
Everted rim, orange clay	9	14.5%	6.6%
Everted rim, brown clay	4	6.5%	3.0%
Everted rim, black burnt covering	1	1.6%	0.7%
Everted rim, small black and small white grit	10	16.1%	7.4%
Everted rim, small white grit	9	14.6%	6.6%
Everted rim, large white grit	3	4.8%	2.2%
Everted rim, large and small black grit	1	1.6%	0.7%
Everted rim, large white grit	1	1.6%	0.7%
Everted rim, large black grit	1	1.6%	0.7%
TOTAL CASSEROLES	62	100.0%	45.5%
COMBINED TOTALS	136	100%	100%

GLOBULAR COOKING POTS

The globular cooking pot is the most common cooking pot that exists in the excavations of the Hellenistic–Roman periods in the land of Israel. The gloublar shape derives from cooking pots of Iron Age II (tenth century BCE) that are equipped with two handles that emerge from the rim and are attached to the shoulders. While Iron Age II cooking pots have thick walls, a number of Early Roman cooking pots have thin walls made of very fine clay that are highly fired and clink like metalware. They are equipped with ridges along the walls and the shoulders (fig. 1).)

Fig. 1. Hellenistic Cooking Pot from Bethsaida, with tall neck; dark brown, burnished slip (?) burnt; fine clay, well-fired. Pot is reconstructed from approximately sixty-five shards

Cooking Pot–Short Neck with Lid Device

This cooking pot (fig. 2) is found to have a short neck with an average height of 2 centimeters; it has one groove that perhaps indicates a lid. Twenty-nine shards were discovered in 1992; seventeen of these were red clay, eleven were orange clay, and one was made of brown clay. Most were tempered with a mixture of small black and small white grits. The rims range in diameter from 4 to 12 centimeters. This type is, according to A. Berlin, "abundantly paralleled throughout the Galilee, where it is the most common type of cookpot in the late first century BC and first century AD assemblages."[1]

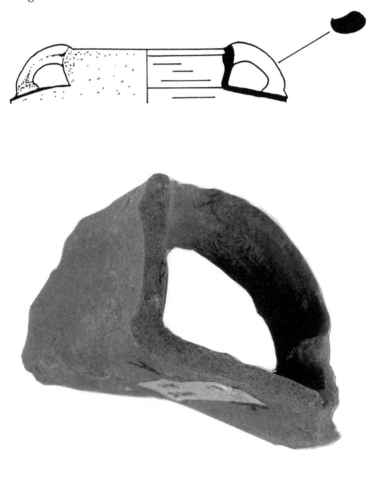

Fig. 2. Cooking pot, short neck with lid device

COOKING POT–TALL NECK STRAIGHT

The characteristic form of this type is a straight neck, with a shoulder appearing at approximately 4 centimeters below a simple rim. Twenty-one shards were uncovered in the 1992 season. Of these, eleven are of red clay, four of orange clay, three are burnt clay, and two are made from brown clay. The black burnt pieces possibly are from the Kefar Hananya kilns.[2] Grit varies from large white grit (in seven pieces), small black and small white (in two pieces), small gray and small white (in three), small white grit (in two), a combination of small and large white grit (in one), and large black and large white grit (in one). Rim diameters range from 8 to 10 centimeters.

Parallels include Herodium pls. 5 and 7,[3] Oboda PW22051, 22041 (F) and Kefar Hananya Form 4E,[4] and C4B Khirbet Shema' pl. 7.1.[5] Negev (1986) asserts the dating of this type of ceramic at an interval between 4 BCE and 63 CE.[6]

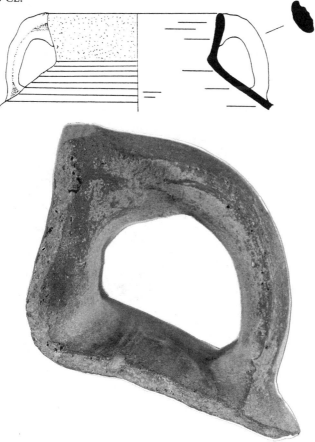

Fig. 3. Cooking pot with tall neck, straight

Cooking Pot– Short Neck Plain

Only seven shards of this type were discovered in the 1992 season. This type has a short, plain neck with a shoulder beginning about 2 centimeters below the rim. The average size of pieces found was 2 centimeters. The colors are red clay (two pieces), orange clay (four pieces), brown clay (one piece). Differences in grit size and color ranged from small white grit (on three), small black and small white grit (one), large white grit (one), small gray and small white grit (one), and small black grit (one). Rim diameters are from 10 to 14 centimeters.

Parallels include Kefar Hananya Form 4E[7] and Khirbet Shema' pl. 7.16.[8] Adan-Bayewitz dates this pottery to early fourth century BCE.

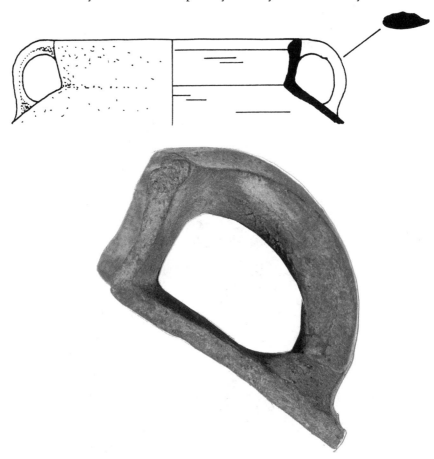

Fig. 4. Cooking pot with short neck, plain

COOKING POT–TRIPLE RIDGE

Nineteen shards of this type were found in the excavation during the 1992 season. The characteristic feature of this rim is three grooves on top of an everted rim. Only two shards show evidence of a shoulder, one at 2.5 centimeters and the other at 2 centimeters. Three of the rims studied have an inverted and everted rim. Nine pieces are from red clay, six from orange clay, and three are from brown clay. The texture of this cooking ware is often fine with no grits, but grit does occur in some instances. This grit is small white grit (four pieces), small black and small white (one piece), and small gray and small white grit (one piece). The rim diameters range from 10 to 12 centimeters.

Parallels to this type include Kefar Hananya Form 4B and 4C,[9] Capernaum Type A5,[10] Khirbet Shema' Types 1.1 and 1.2,[11] Diez Fernández T10.60 and 10.6a,[12] and Golan form G1B.[13] Suggested dating by Adan-Bayewitz is mid-first to mid–second century CE. This type is absent from Tel Anfa.

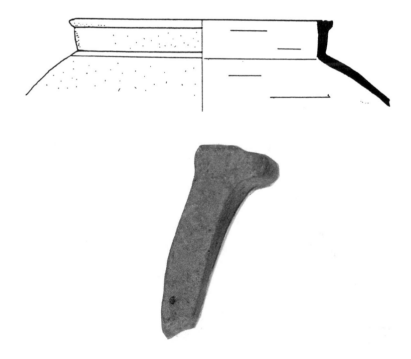

Fig. 5. Cooking pot with triple ridge

CASSEROLES

The casserole is a shallow cooking pot with a hemispherical bottom. Common features shared by cooking pots and casseroles are use of fine, highly fired clay with the clink of metalware and the presence of two handles that extend from the rim to the shoulder. The casserole, however, is more open, while the ceramic cooking pot is a closed vessel.

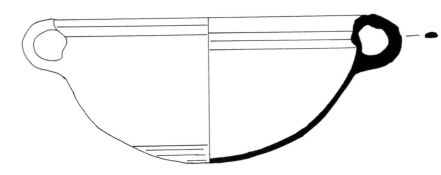

Fig. 6. Hellenistic casserole found at Bethsaida.
Drawing by Rick Baesler (not to scale)

HELLENISTIC CASSEROLE–FLAT SHELF RIM

Twelve casseroles of this type were discovered at this time, approximately 16.5 centimeters in diameter and made of orange fired clay. The piece contains large white and small black grit and has a simple rim.

Parallels are seen in Oboda PW 22041(F). Negev claims, "This group comprises vessels each of which is represented by a few specimens only; sometimes a piece is even unique."[14] Negev dates this type to the Late Hellenistic period.

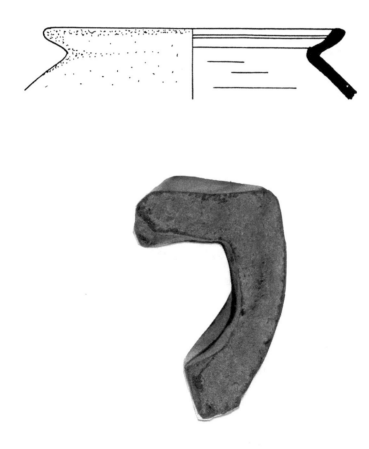

Fig. 7. Hellenistic casserole with flat shelf rim

Casserole–Everted Rim

These casseroles have some distinctive features, but are included in one category. One type has an angled rim, another has a flat shelf rim, a shelf rim with a canal is found, and finally, a casserole with a shelf and lid device is placed in this group. The common factor is the everted rim. Red clay makes up the majority of the finds (eleven pieces), followed by orange clay (nine pieces), and brown clay (four pieces); a black, burnt covering envelopes one shard. Grit content varies, with small black and small white grits (ten pieces), small white grits (nine pieces), large black and large white grits (three pieces), large and small black grits (one piece), and large white grits (one piece). The rim diameters vary, ranging from 17.5 to 22 centimeters, and most are in the upper end of the spectrum.

Parallels to these are found in Kefar Hananya Form 3A, 3B,[15] Capernaum Type A17,[16] Khirbet Shema' P17.12,[17] Diez Fernández T14.1.[18] Adan-Bayewitz dates these forms to Early Roman occupation.

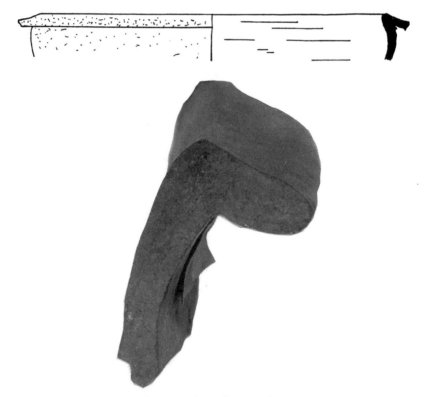

Fig. 8. Casserole with everted rim

Summary

This preliminary study identifies only pieces found in the 1992 excavation season, and it can be assumed that analysis of the many other Late Hellenistic–Early Roman pieces discovered in previous seasons would not change drastically the picture obtained here. It seems that the Bethsaida cooking pots were not all made locally; some were manufactured in places in Galilee and in the Golan. Further analysis will enable us to establish this conclusion.

Datings of samples are taken from other sites. However, these dates do not contradict the other finds from Bethsaida. It seems that at Bethsaida there was gradual development of cooking pots from thick walls and tall necks in the second century BCE to short neck and thinner walls in the first century CE. The triple ridge is perhaps confined to the first part of the first century BCE through the second century CE. The rim diameters indicate that Early Roman cooking ware openings ranged between 4 and 17.5 centimeters.

At this point more research needs to be done on the ceramics of Area B and the ceramics discovered in previous years in Area A. A definite occupation of the area by Late Hellenistic–Early Roman peoples is confirmed by the common artifacts found in ancient Bethsaida.

CATALOG NUMBERS FOR ILLUSTRATIONS

Drawings (by B. Castelhano)				
Fig. No.	Description	Area	Locus	Basket
2	Cooking pot, short neck with lid device	A	712	2078
3	Cooking pot, tall neck straight	A	712	2149
4	Cooking pot, short neck, plain	A	734	2221
5	Cooking pot, triple ridge	B	362	4187
7	Casserole, flat shelf rim	A	713	2069
8	Casserole, everted rim	A	712	?

Photos (by T. Tessaro)				
Fig. No.	Description	Area	Locus	Basket
2	Cooking pot, short neck with lid device	A	720	2144
3	Cooking pot, tall neck straight	?	?	?
4	Cooking pot, short neck, plain	A	735	2238
5	Cooking pot, triple ridge	A	720	2144
7	Casserole, flat shelf rim	?	?	?
8	Casserole, everted rim	A	715	2067

CHAPTER NOTES

1. Berlin 1982, 61–62..
2. Adan-Bayewitz 1993, 24.
3. Negev 1986, 95, 97.
4. Negev 1986, 94.
5. Meyers 1976, 193–196.
6. Negev 1986, 94.
7. Meyers 1976, 193–196.
8. Adan-Bayewitz 1993, 133
9. Adan-Bayewitz 1993, 127, 192.
10. Loffreda 1974, 32.
11. Meyers 1976, 193.
12. Diez Fernández 1983, 120.
13. Loffreda, pl. 9, p. 296.
14. Negev 1986, 97.
15. Adan-Bayewitz 1993, 133.
16. Loffreda 1974, 42.
17. Meyers et al. 1976, 180–181
18. Diez Fernández 1983, 124–125.

LITERATURE CITED

Adan-Bayewitz, D. 1993 *Common Pottery in Roman Galilee: A Study in Local Trade.* Ramat Gan, Israel: Bar-Ilan University Press.

Berlin, A. 1988. *The Hellenistic and Early Roman Common-Ware Pottery from Tel-Anfa.* Ann Arbor: University Microfilms.

Loffreda, Stanislao. 1979. Potsherds from a Sealed Level of the Synagogue at Capharnaum. *LA* 29: 32.

_____. 1982. Ceramica Ellenistico-Romano nel Sottosuola della sinagoga di Carfanao: Studium Biblicum Franciscanorum. *LA* 30.

Meyers, E. M., C. L. Kraabel, and J. F. Strange. 1976. *Ancient Synagogue Excavations at Khirbet Shema', Upper Galilee, Israel 1970-1972.* New Haven: American Schools of Oriental Research (ASOR), *42:* 193–196.

Diez Fernández, Florentino. 1983. *Cerámica Común Roman de la Galilea: Aproximaciones y diferencias con la cerámica del resto de Palestina regiones circundantes.* Madrid: Ed. Biblia y Fe: Escula Biblia.

Negev, Abraham 1986. The Late Hellenistic and Early Roman Pottery of Nabatean Oboda : Final Report. Qedem, no. 22. Jerusalem, Israel : Institute of Archaeology, Hebrew University.

Baruch Brandl

An Israelite Bulla in Phoenician Style from Bethsaida (et-Tell)

T HE BULLA PRESENTED HERE was found during the second (1989) season at the Bethsaida site. The photographs and drawings of the bulla, the description of its use, and the reconstruction of the seal were made under the writer's guidance.[1] An attempt is made to list most of the excavated parallels as a solid basis for the discussion. Parallels from collections have been used when they add to the excavated material. Since this study appears in a report, illustrations of the parallels are not incorporated. Therefore, several references are made to the same items with the hope that some of them are more accessible.

DESCRIPTION

- *Israel Antiquities Authority no. 94-2431.*
- *Reg. no. 2070.*
- *Locus no. 302.*
- *Area:* B.
- *Material:* Light brown clay.
- *Dimensions: (of the bulla):* L. 25 mm; W. 21.5 mm; H. 13 mm.
  (of the seal): L. 17 mm; W. 14 mm.
- *Method of manufacture:* A lump of clay was attached to a rolled papyrus where the string tied it; the clay was then impressed by a seal which was set in a metallic mount (see reconstructions).[2]

This chapter is dedicated to the memory of Professor Nahman Avigad, an outstanding person, teacher, and scholar.

- *Workmanship of bulla:* Mediocre (but of the seal itself, excellent).
- *Technical details:* Finger, seal, and metallic mount impressions on the face; string and papyrus impressions on the back. Not fired.
- *Preservation:* Complete.
- *Seal impression:* Five motifs are arranged in three undelimited registers and enclosed in a vertical oval that serves as a frame. In the upper register is a recumbent winged and crowned griffin. In the central register is a bird with stretched wings standing on two antithetic cobras, and in the lower register is a motif that looks like a basket or shallow bowl.

Iconography

The bulla contains what appears to be classic Egyptian iconography, which might lead one to assume an Egyptian origin.

The Griffin

The griffin (or falcon-headed sphinx) was adopted by the Egyptians in an early period,[3] and sometimes represented the god *Mnṯw* (Mont) of Hermonthis (Armant), Thebes, and others.[4]

The crown on the griffin's head is the *shmty,* or "double crown" of Upper and Lower Egypt,[5] and its own shape was used as a determinative for its name.[6]

The Bird

A bird of this type, with outstretched wings, is represented many times in Egyptian miniature art and has been identified as a hawk,[7] a falcon,[8] a vulture,[9] or a wryneck.[10]

The Cobra (Uraeus)

The cobra is inter alia native also in Egypt, where two of its species are found. The Spitting Cobra (*Naja mossambica*) inhabits the Upper Egyptian Nile valley, while the Egyptian Cobra (*Naja haje*) inhabits the Nile Valley south of the *Idfu* area and the western Nile Delta.[11] Both species are well known in Egyptian mythology.[12] The Greek name for the Egyptian Cobra, υραευσ (*uraeus*) derived from its Egyptian name *i'rt*.[13]

The Basketlike Motif

This motif can be identified as the Egyptian hieroglyph *nb,* whose meaning is "lord" or "all."[14]

Fig. 1. Israelite bulla in Phoenician style. Photo by Mariana Salzberger; used by permission of Israel Antiquities Authority.

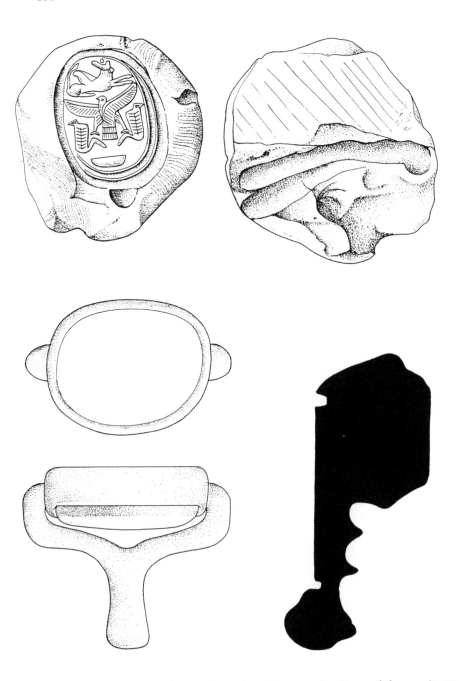

Fig. 2. Israelite bulla in Phoenician style, with reconstructions of the way it was used and the seal's shape.

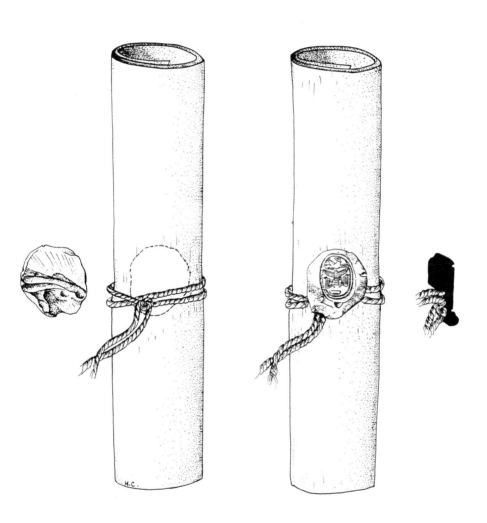

Drawings by Carmen Hersch; used by permission

STYLISTIC ORIGINS

Despite the identification of these five components as Egyptian, there are enough details to prove that the seal from which the impression was made is not an Egyptian product, but rather a Phoenician or Israelite product.[15] Some of the reasons for this conclusion are listed here.

THE GRIFFIN

The griffin (or falcon-headed sphinx) is one of the most popular among the Egyptianizing motifs.[16] The crown of the griffin is a flattened version of the Egyptian "double crown," and is typical of Phoenician art.[17] This form of crown is found in monumental art on sphinxes. One example is that on "the sphinx orthostat" from Hadad's Temple at Damascus;[18] another is on the alabaster relief from Aradus.[19] In the miniature art of ivories it appears on various figures, such as:

- *Sphinxes:* on those from Arslan Tash,[20] Samaria,[21] Nimrud,[22] and Salamis.[23]
- *Human figures:* on those from Arslan Tash[24] and Nimrud.[25]
- *Winged human figures:* on those from Arslan Tash[26] and Khorsabad.[27]

Griffins in their Phoenician form appear on both Phoenician and Israelite seals.[28] However, the recumbent griffin seems to be more typical of the Israelite seals than of the Phoenician seals. It can be seen on the following seals: *lzkr hwš'* [29] *lhym,*[30] *yhzq,*[31] or *lrp'.*[32]

THE BIRD

Although the wings look stretched, they are depicted in a special asymmetrical manner. The wing at the right side is actually stretched behind the bird's back and is shown in profile; one can compare it with the *hmn* seal[33] and with an unepigraphic seal from Nazareth.[34] The wing on the left side is shown en face. The same phenomenon appears on ivories, and one can compare between two ivory panels from Nimrud.[35]

Again, depictions of this kind are typical in Phoenician art; they appear on ivories as in Nimrud[36] and on several Phoenician seals, such as the *hmlk* seal which bears a Hebrew or Moabite script,[37] an unepigraphic seal in the Ward collection,[38] the *br'tr* seal which bears an Aramaean name,[39] an unepigraphic scarab in the Israel Museum,[40] and an unepigraphic scaraboid from Tell el-Far'ah (south).[41] It seems that both the

Phoenician and Israelite seal cutters had difficulty depicting wings that were not in profile.[42]

THE URAEUS.

The head of the *uraeus* is depicted in a special way. It is triangular and is stretched from the reptile's inflated chest, instead of being located above it. This form is found on Phoenician seals such as the *yzbl* seal,[43] the *'bdb'l* seal,[44] the *b'lntn* seal that is iconographically Phoenician with a Hebrew inscription,[45] and on "Hebrew" seals, such as *l'z' bn ḥts,*[46] that Lemaire identified as Israelite.[47]

THE BASKETLIKE MOTIF

It is a common spacefiller on the Phoenician seals, and is often used as an exergue.[48]

The recumbent griffin is a crucial point for making the decision to place this bulla as an Israelite product in Phoenician style rather than as a Phoenician original.

INTERPRETATION

The identification of the bulla's origin obliges us to interpret its composition by comparison with other Phoenician and Israelite seals.The closest parallels will be unepigraphic seals (or those to which inscriptions were added later) with three undelimited registers.

Among the Phoenician seals are the *b'lntn* seal that also contains a Hebrew inscription,[49] the *yzbl* seal,[50] and a scaraboid bought by J. G. Chester in Beirut and now in the Ashmolean Museum.[51]

Among the Israelite seals are: a scaraboid bought by Chester in Nazareth and now in the Ashmolean Museum,[52] the *l'z' bn ḥts* seal,[53] a scaraboid from Shechem,[54] and a scarab from Megiddo.[55]

It seems that all these seals have various compositions, made from several motifs. Therefore, these compositions should not be interpreted as reflecting a known mythological scene, but as independent choice by the seal cutters from a common source or pattern collection.

USE AND FREQUENCY OF BULLAE IN THE ANCIENT NEAR EAST

The frequent use of bullae for sealing papyri started in Egypt during the late Eleventh or early Twelfth Dynasty.[56] From Egypt, the use of bullae spread to Canaan and beyond its borders. The latest pre-Persian bulla from the Levant is a Babylonian bulla from Tell el-Ajjul (Philistia), which was originally identified by the excavator as Persian,[57] and which can be compared with a seal in the Bibliothèque Nationale.[58]

Even though most of these bullae were used to seal papyri, a few were used for other purposes. A seal impression from Beer-Sheba[59] served for the sealing of a consignment or as a stopper for a large storage jar. A bulla from Tell el-'Umeiri in Ammon[60] served as a juglet stopper. Recently, the late Professor Nahman Avigad published two bullae that most probably had been attached to various kinds of goods.[61] Such uses were common in Assyria.[62]

During the first half of the first millennium bullae were found in most of the political entities that existed in the Near East, but in some places later than in others. Among them are:

- *Phoenicia*. All the early Phoenician bullae are from Tell el-Fuḫḫar [Acco][63] and the ex-Lefkovitz collection.[64]
- *Carthage*. As described by Sznycer, Gubel, Redissi, and Kracht.[65]
- *The Kingdom of Israel*. Until recently all Israelite bullae from a known site were found at Samaria, the capital of the kingdom.[66]
- *Urartu*. Ayanis.[67]
- *Three Aramaic Independent Kingdoms Samal*. Zenjirli = *lbrrkb br pnmw*.[68]
- *The Aramaic Kingdom Guzana*. Tell Halaf.[69]
- *The Aramaic Kingdom Hamat*. Hama.[70]
- *Arameans in the Assyrian Empire*. (1) Nineveh: five *l'tr'zr* Aramaic or Phoenician bullae with an Aramaic name;[71] (2) Khorsabad: a bulla written in Aramaic[72] with a new reading of its owner's name *pn'srlmr*;[73] (3) Horvat 'Uzza: a bulla made from a Syro-Palestinian seal with the symbol of the Aramaic moon god Sin.[74]
- *The Assyrian Empire*. Nineveh,[75] Samaria,[76] Khorsabad,[77] Nimrud,[78] and an unknown provenance.[79]
- *Edom*. Umm el-Biyara: *qwsg[br] mlk 'd[m]*.[80] Buseirah: *lmlk lb' 'bd hmlk*.[81]
- *Moab* (?). *km š'z hspr*.[82]
- *Philistia*. Tell Abu Salima (Sheikh Zuweid)[83] and Tell Jemme.[84] Despite their locations both seem to be of Hebrew origin, and they compare favorably to a bulla in a private collection.[85]
- *Tell el-Ajjul*. The above-mentioned Babylonian bulla.
- *Cyprus*. Kition.[86]
- *Tarsus*. Tarsus.[87]
- *The Kingdom of Judah*. Among all these political entities, the one with

the most frequent use of the bullae was the Kingdom of Judah. Most of the impressions had inscriptions;[88] however, bullae were also found there that had impressions of unepigraphic seals, such as those from Lachish,[89] or even blank bullae from the same site.[90] Seven additional epigraphic bullae from the Kingdom of Judah are listed in the next section.

Bullae Impressed with Seals in Metallic Mounts

Many of the bullae were made from seals that were set in metallic mounts but only several cases were described by the publishers:

- *The Kingdom of Israel (?). dlh.*[91]
- *The Kingdom of Que. Tarsus.*[92]
- *Neo-Hittites in the Assyrian Empire. Nineveh.*[93]
- *Carthage. Carthage.*[94]
- *The Kingdom of Judah.* Avigad,[95] who originally overlooked this fact while describing seal no. 10a in Avigad 1976 and Avigad 1977,[96] and most recently *lšm'yhw 'bd hmlk.*

Other cases of bullae made from seals in metallic mounts that were overlooked by their publishers are:

- *Phoenicia.* Acco, ex-Lefkovitz collection.[97]
- *Assyria.* Nineveh, five *l'tr'zr* Aramaic or Phoenician bullae with Aramaic name.[98]
- *Carthage.* Carthage, Dermech.[99]
- *The Kingdom of Israel.* Samaria[100] and probably the additional six that were only mentioned.[101]
- *Edom.* Umm el-Biyaza. *qwsg[br] mlk 'd[m].*[102]
- *The Kingdom of Judah. lhlqyhw bn m's/m'ps;*[103] *lgdlyhw 'sr 'l hbyt;*[104] *"lyhwzrh bn lqyhw 'bd ḥzqyhw;*[105] *ldml';*[106] *sr h'r* [no. 1];[107] *sr h'r* [no. 2],[108] *lmbthyhw 'bd hmlk.*[109]

Typology of the Seal and Its Metallic Mount

In spite of having found only the seal impression, one can reconstruct the seal's shape and relate it to a definite group. From the compositional scheme of the seal impression (three horizontal registers) and on the basis of the identification of its origin (Israelite in Phoenician style), it is obvious that the seal was in the shape of a scaraboid.[110]

From the impression itself it is clear that the scaraboid was set in a looped metallic mount of a very definite type.[111] This type was defined as Phoenician and discussed at length by Culican (1977), who included in it the following seals: Khorsabad,[112] Zenjirli,[113] Nimrud,[114] Khaldeh, Palestine, Lebanon, and unknown sources in private collections.[115] An additional seal is in the Bibliothèque Nationale.[116]

It is possible to add to this group an overlooked seal from Megiddo[117] and several seals that originally were identified as Egyptian as well as some which were dated even to the second millennium BCE:[118] Gezer,[119] Queen Alia International Airport Cemetery,[120] ex-Matouk collection.[121] Two neo-Assyrian imitations in stone that are dated to the seventh century BCE are in the Ashmolean Museum.[122]

From an extensive distribution list of this type of seal, it is clear that it was adopted also by the artists of the Kingdom of Israel.[123]

Dating

The bulla from et-Tell (Bethsaida) and its seal should be dated to the ninth century BCE. This conclusion is based on the following points:

• Stratigraphy and Archaeological Context

The bulla was found two meters north of the northern wall of a monumental building dated to the ninth century BCE in a space whose exact function is not yet definite. The locus, which contained Iron Age II pottery shards from the same period as the building, was partially disturbed by a Hellenistic pit.

• Typology of the Seal Setting

The seals from Megiddo and Khaldeh, and one of the Zenjirli seals, are dated to ninth century BCE.[124]

- THE GROUP OF THREE UNDELIMITED REGISTERS

Unfortunately, all the members of this group are without good archaeological context. Even the seals that have a known site, those from Shechem and Megiddo, are missing a context. However, there is general agreement among scholars as to their dates. Local art products, including seals with Egypto-Phoenician iconography, to which this small group could be related, are attributed to Iron Age II B or to the ninth and eighth centuries BCE.[125]

The seal referred to most often among those from the same time period that belong directly to our smaller group is the *yzbl* seal that was dated by Avigad to the ninth to eighth centuries BCE.[126]

- THE ICONOGRAPHIC DEVELOPMENT PHASE

The bulla and its scaraboid belong to a small but distinctive group that contains several Egyptian motifs which were transformed into Phoenician style and ordered differently, but always in three registers. Such free arrangement points, in the writer's view, to an early stage in the development of Phoenician iconography, before the appearance of its canonical order, or what Uehlinger labels "Phoenician symbolism."[127]

CONCLUSIONS

1. This bulla is most probably the first seal impression made from a scaraboid in a metallic looped setting.

2. Moreover, it is made from an Israelite seal that reflects the Phoenician cultural impact on local art.

3. The bulla represents the importance of the site and its direct connections with Samaria, the capital of the Kingdom of Israel, during the ninth century BCE after its conquest by King Ahab.[128]

CHAPTER NOTES

1. The reconstructions are given here, following the desirable standards for published sealings, as expressed in Ferioli and Fiandra 1990, 221.

2. The impression of the metallic mount is partial as a result of the shape of the clay lump, and therefore one of the ring's edges is missing. Such a phenomenon could be seen on modern impressions of the "Nimrud Jewel" (Mallowan 1966, 114, fig. 58) and of a seal from the cemetery at Queen Alia International Airport (Ibrahim, Gordon et al. 1987, pl. 37:1).

3. Staples 1931, 51-61; Leibovitch 1955; Barnett 1957, 73-77; Klähn 1957, 634; Bisi 1965, 21-38.

4. Pilcher 1913, 145; Gardiner 1973, 569.

5. Straus 1980, col. 813.

6. Gardiner 1973, 504 (Sign-list S-5).

7. di Cesnola 1884, 137, fig. 149; Hall 1913, no. 124.

8. Hayes 1959: 77, fig. 41 center.

9. Giveon and Kertesz 1986, no. 49.

10. Tufnell 1983.

11. Beaux and Goodman 1993, 116–119.

12. Martin 1985.

13. Gardiner 1973, 476 (Sign-list I–12).

14. Gardiner 1973, 525 (Sign-list V–30).

15. I am inclined to separate the Hebrew seals into Israelite and Judaean groups (for the definition of the Israelite group see Garbini 1982, Avigad 1988, 15, and epigraphically, Lemaire 1990, 16). This separation could lead us to the distinction between the Phoenician seals and their Israelite derivatives.

16. Buchanan and Moorey 1988, 41, with bibliography.

17. I do not agree with the idea that this shape is a result of the artist's misunderstanding of the crown's details, degeneration, or lack of sufficient room (Giveon 1971, 95–96, fig. 8; Avigad 1973, 77; Giveon 1978, 44, fig. 17; Winter 1976, 10–11, pl. 6:c-d), both because of the frequency of such a shape alongside the Egyptian traditional form in Phoenician art. It seems that this shape should be considered as a typical Phoenician product, expressing the eclectic nature of Phoenician art that combines elements of different sources into a new form.

18. Abd el-Kader 1926; Avi-Yonah 1954: col. 675; Winter 1973, 272, fig. 11; Winter 1976, 7, pl. 3:d; winter 1981, 102, pl. 6:a; Caubet 1993, 264-265.

19. Moscati 1968, illus.3; Gubel 1987, pl. 47:170.

20. Thureau-Dangin et al. 1931, 102–105, pls. 27: 22, 28: 25, 30: 29–30, 31: 31; de Mertzenfeld 1954, 133–134, pls. 79 (868–870), 80 (872, 875); Thimme 1973a, illus. 4; Thimme 1973b, xx, pls. 1-4; Winter 1976: 8, pl. 4:a; Winter 1981, 105, 111-112, pl. 12:a and d.

21. Crowfoot, Crowfoot and Sukenik 1938: 20-21, pls. 5-6: 2; de Mertzenfeld 1954: 67-68, pls. 9 [94-95], 10 [96, 98-110], 21 [95]; Winter 1981: 111, 112, 115–118, pl. 12:b and c.

22. Davies 1975, 235, pls. 133, Suppl. 37, 134, Suppl. 33.

23. Karageorghis 1968, 156, pl. 127; Karageorghis 1973, 87, 91–2, 94–96; Karageorghis 1974, 37, pls. A, B: 1–2, 62, 241 (no. 258); Winter 1976, 8, pl. 4:b.

24. Thureau-Dangin et al. 1931, 99–102, pl. 26:20–21; de Mertzenfeld 1954, 129, pl. 26 [836–837]; Winter 1981, 105, 115 n. 108, pl. 8:d.

25. Mallowan 1966, 524, Figs. 431-432; Davies 1975, 234, pl. 135, suppl. 28; Winter 1976, 2-3, 6-7, pl. 1:a; and 10–11, pl. 6:c-d.

26. Thureau-Dangin et al. 1931, 97, pls. 24:15-16, 25: 17; Thimme 1973b, xx–xxi, pls. 8–11; Winter 1981, 104, pl. 8:a; Muscarella 1981, nos. 256-258.

27. Loud and Altman 1938, 97, pl. 52:38–39; de Mertzenfeld 1954, 143, pls. 100 (949), 101 (1118); Winter 1981, pl. 8:b.
28. See also Sass 1993, 226 [E1].
29. Levy, 1869, pl. 3:9 = Galling 1941, 174, pl. 5:10 = Sass 1993, 226, fig. 121, pl. 1:6.
30. Petrie and Tufnell 1930, 10, pl. 35:427 = Diringer 1934, 170, pl. 19:8 = Galling 1941, 174, pl. 5:7 = Hestrin and Dayagi-Mendels 1979, no. 43 = Ahitur 1982, col. 261 = Keel and Uehlinger 1992: 288, 290, fig. 253.
31. Diringer 1934, 241-242, pl. 21:20 = Galling 1941, 174, pl. 5:11 = Lemaire 1993, 7, fig. 14.
32. Reifenberg 1950, 41 = Hestrin and Dayagi-Mendels 1979, no. 121 = Parayre 1990, 272-273, 288, 298, pl. 12:16
33. Staples 1931, figs. 33-34 = Diringer 1934, 165-167, pl. 19:3 = Lamon and Shipton 1939, pl. 67:10 = Sukenik 1942, fig. A1 = Avigad 1958, pl. 3 = Hestrin 1973, no. 126 = Hestrin and Dayagi-Mendels 1979, no. 42 = Sass 1993, figs. 92, 120.
34. Harden 1962, 317, pl. 108:d = Buchanan and Moorey 1988, 43, pl. 9:282.
35. Mallowan 1966, figs. 398 with 403.
36. Mallowan 1966: 500-502, fig. 403.
37. Sukenik 1942, fig. A2 = Reifenberg 1950, no. 12 = Moscati 1951, 52, pl. 11:1 = Avigad 1958, pl. 3 = Sass 1993, 226 n. 75, figs. 105, 125.
38. Ward 1967, 71, fig. 1, pl. 12:1
39. Bordreuil 1986, no. 93 = Parayre 1990, 273, 287-288, 291, 293, 298, pls. 2: 18, 12: 18 = Parayre 1993, 34-35, fig. 30 = Bordreuil 1993, 88, fig. 21 = Gubel 1993, 118, fig. 38.
40. Ben-Tor 1989: 43.
41. Keel and Uehlinger 1992: 287-288, n. 262, fig. 251.
42. Among the strangest results are a scaraboid and a scarab from Israel: Tell el–Far'ah (south); see Starkey and Harding 1932, 30, pl. 73:43; Sa'ar-Giveon 1986, 83, no. 9; 1988, 100-101, pl. 9:120, with the solar disc missing in the drawing.
43. Avigad 1964b = Hestrin 1973, no. 40 = Giveon 1974 = Culican 1974, 198, pl. 36:e = Keel 1977, 97, fig. 63 = Hestrin and Dayagi-Mendels 1979, no. 31 = Giveon 1984 = Parayre 1990, 272, 298, pl. 2:14 = Parayre 1993, fig. 19.
44. Delaporte 1920, 87 [K.12], pl. 57, 15 = Galling 1941, 180, pl. 6:55 = Bordreuil 1986, no. 8 = Parayre 1990, 273–274, 288, 293, 298, pls. 2:21, 12:21 = Parayre 1993, figs. 5 and 21.
45. Diringer 1934, 240-241, pl. 21:18 = Galling 1941, 180, pl. 6:54 = Heltzer 1981, 291 [no. 270] = Parayre 1990: 287, 298, pl. 2:15 = Gubel 1993: 118, fig. 39.
46. Avigad 1954, 237, 238 fig. 1: 2, pl. 21:2 = Avigad 1958, pl. 3 = Parayre 1990, 274, 298, pl. 2: 28 = Sass 1993, 212, figs. 72, 82, 97, 138.
47. Lemaire 1993, 6, fig. 12.
48. Brandl 1991, 154.
49. Diringer 1934, 240-241, pl. 21:18 = Galling 1941, 180, pl. 6: 54 = Helzer 1981, 291 (no. 270) = Parayre 1990, 287, 298, pl. 2:15 = Gubel 1993, 118, fig. 39.
50. Avigad 1964b = Hestrin 1973, no. 40 =Giveon 1974 = Culican 1974: 198, pl. 36:e = Keel 1977, 97, fig. 63 = Hestrin and Dayagi - Mendels 1979, no. 31 = Giveon 1984 = Parayre 1990, 272, 298, pl. 2:14 = Parayre 1993, fig. 19.
51. Buchanan and Moorey 1988: 43, pl. 9:277 = Parayre 1990: 298, pl. 2:13.
52. Harden 1962, 317, pl. 108:d = Buchanan and Moorey 1988, 43, pl. 9:282.
53. Avigad 1954: 237, 238 fig. 1:2, pl. 21: 2 = Avigad 1958, pl. 3 = Parayre 1990, 274, 298, pl. 2: 28 = Sass 1993, 212, figs. 72, 82, 97, 138 = Lemaire 1993, 6, fig. 12.
54. Rowe 1936, 221, pl. 25 [no. SO. 3] = Keel and Uehlinger 1992, 292, fig. 258c = Parayre 1990, 274, 288, 298, pl. 3:34 = Parayre 1993, fig. 24. The dot border of this scaraboid points to its "Hebrew" origin (Sass 1993, 206, n. 29), or if to be more specific, to its Judaean or Israelite origin (Hübner 1993, 143).

55. Lamon and Shipton 1939, pl. 67:7 = Parayre 1990, 273, 298, pl. 2:11 = Keel and Uehlinger 1992, 292-294, fig. 259a.
56. Williams 1977, 135-136.
57. Petrie 1933, 4, pl. 4:197; Galling 1937, cols. 485-486, no. 26.
58. Delaporte 1910, 308, pl. 36:565.
59. Aharoni 1973, 75-76, pl. 32:1.
60. Herr 1985, 1989; Younker 1985, 1989 = Bordreuil 1992, cols. 154-160, fig. 1012.34.
61. Avigad 1990.
62. Herbordt 1992: 33-70 [chap. 3, Siegel praxis].
63. Avigad 1964a, 194, pl. 44:D.
64. Culican 1968, 103, pl. V:B = Giveon and Kertesz 1986, no. 125 = Parayre 1990, 275, 298, pl. 2:24. Also, Giveon and Kertesz 1986, no. 173.
65. Sznycer 1969; Gubel 1986, 227, nos. 263-264; Redissi 1991; Kracht 1991, 292-294. For a general discussion on bullae with Phoenician and Punic script including later material, see Gubel 1993, 113.
66. Reisner, Fisher, and Lyon 1924, 378 (IV 2, 3), pl. 57:d3, h3. Also, Rowe 1936, nos. S.100-102 = Crowfoot 1957: 2, 88, nos. 29-31, pl. 15:29 = Keel and Uehlinger 1992, 290-292, fig. 257a = Sass 1993, 214, fig. 86, and additional six that were only mentioned (Crowfoot; Kenyon and Sukenik 1942,108 = Crowfoot 1957: 2, 88. nos. 32-37). See further, Rowe 1936, no. S.103 = Crowfoot 1957, 2, 88, no. 38, pl. 15:38. [It seems that the Israelites stamped not only clay lumps (bullae) but also jar handles as is the case, in my view, in Shechem; see Horn 1966, 55, fig. 1: 54, pl. 6:54 = Parayre 1990, 298, pl. 3:37.]
67. Çiligiroğlu 1994, 68.
68. von Luschan and Andrae 1943, 73-74, 159, pl. 38:b = Bordreuil 1993, 88, fig. 19 = Parayre 1990, 280, 282, 287-288, 300, pls. 7:87, 12:87 = Parayre 1993, fig. 32.
69. von Oppenheim and Hrouda 1962, 32, pl. 28:c
70. Riis 1990, 89-96, Nos. 154-167, Otzen 1990, 276-281, Aramsig 1-2.
71. Layard 1853, 131 = Galling 1941, 146, 181, pl. 6:62 = Millard 1965, 14, n. 7 = Barnett 1967, 5*-6* n.27, pl. 7:4 = Bordreuil 1992, col. 151 = Herbordt 1991, pls. 18:24-25 = Lemaire 1993: 18 = Bordreuil 1993, 92 = Sass 1993: 213.
72. Sprengling 1932.
73. Kaufman 1984, 94 = Bordreuil 1992, col. 151, fig. 1010.28 = Herbordt 1992, 9, 122, 170, pl. 27:3 = Watanabe 1993, 116, pl. 4:6.7.
74. Beck 1986 = Keel 1994, 155, 189, fig. 37..
75. Layard 1853, 130-131; Sachs 1953; Millard 1965; Collon 1990, 17, 19, 24-25, 41 and 51 fig. 2B.
76. Reisner, Fisher, and Lyon 1924, 378 [IV: 1], pl. 56:a; Sachs 1953, 168, 170 [no. 40], pl. 19: 3; Tadmor 1973: 71-72, pl. 5:2
77. Delaporte 1910, xviii, pl. B (5922 and 5294); 1920: 86 (K.5]) pl. 57:10 and 14; Loud and Altman 1938, 98, pl. 58 (nos. 113-122); Sachs 1953: 168-169 (nos. 9-20), pls. 18:6, 19: 4-6
78. Parker 1962,36-37,pl. 19:2 and 5; Buchanan and Moorey 1988, 8-9, pl. 2, 64-67; 55-56.
79. Millard 1978.
80. Bennett 1966, pl. 22:b = Millard 1991, 143, pl. 165 = Bordreuil 1992, cols. 133, 163, 194, fig. 1013.38a (erroneously related to Buseirah) = Lemaire 1993, 5, fig. 6 = Bienkowski 1993, 1489.
81. Bennett 1974a, 76, pl. 4b; 1974b: 18-19, fig. 17, pl. 6:b = Puech 1977: 12-13, fig. 2, pl. 4:B-C = Layton 1991 = Bordreuil 1992, col. 163, fig. 1013.39 = Reich 1993: 265-266.
82. Avigad 1992.
83. Petrie and Ellis 1937:pl. 6:55.
84. Van Beek 1986, 32 = Van Beek 1987, 55.

85. Keel-Leu 1991, no. 94.
86. Clerc et al. 1976, 114-116.
87. Porada 1963, 347-348, 356, pls. 162:1, 165:1, 167:1.
88. Bliss 1900, 221-222, pl. 7:10-11 = Bliss and Macalister 1902, 122, figs. 44-45 = Diringer 1934, 138-139, 142-143, pl. 17:2, 9 = v. s. Shemer *EB* VIII 1982, cols. 139-140 = Sass 1993, 200, 204, 214, figs. 9, 83. Sellers 1933, 59-61, figs. 50: 12, 52 = Diringer 1934, 127, 341, fig. 41, pl. 14:12 = Hestrin 1973, no. 21 = Hestrin and Dayagi-Mendels 1979, no. 7.   Sellers 1933: 59-60, fig. 51: 13. Avigad 1964a: 193-194, pl. 44:C. Avigad 1969, 4, pl. 1:8 = Hestrin and Dayagi-Mendels 1979, no. 26. Aharoni 1975: 19-22, pls. 20-21 = Hestrin 1973, nos. 26-31. Bordreuil and Lemaire 1976, 53, pl. 5:21-23; O'Connell 1977 = O'Connell, Gleen Rose and Toombs 1978: 78-80, pl. 9:B = Fargo and O'Connell 1978: 176, 178. Avigad 1978b = Avigad 1978c = Avigad 1979a = Avigad 1979b = Avigad 1987, nos. 1-2; = Bordreuil 1992, col. 134, figs. 1005.10-11. Avigad 1986; Bordreuil 1992, col. 186, fig. 1015.45. Shiloh 1984, 19-20, Figs. 25-26, pl. 35 = Shiloh 1985 = Shiloh 1986a = Shiloh 1986b = Shiloh and Tarler 1986 = Shoham 1994 = Schneider 1988a = Schneider 1988b = Schneider 1991= Bordreuil 1992: col. 134, fig. 1005: 12 = Schneider 1994; - Avigad 1988: 10, with the new title *l'zryhw šh'r hmsgr*; Deutsch and Heltzer 1994, 41-42, fig. 14. Thirteen years later Avigad published the seal from which Bulla no. 21, *lpltyhw hlqyhw*, was stamped; see Avigad 1989b, 92, no. 6, n. 26. Until recently this was the only discovery of a Hebrew seal and its impression; Sass 1993, 197, n.9).
89. Murray 1953: 373, pls. 44A-45: 164-166; Diringer 1953: 347.
90. Aharoni 1975, 20, 22, pl. 21:14-17.
91. Avigad 1989a, 12-13 [no. 10].
92. Porada 1963, 347-348, 356, pls. 162:1, 165:1, 167:1.
93. Bossert 1942: 77, 251 (nos. 9755-932).
94. Redissi 1991, 61.
95. Avigad 1986, nos. 1, 2, 6, 10a, 10b, 50, 83 and 125.
96. Deutsch and Heltzer 1994, 38-39, fig. 12.
97. Culican 1968: 103, pl. V:B, = Giveon and Kertesz 1986, no. 125 = Parayre 1990;275, 298, pl. 2:24. Also, Giveon and Kertesz 1986, no. 173
98. Layard 1853, 131 = Galling 1941, 146, 181, pl. 6:62; Millard 1965: 14, n. 7 = Barnett 1967, 5*-6* n.27, pl. 7:4 = Bordreuil 1992: col. 151 = Herbordt 1992: 122, pl. 18:24-25 = Lemaire 1993, 18 = Bordreuil 1993: 92 = Sass 1993, 213.
99. Gubel 1986, 227, nos. 263-264; Kracht 1991, 292-294.
100. Rowe 1936: nos. S.100-102=Crowfoot 1957: 2,88, nos. 29-31, pl. 15:29= Keel and Uehlinger 1992, 290-292, fig. 257a = Sass 1993, 214, fig. 86.
101. Crowfoot; Kenyon and Sukenik 1942, 108; Crowfoot 1957, 2, 88, nos. 32-37.
102. Bennett 1966, pl. 22:b; Millard 1991, 143, pl. 165 = Bordreuil 1992: cols. 133, 163, 194, fig. 1013:38a [erroneously related to Buseirah] = Lemaire 1993, 5, fig. 6 = Bienkowski 1993, 1489.
103. Moscati 1951, 62, pl. 13:7 = Diringer 1953, 347-348, pls. 44A-45: 172 = Hestrin and Dayagi-Mendels 1979, no. 27.
104. Hooke 1935: 195-196, fig. 1, pl. 11 up. = Moscati 1951,61-62, pl. 13:6 = Diringer 1953, 347-348, pls. 44A-45:173, = Liver 1954: col. 441 = Avigad 1958, pl. 4 = Hestrin 1973, no. 15.
105. Hestrin and Dayagi 1974a, Hestrin and Dayagi 1974b = Yeivin 1978 = Hestrin and Dayagi-Mendels 1979, no. 4 = Bordreuil 1992: col. 145, fig. 1014: 41 = Sass 1993, fig. 22 = Uehlinger 1993b, fig. 20.
106. Avigad 1975, 70-71, pl. 14:18 = Hestrin and Dayagi-Mendels 1979, no. 47.

107. Avigad 1976 = Avigad 1977 (but see Avigad 1986, no. 10a) = Mazar and Cornfeld 1975: 179 = Keel and Uehlinger 1992, 409, fig. 346 = Bodreuil 1992: col. 192, fig. 1017:50 right = Ornan 1993, 71, fig. 66 = Sass 1993: 237-238, fig. 146 = Avigad 1994.
108. Barkay 1977 = Avigad 1978a = Avigad 1986, no. 10b = Keel and Uehlinger 199,: 409, fig. 346 = Sass 1993: 238 = Barkay 1994 = Bordreuil 1992: col. 192, fig. 1017: 50 left.
109. Deutsch and Heltzer 1994: 39–41, fig. 13.
110. Gubel 1988, 148.
111. Many of the Phoenician and Israelite scaraboids were not perforated since they were set in a metallic mount; Avigad 1954, 237.
112. Delaporte 1920: 87, pl. 57:18a-b [K.16]. According to Culican 1977, 2, pl. 1:a-b, it was found at Kuyunjik (Nineveh).
113. von Luschan and Andrae 1943,73, 159, pl. 38: e and 101, 116, pl. 45, n.
114. Mallowan 1966,114, fig. 58.
115. Culican 1977.
116. Bordreuil 1986,32 [no. 20] = Gubel 1993, 124, fig. 70.
117. Loud 1948, pls. 153: 235, 159: 235 = Keel 1977, 103, fig. 82
118. I intend to discuss this group in detail elsewhere.
119. Giveon 1985: 130–131 (no. 63).
120. Ibrahim; Gordon et al. 1987,22, 57, pls. 37:1, 51:3.
121. Uehlinger 1990: 63, fig. 80d, pl. 12.
122. Buchanan and Moorey 1988, 38, 63, pl. 14:428-429.
123. For another type of metallic ring used in the kingdom of Israel, see a find from its capital Samaria; Reisner, Fischer, and Lyon 1924, 366, C 7a; 377, A II: 17, pl. 56:d, and the "*lšpt*" seal; Ben–Dor 1945, pl. 2:2 upper = Ben–Dor 1948, 64–66, pl. 27:1 = Moscati 1951, 57, pl. 12:5 = Ward 1968, 136, fig. 1:4 = Hestrin 1973, 59, no. 124 = Keel 1977, 107. 110, fig. 93 = Hestrin and Dayagi–Mendels 1979, 61, no. 37 = Cohen 1982: col. 247 = Sass 1993, 200, figs. 12 and 25)
124. The other excavated seals—those from Zenjirli, Nimrud, and Khorsabad—are later and are dated from the eighth to the seventh centuries CE.
125. Buchanan and Moorey 1988, 38; Keel and Uehlinger 1992, 199-321; Sass 1993, 199.
126. Avigad 1964b.
127. Uehlinger 1993a, xvii, n. 25.
128. It should be emphasized that the seal's production date should be considered as a terminus post quem.

Literature Cited

Abd el-Kader, Dj. 1949. Un Orthostate du Temple de Hadad à Damas. *Syria* 26: 191–195.

Aharoni, Y. 1975. Chapter 4: The Stratum II Store. In: Aharoni, Y. et al. 1975. *Investigations at Lachish: The Sanctuary and the Residency* (Lachish V). Tel Aviv: 19–25.

_____, ed. 1973. Chapter 16: The Hebrew Inscriptions, pp. 71–78. In *Beer-Sheba I: Excavations at Tel Beer-Sheba 1969–1971 Seasons.* Ed. Y. Aharoni. Tel Aviv.

Ahituv, S. 1982. *S.v.* Sharuhen. *Encyhclopedia Biblica* 8: cols. 259–263. Jerusalem (Hebrew).

Avigad, N. 1954. Three Ornamented Hebrew Seals. *Israel Exploration Journal* 4: 236–238.

_____. 1958. *S.v.* Seal. *Encyclopedia Biblica* 3: cols. 68–86. Jerusalem (Hebrew).

_____. 1964a. Seals and Sealings. *Israel Exploration Journal* 14: 190–194.

_____. 1964b. The Seal of Jezebel. *Israel Exploration Journal* 14: 274–276.

_____. 1969. A Group of Hebrew Seals. *Eretz-Israel* 9: 1–9, 134* (Hebrew and English summary).

_____. 1973. The Ivory House which Ahab Built. In *Eretz Shomron: The Thirtieth Archaeological Convention, September 1972,* ed. Y. Aviram. Jerusalem: Israel Exploration Society. 75–85, XV–XVI. (Hebrew and English Summary).

_____. 1975. New Names on Hebrew Seals. *Eretz-Israel* 12: 66–71, 120*–121* (Hebrew and English summary).

_____. 1976. The Governor of the City. *Israel Exploration Journal* 26: 178–182, pl. 33:D.

_____. 1977. "The Governor" (Sar Ha-'Ir). *Qadmoniot* 10 (38–39): 68–69 (Hebrew).

_____. 1978a. On "A Second Bulla of a Sar Ha'ir." *Qadmoniot* 11 (41): 34 (Hebrew).

_____. 1978b. Baruch the Scribe and Jerahmeel the King's Son. *Israel Exploration Journal* 28: 52–56.

_____. 1978c. Baruch the Scribe and Jerahmeel Son of the King. *Qadmoniot* 11 (44): 113–114 (Hebrew).

_____. 1979a. Jerahmeel & Baruch—King's Son & Scribe. *Biblical Archaeologist* 42: 114–118.

_____. 1979b. Baruch the Scribe and Jerahmeel the King's Son. *Beth Mikra* 78: 251–254 (Hebrew).

_____. 1986. *Hebrew Bullae from the Time of Jeremiah: Remnants of a Burnt Archive.* Jerusalem.

_____. 1987. On the Identification of Persons Mentioned in Hebrew Epigraphic Sources. *Eretz-Israel* 19: 235–237, 79*. (Hebrew and English Summary).

_____. 1988. Hebrew Seals and Sealings and Their Significance for Biblical Research. In: *Congress Volume, Jerusalem 1986,* ed. J. A. Emerton. Supplement to Vetus Testamentum, 40. Leiden: Brill. 7–16.

_____. 1989a. Another Group of West-Semitic Seals from the Hecht Collection. *Michmanim* 4: 7–21.

_____. 1989b. Two Seals of Women and Other Hebrew Seals. *Eretz-Israel* 20: 90–96, 197* (Hebrew and English summary).

_____. 1990. Two Hebrew 'Fiscal' Bullae. *Israel Exploration Journal* 40: 262–266.

_____. 1992. A New Bulla of a Moabite Scribe *Eretz-Israel* 23: 92–93, 149* (Hebrew and English summary).

_____. 1994. The "Governor of the City" Bulla. In: Geva 1994 (*q.v.*): 138–140.

Avi-Yonah, M. 1954. *S.v.* Damascus. *Encyhclopedia Biblica* 2: cols. 672–675. Jerusalem (Hebrew).

Barkay, G. 1977. A Second Bulla of a Sar Ha-'Ir. *Qadmoniot* 10 (38–39): 69–71. (Hebrew).

_____. 1994. A Second "Governor of the City" Bulla. In: Geva 1994 (*q.v.*): 141–144.

Barnett, R. D. 1957. *A Catalogue of the Nimrud Ivories with other examples of Ancient Near Eastern Ivories in the British Museum.* London: British Museum.

_____. 1967. Layard's Nimrud Bronzes and Their Inscriptions. *Eretz-Israel* 8: 1*–7*.

Beaux, N., and S. M. Goodman. 1993. Remarks on the Reptile Signs Depicted in the White Chapel of Sesostris I at Karnak. *Cahiers de Karnak* 9 (1993) Paris: 109–120.

Beck, P. 1986. A Bulla from Ḥorvat 'Uzza, *Qadmoniot* 19 (73–74): 40–41 (Hebrew).

Ben Dor, I. 1945. A Hebrew Seal in Gold Ring. *Bulletin of the Jewish Palestine Exploration Society* 12: 43–45 (Hebrew).

_____. 1948. Two Hebrew Seals. *Quarterly of the Department of Antiquities in Palestine* 13: 64–67.

Bennett, C.-M. 1966. Fouilles d'Umm el-Biyara. Rapport préliminaire. *Revue Biblique* 73: 372–403.

_____. 1974a. Chronique Archéologique: Buseira. *Revue Biblique* 81: 73–76.

_____. 1974b. Excavations at Buseirah, Southern Jordan, 1972: Preliminary Report. *Levant* 6: 1–24.

Ben-Tor, D. 1989. *The Scarab: A Reflection of Ancient Egypt*. Israel Museum Catalogue 303. Jerusalem.

Bienkowski, P. 1993. S.v. Umm El-Biyara" *New Encyclopedia of Archaeological Excavations in the Holy Land* 4: 1488–1490.

Bisi, A. M. 1965. *Il Grifone: Storia di un motivo iconografico nell'àntico Oriente mediterraneo*. Studi Semitici, 13. Rome: Centro di studi semitici, Istituto di studi del Vicino Oriente, Università Roma.

Bliss, F. J. 1900. Second Report on the Excavations at Tell ej-Judeideh. *Palestine Exploration Fund, Quarterly Statement* 33: 199–222.

_____, and R. A. S. Macalister. 1902. *Excavations in Palestine: during the Years 1898–1900*. London: Palestine Exploration Fund.

Bordreuil, P. 1986. *Catalogue des sceaux ouest-sémitiques inscrits de la Bibliothèque Nationale, du Musée du Louvre et du Musée biblique de Bible et Terre Sainte*. Paris.

_____. 1992. S.v. Sceaux inscrits des pays du Levant. *Dictioinnaire de la Bible, Supplément* vol. XII, fasc, 66. Paris: cols 86–212.

_____. 1993. Le répertoire iconographique des sceaux araméens inscrits et son évolution. In: Sass and Uehlinger (*q.v.*) 1993: 74–100.

_____, and Lemaire, A. 1976. Nouveaux sceaux hébreux, araméens et ammonites. *Semitica* 26: 45–63.

Bossert, H. Th. 1942. *Altanatolien: Kunst und Handwerk in Kleinasien von den anfängen bis zum völligen aufgehen in der Griechischen Kultur*. Berlin: Wasmuth.

Brandl, B. 1991. A Phoenician Scarab from Lohamei HaGeta'ot. *'Atiqot* 20: 153–155.

Buchanan, B., and Moorey, P. R. S. 1988. *Catalogue of Ancient Near Eastern Seals in the Ashmolean Museum III: The Iron Age Stamp Seals (c. 1200–350 BC)*. Oxford: Oxford University Press.

Caubet, A. 1993. Sphinx 228. In: *Syrie Mémoire et Civilisation: Exposition présentée à l'Institut du Monde Arabe du 14 septembre 1993 au 28 février 1994*. Paris: 264–265.

di Cesnola, A. P. 1884. *Salamina (Cyprus): The History, Treasures, & Antiquities of Salamis in the Island of Cyprus*. 2d ed. London.

Çiligiroğlu, A. 1994. Decorated Stone Vessels from the Urartian Fortress of Ayanis. *Tel Aviv* 21: 68–76.

Clerc, G., V. Karageorghis, E. Lagarce, and J. Leclant. 1976. *Fouilles de Kition II: Objets Égyptiens et Égyptisants: Scarabées, amulettes et figurines en pâte de verre et en faïence, vase plastique en faïence. Sites I et II, 1959–1975*. Nicosia: Republic of Cyprus.

Cohen, G. 1982. S.v. Shaphat. *Encyhclopedia Biblica* 8: cols. 247–248. Jerusalem (Hebrew).

Collon, D. 1990. *Near Eastern Seals*. London: The British Museum.

Crowfoot, J. W. 1957. Chapter VI: Scarabs, Seals and Seal Impressions. In: *The Objects from Samaria*, ed. Crowfoot, J. W., and G. M. Crowfoot, K. M. Kenyon. Samaria-Sebaste Series, 3. London: Palestine Exploration Fund.

———, G. M. Crowfoot, and E. L. Sukenik. 1938. *Early Ivories from Samaria*. Samaria-Sebaste Series, 2. London: Palestine Exploration Fund.

———, K. M. Kenyon, and E. L. Sukenik. 1942. *The Buildings at Samaria*. Samaria-Sebaste Series, 1: Reports of the Work of the Joint Expedition in 1931–1933 and of the British Expedition in 1935. London: Palestine Exploration Fund.

Culican, W. 1968. The Iconography of Some Phoenician Seals and Seal Impressions. *Australian Journal of Biblical Archaeology* 1: 50–103.

———. 1974. A Phoenician Seal from Khaldeh. *Levant* 6: 195–198.

———. 1977. Seals in Bronze Mounts. *Rivista di Studi Fenici* 5: 1–4.

Davies, L. G. 1975. Supplementary Catalogue. In: Barnett, R. D. 1975. *A Catalogue of the Nimrud Ivories, with other examples of Ancient Near Eastern Ivories in the British Museum*, ed. R. D. Barnett (first published 1957, 2d ed. rev. and enlarged). London: British Museum. 231–240.

Delaporte, L. 1910. *Catalogue des cylindres orientaux et des cachets assyro-babyloniens, perses et syro-cappadociens de la Bibliothèque Nationale*. Paris: Bibliothèque Nationale.

———. 1920. *Musée du Louvre, Catalogue des cylindres cachets et pierres gravées de style oriental I: Fouilles et missions*. Paris.

Deutsch, R., and M. Heltzer. 1994. *Forty New Ancient West Semitic Inscriptions*. Tel Aviv–Jaffa.

Diringer, D. 1934. *Le iscrizioni àntico-ebraiche palestinesi*. Publicazioni della R. Università degli Studi di Firenze. Facolta di lettere e filosofia III/2. Florence.

———. 1953. Chapter 10: Early Hebrew Inscriptions. In: Tufnell, O., et al. 1953: 331–359.

Fargo, V. M., and K. G. O'Connell. 1978. Five Seasons of Excavation at Tell el–Hesi (1970–77). *Biblical Archaeologist* 41: 165–182.

Ferioli, P., and E. Fiandra, E. 1990. The Use of Clay Sealings in Administrative Functions from the Fifth to First Millennium B.C. in the Orient, Nubia, Egypt, and the Aegean: Similarities and Differences. *Aegaeum* 5: 221–232 (= Aegean Seals, Sealings and Administration: Proceedings of the NEH–Dickson Conference of the Program in Aegean Scripts and Prehistory of the Department of Classics, University of Texas at Austin, January 11–13, 1989).

Galling, K. 1937. *Biblisches Reallexikon*. Tübingen.

———. 1941. Beschriftete Bildsiegel des ersten Jahrtausends v. Chr. vornehmlich aus Syrien und Palästina. Ein Beitrag zur Geschichte der phönikischen Künst. *Zeitschrift des Deutschen Palästina-Vereins* 64: 121–202.

Garbini, G. 1982. I sigilli del regno di Israele. *Oriens Antiquus* 21: 163–176.

Gardiner, A. H. . 1957 (1973 printing). Egyptian Grammar. 3d ed. rev. London: Ashmolean Museum/Oxford University Press.

Geva, H., ed. 1994 (ed.). *Ancient Jerusalem Revealed*. Jerusalem: Israel Exploration Society.

Giveon, R. 1971. Ivories in the Israelite Period: The Samaria Ivories. In *Shomron (Samaria): A Collection of Source Material and Essays*, ed. S. Dar, S. and Y. Roth, Y. Tel-Aviv. 88–99 (Hebrew).

———. 1974. The Seal of Jezebel. In *Footsteps of the Pharaohs in Canaan: Essays on the Relations between the Land of Israel and Ancient Egypt*, ed. R. Giveon. Tel Aviv 151 (Hebrew).

———. 1978. The Samaria Ivories. In *The Impact of Egypt on Canaan: Iconographical and Related Studies*, ed. R. Giveon. Orbis Biblicus et Orientalis 20. Freiburg/Schweiz: Universitätsverlag; Göttingen: Vandenhoeck & Ruprecht. 34–44.

———. 1984. The Seal of Jezebel. In *Footsteps of Pharaoh in Canaan: Essays on the Relations between the Land of Israel and Ancient Egypt*, ed. R. Giveon. Tel Aviv: 147–148 (Hebrew).

_____. 1985. *Egyptian Scarabs from Western Asia from the Collections of the British Museum.* Orbis Biblicus et Orientalis, Series Archaeologica 3. Freiburg/Schweiz: Universitätsverlag; Göttingen: Vandenhoeck & Ruprecht.

_____. 1986. Egyptian Seals from the Western Galilee. In: M. Yedaya, ed. *Western Galilee Antiquities.* Tel Aviv: Ministry of Defence Publishing House and the Regional Council "Mateh Asher." 78–84 (Hebrew).

_____. 1988. *Scarabs from Recent Excavations in Israel.* Orbis Biblicus et Orientalis 83. Freiburg/Schweiz: Universitätsverlag; Göttingen: Vandenhoeck & Ruprecht.

_____, and T. Kertesz. 1986. *Egyptian Scarabs and Seals from Acco.* Freiburg/Schweiz: Universitätsverlag.

Gubel, E. 1986. Deux Bulles. In *Les Phéniciens et le monde Méditerranéen,* ed. E. Gubel et al. Brussels. 227.

_____. 1987. *Phoenician Furniture.* Studia Phoenicia 7. Leuven.

_____. 1988. Phoenician Seals in the Allard Pierson Museum, Amsterdam. The Corpus Glyptica Phoenician Project, 3. *Rivista di Studi Fenici* 16: 145–163.

_____. 1993. The Iconogaphy of Inscribed Phoenician Glyptic. In: Sass and Uehlinger (q.v.), 1993, 101–129.

Hall, H. R. 1913. *Catalogue of Egyptian Scarabs, Etc., in the British Museum.* Vol. 1: *Royal Scarabs.* London: British Museum.

Harden, D. 1962. *The Phoenicians.* London: Thames & Hudson.

Hayes, W. C. 1959. *The Scepter of Egypt: A Background for the Study of the Egyptian Antiquities in the Metropolitan Museum of Art.* Volume 2: *The Hyksos Period and the New Kingdom* (1675–1080 B.C.). New York: Harper/Metropolitan Museum of Art.

Heltzer, M. 1981. Inscribed Scaraboid Seals [nos.266–273]. In *Ladders to Heaven: Art Treasures from Lands of the Bible,* ed. O. W. Muscarella. Toronto: McClelland and Stewart. 290–293.

Herbordt, S. 1992. *Neuassyrische Glyptik des 8.-7. Jh. v. Chr.: unter besonderer Berücksichtigung der siegelungen auf Tafeln und tonverschlüssen.* Helsinki.

Herr, L. G. 1985. The Servant of Baalis. *Biblical Archaeologist* 48: 169–172.

_____. 1989. Chapter 21: The Inscribed Seal Impression. In *Madaba Plains Project 1: The 1984 Season at Tell el-'Umeiri and Vicinity and Subsequent Studies,* ed. L. T. Geraty, et al. Berrien Springs, Mich.: Andrews University Press/Institute of Archaeology. 369–374.

Hestrin, R. 1973. First Temple and Persian Periods. In *Inscriptions Reveal: Documents from the Time of the Bible, the Mishna and the Talmud,* ed. R. Hestrin, Y. Israeli, Y. Meshorer. and A. Eitan. Rev. 2d ed. of Hebrew version. Israel Museum Catalog no. 100. Jerusalem: Israel Museum. 14–71.

_____, and M. Dayagi. 1974a. A Seal Impression of a Servant of King Hezekiah. *Israel Exploration Journal* 24: 27–29, pl. 2:B–C.

_____. and M. Dayagi. 1974b. A Seal-Impression of a "Servant" ('Ebed) of King Hezekiah. *Qadmoniot* 7 (27–28): 104–105. (Hebrew).

_____. and M. Dayagi-Mendels. 1979. *I nscribed Seals: First Temple Period Hebrew, Ammonite, Moabite, Phoenician and Aramaic from the Collections of the Israel Museum and the Israel Department of Antiquities and Museums.* Jerusalem (Translation of 1978 Hebrew version).

Hooke, S. H. 1935. A Scarab and Sealing From Tell Duweir. *Palestine Exploration Fund, Quarterly Statement* 67: 195–197.

Horn, S. H. 1966. Scarabs and Scarab Impressions from Shechem, II. *Journal of Near Eastern Studies* 25: 48–56.

Hübner, U. 1993. Das ikonographische Repertoire der ammonitischen Siegel und seine Entwicklung. In: Sass and Uehlinger (*q.v.*) 1993: 130–160.

Ibrahim, M. M., and R. L. Gordon, et al. 1987. *A Cemetery at Queen Alia International Airport.* Yarmouk University Publications, Institute of Archaeology and Anthropology, 1. Wiesbaden: Harrassowitz.

Karageorghis, V. 1968. *Archaeologia Mundi: Cyprus.* Geneva.

_____. 1973. *Excavations in the Necropolis of Salamis* III (Text). Nicosia: Cyprus Dept. of Antiquities.

_____. 1974. *Excavations in the Necropolis of Salamis* III (plates). Haarlem.

Kaufman, S. A. 1984. On Vowel Redaction in Aramaic. *Journal of the American Oriental Society* 104: 87–95.

Keel, O. 1977. *Jahwe-Visionen und Siegelkunst: Eine neue Deutung der Majestätsschilderungen in Jes 6, Ez 1 und 10 und Sach 4.* Stuttgarter Bibelstudien 84/85. Stuttgart.

_____. 1994. *Studien zu den Stempelsiegeln aus Palästina/Israel* IV. Orbis Biblicus et Orientalis 135. Freiburg/Schweiz: Universitätsverlag; Göttingen: Vandenhoeck & Ruprecht.

_____, and Ch. Uehlinger. 1992. *Göttinnen, Götter und Gottessymbole: Neue Erkenntnisse zur Religionsgeschichte Kanaans und Israels Aufgrund Bislang Unerschlossener Ikonographischer Quellen.* Fribourg, Basel, Vienna: Herder.

_____, and Ch. Uehlinger, et al. 1990. *Altorientalische Miniaturkunst. Die ältesten visuellen Massenkommunikationsmittel. Ein Blick in die Sammlungen des Biblischen Instituts der Universität Freiburg Schweiz.* Mainz am Rhein: P. von Zabern.

Keel-Leu, H. 1991. *Vorderasiatische Stempelsiegel: Die Sammlung des Biblischen Instituts der Universität Freiburg Schweiz.* Orbus Biblicus et Orientalis, 110. Freiburg/Schweiz: Universitätsverlag; Göttingen: Vandenhoeck & Ruprecht.

Klähn, J. B. 1957. Grief. *Reallexikon der Assyriologie* 3: 633–639.

Kracht, P. 1991. Die Aktivitäten des Deutschen Archäologischen Instituts während der letzten Grabungssaison. *Antike Welt* 22: 291–296.

Lamon, R. S., and Shipton, G. M. 1939. *Megiddo* I: *Seasons of 1925–34, Strata I–V.* Oriental Institute Publications, 42. Chicago: University of Chicago Press.

Layard, A. H. 1853. *Discoveries among the Ruins of Nineveh and Babylon, with Travels in Armenia, Kurdistan and the Desert: Being the Result of a Second Expedition, undertaken for the Trustees of the British Museum.* New York.

Layton, S. C. 1991. A New Interpretation of an Edomite Seal Impression. *Journal of Near Eastern Studies* 50: 37–43.

Leibovitch, J. 1955. Le Griffon dans le Moyen–Orient Antique. *'Atiquot* 1: 75–88.

Lemaire, A. 1990. Trois sceaux inscrits inédits avec lion rugissant. *Semitica* 39: 13–21.

_____. 1993. Les critères non–iconographiques de la classification des sceaux nord–ouest sémitiques inscrits. In: Sass and Uehlinger (*q.v.*) 1993: 1–26.

Levy, M. A. 1869. *Siegel und Gemmen mit aramäischen, phönizischen, althebräischen, himijarischen, nabathäischen und altsyrischen Inschriften.* Breslau: Schletter'schen Buchhandlung.

Liver, J. 1954. *S.v.* Gedaljahw Ben Ahikam. *Encyhclopedia Biblica* 2: cols. 440–442. Jerusalem (Hebrew).

Loud, G. 1948. *Megiddo* II: *Seasons of 1935–39.* Oriental Institute Publications, 62. Chicago: University of Chicago Press.

von Luschan, F., and W. Andrae. 1943. *Ausgrabungen in Sendschirli.* Vol. 5: *Die Kleinfunde von Sendschirli.* Staatliche Museen zu Berlin, Mitteilungen aus den orientalischen Sammlungen, 15. Berlin.

_____, and C. H. B. Altman. 1938. *Khorsabad II: The Citadel and the Town.* Oriental Institute Publications 40. Chicago: University of Chicago Press.

Mallowan, M. E. L. 1966. *Nimrud and Its Remains.* London: Collins. [Emended impression, with 6 pages of Addenda and Corrigenda, 1975.]

Martin, K. 1985. Uräus. *Lexikon der Ägyptologie* 4: cols. 863–868.

Mazar, B., and G. Cornfeld. 1975. *The Mountain of the Loard.* Garden City, N.Y.: Doubleday.

de Mertzenfeld, C. D. 1954. *Inventaire commenté des Ivoires Phéniciens et apparentés découverts dans le proche-orient.* Paris: E. de Boccard.

Millard, A. R. 1965. The Assyrian Royal Seal Type Again. *Iraq* 27: 12–16.

_____. 1978. The Assyrian Royal Seal: An Addendum. *Iraq* 40: 70

_____. 1991. Writing in Jordan: From Cuneiform to Arabic. In *Treasures from an Ancient Land: The Art of Jordan.* National Museums and Galleries on Merseyside (Liverpool), ed. P. Bienkowski. 133–149.

Moscati, S. 1951. *L'epigrafia ebraica antica, 1935-1950.* Biblica et Orientalia, 15. Rome: Pontificio Instituto Biblico .

_____. 1968. *The World of the Phoenicians.* London: Weidenfeld and Nicolson.

Murray, M.A. 1953. Chapter 11: Hieroglyphic and Ornamental Seals. In: Tufnell et al. (*q.v.*). 360–373.

Muscarella, O.W. 1981. Ivories from Arslan Tash [nos. 243–262]. In *Ladders to Heaven: Art Treasures from Lands of the Bible,* ed. O. W. Muscarella. Toronto: McClelland and Stewart. 274–284.

O'Connell, K. G. 1977. An Israelite Bulla from Tell el-Ḥesi. *Israel Exploration Journal* 27: 197–199.

_____, D. Glenn Rose, and L. E. Toombs. 1978. Tell el- Ḥesi, 1977. *Palestine Exploration Quarterly* 110: 75–90.

von Oppenheim, M. F., and B. Hrouda. 1962. *Tell Halaf 4: Die Kleinfunde aus Historischer Zeit.* Berlin:

Ornan, T. 1993. The Mesopotamian Influence on West Semitic Inscribed Seals: A Preference for the Depiction of Mortals. In: Sass and Uehlinger (*q.v.*), 52–73.

Otzen, B. 1990. Appendix 2: The Aramaic Inscriptions. In: P. J. Riis, et al., *Hama: Fouilles et recherches de la Fondation Carlsberg 1931-1938,* 2, pt. 2: *Les ojets de la période dite Syro-Hittite (Âge du Fer).* Copenhagen: 265–318.

Parayre, D. 1990. Les cachets ouest-sémitiques à travers l'image du disque solaire ailé (perspective iconographique). *Syria* 67: 270–301.

_____. 1993. A propos des sceaux ouest-sémitiques: Le rôle de l'iconographie dans l'attribution d'un sceau à une aire culturelle et à un atelier. In: Sass and Uehlinger (*q.v.*) 1993: 27–51.

Parker, B. 1962. Seals and Seal Impressions from the Nimrud Excavations, 1955-58. *Iraq* 24: 26–40.

Petrie, W. M. Flinders. 1933. *Ancient Gaza* III: *Tell el Ajjul.* London: British School of Archaeology in Egypt.

_____, and J. C. Ellis. 1937. *Anthedon.* London: British School of Archaeology in Egypt.

_____, and O. Tufnell. 1930. *Beth-Pelet* I *(Tell Fara).* London: British School of Archaeology in Egypt.

Pilcher, E. J. 1913. Old Hebrew Signets from Gezer. *Palestine Exploration Fund, Quarterly Statement* 45: 143–146.

Porada, E. 1963. Chapter 4: Seals. In: *Excavations at Gözlü Kule, Tarsus* III: *The Iron Age,* ed. H. Goldman. Princeton: Princeton University Press. 347–358.

Puech, E. 1977. Documents épigraphiques de Buseirah. *Levant* 9: 11–20.

Rabin, H. 1982. *S.v.* Sar. *Encyhlopedia Biblica* 8: col. 387. Jerusalem (Hebrew).

Redissi, T. 1991. Rapport préliminaire. In: *Ein punisches Heiligtum in Karthago und sein römishscher Nachfolgebau*, In: F. Rakob, Erster Bericht *Mitteilungen des Deutschen Archaeologischen Instituts, Roemische Abteilung* 98: 33–80. Pp. 59–61, pl. 27.

Reich, R. 1993. *S.v.* Bozrah. *New Encyclopedia of Archaeological Excavations in the Holy Land* 1: 264–266.

Reifenberg, A. 1950. *Ancient Hebrew Seals*. London: East and West Library.

Reisner, G. A., C. S. Fisher, and D. G. Lyon, 1924. *Harvard Excavations at Samaria 1908-1910*. Cambridge, Mass.: Harvard University Press.

Riis, P. J. 1990, Chap. III: Les sceaux et les scellements. In: P. J. Riis, et al., *Hama: Fouilles et recherches de la Fondation Carlsberg 1931-1938*, 2, pt. 2: *Les objets de la période dite Syro-Hittite (Âge du Fer)*. Copenhagen: 82–96.

Rowe, A. 1936. *A Catalogue of Egyptian Scarabs, Scaraboids, Seals and Amulets in the Palestine Archaeological Museum*. Cairo.

Sachs, A. J. 1953. The Late Assyrian Royal-Seal Type. *Iraq* 15: 167–170.

Sass, B. 1993. The Pre-Exilic Hebrew Seals: Iconism vs. Aniconism. In: Sass and Uehlinger (*q.v.*) 1993: 194–256.

Sass, B., and Ch. Uehlinger, eds. 1993. *Studies in Iconography of Northwest Semitic Inscribed Seals: Proceedings of a symposium held in Fribourg on April 17-20, 1991*. Orbis Biblicus et Orientalis 125. Freiburg/Schweiz: Universitätsverlag; Göttingen: Vandenhoeck & Ruprecht.

Schneider, Ts. 1988a. "Azariahu ben Hilqiahu" (the Priests?) on a Bulla from the City of David. *Qadmoniot* 21 (81-82): 56 (Hebrew).

_____.1988b. Azariahu Son of Hilkiahu (High Priest?) on a City of David Bulla. *Israel Exploration Journal* 38: 139–141.

_____. 1991. Six Biblical Signatures: Seal and Seal Impressions of Six Biblical Personages Recovered. *Biblical Archaeology Review* 17(4): 26–33.

_____. 1994. A Biblical Name on a City of David Bulla: Azariah son of Hilkiah (High Priest?). In: Geva (*q.v.*) 1994: 62–63.

Sellers, O. R. 1933. *The Citadel of Beth-Zur*. Philadelphia: Westminster Press.

Shiloh, Y. 1984. *Excavations at the City of David I, 1978-1982: Interim Report of the First Five Seasons*. Qedem 19. Jerusalem: Hebrew University Institute of Archaeology.

_____. 1985. A Hoard of Hebrew Bullae from the City of David. *Eretz-Israel* 18: 73–87, 68*. [Hebrew and English summary.]

_____. 1986a. A Hoard of Israelite Seal-Impressions on Bullae from the City of David. *Qadmoniot* 19 (73-74) 2–11 (Hebrew).

_____. 1986b. A Group of Hebrew Bullae from the City of David. *Israel Exploration Journal* 36: 16–38.

_____, and D. Tarler. 1986. Bullae from the City of David: A Hoard of Seal Impressions from the Israelite Period. *Biblical Archaeologist* 49: 197–209.

Shoham, Y. 1994. A Group of Hebrew Bullae from Yigal Shiloh's Excavations in the City of David. In: Geva (q.v.) 1994: 55–61.

Sprengling, M. 1932. An Aramaic Seal Impression from Khorsabad. *American Journal of Semitic Languages* 49: 53–55.

Staples, W.E. 1931. Chapter 3: An Inscribed Scaraboid from Megiddo. In: *New Light from Armageddon: Second Provisional Report (1927-29) on the Excavations at Megiddo in Palestine*, P. L. O. Guy and W. E. Staples. *Oriental Institute Communications* 9, Chicago: 49–68.

Straus, Ch. 1980. Kronen. *Lexikon der Ägyptologie* III: cols. 811–816.

Sukenik, E. L. 1942. A Further Note on Hebrew Seals. *Kedem* 1: 46, vi. [Hebrew and English summary.]

Sznycer, M. 1969. Punic Literature. *Archaeologia Viva* 1: 141–148.

Tadmor, H. 1973. On the History of Samaria in the Biblical Period. In: *Eretz Shomron: The Thirtieth Archaeological Convention, September 1972.* Jerusalem: Israel Exploration Society, 67–74. XV [Hebrew and English summary].

Thimme, J. 1973a. Phönizische Elfenbeine in Karlsruhe. *Antike Welt* 4: 21–27.

_____. 1973b. *Phönizische Elfenbeine.* Karlsruhe.

Thureau–Dangin, F., A. Barrois, G. Dossin, and M. Dunand. 1931. *Arslan-Tash* . Paris: Paul Guethner.

Tufnell, O. 1983. Some Gold Bird Ornaments, Falcon or Wryneck. *Anatolian Studies* 33: 57–66.

_____, et al. 1953. *Lachish III (Tell-ed-Duweir): The Iron Age.* London: Published for the Trustees of the late Sir Henry Wellcome by the Oxford University Press.

Uehlinger, C. 1990. III. *Die Sammlung ägyptischer Siegelamulette (Skarabäensammlung Fouad S. Matouk).* In Keel, Uehlinger, et al. 1990 (*q.v.*), 58–85.

_____. 1993a. Introduction: The Status of Iconography in the Study of Northwest Semitic Inscribed Seals. In: Sass and Uehlinger (*q.v.*) 1993: xi–xxiii.

_____. 1993b. Northwest Semitic Inscribed Seals, Iconography and Syro–Palestinian Religions of Iron Age II: Some Afterthoughts and Conclusions. In: Sass and Uehlinger (*q.v.*) 1993: 257–288.

Van Beek, G. 1986. Tell Jemmeh – 1984. *Hadashot Arkheologiyot (Archaeological Newsletter)* 88: 32 (Hebrew).

_____. 1987. Tell Jemmeh – 1984. *Excavations and Surveys in Israel* 5: 54–55.

Wantanabe, K. 1993. Neuassyrische Siegellegenden. *Orient* 29: 109–129.

Ward, W. A. 1967. Three Phoenician Seals of the Early First Millennium B.C. *Journal of Egyptian Archaeology* 53: 69–74.

_____. 1968. The Four-Winged Serpent on Hebrew Seals. *Rivista degli Studi Orientali* 43: 135–143.

Williams, B. 1977. Aspects of Sealing and Glyptic in Egypt before the New Kingdom. In *Seals and Sealing in the Ancient Near East,* ed. M. Gibson, and R. D. Biggs. *Bibliotheca Mesopotamica* 6. Malibu. 135–140, 158.

Winter, I. J. 1973. *North Syria in the Early First Millennium B.C., with Special Reference to Ivory Carving.* Ph.D. dissertation, Columbia University.

_____. 1976. Phoenician and North Syrian Ivory Carving in Historical Context: Questions of Style and Distribution. *Iraq* 38: 1–22.

_____. 1981. Is There a South Syrian Style of Ivory Carving in the Early First Millennium B.C.? *Iraq* 43: 101–130.

Yeivin, S. 1978. A Seal-Impression of a 'Servant' ('Ebed) of King Hezekiah. *Qadmoniot* 11 (41): 34–35 (Hebrew).

Younker, R.W. 1985. Israel, Judah, and Ammon and the Motifs on the Baalis Seal from Tell el-'Umeiri. *Biblical Archaeologist* 48: 173–180.

_____. 1989. Chapter 22: Historical Background and Motifs of a Royal Seal Impression. In: *Madaba Plains Project 1: The 1984 Season at Tell el-'Umeiri and Vicinity and Subsequent Studies,* ed. L. T. Geraty et al. Berrien Springs, Michigan: Andrews University, 375–380.

Acknowledgments

Special thanks are due Dr. Benjamin Sass for adding the references to bullae from Carthage, Hama, and Khorsahad; to Mrs. Mariana Salzberger for the photographs; and to Mrs. Carmen Hersch for the drawings and reconstructions.

Fred Strickert

The Coins of Philip

I N THE SUMMER OF 1992 a private Christian newspaper in Jerusalem
ran a front page picture from our archaeological site with the caption "Head Of King Herold Found On Coin At Bethsaida." Coin discoveries
can generate all kinds of excitement, but of course there was no King
Herold (unless, perhaps, a Bethlehem angel). If the caption meant Herod
the Great, as I assume, this was indeed exciting news because we have no
visual representations of him, certainly not on coins. However, what was
shown in the picture was a coin minted, not by Herod the Great, but by
Philip, his son, who in 4 BCE inherited the tetrarchy northeast of the Sea
of Galilee, including the town Bethsaida.

Since excavations began in 1987, some seventy-six coins have been
discovered that cover a wide range of history, from a fifth-century-BCE.
Tyrian Obol to nineteenth- and twentieth-century coins of the Ottoman
empire. Among those seventy-six coins, two are of special interest because
they originated in the mints of Philip himself. By concentrating on these
two coins and the other coins of Philip that have been discovered over the
years, I hope to share the excitement over discovery of the coins, and to
show how coins can provide a wealth of information about the rule of
Philip and even about the town of Bethsaida.

It is immediately apparent that the two coins in question are not
well preserved, which is characteristic of all of Philip's coins. Ya'akov Meshorer writes: "Because of the poor alloy of bronze from which they
[Philip's coins] were struck, those that have survived are mostly in a poor
state of preservation."[1] This tells us something about the second-class
nature of the region inherited by Philip. He was, after all, granted the

smallest allowance from the estate of Herod. Nevertheless, he began issuing coins twenty years prior to his brother Antipas in Galilee, and he offered twice as many issues.

Human Images

The two Bethsaida finds are characteristic of the most common coin type minted by Philip. The head of the emperor is found on the obverse; the facade of a tetrastyle temple is on the reverse. This type of coin was produced in each of the eight years that Philip minted coins (fig. 1). Philip

Fig. 1. Coin of Philip: Emperor Tiberius on obverse, facade of tetrastyle temple on reverse.

was the first ruler of the Jews to use human images on Jewish coins. While the most common type of coins used the image of the emperor (first Augustus and then Tiberius), Philip minted coins with images of himself, with Livia/Julia (wife of Augustus), and with an image of both Augustus and Livia.

Prior to this time, all Jewish coinage had been affected by the Commandment forbidding graven images.[2] Pilate's activities during his first years in office are well known from the reports of Josephus and Philo, which include various incidents of Pilate's insensitivity to Jewish custom, including his bringing to Jerusalem the Roman standards with the image of the emperor Tiberius Caesar, his erecting commemorative shields at Herod's Jerusalem palace, and his taking money from the Temple treasury to build an aqueduct.[3] The Hasmoneans, Herod the Great, Archelaus, and the procurators all used common symbols on their coins instead of human images. One must note the influence of the Hasmoneans on Bethsaida, where no less than seven coins from that era were discovered. Even in Galilee, when Antipas first issued coins in 20 CE, he did not include human images even though his brother had been minting such coins for several decades. In subsequent mintings, he used other symbols; only in his final year, 39 CE, did he include the name of the emperor on his coins.[4]

Philip's freedom to use human images on coins was a result of both a low concentration of Jewish population in his region[5] and their less stringent attitude toward the Law. In fact, Philip was influenced by Lysanias and Zenodorus (r. 30–20 BCE) in his decision to use images for his initial coinage. In 27 BCE, Zenodorus issued a coin with his own portrait on the front and with a portrait of Octavian on the reverse.[6] The oldest coins of Philip include images both of himself and Augustus. This practice was then abandoned in favor of using only the emperor's image on the obverse and a tetrastyle temple on the reverse. Meshorer sees this as evidence of Philip's positive attitude toward Augustus and toward his own position as tetrarch. This stands in sharp contrast to both Archelaus and Antipas, who resented the distribution of their father's will.[7] Philip was the first ruler of the Jews to make use of this practice of using human images on the coins, especially the image of Augustas, and there is no sign that he met with disapproval. In fact, he was the most popular ruler of Herod's sons.

THE TEMPLE OF AUGUSTUS

More striking than the use of human images is Philip's depiction of a pagan temple on coins. While none of the coins specifically identifies this temple, there is no doubt that it represents the temple to Augustus in Paneas/Caesarea Philippi. Josephus reports that this temple was constructed by Philip's father, Herod the Great, when Augustus visited this territory and annexed it to the kingdom of Herod. After accompanying Augustus to the coast, Herod returned to carry out its construction in Augustus' honor.[8] The significance of this temple was not lost on Philip, who renamed the city Caesarea Philippi to parallel the coastal city of Caesarea, where Herod had built a second temple to Augustus.

The description in Josephus' *Antiquities* states only that the temple was constructed of beautiful white limestone. Philip's coins offer our only visual representation of the temple. The depiction is rather consistent throughout all mintings. It shows a tetrastyle temple with four Ionic columns supporting a pediment. On several coins the temple is presented on a high foundation, with a staircase.

While the use of human images and the depiction of a temple are striking, one must complete the picture by noting the absence of any Jewish symbols. The one exception is a lily which appears on the temple pediment in the first issue of this coin type. This may well have been a prominent decoration of the Paneas temple; however, on Jewish coins the lily often represents the Jerusalem Temple. Meshorer notes the numerous descriptions of lily decorations during both the First Temple and the Second Temple eras.[9] Interestingly, despite the first issue of Philip's temple coin with a lily in the pediment, the lily is replaced in later coins with a simple dot. This could suggest that Philip was testing the waters with his first issue. If he received too much criticism, he could claim that the lily represented not the Augusteum, but the Jerusalem Temple. The omission of the lily from later coins might indicate an initially unfavorable reception of this coinage in his territory.

One cannot overemphasize the significance of the imagery on Philip's coins when discussing the environment of Christian origins. A case is often made from silence that Jesus avoided cultural centers like Tiberias. However, Jesus clearly frequented Bethsaida and also traveled to Caesarea Philippi. These were the two main centers of Philip's rule and the coins from those areas reflect a less conservative brand of Judaism and a prevalence of pagan ideas. It is interesting that the first question addressed to Jesus upon returning to Galilee concerns coinage and the payment of taxes,[10] and that the issue resurfaces once he reaches Jerusalem.[11]

Dating Philip's Coins

With one exception, dates are included on all of Philip's coins. A Roman "L" standing for "Year" is followed by one or two Greek letters. This of course represents the year of Philip's rule, which began after Herod's death in 4 BCE, or possibly not until 3 BCE. On the majority of coins the date is located between the columns of the temple; on several coins it is found in the field next to the image.

Despite the poor condition of these coins, the dates are often legible. Of the two found at Bethsaida, one dates to year 33 of Philip, or 29 CE;[12] the date of the other is effaced. It would appear that Philip minted coins in eight of the thirty-seven years of his rule. There is some debate concerning those coins minted at the beginning of his rule. According to Meshorer, the earliest coins read "LE" or "year 5" (1 CE).[13] Jacob Maltiel-Gerstenfeld argues that the "E" is a Gamma, which would read "year 3" (2 BCE); for one other coin, he reads "year 6" (or 2 CE).[14] I prefer to follow Meshorer's readings. It is worthwhile to pay attention to the dates of mintings:

Table 1. Coin Mintings and Significant Events

Year	Coins of Philip	Event	Coins of Herod Antipas
4 BCE		Philip begins reign	
1 CE	1st issue	Caesarea celebrated	
6 CE		Coponius, procurator, issues coins	
8 CE	2d issue	(reaction to taxation)	
9 CE		Ambibulus, Procurator	
12 CE	3d issue	Annius Rufus, procurator	
15 CE	4th issue	Valerius Gratus, procurator	
20 CE		Tiberias founded	1st issue
26 CE	5th issue	Pontius Pilate, procurator	
29 CE	6th issue	1st Pilate coins	3d issue
30 CE	7th issue	2d Pilate coins	
31 CE		3d Pilate coins	
33 CE	8th issue		4th issue
34 CE		Death of Philip	

Why did Philip issue coins only in four of his first twenty-nine years as ruler and then four more times in the last eight years of his reign (26/27 to 33/34 CE; see table 1)? The answer to this question will tell us much about Philip. For New Testament scholars, the matter is significant because it concerns the time of Jesus' activity in and around Bethsaida.

Procurators, Pontius Pilate, and Philip's Product

The timing of Philip's first four mintings are quite logical (see Table 1). Perhaps he did not mint coins during the first years of his rule until the city of Caesarea Philippi had become well established. (Antipas did not mint his first coins until 20 CE, after Tiberias was established.) It is not difficult to see that subsequent mintings were made not only to satisfy monetary needs, but also for political purposes. The second minting may have been a reaction to the introduction of the procurators in Judea. Upon his arrival in Judea in 6 CE, the first procurator, Coponius, issued his own coinage. This was a time of great unrest, when Judas of Galilee, a Zealot leader and radical revolutionary, raised an insurrection against the taxation census (Acts 5:37).[15]

In 8 CE, Philip's decision to mint a new series of coins may well reflect his attempt to reassert the independence of his rule from the Roman procurators in Judea. Each of the next three mintings by Philip occurred in a year in which a new procurator arrived in Judea: 12 CE (Annius Rufus), 15 CE (Valerius Gratus), and 26 CE (Pontius Pilate).[16] It would seem that issuing coins served to publicize the legitimacy of one's own authority in the face of foreign domination. It is significant that while a coin of Archelaus was found at Bethsaida, no coin from the Roman procurators was found at this writing.

There was an eleven-year break between Philip's fourth and fifth mintings, which coincides with the longest tenure of the procurators by Valerius Gratus (15 to 26 CE). However, during the ten-year rule of Pilate (26 to 36 CE) Philip minted coins in four different years: 26, 29, 30, and 33 CE. In this situation, one might expect that the number of denominations of currency, up to this point two per minting, would have decreased. Instead, Philip continued to mint two denominations in 26 and 29 CE and even increased the number of denominations to three or four in both 30 and 33 CE. Philip died in 34 CE, two years before Pilate left office. It is obvious that the most productive minting period for Philip was during the time of Pontius Pilate's procuratorship.

A similar pattern occurs with respect to the coins of Herod Antipas. Even though he ruled longer than Philip, he issued coins during only five years of his reign: in 20 CE, after the founding of Tiberias; in 39 CE, shortly before his death; and in 29, 30, and 33 CE, during three years of Pilate's rule (the same three years that his brother Philip minted coins). Meshorer notes the nine-year gap between the first and second mintings of Antipas and explains this as the result of a saturation of the market with the bronze coins of the procurators.[17] He goes on to credit Pilate's antagonism towards the Jewish populace as the catalyst for the flurry of new mintings. There is no reason not to associate this phenomenon with Philip as well. Both Josephus and Philo report the dissatisfaction of the general public with Pilate. Philo even makes clear that the sons of Herod—Antipas and Philip—sided with the populace and led the opposition that forced Pilate to retreat.

Pilate issued relatively large quantities of coins in three consecutive years, 29, 30, and 31 CE, which may have been a deliberate attempt by him to monopolize the market.[18] Nevertheless, both Philip and Antipas followed suit by minting coins in 29, 30, and 34 CE in order to "emphasize their legitimate rights as Jewish rulers."[19] The absence of coinage minted by the tetrarchs in 31 CE may reflect a lack of financial resources which prevented them from competing with Pilate. One must also note the report in the Gospel of Luke that cooperation in the crucifixion of Jesus served to mend fences between Antipas and Pilate.[20] The final incident reported by Josephus, Pilate's massacre of Samaritans at Mount Gerizim,[21] helped to unite Antipas and Philip against Pilate. This may help explain why they both began issuing coins again in 33 CE.

The Philip and Julia Coins

Recent discoveries have brought to light two new coin types minted by Philip which date to this period. Up until 29 CE, Philip's coins were relatively standard, depicting the image of the emperor and the Paneas temple.[22] However, in both 30 and 33 CE, Philip issued a coin with his own image and another with the image of Livia/Julia.[23] Careful analysis will illustrate that these particular coins were produced with Pilate's coinage in mind.

In the year 29 CE, Pontius Pilate issued his first coin on which, as was the custom of the procurators, he made use of symbols rather than human images, surprising in light of his previous record. The obverse of the coin (fig. 2) shows a *simpulum*, which is a ladle used by Roman priests to pour wine over sacrificial animals. The reverse shows what appears to be a common neutral symbol: three ears of grain bound by stalks.[24] Although Meshorer notes that the Roman cultic *simpulum* is unique and carries what would seem to be an offensive message in Jerusalem, the presence of the three ears leads him to conclude that "the intentions of the procurator were not consistently negative or destructive, but rather may simply reflect his ignorance of local customs."[25] In other words, Pilate may have believed that the *simpulum* was used at the Jerusalem Temple and meant no harm.

Fig. 2. Coin of Pilate: *Simpulum* on obverse, ears of grain on reverse

In spite of his many accurate insights, Meshorer here misses the point. The key to understanding this coin is the inscription on the reverse: ΙΟΥΛΙΑ ΚΑΙΣΑΡΟΣ. The year 29 CE marked the death of Julia, and this coin was produced to commemorate her death. A different coin type was produced in both 30 and 31 CE. Although ears of grain previously had been used on Jewish coinage,[26] they were not so prominent. It is also significant that the two outer ears are drooping. This may signify that Julia was dead. Gertrude Grether notes that Livia was frequently associated with Abundantia (ΕΥΘΕΝΙΑ), the goddess of agricultural plenty. In fact, coins of Augustus from 2 BCE to 14 CE depict Livia seated, holding ears of corn and a scepter.[27] Thus the symbolism of Pilate's coin is quite appropriate for Julia/Livia. A second artistic tendency with regard to Livia, according to Grether, was to depict her role as priestess of Augustus.[28] Thus, the obverse depiction of a Roman cultic theme is quite appropriate for this memorial for Livia. It would seem that Pilate was shrewd even when issuing coins. After failing in his efforts to bring to Jerusalem the Roman standards with the image of Tiberius and a dedicatory inscription on commemorative shields, he was able to commemorate the death of Julia on coin. Whether this symbolism was lost on the Jewish populace is unknown; neither Josephus nor Philo mentions any reaction. Philip seems to have been influenced by Pilate's coin. Philip's 30 CE coin (fig. 3) presents a draped image of Julia/Livia, perhaps depicting her priestly role. Her image is surrounded by the inscription: ΙΟΥΛΙΑ ΣΕΒΑΣΤΕ. On the reverse, Philip also used the three ears of grain. There are two differences between Philip's and Pilate's coins. First, in Philip's coin the hand of Julia is holding the ears—she is fulfilling her role as goddess of abundance. The inscription reads ΚΑΡΠΟΦΟΡΟΣ. Second, the grain is not drooping. Like the coin of Pilate, this coin depicts Julia in her dual role as priestess and goddess of agriculture. Ironically, Philip was able to do something that Pilate could not do: use the image of Julia.

Fig. 3. Coin of Philip: Julia/Livia on obverse, holding ears of corn on reverse

In 30 and 31 CE, Pilate issued another coin type with a different symbol from the Roman cult, called a *lituus* (fig. 4).This augural staff represented the authority of the Roman state. The staff is surrounded by the inscription ΤΙΒΕΡΙΟΥ ΚΑΙΣΑΡΟΣ. On the reverse is only the date within a wreath, another symbol associated with the Caesars.[29]

Fig. 4. Coin of Pontius Pilate: *Lituus* staff on obverse, wreath with date on reverse

For the first time since his initial mint, Philip issued in 30 CE and again in 33 CE a coin with his own image on the obverse and the date within a wreath on the reverse (fig. 5). It is not difficult to see the connection between this coin and the coin of Pilate. Philip simply substituted his own image for the *lituus*—both symbols of authority. The reverse with the date inside a wreath is virtually identical to Pilate's coin.

Fig. 5. Coin of Philip: image of Philip on obverse, wreath with date on reverse

One can conclude that Philip was influenced highly during these years by the minting patterns of Pontius Pilate, both with regard to the frequency of issue and the use of symbols. As mentioned earlier, Antipas also was influenced by Pilate's coins, but the coin type produced by Antipas during these years was totally independent—the symbol of a palm tree.

Denominations

The Pilate coins also affected another aspect of Philip's coinage: their size. Prior to the year 30 CE, Philip produced two denominations per year, with the smallest coin weighing 3.8 grams, with a diameter of 16 mm. In both the years 30 CE and 33 CE Philip produced three or four denominations of coins, and introduced smaller coins for the first time. The four coins with an image of Philip or with an image of Julia weigh 1.61, 1.75, 2.51, and 3.5 grams and have diameters of 10.5, 11.7, 14.0, and 15.2 mm respectively.[30] The radical change in minting patterns appears to be a response to Pilate's flooding the market with small coins that weighed from 1.2 to 2.3 grams and had diameters from 14 to 16 mm.[31]

A brief word must be inserted here about denominational standards for ancient mints. The Roman system of this time was made up of five denominations:

Denomination	Weight
1. *Sestertius*	27.0 grams
2. *Dupondius*	14.0 grams
3. *As*	7.0 grams
4. *Semis*	3.5 grams
5. *Quadrans*	1.8 grams

Table 2. Roman Denominational Standards during Reign of Philip

The precision of these measurements was due to the use of a yellow alloy of copper and zinc called orichalcum.[32] Since this alloy was unavailable in Palestine, such precision there was impossible, but an effort was made to follow the Roman standard to some degree. Both Herod the Great[33] and Antipas (see table 3)[34] consistently minted four denominations:

Denomination	Weight
1. *As*	12.58–17.75 g
2. *Semis*	5.78– 8.25 g
3. *Quadrans*	3.05– 3.95 g
4. *Half Quadrans*	1.39– 1.95 g

Table 3. Mintings by Antipas

It is not so easy to be conclusive about the denominations of Philip owing to the poor quality of specimens available for study.[35] However,

careful analysis reveals a clear pattern. In six mintings through 29 C.E,
Philip issued coins in two denominations: the *As* and the *Semis*. The evi-
dence from the first two issues (1 C.E and 8 C.E)[36] is clearest because
Philip issued two different coin types in each year, as demonstrated by the
Maltiel-Gerstenfeld Catalog and the Meshorer Catalog:

Year	Denomination	Obverse	Reverse	Weight	Diameter
1 BCE	As	Philip	Augustus	9.39 grams	23.4 mm
	Semis	Philip	Temple	3.82 grams	18.0 mm
	As	Augustus Head, *r.*	Temple	9.61 grams	22.0 mm
8 CE	As	Augustus Head, *r.*	Temple	8.90 grams	21.0 mm
	Semis	Augustus Head, *l.*	Temple	5.96 grams	18.0 mm

Table 4. Coins of Philip according to Maltiel-Gerstenfeld Catalog[37]

Year	Denomination	Obverse	Reverse	Weight
	As	Philip	Augustus	7.50 g
1 BCE	*As*	Philip	Augustus	7.12 g
	Semis	Philip	Temple	3.82 g
	As	Augustus Head, *r.*	Temple	9.61 g
	As	Augustus Head, *.r*	Temple	8.93 g
8 CE	*As*	Augustus Head, *r.*	Temple	8.63 g
	Semis	Augustus Head, *l.*	Temple	6.39 g
	Semis	Augustus Head, *l.*	Temple	5.31 g

Table 5. Coins of Philip according to Meshorer Catalog[38]

On the basis of this comparison, we get a picture of the general standard
used by Philip:

Denomination	Weight	Diameter
As	7.12–9.61 g	21–23.4 mm
Semis	3.82–6.50 g	16–18 mm

Table 6. Standards for Philip's Coins

For the years 12, 15, 26, and 29 CE, analysis of denominations is complicated by the fact that only one coin type is used, with the head of the emperor on one side and the temple on the reverse. For the years 26 and 29 CE, however, there is one slight difference in coins: some display a laurel branch to the lower right of Tiberius' image, others omit the branch. In all cases the laurel branch coin weighs less.[39] Note the following comparison of these coins using Meshorer's weights:[40]

With Laurel	26 ce	29 ce
No	7.41 g	6.70 g
No	6.80 g	—
Yes	3.80 g	5.59 g

Table 7. Tiberius Coin of Philip

The only examples cited by Maltiel-Gerstenfeld for these two years do not show a laurel branch and weigh 6.5, 6.85, and 7.71 grams.[41] The two Philip coins found at Bethsaida are important to note here. Although both are effaced, I observed slight traces of the laurel branch on the coin dated 29 CE. It weighs 4.67 grams and has a diameter of 17.5 to 18 mm. The other coin, too badly damaged to note either date or laurel branch, weighs 3.9 grams and has a diameter of 17.5 to 19 mm.[42]

On the basis of this evidence one can conclude that the laurel branch designates the *Semis,* and the coins without the branch are in the *As* denomination. When we place them alongside the earlier coins, we begin to get a better picture of the range of weights in these denominations.

Denomination	1 CE–8 CE	26 CE–29 CE
As	7.12–9.61 g	6.50–7.71 g
Semis	3.82–6.50 g	3.80–5.59 g

Table 8. Weight Ranges of Four Mintings by Philip

It would appear as though Philip slightly lowered the standard of weights between these two periods.

The years 12 CE and 15 CE pose more of a problem because none of the examples includes the laurel branch or any other markings that distinguish between denominations. One might conclude that Philip issued only one denomination during these years, but different denominations of the same coin type might have been distinguished only by size (as was the case with the coins of Antipas).[43] The following charts attempt to analyze the data presented by Meshorer and Maltiel-Gerstenfeld:

By Meshorer[44]		Suggested Denomination based on Wgt	By Maltiel-Gerstenfeld[45]	
12 ce	15 CE		12 CE	15 CE
—	—	*As*	—	8.12 g
—	—	*As*	6.42 g	—
—	6.30 g	*As*	—	—
6.15 g	6.15 g	*As*	—	—
—	6.12 g	*As*	—	—
—	6.05 g	*As*	—	—
—	—	*Semis*	—	5.48 g
5.37 g	—	*Semis*	—	—
—	4.29 g	*Semis*	—	—
—	—	*Semis*	—	4.19 g

Table 9. Analysis of Two Mintings by Philip

There is no doubt that two denominations are also represented here. The large coin, 8.12 grams with a diameter of 22.8 mm, is clearly an *As*.[46] The smaller coins are certainly *Semis*. The only question is where to draw the line. I would suggest that all coins above 6.0 grams fit into the *As* denomination while the *Semis* range from 4 to 6 grams. We can therefore suggest the following distribution:

Denomination	1 CE/8 CE	12 CE / 15 CE	26 CE / 29 CE
As	7.12–9.61 g	6.05–8.12 g	6.50 –7.71 g
Semis	3.82–6.50 g	4.19–5.48 g	3.80–5.59 g

Table 10. Distribution of Six Mintings by Philip

We can conclude that Philip consistently issued two denominations in each of the six years that coins were minted from 1 CE to 29 CE. For each of these years we have examples of both the *As* and the *Semis*.

As we stated at the beginning of this section, Philip changed his minting pattern in 30 CE. In both 30 and 33 CE, he issued two additional denominations, the *Quadrans* and the *Half Quadrans,* while continuing to issue a *Semis*.

Denomination	Obverse	Weight	Diameter
As	?	?	?
Semis	Tiberius	5.16 g	18.5–19.0 mm
Quadrans	Julia	3.50 g	15.0–15.2 mm
Half Quadrans	Philip	1.61 g	11.7 mm

Table 11. Coins of Philip Minted in 30 CE

Denomination	Obverse	Weight	Diameter
As	?	?	?
Semis	Tiberius	7.05 g	19 mm
Quadrans	Julia	2.51 g	13–15 mm
Half Quadrans	Philip	1.75 g	10.5 mm[47]

Table 12. Coins of Philip Minted in 33 CE

The Tiberius coin (*Semis*) is a continuation of the most common coin type with the temple on the reverse. The example from 30 CE weighing 5.16 grams fits the standard for the *Semis*, although the 33 CE coin weighing 7.05 grams reaches the upper limit. Note, however, that both of these coins include the laurel branch, which as we argued above, designated the *Semis* in 26 and 29 CE.

In both 30 and 33 CE, therefore, Philip issued at least three denominations. Only the *As* appears to be missing, which would complete four full denominations—the minting pattern of both Herod and Antipas. Following a suggestion by Maltiel-Gerstenfeld, I would argue that we also have the *As* for 30 CE.

COINS WITH NO DATE

There is a final type of coin by Philip which does not include a date (fig. 6). This coin has the tetrastyle temple on the reverse, but a double image of Augustus and Livia on the front. It is coin type 6 in Meshorer's catalog,[48] and no. 118 in Maltiel-Gerstenfeld's list.[49] According to Maltiel-Gerstenfeld, this coin should be classified as an *As*.[50] The examples he lists weigh from 7 to 8 grams with a diameter ranging from 19 to 24 mm. The two examples cataloged by Meshorer at 5.63 and 5.37 grams may raise questions, but in the text he cites another example weighing 13.71 grams.[51] Unfortunately, Meshorer does not include the diameter measurements, but close examination of plate 7 in Meshorer shows that this was one of the largest coins minted by Philip. Clearly, it should be classified as an *As*. The most logical date for this coin is 30 CE. As we saw above, all six issues of coins from 1 to 29 CE already include both an *As* and a *Semis*, while only in 30 and 33 CE is an *As* missing. One must not exclude the possibility that this coin was issued in a different year from the eight mintings studied. On the basis of the present corpus of coins, that is unlikely; however, the coin must be examined carefully.

Fig. 6. Coin of Philip: Augustus and Livia on obverse, tetrastyle temple on reverse

The inscription ΣΕΒΑΣΤΩΝ rules out an early date since Livia was not adopted into the Julian gens and granted the title of *sebaste* until after Augustus' death in 14 CE.[52] Thus one can discard easily Hendin's date of 5 CE (based on his assumption that the round object in the center of the temple must be the Greek letter theta [Θ]).[53] Meshorer dates this coin to shortly after Augustus' death, partly on the basis of a countermark.[54] Since countermarks were added after the coin was in circulation, this evidence should not override evidence from the original minting. The reverse inscription reads ΕΠΙ ΦΙΛΙΠΠΟΥ ΤΕΤΡΑΡΞΟΥ, which does not occur on any other coins through 15 CE. Rather, ΦΙΛΙΠΠΟΥ ΤΕΤΡΑΡΞΟΥ is the usual inscription. Beginning with coins of 26 CE, however, the longer inscription was used consistently. There is no reason to date this coin earlier than 30 CE.[55] Therefore, the year 30 CE, unlike the previous six years that coins were minted, includes four different denominations:

Denomination	Obverse	Weight	Diameter
As	Augustus/Julia	7.0 g	19.0–24.0 mm
Semis	Tiberius	5.16 g	18.5–19.0 mm
Quadrans	Julia	3.5 g	15–15.2 mm
Half Quadrans	Philip	1.61 g	11.7 mm

Table 13. Coins of Philip Minted in 30 CE

Why then was the date omitted on this particular coin? Not only does it differ from other coins in previous years, but it also differs from the three other coins minted in 30 CE, which did include dates. One must assume that the omission was not accidental. Like most coins of Philip, this coin portrays the Paneas temple on the reverse. Yet instead of including the date between the four columns, the inner columns have been moved adjacent to the outer columns, leaving no space in between for the date. This alteration was deliberate in order to depict a round object in the center of the temple—an object which is not depicted on any of the dated coins. Meshorer's conclusion reflects a general feeling of puzzlement: It is "an enigmatic round shape, which perhaps represents a decoration on the entrance door."[56] Maltiel-Gerstenfeld, however, is more specific in referring to it as a "shield."[57]

One must assume that the object in question was identifiable by the populace in Philip's day and that it was related to a particular event near the time of minting since the image was never repeated on any of the other issues of this coin. With these assumptions, I believe Maltiel-Gerstenfeld is on the right track. One event that is well known from this particular period is the famous "shields episode," when Pilate attempted to set up commemorative shields in Jerusalem. Philo relates these events as follows:

One of his lieutenants was Pilate, who was appointed to govern Judaea. He, not so much to honour Tiberius as to annoy the multitude, dedicated in Herod's palace in the holy city some shields coated with gold. They had no image work traced on them nor anything else forbidden by the law apart from the barest inscrip-

inscription stating two facts, the name of the person who made the dedication and of him in whose honour it was made.[58]

There are two less familiar, yet important, details reported by Philo. First, Philip and the other sons of Herod were instrumental in persuading Pilate to back down:

> But when the multitude understood the matter which had by now become a subject of common talk, having put at their head the king's four sons, who in dignity and good fortune were not inferior to a king, and his other descendants and the persons of authority in their own body, they appealed to Pilate to redress the infringement of their traditions caused by the shields and not to disturb the customs which throughout all the preceding ages had been safeguarded without disturbance by kings and by emperors.[59]

Thus, the story was probably well known among the inhabitants of Philip's region. In light of our previous discussion, it is apparent that there was a rivalry between Philip and Pilate, and that Philip saw his own coins as important propaganda devices. It is also worth noting what happened to those shields taken to Jerusalem. Philo concludes his account by stating that they were returned to Caesarea, where they were hung in the Temple of Augustus:

> For at once without even postponing it to the morrow he [Tiberius] wrote to Pilate with a host of reproaches and rebukes for his audacious violation of precedent and bade him at once take down the shields and have them transferred from the capital to Caesarea on the coast surnamed Augustus after your great-grandfather, to be set up in the temple of Augustus, and so they were.[60]

We should not confuse two distinct temples, but the fact remains that Philip's father, Herod, built two temples in honor of Augustus, both in cities named Caesarea. Would not a symbolic depiction of a shield in a Temple of Augustus on Philip's coin serve to remind people of Pilate's fiasco and Philip's triumph? Since this event probably took place around 29 or 30 CE, there would have been great interest when the coins of Philip were issued in 30 CE.

THE KTISTES COIN

Another coin in the 30 CE series is of special interest. The *Semis*, which depicts the image of Tiberius and the tetrastyle temple, includes a unique inscription. There are basically three types of inscriptions which mention the name of Philip on this common coin type:

ΦΙΛΙΠΠΟΥ ΤΕΤΡΑΡΞΟΥ	Years 1, 8, 12, 15 CE
ΕΠΙ ΦΙΛΙΠΠΟΥ ΤΕΤΡΑΡΞΟΥ	Years 26, 29, 30, 33 CE
ΕΠΙ ΦΙΛΙΠΠΟΥ ΤΕΤΡΑΡΞΟΥ ΚΤΙΣ	Years 30 CE

This last inscription is of special interest since the additional ΚΤΙΣ is an abbreviation for κτίστης, or "founder." This coin calls attention to the role of Philip as the founder of cities. In fact, this is the very word used by Josephus in his description of the founding of Caesarea and Julias: "Philip founded [κτίηει] the city Caesarea at the sources of the Jordan in Paneas and Julias in lower Gaulantis."[61] In a parallel passage, Josephus gives much more detail:

> Philip for his part made improvements at Paneas, which is situated at the headwaters of the Jordan, and called it Caesarea; he further granted to the village Bethsaida on the Sea of Galilee both by means of a large number of settlers, and through expansion of strength, the rank of a city and named it after Julia, the daughter of Caesar.[62]

While he does not use the term κτίηει in this passage, Josephus refers to the founding process not so much as the creation of new cities but rather as a change in status. This involves "improvements" and "expansion" and the name changes—from Paneas to Caesarea and from Bethsaida to Julias. With regard to Julias he is explicit in referring to a change from the status of village (κώμη) to city (πόλις).

The literature on coins has generally noted the ΚΤΙΣΤΗΣ inscription as a reference to the founding of Caesarea Philippi.[63] This, however, seems to ignore the fact that ΚΤΙΣΤΗΣ occurs only on a single issue of coin in 30 CE.[64] Caesarea was founded in the early years of Philip's rule.[65] Why was ΚΤΙΣΤΗΣ not used on earlier coins? There is no reason to continue interpreting the inscription as a reference to Caesarea.

It is more logical to conclude that the occurrence of ΚΤΙΣΤΗΣ on a single coin refers to the founding of a city in the very year that the coin was issued, 30 CE. This is supported by the presence of the ΚΤΙΣΤΗΣ coin as part of a series of four coins in the only year that Philip issued four denominations. The series not only includes coins with the image of the emperor and Philip himself—something that had been done previously—but also includes two new coin types: one with Julia alone and the other with Julia alongside Augustus. The attention given to Julia in this series is a strong argument in support of the view that this issue of coins was made to commemorate the founding of Bethsaida/Julias. Every indication indicates that the founding of this city was designed as a grand celebration.

My colleagues, Rami Arav and Heinz-Wolfgang Kuhn, have already demonstrated that Josephus was mistaken in connecting the name Bethsaida/Julias with Julia, daughter of Augustus. Since she was banished in 2 BCE, it is quite clear that the city was not named for her, but rather for Livia/Julia, wife of Augustus.[66]

Livia, of course, had been a widely popular figure, who was honored along with her husband, Augustus, in the imperial cult. Upon his death in 14 CE, she was adopted into the Julian clan according to the directive of the will of Augustus. She thus received the title Augusta/Sebaste and the name Julia, which, while guaranteeing succession to her son Tiberius, also raised her to the level of equality with the next emperor.[67] As a close friend of the Herod family it is no accident that her honors extended to their territory. Antipas had already rebuilt the town Betharamatha in Perea and named it Livia, later to be changed to Julia.[68] Salome bequeathed territories on the southern coast to Julia.[69] Even the procurators honored Julia with inscriptions on six different coins minted between the years 15 and 24 CE.[70] It was only fitting for Philip to honor her as well.

The timing of this celebration is significant. One might expect the naming of the town Julias to have occurred in 29 CE, the actual year of Julia/Livia's death. Why did it take place a year later? One must understand that her death was not without controversy. While she personally sought deification as had been the case with Augustus, this was not granted by her son Tiberius.[71] In fact, because he was away from Rome at the time of her death, only a simple funeral was carried out without him. In contrast to Tiberius's command that mourning be forbidden following the death of Augustus (implying subsequent deification),[72] Tiberius ordered that the populace mourn Julia's death—a recognition of her mere humanity.[73] The coin with her name issued by Pilate in 29 CE (see fig. 2, p. 171 above) shows that this mourning was taken seriously throughout the empire. Even the ears of grain are drooping on that coin. Pilate was responding favorably to his political appointment by Tiberius.

The actions of Philip, however, suggest that he did not mourn Livia/Julia as a mere human. Rather, like many others, he favored her deification—a process which would eventually occur during the rule of Claudius in 41 CE.[74] Thus the absence of a Julia coin in 29 CE is not surprising. Philip would not produce a coin which focused on themes of mourning.

At the same time, he could not offend Tiberius by publicly disregarding the period of mourning.

A year later, however, such honors for Livia/Julia could be considered appropriate. The coin of Julia not only honors her following her death, but also emphasizes her divinity with the representation of the hand holding ears of grain—the goddess Abundantia *continuing* to provide blessings. The depiction of her hand is itself rather interesting and may represent a copy of a statue of Livia/Julia, perhaps erected in a prominent location in Bethsaida.[75] Likewise a second coin which juxtaposes Julia and Augustus and the inscription ΣΕΒΑΣΤΩΝ connotes equality in status. This coin is also an important reminder that Philip had initially received his rule not from Tiberius, as was the case with Pilate, but from Augustus, who favored honors for Julia. It is ironic that the ΚΤΙΣΤΗΣ inscription occurs on the coin in that series which displays the image of Tiberius. The ultimate honor bestowed by Philip on Livia/Julia was not the issuing of coins, but rather the founding of a city in her honor.

Grether reports that, in spite of the wishes of Tiberius, among the honors which continued in the years following her death was the public celebration of Livia/Julia's birthday.[76] One would assume that this took place, as during her lifetime, not on the anniversary of her birth, but on September 21, when she was honored together with Augustus.[77] This would also explain the occurrence of the Livia/Augustus coin in 30 CE. Therefore, the most likely time for the founding of Bethsaida/Julia is on September 21, 30 CE. This dating of the refounding of Julias may explain the absence of the name "Julias" in the Gospels. The Gospels record events ending with the crucifixion of Jesus on April 7, 30 CE. If the name Julia had appeared appended to the name Bethsaida in the Gospels, readers would have recognized it as anachronistic. The issue concerning the terminology and the timing of the refounding of the city has additional implications. While Mark correctly refers to Bethsaida as a village at that time, Luke and John use the later designation πόλις.[78]

It was probably no accident then that the Julia coin was reissued in 33 CE, the ninetieth anniversary of Livia's birth and the seventieth anniversary of her marriage to Augustus. It is possible that the undated coin was reissued that year as well, which might explain the variations of sizes for that coin. What is clear is that the final two mintings of coins by Philip gave special attention to Livia/Julia and thus must be related closely to the founding of the city Bethsaida/ Julias.

MINT

Unlike Antipas, Philip did not name his mint on coins. It is generally assumed that Philip minted his coins at Caesarea Philippi.[79] There are several reasons for this assumption:

- There are later references to a mint at Caesarea Philippi.
- The city of Caesarea Philippi was founded at an early date.
- There is no clear evidence for a mint at another location.

I would like to suggest that Philip had two mints. During the first four issues (1 CE to 15 CE) coins were minted at Caesarea Philippi. In 26 CE, however, the mint was moved to Bethsaida. It is necessary to note that the founding of the city in 30 CE does not preclude this. As was often the case, the actual founding of cities took place after years of building and improvements.[80] Thus, the expansion of Bethsaida may have been partially completed years before its official founding. It does appear that Philip showed more favor toward Bethsaida/Julias in his later years and as a result he chose this site for his tomb.[81] To support this theory, I offer several bits of evidence:

- There is greater precision in the minting of coins from 26 CE on.
- There is a shift in inscriptions in 26 CE from ΦΙΛΙΠΠΟΥ ΤΕΤ–ΡΑΡΞΟΥ prior to this date to ΕΠΙ ΦΙΛΙΠΠΟΥ ΤΕΤΡΑΡΞΟΥ following this date.
- The major mintings in the years 30 and 33 CE would make more sense if the minting was done in the city of Julias itself.
- During the years 26, 29, 30, and 33 CE, many coins of Tiberius show what we described earlier as a laurel branch. It does not occur on any of the earlier coins. Is it possible that this represents not a laurel, but a reed, which is used to symbolize a body of water? Antipas, in fact, made use of the reed on his coins which were minted at the lakeside city of Tiberias.[82] The symbol may denote the change of minting site to the seaside city of Bethsaida/Julias.

We must pay close attention to future coin finds in order to see if there are any distribution patterns which may offer further clues concerning the mint. At present, Philip coins have been discovered in excavations at Bethsaida, Gamla, Ginnosar, and Tel Anafa. None has been discovered at Caesarea Philippi, where the mint of Philip was supposedly located. The discovery of Philip coins at Bethsaida enhances our understanding of this ancient city.

CHAPTER NOTES

1. Meshorer 1982, 2:49.
2. Exod. 20:4; Meshorer 1982, 2:42.
3. Josephus, *Ant* 18.55–62, *JW*, 2.167–177. Philo, *Embassy to Gaius*, 38.299–305.
4. Meshorer 1982, 2:40.
5. Josephus, *Ant* 17.188. Josephus refers to a "mixed population of Jews and Syrians" in this region (*JW* 3.58) and he describes how Herod settled both Babylonian Jews (*Ant* 17.2.1-5) and Idumaeans (*Ant* 16.9.2) in this area. See also Meshorer 1982, 2:45.
6. Kindler 1971, 162.
7. Meshorer 1982, 2:45, lists this coin only for the first minting. It is also included for a second minting according to Maltiel-Gerstenfeld 1982, 145.
8. Josephus, *Ant* 15, 363; *JW* 1.404.
9. In the First Temple, the pillars of Jachin and Boaz were decorated with the lily. The brim of the molten sea is compared to a lily (1 Kgs. 7:26); it is suggested that the menorah was adorned with the lily (Exod. 25:33) and this theme is carried over in synagogue depictions. During the Second Temple period, Ptolemy Philadelphus made a gift of a lily-decorated table to the Jerusalem Temple (*Letter of Aristeas*); see Meshorer 1982, 1:29–30.
10. Matt. 17:24-27.
11. Mark 12:13–17.
12. The catalogs give a two-year range for Philip's coins. For the sake of simplicity I list only the earliest year:
    1 CE to 1/2 CE
    8 CE to 8/9 CE
    12 CE to 12/13 CE
    15 CE to 15/16 CE
    26 CE to 26/27 CE
    29 CE to 29/30 CE
    30 CE to 30/31 CE
    33 CE to 33/34 CE
13. Meshorer 1982, 2:48.
14. Maltiel-Gerstenfeld 1982, 89.
15. Judas, the leader of the revolt in Judea, was from Gamla (Josephus, *Ant* 18. 3). He is credited by Josephus with founding the Zealot movement, the "Fourth Philosophy" (*Ant* 18. 1). Note that the large number of Idumaeans in this area would have their sympathies with those under the procurators' rule. See also J. T. Greene's chapter in this volume.
16. The year 15 CE is also significant since Augustus died in 14 CE. New coins of Philip would demonstrate his allegiance to the new Emperor Tiberius.
17. Meshorer 1982, 2:38.
18. Meshorer 1982, 2:180.
19. Meshorer 1982, 2: 38.
20. Luke 23:12.
21. Josephus, *Ant* 18.85–89.
22. The first year is the only exception.
23. Unless specifically noted, reference to Julia in this chapter will always mean Livia, wife of Augustus and mother of Tiberius. Livia received the name Julia upon adoption into the Julian gens after the death of Augustus in 14 CE. See Tacitus, *Annals,* 1.8.14; Dio 56.32.1; 56.46.1; 57.12.2; Suetonius *Augustus,* 101.2. See also Giacosa 1983.
24. Meshorer 1982, 2:180, 283.
25. Ibid., 2:180.

26. Ibid., 1:63, 89.
27. Grether 1946, 226, 232.
28. Ibid., 245.
29. Meshorer 1982, 2:180, 283.
30. Ibid., 1:245–246; Maltiel-Gerstenfeld 1982, 278.
31. Ibid., 2:282.
32. Ibid., 2:37.
33. Ibid., 2:15.
34. Ibid., 2:242. Meshorer uses the terminology "whole, half, quarter, eighth" for these denominations.
35. E.g., coin no. 108 in Maltiel-Gerstenfeld 1982 weighs 3.82 grams and has a diameter of 18 mm. The following coins are listed at 18 mm but are much heavier: no. 112 (5.96 g), no. 113 (6.42 g), no. 117 (6.85-7.71 g). On the other hand, the weight of no. 120 (3.184–3.43 g) is similar to no. 108, but it has a smaller diameter (15.2 mm). Unfortunately, Meshorer does not list the diameters for comparison.
36. The dating of Meshorer 1982 is followed here. Maltiel-Gerstenfeld 1982, 89, argues that Philip first issued coins in 2 BCE. This will not affect our argument.
37. Maltiel–Gerstenfeld 1982, 144–146.
38. Meshorer 1982, 2:244–245.
39. Ibid., 2:45.
40. Ibid., 2:245.
41. Maltiel-Gerstenfeld 1982, 147. Note that he identifies these as *Semis*.
42. Similar to Meshorer 1982, no. 9, 26 CE.
43. Meshorer 1982, 2:242–243.
44. Ibid., 2:244–245.
45. Maltiel–Gerstenfeld 1982: 146–147.
46. Maltiel-Gerstenfeld 1982, 146, no. 114.
47. Meshorer 1982, 2:246; Maltiel-Gerstenfeld 1982, 148–149.
48. Meshorer 1982, 2:245.
49. Maltiel-Gerstenfeld 1982, 148.
50. Ibid., 143, 148.
51. Meshorer 1982, 2: 49.
52. Grether 1946, 233.
53. Hendin 1987, 70. Note that there is no symbol "L" for "Year," nor does the figure look like a theta.
54. Meshorer 1982, 2:48.
55. Maltiel-Gerstenfeld 1982, 143.
56. Meshorer 1982, 2:46.
57. Maltiel-Gerstenfeld 1982, 143.
58. Philo, *Embassy to Gaius*, 38.299.
59. Ibid., 38.300.
60. Ibid., 38.305.
61. Josephus, *JW* 2.168.
62. Josephus, *Ant* 18.28.
63. Meshorer 1982, 2:42; Hill 1965/1914, xcvii; Maltiel-Gerstenfeld 1982, 143.
64. Meshorer 1982, 2:49, suggests that this commemorates the thirtieth anniversary of the founding of Caesarea.
65. Schuerer 1973, 2:170.
66. Kuhn and Arav 1992, 77–106. I am indebted for their suggestion that the ΚΤΙΣΤΗΣ coin points to the founding of Bethsaida. This suggestion was originally made by Professor

Arie Kindler in a lecture given in a congress "On the House of Herod" at the Haifa University on April 9–10, 1986, based on his reading of the numismatic evidence of Philip coins available then. See also Kindler 1989.
67. Grether 1946, 233.
68. Josephus, *JW* 2.168.
69. Ibid., 2.167.
70. Meshorer 1982, 2:173.
71. Dio, 58.2; Suetonius, *Tiberius,* 51; Tacitus, *Annals,* 5.1–2.
72. Dio, 56.41.
73. Ibid., 58.2.
74. Suetonius, *Claudius,* 11; Dio, 60.
75. I am indebted to Dr. Robert Wenning of Münster, Germany, for this suggestion.
76. Grether 1946, 247.
77. Tacitus, *Annals,* 4.37; Dio, 51.20.
78. There are, of course, other solutions to these questions and the dating of the crucifixion is by no means a closed question, but this solution is highly suggestive because of Mark's terminology as well. The use of the terms κωμη and πόλις are not altogether standard in this period.
79. Meshorer 1982, 2:42–43.
80. As with Caesarea Maritima and Tiberias. See Avi-Yonah 1950–1951, 168–169.
81. Josephus, *Ant.,* 18.106–108.
82. Meshorer 1982, 2:36–37.

LITERATURE CITED

Avi-Yonah, M 1950–1951. "The Foundation of Tiberias," *Israel Exploration Journal* 1.

Dio, Chrysostom. [*Works*. English & Greek. 1932.] With an English translation by J. W. Cohoon and H. Lamar Crosby. Loeb Classical Library. London, W. Heinemann

Josephus, Flavius. [*Works*, English & Greek, 1958–]. Loeb Classical Library. 9 vols. Cambridge, Mass.: Harvard University Press; London: W. Heineman, 1958–1965.

Giacosa, Giorgio. 1983, *Women of the Caesars: Their Lives and Portraits on Coins*. Tr. R. Ross Holloway. New York: Arte e Moneta Publishers.

Grether, Gertrude. 1946. "Livia and the Roman Imperial Cult." *AJP* 67: 222–252.

Hendin, David. 1987. *Guide to Biblical Coins*. New York: Amphora Books.

Hill, George Francis. 1914/1965 Catalogue of the Greek Coins of Palestine (Galilee, Samaria, and Judaea). Ed. British Museum. Dept. of Coins and Medals. Bologna: A. Forni (reprint of the 1914 ed.).

Kindler, A. 1971. "A Coin of Herod Philip—the Earliest Portrait of a Herodian Ruler," *Israel Exploration Journal* 21: 162.

_____. 1989. "The Coins of the Tetrarch Philippus and Bethsaida," *Cathedral for the History of Eretz Israel and its Yishuv* (September) no. 53. Jerusalem (Hebrew).

Kuhn, H. W., and R. Arav. 1991. "The Bethsaida Excavations: Historical and Archaeological Approaches." In *The Future of Early Christianity*, ed. Birger A. Pearson. Minneapolis: Fortress Press.

Letter of Aristeas. 1917. Trans. H. St. J. Thackeray. Translations of Early Documents, ser. 2, Hellenistic-Jewish Texts.

Maltiel-Gerstenfeld, Jacob. 1982. *260 Years of Ancient Jewish Coins* (Tel Aviv: Kol Printing Service Ltd.).

Meshorer, Ya'akov. 1982. *Ancient Jewish Coinage*, 2 vols. Vol. 1, *Persian Period through Hasmoneans*, Vol. 2, *Herod the Great through Bar Cochba* (Dix Hills, N.Y.: Amphora Books).

Philo, of Alexandria. [*Works*. English and Greek]. English tr. F. H. Colson and G. H. Whitaker. Loeb Classical Library. Cambridge, Mass.: Harvard University Press; London: Heineman, 1929–1962.

Schuerer, Emil. 1973. *The History of the Jewish People in the Age of Jesus Christ*, vol. 1. Rev. ed. G. Veames and F. Millar. Edinburgh: Clark.

Suetonius. 1939. *Divi Augusti vita*. Macmillan's Classical Series for Schools and Colleges. Ed Michael Adams. London, Macmillan, 1939.

_____. 1979. *Suetonius on the Life of Tiberius*. Latin Texts and Commentaries. New York: Arno Press, 1941; reprinted 1979. Reprint of the ed. of chapters 1-23 edited by M. J. Du Four and originally presented as her thesis, University of Pennsylvania, 1940, and of the 1928 ed. of chapters 24–40 edited by J. R. Rietra and published by H. J. Paris, Amsterdam.

Tacitus, Cornelius. 1989. *Annals*. Book IV. Cambridge Greek and Latin Classics. Ed. R. H. Martin and A. J. Woodman. Cambridge: Cambridge University Press.

ACKNOWLEDGMENT

I am grateful to Dr. Ya'akov Meshorer, the Tamar and Teddy Kollek Chief Curator at The Israel Museum, who provided from his personal files all photos of coins used in this chapter.

Part 2

Literature of Bethsaida

Rami Arav

Bethsaida, Tzer, and the Fortified Cities of Naphtali

T HE BIBLICAL VERSES WHICH DESCRIBE the boundaries and the fortified towns of Naphtali (Josh. 19:32–39) have been the subject of
much research.[1] Particularly controversial is Josh. 19:35, which lists the
fortified cities of the tribe of Naphtali. Through the ages it has received
different translations and interpretations. The literal translation of this
verse is: "The fortified towns of the Tziddim [are] Tzer, and Hamat, Raqat,
and Kinneret." According to my analysis, the verse can be divided into two
sections: (1) an opening phrase of definition, "The fortified towns of the
Tziddim," and (2) a short list of towns that are located around the Sea of
Galilee, "Tzer, and Hamat, Raqat, and Kinneret." This chapter will survey
the prominent views of this phrase and introduce a new theory suggesting
that the phrase deals with fortified towns inhabited by fishermen along
the shores of the Sea of Galilee.

FROM THE MASORETIC TEXT TO THE SEPTUAGINT

It is important to note the Septuagint translation. Two words in this
phrase, *[the] Tziddim* (הצדים) and *Tzer* (צר), appear to have been unfamiliar
to the Septuagint translators and so the phrase was rendered: "And the fortified towns of the Tyrians: Tyre and Omatha, Daketh and Keneret." The
difference between the Septuagint and the Masoretic Text is clear. A mis-
translation, mistransliteration, or misinterpretation has occurred primarily on two levels: an interchange of letters and a misunderstanding of the
Masoretic Text.

The unknown word הצדים was "metamorphosed" by the Septuagint as *Tyrians*, probably because the letter *dalet* (ד) was read as the letter *resh* (ר). This interchange resulted in the reading הצרים, which in Hebrew may indeed mean [*the*] *Tyrians*. The word, צר, contains only a slight change, but it is a significant one. The Masoretic Text reads *Tzer* and not *Tzor* for Tyre. In no other place in the Bible does the reading צֵר (Tzer) stand for צֹר (Tzor).

The Septuagint appears to have ignored the Hebrew definite article ה prefixed to the word: הצדים. Reading the word הצדים (*HaTziddim*, with the definite article) would mean that the word was not understood as a proper name in Hebrew. The definite article here would indicate a noun. Seemingly the Septuagint translators preferred to omit this difficulty.

There seems to be a consistent series of changes by the Septuagint translators in Joshua 19:35, perhaps to facilitate the use of letters, names, or designations that were more familiar to readers than those found in the Masoretic Text. Another interesting interchange appears in the reading of the place name *Raqat*. Here the Septuagint transliterated it (in the version known as B) as דקת, i.e., *Dakkath* rather than the Masoretic Text רקת. This phenomenon is a common mistake of interchanging the Hebrew *dalet* (ד) with *resh* (ר).

Noteworthy is the rendering of the towns of חמת (*Hamat*) and כנרת (*Kinneret*). No change is found here, presumably because these continued to exist in the period of the translators or for various reasons were known to the translators.[2] However, it is remarkable and contrary to what might be expected, since the articulation of the place name *Hamat* is rendered as *Ammath*, and not as *Emmaus* as in the case of Emmaus near Jerusalem.[3] It is interesting that *Kinneret* is not rendered as *Genosareth*, as might be expected.

From the Septuagint to the Vulgate

The Vulgate does not agree with the Septuagint on the interpretation of this verse, and translates it as: "Civitates munitissimae Aseddim Ser et Ammath Recchath Chenereth." הצדים and צר are not identified with the Tyrians and Tyre, but rather with two unknown cities, Aseddim and Ser. The definite article is treated as part of the proper name of the town, perhaps because of the translator's attempt to create a simple list of cities (which may have been unknown in this period), perhaps because of the confusion raised by the Septuagint rendering, or simply because of an insufficient command of the Hebrew language. The Vulgate does not copy the interchanging of *dalet* (ד) and *resh* (ר) of the Septuagint and appears to have been prepared from the Masoretic Text. It should be noted that, similar to the Septuagint, *Hamat* is rendered as *Ammath* and not *Emmaus*. Likewise, *Kinneret* is rendered as *Chenereth*, a good approximation of the Masoretic Text version.

The following table summarizes the three (or four) versions:

Masoretic Text	Septuagint Version A	Septuagint Version B	Vulgate
הצדים	Τυριων	Τυριων	Asseddim
צר	Τύρος	Τύρος	Ser
חמת	Αμαθα	Ωμαθα	Ammath
רקת	Ρεκκαθ	Δακεθ	Recchath
כנרת	Χενερεθ	κενερεθ	Chenereth

From the Masoretic Text to the Septuagint to the Vulgate

A Short Survey of Opinion: Interpretations and Explanations of the City Designations

The Talmud does not agree with the Septuagint or the Vulgate, and it identifies the two locations with places which seem to have been known to the rabbis of this area at a later time. It proposes an interesting equation in its typical condensed style: *Tziddim* = *Kefar Hitayya*, *Tzer* adjoining, *Hamat* is *Hamata*, *Rakkat* is *Tiberias*, *Kinneret* is *Genosar* (*Gennesaret*).[4] Of all these named places, only *Hamat* (*Hamata*) reflects the archaeological record. Rakkat is not the former Tiberias,[5] but rather has been identified with Tel Quneitra, which is 2.4 kilometers north of Tiberias. Genosar/Gennesaret has been identified as slightly south of Tel el-Oreimeh, at the northern end of the Genosar plain.[6]

F. M. Abel, for lack of information on how to date sites, accepts the Talmudic identification and places Tziddim at Hattin el-Qadim near Hittim. He suggests linking Tzer with Jezer (Gen. 46:23), whose name is immediately after Guni in the list of the sons of Naphtali. Guni is identified by him with Umm Junnieh, near the place where the Jordan River emerges from the Sea of Galilee; therefore, Tzer, according to Abel, should be found in this area.[7] A. Saarisalo suggests that Tziddim and Tzer do not represent names of towns at all.[8]

A. Alt hypothesizes that this phrase is a corrupted version of two phrases that appear before verse 35, "to Great Sidon" (v. 28) and "to the fortress of Tyre" (v. 29). He proposes that the original text should have been: "From the fortress of Tyre to Great Sidon."[9] This hypothesis is not tenable for two reasons: (1) The list of towns that follow this phrase are located around the Sea of Galilee and not on the Phoenician coast, and (2) this sort of corruption has no basis in the Biblical period. Y. Aharoni concurs partially with our hypothesis, having proposed that the version of the Septuagint is an attempt to explain the difficulty of the text and does not derive from a different source.[10]

M. Kochavi proposes that the Septuagint version reflects the original text and the "fortified cities" are the fortresses that the Tyrians and Sidonians had built in Galilee.[11] Archaeological excavations have uncovered several Phoenician fortresses in upper and western Galilee such as Har Adir and Har Meron.[12] These fortresses present, according to him, a Phoenician attempt to strengthen their hillside hinterland. This interpretation has some difficulties: (1) Most scholars reject the interpretation of the Septuagint and maintain that the Masoretic Text is the correct version. It has been shown that the Septuagint mistake is in fact a typical interchange of the letters *dalet* (ד) and *resh* (ר), and (2) the towns listed after the opening phrase are located around the Sea of Galilee, far from the Tyrian and Sidonian fortified hinterland.

Suggestion for a New Reading

I wish to propose a new suggestion regarding this designation in Josh. 19.35. The word הצדים may be derived from the Aramaic *the fisherman*. Therefore, verse 35 contains a list of fishing villages equipped with fortifications which were located around the Sea of Galilee. This list was inserted into a larger town list of the tribe of Naphtali.[13] The fishermen town list is arranged in a clockwise direction (see fig. 1). The suggested translation would then be: "and the fortified cities of the fishermen are Tzer (Tzed?), Hamat, Raqat, and Kinneret."

The word הצדים means *fishermen* in several Semitic languages, including Aramaic, Arabic, and Hebrew. A few examples are referred to in the Masoretic Text Hebrew, such as Eccl. 9:12, "like fish caught in an evil net" (net = מצודה; the Hebrew root is צוד); Eccl. 7:26, "the woman, whose heart is a snare [*herem* = drag net] and nets [מצודים]." The Masoretic Text describes this woman's heart by using two fishing implements: *Herem* = drag net (Hab. 1:15-17; Ezek. 32:3) and *metzodim* = "a trap" (Hebrew root:

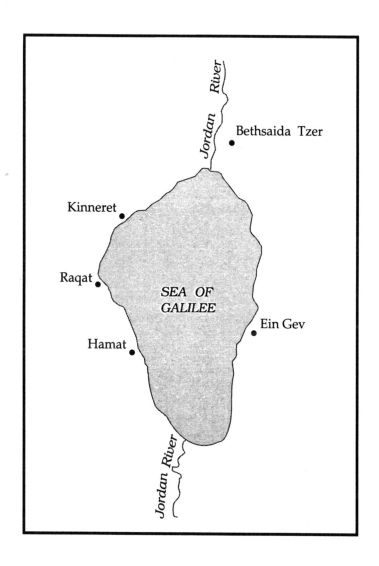

Fig. 1. Map, with fishermen towns (read clockwise)

צוד). Jer. 16:16 refers to fishing and hunting in the same verse: "I shall send for many fishermen, says the Lord, and they will fish for them. After that I shall send for many hunters, and they will hunt for them."

The unidentified town in this list is Tzer. It is suggested here that with the above-mentioned interchange of *resh* and *dalet*, the reading of *Tzer* could have been *Tzed*. It is the suggestion of this author to identify the Iron Age Tzer/Tzed with the town Bethsaida mentioned in Josephus and the New Testament, and to situate it on the ancient northern shores of the Sea of Galilee.[14] Two facts support this suggestion: (1) The toponym Bethsaida in Aramaic means "the house of fishermen," and (2) there are several First Temple period place names to which the word בית (house) was added during the Second Temple period. These are Gilgal (Deut. 11:30; Josh. 4:19, 5:9–10; etc.) and Beth–Gilgal (Neh. 12:29); Succoth (Gen. 33:17; Josh. 13:27; etc.) and Beth Socoth (Hieronymus, *Quaest. in Gen.* 53:8).[15] In this manner Tzer/Tzed was transformed into Bethsaida during the Greco-Roman period.

ARCHAEOLOGICAL FINDS FROM THE IRON AGE AT TELL BETHSAIDA
The position of *Tzer* at the head of the list may indicate the relative importance of the city. The archaeological site of Bethsaida has already proven to be the largest of all Iron Age cities around the Sea of Galilee (80 dunams as compared with 60 dunams of Tel el-Oreimeh and 30 dunams of Ein Gev). Archaeological excavations at Bethsaida reveal that the Iron Age city contained a palace and perhaps a temple, with a piazza extending in between these impressive buildings. The buildings were constructed from massive boulders and were undoubtedly in service to the entire region (fig. 2). Among the finds at Bethsaida is an Aramaic ostrakon bearing the name AQBA (Aqiba).[16] This find is in addition to another Aramaic ostrakon that was found at Ein Gev mentioning the position of cupbearer, LSKYA.[17] It seems plausible that the Aramaic language was spoken in this region already during the seventh century BCE. It is, therefore, no wonder that Josh. 19:35 uses Aramaic terms for positions and places in this area.[18] These finds, in conjunction with the pottery, architecture, and Iron Age fishing gear, suggest that in the Iron Age the ancient city of Tzer/Tzed was already an important site located on the ancient coastline of the Sea of Galilee.

Fig. 2. Stone walls at Bethsaida, built from massive boulders

CHAPTER NOTES

1. See latest views in Frenkel 1992.
2. Hamat was a town to the south of Tiberias. A site has been identified as Hamat and did exist during the Hellenistic-Roman period. Its northern walls were perhaps the southern walls of Tiberias. See Dothan 1985, 10–14, who maintains that the town was founded not earlier than 170 BCE. However, a Ptolemaic coin that was discovered at the site indicates some sort of settlement located there during the 3d century BCE.

     Chinnereth/Kinneret was identified with Tel el-'Oreimeh. Excavations unearthed a small settlement on the top of the mound of el-'Oreimeh, dating from the Hellenistic period. V. Fritz, the excavator of the site, maintains that Gennesaret was founded only during the Roman period and is located 0.5 km south of tel el-'Oreimeh. See: Fritz 1992; Avi-Yonah 1976, 55.
3. See Avi-Yonah 1976, 55.
4. PT Megillah 1.1; 70a.
5. Aharoni 1962, 353.
6. Fritz 1992.
7. Abel 1933–38, 2:457, 460–461.
8. Saarisalo 1927, 128 n.1.
9. Alt, 4:59–81.
10. Ahituv 1971, 6:765.
11. Kochavi 1984, 19–84.
12. Recently another fortress was discovered at Western Galilee, Khurvat Rosh Zait; see Gal 1990, 74–98.
13. See support for this idea: White 1992.
14. On the identification and the excavations of Bethsaida, see: Arav 1988, 187–188; idem 1989, 99–100; idem 1991a, 184–185; idem 1991b, 172–175; idem 1992, 252–254; Arav and Rousseau 1991, 1–4; Kuhn and Arav 1991, 77–107;
15. Avi-Yonah 1984, 167.
16. Arav 1991b, 172–175.
17. Mazar, et al. 1964, 1–49.
18. The people of Geshur who inhabited the eastern shores of the Sea of Galilee were under the influence of the Arameans and presumably used a great deal of their language. See also Mazar 1975, 190–202.

LITERATURE CITED

Abel, F.-M. 1933–38. *Géographie de la Palestine.* Vol. 1, *Géographie physique et historique;* Vol. 2, *Géographie politique. Les villes.* Paris: Librairie Lecoffre.

Aharoni, Y. 1962. *The Land of Israel in Biblical Times: A Historical Geography.* Jerusalem (Hebrew).

Ahituv, S. 1971. *S.v.* Tzer, in *Encyclopedia Biblica.* Jerusalem, 6:765 (Hebrew).

Alt, A. Eine galiläische Ortsliste in Jos. 19. *ZAW* 4:59-81.

Arav, Rami. 1988. 1988, Et-Tell and el-Araj, *Israel Exploration Journal* 38, no. 3, 187-188.

_____. 1989. Et-Tell, 1988, *Israel Exploration Journal* 39, nos. 1-2, 99–100.

_____. 1991a. Bethsaida, *Israel Exploration Journal* 41, nos. 1-3, 184–185.

_____. 1991b. The City of Bethsaida. In *Lake Kinneret.* Ed. Gofen. Tel Aviv.

_____. 1992. Bethsaida, *Israel Exploration Journal* 42, nos. 3-4, 252–254.

_____, and J. J. Rousseau. 1991. Elusive Bethsaida Recovered, *The Fourth R* 4, no. 1 (January), 1-4.

Avi-Yonah, M. 1976. Gazetteer of Roman Palestine, *Qedem* 5.

_____. 1984. *Historical Geography of Palestine.* Jerusalem: Institute of Archaeology, Hebrew University of Jerusalem and CARTA (Hebrew).

Dothan, M. 1985. *Hamath Tiberias.* Jerusalem: Institute of Archaeology, Hebrew University of Jerusalem and CARTA.

Frenkel, R. 1992. *S.v.* Ziddim, in *Anchor Bible Dictionary* (New York: Doubleday).

Fritz, V. 1992. *S.v.* Chinnereth, in *Anchor Bible Dictionary* (New York: Doubleday).

Gal, Z. 1990. *Lower Galilee, Geographical History during the Biblical Period.* Tel Aviv: Hakkibutz Nameunad (Hebrew).

Kochavi, M. 1984. The Period of the Settlement, in *The History of Eretz Israel.* Vol. 2, *Israel and Judah in the Biblical Period.* Ed. I. Ephal. Jerusalem (Hebrew).

Kuhn, H.-W., and R. Arav. 1991. Bethsaida Excavations: Historical and Archaeological Approaches, in *The Future of Early Christianity.* Ed. Pearson. Philadelphia: Fortress Press 77-107.

Mazar, B. 1975. Geshur and Maachah, in *Cities and Districts in Eretz Israel.* Jerusalem: Israel Exploration Society and Bialik Institute.

_____, A. Biran, M. Dothan, I. Dunayevsky. 1964. *Israel Exploration Journal* 14, 1–49.

Saarisalo, A. 1927. *The Boundary between Issachar and Naphtali.* Helsinki.

White, S. Ann. 1992. *S.v.* Rakkat, *Anchor Bible Dictionary* (New York: Doubleday).

John T. Greene

Bethsaida-Julias in Roman and Jewish Military Strategies, 66-73 CE

U PON THE HEIGHTS TO THE WEST OF MODERN TIBERIAS is an impressive set of ruins, the vestiges of a Byzantine monastery. Many tour guides in the region tell visitors that these are the ruins of "Berenice's house." The Berenice referred to was the sister-consort of King Herod Agrippa II. Indeed, for a time their principle residence was at Tiberias, but it did not remain there. And, an old family estate of theirs in Jerusalem, some seventy-five miles to the south-southwest, would also be lost to them. This king, his sister, and many of their supporters—the so-called Herodians—were not only divested of much of their real estate and other possessions; they also lost their lives. Three main groups—the Zealots, the Sicarii, and the Galileans—who saw themselves as Jewish patriots and freedom fighters, with loyalty only to the reign of the God of Israel, would be primarily responsible for the problems that eventually befell the so-called Herodians (employing that term in its broadest sense).

While the Zealots and the Sicarii were known to have been active in the province of Judah, Agrippa's fiercest opposition came from the rebelling Galileans in the northern part of Jewish Palestine. A contingent of disaffected Jews who resided in Herod-ruled Gaulanitis also opposed Agrippa's hegemony.

Located so close to the western border of Gaulanitis that some ancient and modern writers claim it was located in Galilee, the former fishing village, that was upgraded to the *polis*, of Bethsaida–Julias was the locus of hostilities engaged in against their opponents by forces loyal to Agrippa.

203

Bethsaida–Julias was recently rediscovered. On at least one occasion, it was witness to an engagement between the Galilean rebel forces led by Jeremiah (one of Josephus' officers) and the Rome–loyal Herodian forces led by Sylla. Because the battle took place there, Bethsaida–Julias must have played a role in both the rebel Jewish and in the Roman (and Roman–loyal) strategies for control of the Galilee–Golan during the rebellion of 66–73 CE. What follows is an exploration of the role of Bethsaida in light of the available literature, the research in the present anthology, and the current excavations at the site.

THE PROBLEM

The contest for the Galilee–Golan during the first Jewish rebellion against Roman overlordship (which included King Herod Agrippa II and his forces) was an important chapter in both Roman and Jewish military history. Although Jerusalem was the obvious target for crushing such a large-scale rebellion, the initial brunt of the Roman attack southward was experienced by the Jewish defenders in the Galilee and in Gaulanitis. It was there that several large and influential Jewish towns had refused to accept Roman-led overlordship and openly supported general rebellion. Among them were to be counted Tiberias, Taricheae, Gishala, Gamla, and perhaps Bethsaida–Julias. Yet the official documents and the diaries of the major Roman participants have not been available to modern researchers to allow for a reconstruction of events from a purely Roman point of view.[1] In the face of this paucity of official Roman documentation, one Jewish observation has been distilled and presented in several iterations, mirroring several different foci through the copious writings of the Jewish priest-politician - statesman - soldier - historian - author - apologist, Yoseph ben Mattittiyahu, better known as Flavius Josephus. Josephus tells his readers that he was at many of these places (Gamla) as observer and as Jewish commander of the rebellious forces defending the Galilee at Bethsaida. We thus have coverage from two points of view from the same source. The histories and falls(!) of Bethsaida and Gamla were inextricably joined; 67 CE was a fateful year for both. I propose to discuss both cities against the backdrop of the first Jewish Rebellion against Rome.

LITERARY SOURCES AND THEIR TREATMENT

The major literary sources for our discussion consist of the four Gospels and the copious writings by Josephus about the general war for the Galilee. His methods have cast numerous aspersions on the reliability of the contents of his writings, however. This is wolfbane to the historian. It is also a general embarrassment of history writing viewed from a modern critical standpoint. Yet the physical presence of possible ballistas, several arrowheads, and a spearhead as well as numerous ash layers and patches of collapsed and burned mudbrick, smashed pottery, burned detritus in general, scorched loom weights and collapsed walls all attest to a violent end to some parts of the dwelling place that was et-Tell. The dilemma is this: The literary evidence from the Late Hellenistic/Roman era is garbled, inconsistent, contradictory, and from the pen of one recorder of events who cannot be adjudged impartial. The literary sources must be employed gingerly, even those that are being or have been hypothesized. In the end, we must all become students of the ancient dirt and take copious notes during its silent, yet eloquent lectures. Et-Tell's singed strata, not literary records alone, must help tell the military history of a locus which is mentioned in ancient Jewish, Jewish-Christian, and hypothesized Roman documents.[2]

So much has been written by Flavius Josephus and about his accounts of the war for the Galilee/Golan during the first Roman-Jewish War that one is hesitant to tread those literary battlefields once more in search of any *objets de guerre* which may have been left. Having participated in the excavations of Gamla in 1985 and since 1988 at Bethsaida–Julias, I find that the actual battlefields still have a thing or two to yield up to the researcher. I propose to share some of the results of my work at both places as I proceed along lines of inquiry concerning what these two sites have contributed to studies concerning (1) the reliability of the Josephan accounts concerning battles or engagements which occurred there, (2) the Josephan emphasis on who engaged in military engagements at Bethsaida–Julias and Gamla, and (3) whether those engagements described in his accounts really reflect the era in which they are purported and reported to have taken place. These issues are addressed in an intertwined and sustained treatment that includes recent scholarship concerning the problem of identifying the revolting "Galileans." The two sites, some 10.2 kilometers apart, yet able to signal each other by fires, are like *hapax legomena* in a literary piece. That is, since battles occurred at each, one is tempted to deal with each as sui generis. I disagree. Just as Bethsaida–Julias, Chorazin, and Capernaum may be said to form a sort of rebellious triangle with Bethsaida and Capernaum forming opposing positions at its base, so too Gamla, Bethsaida, and Scythopolis (Bethshean) form another uneven but more politically coherent triangle. The geographical gives way, therefore, to the strategic-geometrical. The reasons will become clear presently.

MILITARY SIGNIFICANCE OF THE TELL

Initial probes of et-Tell reveal four main strata of occupation: (1) Early Bronze, (2) Iron, (3) Hellenistic, and (4) Roman periods. Sitting astride the ancient Via Maris proved to be both an ideal and strategic location for those who occupied it.[3]

The results of the Gamla and Bethsaida–Julias excavations to date provide additional data concerning the military significance and contributions of the ancient cities occupying these sites. In addition, they address in an adroit way the three lines of inquiry mentioned above.

BACKGROUND TO THE OUTBREAK OF HOSTILITIES

The latter part of the year 66 CE and much of the following year witnessed much military activity in the Galilee and in Gaulanitis. Therein, several major cities refused to be dominated either by the Roman-controlled army of King Herod Agrippa II, or by more ominous military threats presented by the Roman forces in the nearby Province of Syria. By the year 67 CE, the cities of Gamla and Bethsaida–Julias, having undergone loyalty crises, were once again in the hands of Roman and pro-Roman forces.

Vespasian and his son Titus were not the first Roman commanders to fight against the rebellious Jews of the Galilee–Golan region. Earlier, Gallus, commander of the Twelfth Legion, was sent by Cestius Gallus, governor of the Province of Syria, to subdue this region. Once the Roman-loyal inhabitants of Sepphoris received Vespasian openly, the remaining cities offered no resistance. But some rebel forces assembled on Mount Asamon opposite Sepphoris and did engage Gallus' forces. Josephus writes that more than two thousand rebels were killed in what could be termed the first battle for the Galilee region. Gallus was convinced that this was the only attempt at resistance; he consolidated his forces and retired to Caesarea to join forces with Cestius, who was about to move on Jerusalem. The year was 66 CE.

One significance of Bethsaida must be understood within the framework of the first Jewish rebellion against Rome.[4] The Jewish rebels lost this conflict. With it, Bethsaida was lost also, a loss which became one of the turning points in Jewish history of the first century CE for both pro- and anti-Roman factions.

In this attempt, the first of two noteworthy attempts to throw off the shackles of Roman overlordship, the regions of the Galilee–Golan played an important role. Receiving some of the initial brunt of the Roman military redress, several cities of this region reciprocated military aggressions and were among the first to both challenge and become victimized by Roman military might and ambitions for retention of empire. While many begin their study of this period by questioning whether this conflict could have been avoided, we assume that reasonable people of mutual goodwill can always avoid such conflicts, and begin our study with the view toward what apparently happened, and why.

The major reason for the conflict is as easily recoverable as it is understandable. Jews resented being an occupied people. Whether the occupation was obvious, as in the physical presence of the Roman troops in Judea and Samaria, or less obvious, as in the puppeteering of their client-king, Herod Agrippa II, the desire for freedom was just as great; freedom was not some will-o'-the-wisp idea. For many Jews, freedom was a state of existence in their recent memories. It was, after all, as recent as 58 BCE that the Roman strongman Pompey had annexed the formerly free, but civil-war-torn kingdom of the Jews as a portion of the Roman-controlled Province of Syria. The Israelite/Judaite peoples had memories of many of their previous overlords, including the Canaanites, Ammorites, Arameans, Egyptians, Neo-Assyrians and Babylonians, and the Greco-Hellenists of Egypt and Syria which provided an already embarrassingly long list of previous, major overlords. The brief interlude between 160 and 58 BCE had inculcated in Jews, especially those residing in the then free kingdom, and their now-chafing, once-more-ruled-by-outsider descendants, an appreciation for what it meant to have been (as their collective traditions had taught and maintained) a delivered people. It can be imagined readily, therefore, that each time between 58 BCE and 66 CE that Jews observed the festivals of Pesach or Sukkot, festivals which celebrate freedom from foreign overlordship, they felt an obvious embarrassment, for they celebrated a past period of freedom as a presently dominated people!

Historians tend to agree that it was Florus, the last procurator (*Epitropos*) of Judea, to whom the most immediate series of events which caused the outbreak of hostilities in 66 CE may be traced. To be more accurate, he was merely the last in a series of straws which had already weighed too heavily on the back of contemporaneous Judaism. But while this might have contributed to explaining why Jews were distraught, it does not contribute to a fuller explanation of why Jews rebelled. For that, other stressful issues must be highlighted. Jews in Palestine felt that they could count on Jews elsewhere in the Roman Empire to be just as disaffected as they were. They also felt that Jews in Parthia, Rome's competitor in Asia Minor and the Middle East, would also help further their efforts should they rebel. Moreover, many aristocratic Romans themselves had become disaffected after having been subjected to the shenanigans and peccadilloes of first Gaius Caligula, then later those of the equally mad Nero. Ideally, then, they thought they had powerful potential allies within and without the Roman Empire. There was one final ingredient: past history had shown that civil war within the Syrian Greek ranks had earlier aided Jews in their fight for both religious and political freedom during the days of the Maccabee/Hasmonean revolt. With the Parthian threat from without and the potential aristocratic threat from within, external aggression and civil war, it was thought, could once again serve the cause of Jewish independence, self-rule, and self-respect.

Returning to Florus, but now in a more understandable context, we view the human flame which ignited the explosive situation described above. While Flavius Josephus provides a blow-by-blow explication of Florus' personal ambitions and deportment, several key events need to be listed here. In the year 66 CE, Florus robbed the Jerusalem Temple. This was both a religious and an economic crime.[5] As such, it brought together many disparate Jewish antagonistic groups: the religious, the artisans, the business class, the middle class, and the wealthy (the latter two groups had money in the Temple). When Jews mocked him by taking up a collection of small coins for "poor Florus," he reacted by ordering his troops to attack the crowd; thousands were slaughtered. Several other encounters with this procurator ensued, each time marked by senseless violence and Jew-baiting.

Meanwhile, King Agrippa II, who ruled as puppet-prince in a portion of Palestine, traveled to Jerusalem to speak with Jewish leaders there. Misreading the gravity of the situation, he suggested placating Florus with apologies, rather than sending a deputation to Rome enumerating Florus' wrongs and their grievances. As a result Agrippa lost the support he might have enjoyed from the lower classes, the wealthy middle class, and the revolutionaries. He appeared in their eyes as the protector of a thief from Rome and not of the Jewish people. He and his sister Berenice, who had accompanied him, managed to leave Jerusalem with great difficulty at the threat of their lives. When open hostilities broke out, Agrippa and his military forces fought on the side of the Roman military forces. The so-called peace parties all over the country and the aristocrats continued to support him.

A widening of the circle of protest to include Rome and the Emperor Nero himself may be traced to a decision on the part of disaffected members within the aristocratic, priestly ranks. One Eleazar, a Temple priest–political activist, saw that the offering of daily sacrifice on behalf of the emperor must be ended. Instead of attacking Rome's symbol of rule—Florus—Rome itself and all it stood for, now was the indisputable target of open rebellion. This signaled to Rome, the Herodian Party, and its supporters among the aristocrats of Palestine, a declaration of independence.[6] When the aristocrats contacted Florus and Agrippa II to solicit support for maintenance of what had been the status quo, it signaled the beginning of a civil war, fought initially along class lines. Florus sent troops from Caesarea to join those already at the fortress Antonia in Jerusalem; Agrippa, as would be expected, also sent an expeditionary force. Before long, all but the walled area of the Temple Mount was under Roman-backed control. Eleazar and his rebels held that securely. Elements of the rebels, especially the masses, killed aristocrats, chased others out of their homes by burning them down, burned Agrippa's palace complex, and fought bitterly against their adversaries in the streets of the city. Ultimately, atrocities were committed on both sides. This violence even spread abroad to Palestinian cities such as Caesarea, where non-Jews slaughtered Jews, and to Alexandria, where non-Jewish rioters all but leveled the Jewish quarter of that city. Jews in Damascus were also set upon and slaughtered wholesale.

If the actions of Florus were the last in a long series of usurpations on the part of "official" Roman activity, the defeat of the forces of Cestius Gallus by rebelling Jewish forces was the first serious response in a long series of rebellious actions on their part. Cestius moved on Jerusalem with a sizable army (the Twelfth Legion supported by numerous cohorts) after having moved down the coast of the Mediterranean to Joppa. This occurred during the Jewish celebration of Sukkot; Jewish pilgrims from numerous countries were in attendance, so the city of Jerusalem was packed with a potential army of disaffected rebels or patriots. Although it has been suggested that Cestius was an incompetent commander (or that Florus bribed some of his key generals so that Jerusalem was not taken), leaving Florus with future opportunities to exploit its wealth and its people simultaneously—he failed to capture the city and had to retreat. When he did so so through the valleys northwest of the city, and retreated in the direction of Beth-horon, Lydda, and Antipatris, Jewish guerrillas attacked the exposed flanks of his army and inflicted serious damage to it. Although an impossible task, the army of Cestius was eventually defeated; Jewish rebels had roundly defeated a Roman army!

The written record of Flavius Josephus attests to innumerable revolts against his regional leadership of the Galilee after he had attempted to organize it for defense against inevitable attack by avenging Roman forces. Among his cleverest opponents (within the Jewish defense forces) was John of the northern city of Gishala. John machined several attempts on Josephus' life, and attempted to discredit him in the eyes of those he governed, as well as among his superiors in Jerusalem who had appointed him governor-general of the Galilee–Golan. Josephus mentions several cities around which he built walls of defense (*JW* 2.20.6) and four of them which revolted against his leadership (2.21.7) and of those four, one which revolted twice (2.30.9). In the end, he tells his readers, all four were recovered to his leadership through effective stratagems. Following a terse rehearsal of the major causes of the outbreak of hostilities between Rome and Jerusalem—accomplished in the preceding paragraphs—the preceding puts the reader/hearer in an advantageous position to assess the appearance of events at Gamla (Gamala), and in light of those, the events which unfolded in and near Bethsaida–Julias.

That Bethsaida–Julias is not mentioned as one of the major cities fortified with walls by Josephus in book 2.20.6 of *JW* need not disturb the reader. Excavations since 1987 likewise do not reveal a Hellenistic/Roman walled city. Numerous cities surrounding Bethsaida–Julias were affected, and the city sat astride a busy thoroughfare and witnessed both Roman and Jewish military and commercial traffic going in both directions. While not mentioned in *JW*, Josephus does mention Julias elsewhere. The city (Bethsaida) is mentioned three times in Josephus' autobiographical account, *Life*. In section 71, one reads that Sylla, a commander of Herod Agrippa II's forces, "pitched his camp at five furlongs' (stades') distance (=3,500 feet) from Julias and set a guard upon the roads, both that which led to Cana and that which led to the fortress Gamla (perhaps as a border city). . . ."

Section 72 contains Josephus' reply to Sylla's move: "I sent 2,000 armed men, and a captain whose name was Jeremiah, who raised a bank a furlong (stade = 700 feet) off Julias, near to the river Jordan. . . ." Eventually, a skirmish ensued with Josephus' forces getting the better of those of Sylla. Unfortunately, Josephus was thrown from his horse, sustained a debilitating wrist injury, and was removed from the area of battle to Capernaum to receive medical attention. Upon hearing this news, Sylla's retreating forces rallied and returned to engage. Devising an ambush stratagem, Sylla's forces routed those of Josephus. Although severely trounced, by the look of things, he writes, "Yet did they not go off with the victory at last; for when they heard that some armed men were sailed from Taricheae (whence Josephus had been removed from Capernaum) to Julias, they were afraid and retired." We do not know whether the Jewish rebels' siege against the city was prosecuted further. We also learn that the city could be approached by water![7]

If Jeremiah's bank was thrown up near the Jordan River at Julias, it was located on the western side of the city, probably in what is presently Jordan Park. It should be noted that since Josephus never mentions Julias in the list of cities he fortified in either *Life 37*, *History of the Jewish War* (*JW*)2.20.6, or in *Antiquities of the Jews* (*Ant*) 18, Sylla's bank, erected at Julias on the south side near the roads to Gamla and Cana (i.e., eastward and westward respectively,) was probably chosen as the site at which the "roadblock" was set up because it was under the control of King Herod Agrippa II.

As to the plausibility of the theory that Bethsaida–Julias was under the control of the Herodian family, one should remember that earlier this, too, was the case. It was Herod Philip who upgraded this fishing village and later town to the status of *polis* (*Ant 18*). A coin found in the Hellenistic house of Area B at Bethsaida minted by Philip states that thirty-one years into his reign (= 27 CE) he founded the city. Josephus relates in *Ant* that Philip also had a tomb built, and that he was buried there. Excavations at the site have yet to verify this. Thus, in light of the Josephan record in three separate works, it appears that Bethsaida–Julias, by the outbreak and well into the first full year of open hostilities in 67 CE, remained a pro-Roman—or at least pro-Herodian—city/town.

Further evidence to support the thesis that Bethsaida–Julias was a city controlled by Agrippa II concerns the (siege) bank that Josephus had built on the western side of the city. Banks, as we see throughout Josephus' accounts of the Roman siege procedures, were offensive in design. Josephus' attitude toward the city was aggressive in nature. He tells us in *JW* 2.20.7 that he emulated their style of warfare and organization. Josephus' Julias and Bethsaida are identical cities as evidenced in *Ant* 18. It is stretching the facts to say that the engagement at Julias was a part of the war between Jews and Romans. Rather, one should be more accurate in saying that the engagement was part of the multifaceted Jewish civil war involving pro-Roman forces against anti-Roman forces framed by intra-Galilee–Golan politics.[8]

A similar situation existed with respect to Gamla. We know that prior to its fall to the forces of Vespasian, this citadel city was certainly under Agrippa's control. In *JW* 2.4.2 Josephus writes that the king had laid siege to the city for some seven months in order to retrieve it from rebel control. An account in *Life* 37 describes the rebellion which netted Gamla into anti-Herodian/Roman hands, as well as how Josephus as governor was invited to build a wall around the city and fortify it.

The battle for the Galilee–Golan occurred in two important phases. These phases correspond to (1) Roman redress for the defeat of Cestius Gallus' forces, and (2) redress for the insult to King Agrippa II in both Jerusalem and in several cities under his control. Altogether, Josephus reports that there were at maximum some sixty thousand soldiers fighting under combined Roman command. This included auxiliaries and troops supplied by Caesar-appointed client-kings such as Agrippa II. A brief review of the battle itinerary is in order.

Phase i: Galilee

Before the outbreak of the war for the Galilee, this region had no central government. From about 38 to 4 BCE, Herod the Great ruled as client-king, supported first by Augustus Caesar, then by Tiberius Caesar. After Herod's death, his sons Antipas and Philip ruled over Galilee and Gaulanitis respectively, bearing the title tetrarch. Gaius Caligula deposed Antipas in 38 CE and for a time a procurator provided Roman administration as was the case after Archelaeus was deposed by Tiberius in 6 CE. Herod Agrippa I received the restored kingdom under Claudius, but by 66 CE Florus was procurator in Judea, Herod Agrippa II ruled parts of Galilee and Gaulanitis (and had a family estate in Jerusalem), and the Roman legate in the Province of Syria, Cestius Gallus, exerted influence over much of what is considered northwestern Israel, including the western Upper Galilee. Solomon Zeitlin succinctly summarizes:

> The people of Galilee were divided. One part was under the rule of Agrippa, and the other was under the hegemony of Rome. There was no central government as in Jerusalem. The revolutionaries were strong and there were many who opposed Agrippa and Rome.[9]

In 167 BCE the Galilee was known as "Galilee of the heathens." This is according to 1 Macc. 15 and Isa. 8:23. The reference is to the doubtful ethnic makeup of numerous people who populated both the upper and lower regions of the Galilee (and even parts of Samaria) from the time of the fall of the kingdom of Israel at the hands of the Neo-Assyrians under Sargon II in 722/1 BCE until ca. 167 BCE.

Between 143 and 134 BCE, Simon the Maccabee/Hasmonean fought against the people of the Galilee who were non-Jewish supporters of the Syrian Greeks. Living among them were Jews whose pedigree was unassailable, whom according to 1 Macc. 5:15, Simon "took back with him . . . with their wives and children and everything which was theirs, and brought them into Judea with great rejoicing." This passage suggests that there were people who were Jewish and people who were not, people who were pro-Syrian Greek and people who were pro-Hasmonean. It suggests further that these people would all have been referred to as Galilean, designating a person who lived in the region.

Zeitlin observes, however, that the designation "Galilean" had a different meaning, especially as employed by Flavius Josephus in his *Life*. Zeitlin writes that it "is an appellative name given to the revolutionaries against Rome and the rulers of Judaea who were appointed by Rome."[10] He cites some thirty-four places where he argues that the term "Galilean" designates a distinct group or "philosophy" on a par with the Zealots and the Sicarii.

Zeitlin's work, and the treatment of the first Jewish rebellion by S. G. F. Brandon in *Jesus and the Zealots*[11] supported the above thesis until 1981. In that year Joseph R. Armenti published a brief note which took Zeitlin and others to task.[12] Armenti's work is nothing less than a deconstruction of Zeitlin's work.

To begin, Armenti discovered that Zeitlin omitted some eleven references to "Galilean" in Josephus' *Life*. The omitted occurrences, when read in context, show clearly that "Galilean" refers to a specific people living in a specific geographical locality. Zeitlin's argument was supported by reference to Josephus having written of the inhabitants of the two capital cities located in the Galilee as the Sepphorites (of Seppphoris) and the Tiberians (of Tiberias) instead of as the Galileans. Again, Zeitlin argues, "Galilean" must designate a political/religious "philosophy," and not an inhabitant of a region.

Armenti counters:

> Josephus seems indeed to be conscious of a difference among
> "Tiberians, Sepphorites, and Galileans." Since Tiberias and Sep-
> phoris are in fact themselves in Galilee, why are Galileans men-
> tioned separately? In this context, I would suggest, the term de-
> notes specifically *the inhabitants of the villages* (over two
> thousand, according to Josephus) scattered throughout Galilee.
> Galileans signifies the peasantry, as distinct from the population
> from the major cities.[13]

It is possible to review the evidence of both Zeitlin and Armenti
and attempt rapprochement. A starting point could be Zeitlin's statement:

> . . . we may conclude that the term "Galilean in *Vita* can not have
> a group connotation but *must refer to a group who propagated war
> against Rome as well as against King Agrippa* who ruled a part of Ga-
> lilee in which Tiberias was the capital.[14] [emphasis mine]

Compared with Armenti's:

> . . . why are Galileans mentioned separately . . . the term denotes
> specifically *the inhabitants of the villages* . . . scattered throughout
> Galilee. Galileans signifies the peasantry, as distinct from the pop-
> ulation of major cities.[15]

Both scholars agree that the Galileans were a designated group who
were enemies of both Rome and Agrippa II. That group was the *ame ha-
aretz*, the "people of the land," as opposed to the city-dwellers of the Gali-
lee.The term "Galileans," therefore, indicates and differentiates between
parties which were indeed rural versus urban. Yet all of this must be understood within the restricted space of what was called the Galilee; to the
Romans, the Samaritans, and the Judeans, however, this argued distinction
would have been meaningless anyway.

Modern scholarship shuns the attempt at rapprochement in this
issue; it prefers an either-or resolution. Thus, immediately following Armenti's note in the *Jewish Quarterly Review* is an even briefer note by the
Josephus scholar Louis Feldman of Yeshiva University. In Feldman's two-
and-one-half page support of Armenti's conclusion he begins, "The preceding paper correctly, I believe, concludes that Josephus did not regard
the Galileans as a distinct political party."[16] He then offers eight supplementary comments, which concern:

1. The area of equating "Galilean" with Zealots in particular;
2. The fact that often when Zeitlin speaks of "the Galilean," the Josephan text merely has "Galilean"—individuals from Galilee;
3. A citation from Josephus' *JW* (2.6.2) where Galileans from one town or another joined him, and in *Against Apion* where he commanded those called Galileans;
4. The question of why, if the "Galileans" indeed constituted a separate political group, they weren't mentioned anywhere outside of Galilee; there was much ado in Samaria, Judea, and Transjordan involving anti-Roman and anti-Herod Agrippa II activity as well;
5. The fact that "Galileans" are mentioned nowhere in the designated five in the revolutionary group in *JW* 2.262–274, where one would most certainly expect them to be listed were Zeitlin's thesis to hold;
6. Whether urban/rural tensions in the Galilee were mirrored through the terms "Galilean," to refer to the peasantry, and Tiberians, Sepphorians, and Gabarans, which referred to urban dwellers;
7. That if "Galileans" refers to a particular rebel group, namely the followers of Josephus' arch rival, John of Gishala—a thesis forwarded by Francis Loftus[17]— then any participating Galileans would have been a part of the Zealots, and John himself is never referred to as a Galilean, nor are his followers, although Gishala was located in the Upper Galilee;
8. The fact that there is no historical link between the Hasmoneans and the Zealots, no link between the brigand chief Ezekias and the aristocrats of Galilee, and therefore no link between the Hasmoneans and the Zealots exists. Moreover, Josephus never refers to Ezekias as an aristocrat, and it is his son, Judas (in 4 BCE), not he, who was considered the founder of the Zealot's Fourth Philosophy in *Ant* 18.23.

Thus no rapprochement was sought by Feldman in his eight supporting addenda to Armenti's arguments against the Zeitlin thesis.

The foregoing notwithstanding, Martin Hengel[18] could still write as late as 1989 a treatment of the place of the term "Galilean" under the heading "The Names of the Jewish Freedom Movement." Hengel attempts to connect the term with the followers, immediate and later, of the 4 BCE freedom fighter Judas, called (for some unknown reason) the Galilean. This appellation apparently underlay the concerns which animated Zeitlin as well. Thus, we are confronted by an attempt to unravel what to modern westerners appears to be an odd way of referencing a certain term as it appeared in Josephus' *Life*, allied writing in his copious corpus, and even in the New Testament, which in fact really begins with an attempt to name and to identify Judas' followers and the organization he apparently founded, and whether that term is synonymous with Zealot.

What exacerbates all this is that, as Baigent and Leigh correctly observe,[19] Judas the Galilean was equally known as having been Judas of Gamla(!), and such a flurry of articles and notes could just as well have been produced to argue for a term "Golanite" or "Gaulanite." Further articles and notes could seek to link the inhabitants with Zealots and Sicarii, or even with other militant, anti-Agrippa, and/or anti-Roman "philosophies." One should ask, however, to what end such studies would strive. Judas the Galilean was actually from Gamla! Now we have something to argue. The real issue should be who gave him this sobriquet.

Judas, regardless of where he was born or lived, became known as Judas the Galilean because of what he did *there* under his leadership, and this based on an understandable belief that, as Hengel observes, "a Jew should recognize no other than the Lord God alone."[20] Judas led a successful raid on the Roman-controlled stockpile of arms stored in the pro-Roman, Hellenistic city of Sepphoris in 4 BCE.[21]

Sepphoris, a city near Nazareth, was the scene of the first trial between Josephus, commander of the rebellious forces of the Galilee, and the Roman tribune, Placidus. Placidus' forces routed those of Josephus. These two adversaries matched strategies a second time at the battle for the important city of Jotapata. Josephus' forces forced those of Placidus to withdraw. It would turn out to be a hollow victory for Jewish forces, however, for it hastened Vespasian's arrival into the area and his entry into the battle for Roman control of the Galilee.

When Vespasian, Cestius Gallus' replacement as Rome's enforcer in the Province of Syria, entered Galilee with his legions and auxiliaries from his initial base at Ptolemais (Acco), Josephus was at Garis (a city east of Sepphoris). Josephus fled, however, to the rebelling city of Tiberias, for his army at Garis had already deserted him upon hearing of Vespasian's arrival. Pressing business in Gadara required Vespasian's attention first. Its citizens, rebellious Jews, were slaughtered once the city was taken in retaliation for Cestius' embarrassment at having failed to capture Jerusalem and having been defeated. Rome had struck the first in what was to be a long series of revenge-gaining blows for that defeat.

Josephus then made his headquarters at the central Galilean city of Jotapata, and decided to face Vespasian there. It proved to be one of the most important and longest sieges of a Galilean city during the rebellion.

So important was the battle for Jotapata that Josephus used it to frame other battles and sieges which affected other Galilean cities such as Japha, Tiberias, and Taricheae. A minor revolt at Mount Gerizim by Samaritans is also highlighted as having occurred about the same time.

Initially at Jotapata, Josephus matched military strategies with advanced Roman units commanded by Placidus the tribune and Ebutius the decurion. Vespasian and Titus arrived presently, however, and the fifty-one-day siege began in earnest. For the first five days of the siege the Jewish defenders fought the Romans outside the walls of the city. The results could be said to have been a draw. Thereafter, Vespasian decided to starve them out, but not actively engage them. To counter this, Josephus devised the stratagem of demonstrating that provisions, especially water, were in abundance in the besieged city. When Vespasian, growing ever frustrated that his siege strategy was not working, began to prosecute the attack once more, Jotopata's defenders sallied forth on several occasions against the advancing siegeworks and engines of Vespasian. Fifty-one days after the siege of Jotapata began, the city fell to Vespasian. Three days later, he moved first to his major base at Ptolemais, then on to Joppa in Judea. With this move, and the success of Jotapata behind him, the first phase of the war between the Jews and Romans for the Galilee was brought to an end.

Standing amid the ruins of a large, late Hellenistic/Early Roman era house on the summit of et-Tell which has now been identified as Beth-saida–Julias, it is not obvious to the researcher that military might was directed against this area for a sustained period. What one may not immediately assert either is that the weaponry which has been discovered there came from Roman or Roman-supported Jewish soldiers. In other areas of the tell under investigation, ballistas, a spearhead, and even a small piece of body armor turn up in these Hellenistic/Roman strata, and they, too, beg the same question.

Late Hellenistic/Early Roman era smashed pottery, including black Athenian ware and beautiful examples of Roman fineware, suggest strongly that Bethsaida's history suffered significant damage in this period. Even more telling is the presence of pieces of spouted lamps, some bearing a sun from which rays emanate, in the Early Roman strata of Areas A and B. They are also known as Herodian lamps. Later than this period they do not appear at Bethsaida. Thus, while they provide no military evidence per se, the spouted lamps mark stratigraphically the end of a historical period, a period during which the human habitation of this Hellenized city may have been interrupted.

The absence of whole pieces of pottery as well as the absence of layers of ash and scorched pottery (other than those found in the two kitchens of the large Hellenistic house in Area B where one would expect scorched pieces) and the general lack of large material remains in either Areas A, B, or C, combine to suggest that the inhabitants of Bethsaida had time to pack up their possessions and leave. Recent discoveries in Area C of ballistas and Roman metal arrowheads similar to the ones discovered at Gamla do indicate, however, that some form of attack did take place from the west. Whither the inhabitants of this area went is open to speculation, both wild and reasonable. Let us speculate.

Wild speculation might suggest that part of Bethsaida's erstwhile inhabitants sought refuge at Gamla to the east in this period. It had recently gained the reputation of being an (almost) impregnable walled city.

Reasonable speculation would suggest that by 67 CE Sepphoris, Tiberias, and Taricheae were in Roman hands. Jotapata and Gishala had likewise been divested of any Jewish rebellious forces. The campaign for the Galilee was open. After the fall of Taricheae during a northward push by Vespasian and Titus, the Roman campaign for the Golan commenced. The Rome-loyal, Jewish (Herodian) campaign had already been well underway. At any rate, Capernaum, and then Bethsaida, would have been the next two cities or towns to encounter Roman troops. This brings us, indeed, to an interesting crossroads.

In *Life*, Josephus writes that after his slight injury at the engagement at Julias he was moved to Capernaum for medical treatment. The Capernaumites appear, at least at that time, to have been in league with the rebels, especially with those of Taricheae where Josephus was moved after having received treatment in Capernaum. Were this still the case when later Taricheae fell, the Capernaumites would have received Vespasian's next visit. If this scenario holds, the inhabitants of Bethsaida–Julias, depending on whether they were pro-Roman/Herodians or rebels, would have been forced to make a decision either to fight or to evacuate their town. To the west, Tiberias, Sepphoris, and several other cities were in Roman hands by this time, and they could have moved there. On the other hand, if the loyalties of Julias' inhabitants had shifted to the cause of the rebels, Gamla would have appeared as the best place of refuge against both Herod Agrippa II and Vespasian. Either way, it appears, all eyes (and hopes) were upon the walls of Gamla and its defenders. The several ballistas and the spearhead of Bethsaida are paralleled by those found in excavations some 10.2 kilometers farther up on the Golan Heights plateau at the site of ancient Gamla.

PHASE 2: GAULANITIS

Battles also were fought outside the rebellious Galilee, such as at Joppa, but Vespasian soon set upon a second phase which was designed to restore to King Herod Agrippa II his fractured kingdom. It is during this phase that the battle for Gamla occurred, and that Bethsaida-Julias' significance became most clear.

Upon his return to the region, Vespasian moved from Caesarea Maritima to Caesarea Philippi (Banias) and rested his army for twenty days. When the Herodian cities of Tiberias and Taricheae revolted against their king, Vespasian removed to Scythopolis (Bethshean) to await Titus and his army which had remained at Caesarea Maritima. After the two joined forces, they moved northward to Sennabris, some distance south of Tiberias, but clearly visible from it. Negotiations for the surrender of the city were held and resulted in its being taken without a fight. To facilitate and speed up the Roman entry into and takeover of the city, the south wall was demolished. Jesus the son of Shaphat, who led the revolt, escaped capture and removed to the city of Taricheae to make a stand there. Rebellious forces there readied themselves for a land battle, a siege of the walled city, and a sea (lake) battle as well.[22] Vespasian pursued Jesus and encamped south of the city. Battles were fought in all three forms before that city, too, was taken and its prisoner inhabitants were slaughtered. The Josephan account in *JW* 2.10.9 is graphic and disturbing. Although there is no mention of this, and since Josephus' account shifts to the siege of Gamla in Gaulanitis, it is safe to suggest that Bethsaida-Julias, once also in rebel control while Josephus commanded, was once more taken by Roman forces and their Herodian allies.[23]

THE BATTLE FOR GAMLA

Just as Josephus employs the siege of Jotapata to frame other simultaneous military engagements by Vespasian, Josephus' siege of Gamla frames the engagement at Mount Tabor. Both Placidus, Vespasian's general in charge of the engagement, and the Jewish rebels who had assembled there planned to appear less threatening in order to lure the other into a trap. Their intention was to fall upon the other and effect a great slaughter. Placidus' ruse worked; the fortification was taken, and the rebel leaders fled to Jerusalem. Gamla is referred to as the "Masada of the north."[24] This is a reference to a report in Josephus that when the siege of Gamla was seen as all but an assured success, many inhabitants (ca. 5,000) threw themselves down the northern escarpment of the "camel's hump" to their deaths (*JW* 4.1.10), rather than be taken prisoner. Viewed chronologically, if the account is reliable, Masada should be referred to as the Gamla of the South (!) since Gamla fell in 67 CE and Masada was not taken until 73 CE.[25] In *Life* 37, Josephus states that one Joseph, the son of a female physician, convinced the leading citizens of Gamla to revolt against Agrippa II, providing the reason why: Agrippa's forces had already besieged the city some seven months before Vespasian, and later Titus, arrived with legions and successfully took the city, causing four thousand casualties.

In August 1985, I participated with Michigan State University students in excavations of both the old (eastern) and new (western) cities of Gamla. Project 67, as it was known, employed British volunteers who worked with an Israeli staff under the direction of Mr. Shemarya(hu) Gutman,[26] who himself had earlier excavated at Masada. One approaches the city from the plateau overlooking the impressive "hump" of an invisible "camel." This plateau position provides an excellent view of the entire city as well as much of its surroundings. Vespasian made his headquarters there, opposite the strong wall and tower (which have been partially restored).

Entering the city through the breach caused by Vespasian's forces, one passes an impressive building on one's left, with the tower at some distance to one's right. Once through the breach, and turning to the right—with Josephus' account in hand—one easily follows the events described in his account of the siege of Gamla. Walking toward the summit, one has no difficulty imagining Vespasian's advance, and understands how he could have suddenly found himself surrounded by hostile defenders of the city, and at some distance from his main body of troops within the walls. One is impressed with the steepness of the slope on the southern face of the mountain and how, indeed, the remains now of the houses and buildings could have appeared to one then as "being suspended in air." The narrow streets can still inculcate a sense of claustrophobia and a desire to gasp for breath, imagining that buildings were standing all around. Everywhere, in both segments of the city and its suburbs, destruction debris is to be seen. So complete was the destruction of structures that only portions of three "oil factories" (two in the eastern city [Hellenistic] and one in the western [Roman era] city), the reconstructed tower and wall, and the lower portion of a large, public building are somewhat clearly reflective of their former function.

Although the precise limits or borders of Herod Agrippa's kingdom appeared to have shifted with the development of political events, loyalties, and betrayals, Gamla seems to have marked and been located at the eastern limits of his influence in Gaulanitis. And while Tiberias figures most prominently as his residential city in the Galilee, the party which backed Jesus ben Shaphat must have caused him to reside temporarily in the Roman-controlled Province of Syria as the head of a government in exile. This being the case, Bethsaida, since the cities along the western and northwestern shore of the Sea of Galilee appeared to have been in rebel hands, grew in importance as the westernmost border outpost of what remained of Agrippa's holdings in Gaulanitis! The appearance of Jeremiah on the western side of Bethsaida–Julias, and his throwing up a bank there, suggest that the rebels were entering a new phase of their strategy to reduce the king's holdings now in the Golan. In essence, the siege of Bethsaida–Julias by the forces under Josephus' command had embarked on a Phase II of their own. Josephus/Jeremiah versus Sylla/Agrippa marked the opening of this second phase.

From Iron to Hellenistic: Et-Tell during Iron Age II

While the 1987 probes revealed occupation levels during the Iron Age, it was not until 1989 that excavations in Areas A (south) and B (north) began to penetrate to this level. Each successive year to 1992 revealed an increasingly wide area of occupation. By the end of the 1992 season something fascinating began to emerge.[27]

In Area A during the 1988 season, the mixture of pottery in the eastern section of this area was heavily late Hellenistic and Iron Age. When enough of it was revealed, the emerging floor plan began to show that either the later, Hellenistic Age occupants employed certain portions of the Iron Age structures to build new ones for themselves, or they incorporated existing Iron Age structures and built onto or expanded them, creating new structures.

By the end of the 1989 season in the same area, but not in the western section, the pattern noted above was evident in that a later, circular silo was built onto the lower portion of an Iron Age structure. And in two 5 x 5 meter squares which were opened on the northeastern side of Area A, a beautifully preserved plastered surface leading southward to an east-west oriented wall with an entrance blocked by detritus was discovered. This plastered surface and entranceway led to more fascinating finds.

In Area B during the 1989 season, excavations which had concentrated on a large, late Hellenistic/Roman dwelling were conducted south-central of the southern, east-west running wall of this structure. This was the first penetration to the Iron Age level in this area. Aside from mixed Hellenistic/Iron II pottery, little of interest was found. Directly east of this 5 x 5 meter opening another locus was opened, still on (and approximately one meter above) the Hellenistic level. By the end of the season, however, excavations had penetrated from modern, Syrian (evidenced by numerous discarded, empty food tins, spent and unspent automatic and semiautomatic rifle shells, and mortar shells), to the already revealed Hellenistic dwelling strata.

It was not until the 1990 season that excavation in this locus penetrated to the Iron II structure located immediately below. The square corresponded almost perfectly to the shape of the room where et-Tells' largest (to date) hoard of intact earthen vessels was discovered.

Concerning the Iron Age stratum in both A and B during the 1991 season, the research on Area A was conducted on the northern and northeastern section to articulate more of the paved surface and the wall, to clear the debris from the entryway, and to determine the intent of the structure and surface which had emerged. In B, the area south of the southern wall of the Hellenistic dwelling, and west of the first 5 x 5 meter square which had yielded Iron Age pottery, was investigated. The northern edge of an east-west oriented wall was revealed. Tracing this wall westward, it ran almost parallel to the southern wall of the Hellenistic dwelling. By the end of the season, the Iron Age wall's northwestern corner was revealed, and the wall was shown to have a western, north-south oriented wall abutting it.

Working southward to expose a considerable portion of the north-south, western wall structure, while simultaneously excavating to expose as much as possible of the east-west wall of the same structure, a series of large rooms and even a long corridor were exposed. By the time the third group of excavators joined the project in June 1992, the previous two groups working that season had exposed four rooms and the corridor. The third group was able to expose the northeastern and east central portion of this large structure.

Corresponding season excavations in Area A's northeastern area continued to reveal more of the surface which had extended to the

northern, east-west wall of the Iron Age structure. As the limits of this surface were sought, it was shown to extend far to the north of the structure's
entrance.

A critical study of the floor plans of both areas in light of known
and similar plans elsewhere (e.g., Jerusalem and in southern Turkey)
strongly suggest the presence of a (royal) residence in Area B which is separated from a temple structure (with a formally blocked, northward-ori-
ented entrance) in Area A by a (now revealed cobblestone) plaza.

Other evidence adds to this assessment. Numerous smashed but re-
storable vessels, a series of loom weights, and a considerable broad area of
ash surrounding them in the central and northeasternmost rooms on the
northern side of the Iron Age structure in Area B illustrate that it was destroyed by violence and fire. It is known that this region, known as Geshur, was militarily strong, with independent Arameans dwelling there in
the tenth and ninth centuries, but as early as the fourteenth century BCE.
The Iron II structure exposed thus far in Areas A and B could have been occupied and controlled by one of King David's fathers-in-law, King Talmai,
who was the father of Maachah (David's wife and Absalom's mother). As a
result of revived independence during the United Monarchy, by the time
of the Neo-Assyrian invasion of the smaller states of the eastern Levant,
Geshur's status most certainly changed. Further excavations will help determine whether Geshur, and what was most probably its royal city, were
destroyed during the first Assyrian march southward in 722/1 BCE (Sargon
II), or on the return trip during the invasion of Sennacherib ca. 701 BCE.
Either way, during this portion of the eighth century BCE this area would
have witnessed much warfare, bloodshed, and devastation.

Conclusions

Located on the northern banks of the Sea of Galilee, Bethsaida–Julias was
one of a number of cities which sat on or near the lake and which became
embroiled in the first Jewish rebellion against Roman overlordship. Were
it not for the account in *Life* written by Josephus we would not be aware
that nearby, and possibly involving it, an important military engagement
took place. If the account is reliable, it tells us that the encounter proved
militarily indecisive. This encounter had to have taken place early in the
rebellion; certainly before the battle for Jotapata, for it was there that Josephus was eventually captured.

Rome-controlled interests located in the Galilee and their retention
were the objects of one phase of their military strategy; returning to

Agrippa II's control rebelling cities located in his kingdom was a second phase. That a siege bank was thrown up on the western side of Bethsaida–Julias by Josephus' forces suggests strongly that an attack against it signaled that both rebellious, Jewish combatants and Rome-loyal forces had organized their strategies into two distinctive phases; the rebels' phase 2, as seen by the siege of Bethsaida–Julias, was certainly earlier.

Examination of the Late Hellenistic/Roman strata at Bethsaida reveals nothing that would suggest that the town came to a violent end. Yet the paucity of whole ceramic pieces and the absence of spouted or Herodian lamps in later strata suggest that the site was not reoccupied to any significant degree after about 67 CE. Thus, whether or not the inhabitants temporarily abandoned the city and sought refuge elsewhere in Roman-controlled Galilee or at Gamla on the Golan, life came to an end at Bethsaida. Shortly before, or shortly thereafter, life also came to an end at Gamla.

Chapter Notes

1. Feldman and Hata 1987, 24, write: "Professor Menahem Stern, in his essay on Josephus and the Roman Empire, raises the question of Josephus' reliability in his *Jewish Wars*, and notes that, despite the fact that Josephus does not mention, in his introduction, his use of Vespasian's and Titus' commentaries, he must have used them." They state further that since Josephus was residing in the Flavian palace he had "access to the Roman archives," and that "it would appear likely that he used the notes of their campaigns in Judea." Consult also Charlesworth 1951, Suetonius 1979, Tacitus 1988, Gichon 1986.

2. The Christian documents of the four New Testament Canonical Gospels. Jewish texts include attestations in Josephus' *Ant, Life,* and *JW,* as well as the Talmud Yerushalmi and the Talmud Bavli. The hypothesized Roman documents are referred to in the previous note. To them may be added authentic Roman documents such as Pliny the Elder, *Natural History* 5.15.17 (a first century CE document), and Ptolemy Claudius, *Geographia,* 5.16.4 (a second century [90-168] CE document). General Flavius Silva's field notes and reports to Caesar Vespasian, his relative, must be considered another hypothesized collection from which the epic of Masada was crafted.

3. The region, known as Geshur (i.e., Bridge), was located in and just north of the area referred to as Bashan, and just south of the region called Maacah. It served as the bridge between the eastern Galilee and the western portion of the Golan plateau. While the Bethsaida Excavations Project should supply information concerning the early Bronze Age settlement(s) (the Early Bronze wall is visible at the base of et-Tell) after future excavations, Geshur is mentioned in Deut. 3:14; Josh. 13:13; 2 Sam. 3:3, 13:37, 15:8; 1 Chron. 2:23 (Late Iron Age); and in the fourteenth century BCE corpus known as the Tell-el Amarna Correspondence, as the result of Egyptian imperial expansion, especially after the campaign of Thuthmose III ca. 1468 BCE.

4. Like Gamla, discussed below, Bethsaida–Julias was an important city to be fought for by the forces of Herod Agrippa II as part of his strategy to retain that portion of his kingdom located in Gaulanitis.

5. As to both the religious and economic significance of the Jerusalem Temple, see Hamilton 1964, 365–372.
6. The Herodians, comprising a strong political party during the rebellion, were vestigial of the first supporters of Pompey among the family of Antipater the Idumean, an advisor to John Hyrcanus II. Antipater, father of Herod the Great, was empowered by Pompey. It marked the beginning of the Herodian family's (and their supporters') long influence, which would last until the death of Herod Agrippa II in 93 CE. See Grant 1977, Hoehner 1980, Jones 1938, Perowne 1956, Sandmel 1967, Fritsch 1955, 173ff. Speculations concerning Bethsaida-Julias' location included other potential locations (e.g. a Dutch priest, Adrichomius, in *Theatrum Terrae Sanctae*, included a map on which he placed "Bethsaida" on the western side of the Jordan and "Julias" on the eastern side). Most medieval and pre-modern assessments began from the assumption that the present size and shape of Lake Kinneret was the same in antiquity. Two other contenders, el-Araj and el-Messadiyye, have been dated no earlier than the fourth century CE (by virtue of the systematic finds found at the site), whereas the systematic finds of et-Tell yield some Early Bronze and Iron Age remains, and large amounts from the Hellenistic and Roman era. Of these three prime candidates, only et-Tell is old enough and in the most reasonable location to meet all of the requirements for identification. In addition, a preliminary, geomorphologicial study demonstrates that the northern shore of the lake extended farther northward than the present shore, and that the Jordan itself was considerably wider in the area of et-Tell. See Moshe Inbar and John Shroder's chapter in this volume on the geology and geography of the area.
7. Speculations concerning Bethsaida-Julias' location included other potential locations. Most medieval and premodern assessments began from the assumption that the present size and shape of Lake Kinneret was the same in antiquity. Two other contenders, el-Araj and el-Messadiyye, have been dated no earlier than the fourth century CE (by virtue of the systematic finds found at the site), whereas the systematic finds of et-Tell yield Early Bronze, Iron Age remains, and large amounts of Hellenistic and Roman era remains. Of these three prime candidates, only et-Tell is old enough and in the most reasonable location to meet all of the requirements for identification. In addition, a preliminary, geomorphological study demonstrates that the northern shore of the lake extended farther northward than the present shore, and that the Jordan itself was considerably wider in the area of et-Tell. See Moshe Inbar and John Shroder's chapter in this volume on the geology and geography of the area.
8. Even among those of us who have been excavating et-Tell and examining the evidence it has yielded, there is friendly, scholarly disagreement, and lively ongoing debate. Arav and Rousseau 1991 hold: "After the disastrous and bloody conquest of Galilee by the armies of Vespasian in 66 CE, only three cities remained unconquered: The Fortress of Gamla ..., Seleucia ... , and Bethsaida." If read out of context—both of the text and of the Roman military strategy for the Galilee–Golan regions—one assumes this city was, like Seleucia and Gamla, in open revolt. This does not seem to have been the case at all. A different case will be argued below.
9. Zeitlin 1974, 201.
10. Ibid., 195.
11. Brandon 1967.
12. Armenti 1981, 45–49.
13. Ibid., 49.
14. Zeitlin 1974, 195.
15. Armenti 1981, 49.
16. Feldman 1981, 50–52.

17. Loftus 1975, 182–183; Loftus 1977–1978, 78–98.
18. Hengel 1989.
19. Baigent and Leigh 1991, 205, 206, 207, 212.
20. Hengel 1989, 57.
21. Some sixty-two years later, the Sepphorites still maintained a fidelity to Roman overlord-ship, for they welcomed, and did not oppose militarily, Gallus' army.
22. Concerning this sea battle at Taricheae-Magdala consult Wachsmann 1988, Adan-Baye-witz 1988, Carmi 1988.
23. Hengel 1989.
24. Gutman 1981. See also Bagh 1958, Dauphin 1982, 129–142; Dauphin and Schonfield 1979–1981, 189–206; Hüttenmeister and Reeg 1977; Levine 1981, Ma'Oz 1987a-c; Urman 1975 and 1985.
25. Cf. Lindner 1992; Cohen 1982; Weiss–Rosmarin 1967, 2–8, 3–32; Weiss-Rosmarin 1969; Feldman 1976, 71; Ladoucer 1987.
26. Gutman 1981. See also Bagh 1958; Dauphin 1982, 129–142; Dauphin and Schonfield 1979–1981, 189–206; Hüttenmeister and Reeg 197; Levine 1981; Ma'Oz 1987a-c; Urman 1975 and 1985.
27. This will be discussed below and is discussed at great length in Dr. Arav's work.

LITERATURE CITED

Adan-Bayewitz, David. 1988. Dating the Pottery from the Galilee Boat Excavation. *BAR* 14, no. 5: 24

Arav, Rami, and John Rousseau. 1991. Elusive Bethsaida Recovered, in *The Fourth R* 4 (January): 1–4.

Armenti, Joseph R. 1981. On the Use of the Term "Galileans" in the Writings of Josephus Flavius: A Brief Note. *JQR* 72, no. 1, 45–49.

Bagh, A. S. 1958. *La Région de Djolan*. Paris: Université de Damas.

Baigent, Michael, and Richard Leigh. 1991. *The Dead Sea Scrolls Deception*. New York: Summit Books.

Brandon, S. G. F. 1967. *Jesus and the Zealots*. New York: Scribner.

Carmi, Israel. 1988. How Old Is the Galilee Boat? *BAR* 14, no. 5:30.

Charlesworth, M. P. 1951. *Documents Illustrating the Reign of Claudius and Nero*. Cambridge: Cambridge University Press.

Cohen, Shaye J. D. 1892. Masada, Literary Tradition, Archeological Remains, and the Credibility of Josephus. *JJS*. 385-405.

Dauphin, C. M. 1892. Jewish and Christian Communities in the Roman and Byzantine Gaulanitis: A Study of Evidence from Archaeological Surveys. *PEQ* 114: 129-142.

_____, and J. Schonfield. 1892. Settlements of the Roman and Byzantine Period on the Golan Heights: Preliminary Reports on Three Seasons of Survey (1979-1981). *IEJ* 33:189-206.

Feldman, Louis. 1976. Josephus as an Apologist to the Greco-Roman World: His Portrait of Solomon, in *Aspects of Religious Propaganda in Judaism and Early Christianity*. Ed. Elizabeth Schüssler Fiorenza. Notre Dame, Ind.: Notre Dame University Press.

_____. 1981. The Term "Galileans" in Josephus. *JQR* 72, no. 1.

_____, and Gohai Hata, eds. 1987. *Josephus, Judaism and Christianity* (Detroit: Wayne State University Press).

Fritsch, C. T. 1955. Herod the Great and the Qumran Community. *JBL* 74, part 3, p. 173ff.

Gichon M. 1986. Who Were the Enemies of Rome on the Limes Palaestinae. *Studien zu den Militärgrenzen Roms* 3.

Grant, Michael. 1977. *Herod the Great*. New York: American Heritage.

Gutman, Shemarya. 1981. *Gamla: The Excavations of the First Eight Seasons*. Israel: Kibbutz Meuhad Publications.

Hamilton, Neil Q. 1964. Temple Cleansing and Temple Bank. *JBL* 83, part 4.

Hengel, Martin. 1989. *The Zealots: Investigations into the Jewish Freedom Movement in the Period from Herod to 70 A.D.* Edinburgh: T. and T. Clark.

Hoehner, Harold W. 1980. *Herod Antipas*. Grand Rapid: Zondervan.

Hüttenmeister, F., and G. Reeg. 1981. *Die antiken Synagogen in Israel*. Wiesbaden: Reichert.

Jones, Arnold H. 1938. *The Herods of Judea*. London: Oxford University Press.

Josephus, Flavius. 1958–1965. [*Works*, English & Greek, 1958–]. Loeb Classical Library. 9 vols. Cambridge, Mass.: Harvard University Press; London: W. Heineman.

Levine, L. I., ed. 1987. *Ancient Synagogues Revealed*. Jerusalem: Israel Explorations Society.

Ladoucer, David. 1987. "Josephus and Masada." In Feldman and Hata, eds.1987.

Lindner, Helgo. 1992. *Die Geschichtsauffassung des Flavius Josephus im Bellum Judaicum. Gleichzeitig ein Beitrag zur Quellenfrage*. Leiden: Brill.

Loftus, Franci. 1975. A Note on Suntagma Ton Galilaion, B. J., IV. 558. *JQR* 65.

_____. The Anti-Roman Revolt of the Jews and the Galileans. *JQR* 68 (1977-78).

Ma'Oz, Z. 1987a. The Art and Architecture of the Synagogue in the Golan. *Jewish Art in Golan Series: The Reuben and Edith Hecht Museum Catalog* 3: 98–115.

_____. 1987b. Synagogues of the Golan. *Jewish Art in Golan Series: The Reuben and Edith Hecht Museum Catalog* 3: 8-20.

Perowne S. 1956. *The Life and Times of Herod the Great*. London: Hodder and Stoughton.

Sandmel, Samuel. 1967. *Herod: Profile of a Tyrant*. Philadelphia: Lippincott.

Suetonius. 1979. *The Twelve Caesars*. Trans. R. Graves. New York: Harmondsworth.

Tacitus. 1988. *The Histories*. Rev. ed. Trans. K. Wellesley. New York: Harmondsworth.

Urman, D. 1975. *S.v*. Golan. *Encyclopedia of Archaeological Excavation in the Holy Land*, ed. M. Avi-Yonah. Jerusalem: Massada.

_____. The Golan, A Profile of a Region during the Roman and Byzantine Periods. BAR International Series 269. Oxford: BAR.

Wachsmann, Shelly. 1988. The Galilee Boat—2,000-Year-Old Hull Recovered Intact. *BAR 14, no. 5:* 18-33.

Weiss-Rosmarin, Trude. 1967. Masada, Josephus, and Yadin. *JSP.* 32, no. 8: 2-8, 31-32.

_____. 1969. Masada Revisited. *JSP* 34, nos. 3-5: 29-32.

Zeitlin, Solomon. 1974. Who were the Galileans? *JQR* 64, no. 3.

Mark Appold

The Mighty Works of Bethsaida: Witness of the New Testament and Related Traditions

H EIR TO A LONG AND ELUSIVE HISTORY, punctuated by periods of great activity that stretch from early settlements in the Bronze Age through Geshurite ventures of the Iron Age, Bethsaida emerged in the Greco-Roman era as a fishing village, and then as a city of some significance, refounded by Philip Herod the Tetrarch and renamed Bethsaida–Julias[1] sometime between 29 and 31 CE.[2] Located on a twenty-acre plateau overlooking the northern edge of the Sea of Galilee, and described in the first century by Pliny the Elder as "one of four lovely cities on the Sea of Galilee,"[3] Bethsaida would play a major role in the ministry of Jesus and in the emergence of early Christianity. Even after its abandonment following the Jewish Revolt in 66/67 CE, its memory was kept alive as witnessed in the continuing Gospel and apocryphal traditions and in scattered references throughout Mishnaic and Talmudic literature.

In this chapter, I assess the significance of Bethsaida on the basis of the New Testament texts and two related apocryphal traditions. The Biblical references are relatively few, even though Bethsaida ranks sixth in terms of those cities most frequently mentioned.[4] The seven Bethsaida references in Gospel tradition (discounting textual variants) are, nonetheless, provocative and suggest connections and developments that move well beyond the level of mere geographic description. It is possible to group the Bethsaida references into four major clusters of tradition, each with its own distinct character and provenance. They include, first of all, the *Q-Logion* of Jesus in Matt. 11:21–23 and Luke 10:13–15 with its harsh word of judgment pronounced over Bethsaida for its refusal to repent and respond to the mighty works, the "deeds of power" (δυναμεις) demonstrated in that city. A parallel tradition of judgment appears in the apocryphal text of 5 Ezra 1:11.

Second, there is the singular Markan account (8:22–26) of the healing of the blind man and a related tradition in the Gospel of the Nazaraeans 27, again with focus on "the mighty works of Jesus." Third, Bethsaida and the surrounding area are associated, either by implication or by direct statement, with the feeding of the multitudes in Mark 6 and 8, Matthew 14 and 15, Luke 9, John 6, and the related epiphany accounts of Jesus' appearance on the water in Mark 6, Matthew 14, and John 6 narratives in the "powerful works" tradition that connect with the post-Easter witness of the early Christian communities in Galilee. And fourth, there is the Johannine listing of Bethsaida as the home of Philip, Andrew, and Peter. The occurrence in John 1:44 is lodged in an earlier level of tradition, postulated by many to be part of a *Semeia (SQ)* source,[5] a pre-Johannine Jewish Christian collection of the works of Jesus that focuses on his powerful deeds, which are seen as demonstrations of his messianic status. The reference in John 12:21, with its emphasis on "seeing Jesus," builds on this tradition.

It should not be surprising that Josephus, too, in the passage already cited (*Ant* 18.2.1), links the descriptive term δυναμεις with Bethsaida. Admittedly, there are difficulties with the translation of this term, and it is not totally clear what Josephus had in mind when using this point of reference. Some would translate τη αλλη δυναμει as a description of "the further expansion of strength" or of Bethsaida's "other grandeur" as a reference to building projects or material enlargement. And yet there is no good reason why such a phrase could not be an oblique reference to the already existing tradition characterizing Bethsaida as the place of "mighty works." This in no way implies a confessional intent on the part of Josephus. It simply suggests the possible use of an unreflected yet commonly accepted perspective that identified Bethsaida as a place of some renown because of the notable religious traditions generally associated with it.

On the basis of these texts I advance the hypothesis that Bethsaida was a place where Jesus was active in a ministry characterized by compelling and demonstrative actions. Overall, it was a ministry that met with resistance and rejection in the face of "powerful works." Because of its rejection, Bethsaida would stand under the heavy hand of judgment.[6] After the death of Jesus in 30 CE, Bethsaida and its environs would emerge as the place of considerable Jewish–Christian mission activity, the area where there was great interest in collecting the sayings and the works of Jesus. Words of judgment would be remembered as Christian prophets and disciples encountered rejection in their mission activity. And yet their work would continue, particularly since this area was associated with the Easter experiences of early disciples, the place to which Philip, Andrew, and Peter, at least initially and in the disruptive aftermath following the crucifixion, would have returned since Bethsaida was their home. The population there was mixed[7] and the movements were marked by diversity. There would be some people who associated with the newly developing Jesus movement and yet remained firmly within the parameters of a Law-oriented Judaism, while others would be more prophetically and charismatically motivated with experiences marked not just by a focus on the words and teachings of Jesus but by a growing response to his works and above all to the story of his crucifixion and resurrection. There would be great upheaval at the time of the revolt and the destruction of the city, when the communities would scatter and relocate. But Bethsaida would remain in the memory on one level of the tradition as an example of conflict, rejection, and judgment. On other levels of the tradition, Bethsaida would be associated with the diverse beginnings of the Jesus movement, and then in the post Second Temple era it would be remembered with great reverence and emerge on occasion as a site of pilgrimage.

The Bethsaida Texts

A survey of the texts involved reveals that both Matthew and Luke contain the well-known "woe" statements of Jesus:

> Woe[8] to you, Chorazin! Woe to you, Bethsaida! For if the deeds of power done in you had been done in Tyre and Sidon, they would have repented long ago in sackcloth and ashes. But I tell you, on the day of judgment it will be more tolerable for Tyre and Sidon than for you. And you, Capernaum, will you be exalted to heaven? No, you will be brought down to Hades. (Luke 10:13-15)

Matthew has virtually the same reference, but records it differently. The redaction of each evangelist is apparent. Matthew uses a different verb (εγενοντο) as compared to Luke's εγενηθησαν. He adds "I say to you," whereas Luke adds "sitting" to the phrase "in sackcloth and ashes."

The immediate contexts are also different. In Luke the "woes" belong to the mission charge to the seventy. In Matthew they are part of a series of narratives illustrating the authority claimed by Jesus. They follow Jesus' mission instruction to the Twelve. Matthew also adds a verse to the "woes" and constructs a doublet to the sequence in Luke by expanding on the Capernaum statement, "For if the deeds of power done in you had been done in Sodom, it would have remained until this day. But I tell you that on the day of judgment it will be more tolerable for the land of Sodom than for you." This is a variation on similar words found in Matt. 10:15 as part of the mission commission given to the Twelve: "Truly, I tell you, it will be more tolerable for the land of Sodom and Gomorrah on the day of judgment than for that town."

In any case, it is clear that the statements of "woe" as they now appear in both Matthew and Luke derive from an earlier level of tradition which was edited to fit the purpose and scheme of each respective evangelist. The secondary nature of the "woe" statements in their present locations has long been noted. David A. Catchpole sums it up with the following: "There is a discrepancy of audience between the missionaries and the towns; woes are pronounced before the disciples have even been in action; and it was easy for Matthew to move the woes to a different context. Therefore the position of Q 10:13–15 is due to an editor." [9] That raises yet another point. These "woe" statements of Matthew and Luke are generally assigned to the Q document, an early Jewish Christian collection of the sayings of Jesus. Since Matthew's version of the "woe" statement is different from Luke's, the question arises, which one comes from Q? Again, there is general agreement that Matthew's rendition shows the marks of greater redaction. The additional verse in 23b–24 lacks any reference to repentance and it includes the characteristically Matthean phrase "μεχρι της σημερον." Also, Luke otherwise shows no adversity to parallelism; in fact, quite the opposite is the case. So there would be no reason for him to omit the couplet, had it already been there in the tradition. All of which says that the original Q text of the "woes" is most likely given to us in the Lucan form of Luke 10:13–15.

That raises a related question. What was the *Sitz im Leben* for this "woe" statement in the Q document? Q scholars have advanced the case that Q material was preserved by people who believed that the words of Jesus had continuing validity for them. They were Jewish Christians with a fairly conservative attitude toward the Law. Eschatological warning, imminent judgment, and the call to repentance dominate much of their thinking. Such thinking is interlaced with sapiential themes. The motif of Wisdom (*sophia*) that is rejected and the Deuteronomic theme of the violent fate suffered by the prophets coalesce (there is no Passion narrative in Q) so that Wisdom herself becomes the agent who sends out the prophets, all of whom suffer persecution and violence (Luke 11:49–51). Q represents a separate tradition, a community of people characterized by a distinct theology. A much discussed feature of Q arises out of Q's version of Jesus' mission charge. It is in this body of material that the "woe" statements are lodged. There is general scholarly agreement that these "woe" statements are intrusive in the Q sequence, suggesting that there were successive recensions of the Q material and that Q had its own history of tradition.[10] Helmut Koester summarizes by saying "the woe against Chorazin and Bethsaida is evidently an intrusion into an older collection of sayings concerning the mission of the disciples. It is an originally independent saying, and it is difficult to judge at which stage of the development of Q it was interpolated."[11] John Kloppenborg and others suggest that this independent saying was incorporated into a second edition of Q (Q^2) when the original collection was overlaid with material that included pronouncements of judgment.[12] Its incorporation, if this is the case, may well reflect the actual mission experiences of the Q community, which may have included wandering prophets or charismatics who had made a radical break with their own homes and went about preaching the message of the kingdom and calling for repentance.[13]

Bethsaida and Judgment

Jesus' judgment on Bethsaida for failure to repent in the face of mighty works done there would be remembered in the mission to Israel, a mission dedicated to the renewal of Israel. In view of the long tradition in the Hebrew scriptures of prophets inveighing against the evils of Tyre and Sidon (Isa. 23; Ezek. 28:11–12, 22–23; Jer. 47:4; Joel 4:4–8), the comparison of these two cities with Bethsaida can only underscore the severity of the judgment incurred. There is also some irony in the relationship of the name Sidon with "Saidan," as Bethsaida was later known in the Rabbinic literature. But that connection is not at stake here, even though the correlation of judgment, simply in terms of the names themselves, is certainly noteworthy. It must have been particularly galling for the original hearers to have the Jewish towns of Bethsaida, Chorazin, and Capernaum compared with notoriously sinful Gentile cities. But the comparison would illustrate the ongoing conflict in the rejection and acceptance experienced by the people of this early Jesus movement who would continue to find new meaning in the eschatological warnings that consigned Bethsaida to divine judgment.

Bethsaida and judgment—that appears as an indelible theme which surfaces in a variety of layers of tradition. One final late example of the persistence of this theme occurs in the Fifth Book of Ezra, a Christian pseudepigraphic, apocalyptic text which appears as an additional unit of two chapters either at the beginning or at the end of the Latin texts of the Fourth Book of Ezra. Linguistic observations, however, point to a Greek original. Dated around the end of the second century CE, this Christian text may have been based on earlier Jewish apocalyptic material and then reworked to reflect polemic against Jewish rejection. Interesting in the two extant chapters is a long history of salvation review presented as a word of God which came to Ezra, son of Chusis, in the days of Nebuchadnezzar. The text recounts the faithlessness of God's people, who nonetheless were brought out of the land of Egypt with great signs and wonders. Then, immediately on the heels of the statement "Pharaoh and his servants and all his hosts have I thrown violently down"(5 Ezra 1:10), follows the chronologically disconnected question, "Have I not for your sake destroyed the city of Bethsaida and burned with fire two cities in the east, Tyre and Sidon?" Without any further explanation, the account of the Exodus is resumed with the reminder that God brought his people "through the sea and in the pathless desert."[14] The Bethsaida interpolation is anachronistic and appears as a blatant intrusion whose only rationale for inclusion is its clear association with judgment. I cite it here only as another indication of the tenacity of the association, now deeply embedded in the tradition of "Bethsaida and judgment," judgment which is linked to the demonstration of powerful deeds, the mighty works, that fail to stimulate repentance.

MARK AND BETHSAIDA

The linkage in the Bethsaida tradition of "mighty works"—δυναμεις, not *kerygma*—and judgment throws light on the next pericope associated with Bethsaida, the healing of the blind man in Mark 8:22–26. Even apart from this Markan pericope, the connection between Bethsaida and the caring and curing works of Jesus is established in the larger tradition. In Luke's redactional addition (Luke 9:10–11) Jesus "withdrew privately to a city called Bethsaida . . . and healed those who needed to be cured." In the Matthean parallel the wording is entirely different, although the connection is the same. If both Matthew and Luke had known of another form of this account, they would likely have used it to modify Mark, who in the parallel location focuses on teaching instead of healing (Mark 6:34). In Mark, however, the general connection between Bethsaida and healing, established in Matthew and Luke, becomes very specific in his singular account of the healing of the blind man in Mark 8:22–26. This narrative occurs only in Mark and appears as a kind of doublet to the healing of the deaf mute in Mark 7:31–35, which likewise occurs only in Mark.

The healing of the blind man pericope is also introduced with a geographical marker: "They came to Bethsaida." A good share of the interpreters see this as only a Markan construction which brings resolution to the instructions of Jesus two chapters earlier in Mark 6:45, where instructions are given to the disciples, following the feeding of the multitudes, "to go on ahead to the other side, to Bethsaida," while he (Jesus) dismisses the crowd. Mark is conceived here as expressing concern for literary balance. From this standpoint the healing of the blind man at Bethsaida would also serve as a prelude to the trip north to Caesarea Philippi, just as later the healing of the blind Bartimaeus at Jericho (introduced the same way: "they came to Jericho") served as a prelude to his entry into Jerusalem. If that were the case, then the healing episode in Mark 8 would be a detached account, devoid of any connection with time and place, an independent piece of tradition, free floating, which Mark (mistakenly) identifies with Bethsaida. On the other hand, to saddle Mark with that kind of literary finesse and concern, not otherwise apparent, seems to be a tour de force. While Mark's redactional concerns are fairly evident, it could hardly be argued that his real aim is to produce a literary production.[15] Contrary to what Eduard Schweizer,[16] Ernst Lohmeyer,[17] and others would say in suggesting that Bethsaida simply does not fit here, it would appear that the Bethsaida connection with the healing of the blind man was already deeply rooted in the tradition and provided an intrinsic link between the "mighty works" of the *Q-Logion* and the geographical place of Bethsaida.

A closer look at the description of Jesus' encounter with the blind man is necessary. The parallel with Hellenistic healing accounts is often drawn. A typical example may be seen in the story of the temple of Asclepios at Epidaurus where the god runs his fingers over the eyes of the blind Alcetas of Halice and "the first things he saw were the trees in the temple precincts." The assertion can thus be made that Mark's account is novelistically styled and that what really interested the writer was the event's symbolic meaning illustrating the gradual opening of the disciples' eyes to the truth about Jesus. Be all that as it may, there are several lingering facets about this account which should not be overlooked, the most important of which is the gradual recovery of sight and the initially half-failed attempt of Jesus to restore sight.

Considering the primary criteria that scholars use to establish levels of authenticity, one could well employ here the criterion of embarrassment. This criterion addresses the sayings or the actions of Jesus that would have embarrassed or created difficulty for the early Church.[18] Embarrassing material would tend to be softened, suppressed, or eliminated in later stages of the Gospel tradition. Is it not reasonable to assume that such a dynamic would be at work in the transmission of this unique Markan account? Could not a core event be rooted in the telling of this account which is more than literary construction, and could not the retelling of this event reflect its place in a fairly unified tradition that linked Bethsaida with the δυναμεις, the mighty works of Jesus? The remark that Jesus dismissed the man and sent him to his home, saying, "Do not even go into the *village*," should pose no problem, considering the fact that Bethsaida, contrary to earlier opinion based on Josephus, was not elevated from village status to city (*polis*) status until somewhere between 29 and 31 CE.

Another witness that cements the relationship between Bethsaida and the place of "mighty works" occurs in a late fragment from the Gospel of the Nazaraeans. The text is given in Hennecke's collection of New Testament apocryphal writings. The issue of Jewish Christian gospels, already broached in the discussion on the Q recensions and the *Semeia* traditions, is a particularly vexing one. Only small fragments and patristic citations are available for reconstructions that allow postulating three later separate textual traditions—the Gospel of the Nazareans, the Gospel of the Hebrews, and the Gospel of the Ebionites.[19] Regardless of what their inner relationships were, it is clear that these materials shed light on earlier developments in the emergence of the Gospel tradition. Much here depends on interpretation of the Jerome references. Although it is difficult to know how far to trust Jerome when he expresses familiarity with a Gospel which, he says, was used by the Nazaraeans (Syrian Jewish Christians), it is within this complex of traditions that we encounter a late fragment from an Irish "Historical Commentary on Luke" which mentions the "Gospel according to the Hebrews (Nazareans)" and gives the following statement: "In these cities (namely Chorazin and Bethsaida) many wonders have been wrought, as their number the Gospel according to the Hebrews gives 53."[20]

Admittedly, this reference is late and tenuous. Moreover, the number 53 as a numeric indicator for the miracles of Jesus is without precedent in the Biblical witness. On the other hand, the number is reminiscent of the Signs Gospel embedded in the Johannine text where vestiges of a numbering pattern clearly emerge in John 2:11 and 4:54.[21] Even more striking is the fact that this unattached fragment occurs in the literature at all and that, parallel to the *Q-Logia*, Bethsaida is linked with Chorazin as the place of "mighty works," but that Capernaum is absent, ruling out any direct replication of the otherwise standard "evangelical triangle" pattern (Bethsaida, Chorazin, and Capernaum) in the Biblical text. At work here is an independent but related tradition. It is a fragment that derives from a larger pool of Jewish-Christian textual traditions in which, at their earliest levels, the Q collection of Jesus' words and the Signs Gospel of Jesus' works would have had their home. A common theme in this trajectory of texts is the linkage on successive levels between Bethsaida and "the mighty works" of Jesus.

The final two clusters of New Testament texts associated with Bethsaida will be dealt with only in summary form. The first of these involves a group of six pericopes (Mark 6 and 8, Matthew 14 and 15, Luke 9, and John 6), two of which focus on Jesus' feeding a crowd of four thousand people, while four focus on the Feeding of the Five Thousand. Matthew, Mark, and John also connect the Feeding of the Five Thousand with a related account of Jesus' epiphany on the water. These feeding episodes are the only accounts of works of Jesus which are narrated unanimously in all four Gospels. They clearly are deeply anchored in the Gospel tradition, as the doublets of the Feeding of the Four Thousand, narrated in parallel fashion, amply testify.

Although the exegesis of these texts is fraught with all kinds of knotty problems, not the least of which are the geographical references, one thing is clear. They all in one way or another are related to Bethsaida either as a point of orientation or as the actual location for the event. Admittedly, the references are at times confusing and contradictory. Mark, for example, when cross-referenced with the other Gospels, appears to have Jesus and his disciples leave by boat for Bethsaida, but then still has them placed on the east side of the Sea of Galilee for the feeding event. It is clear that in the tradition geographical locations no longer have the exact sense of so much distance between one locale and another, but rather are simply remembered for the actions and events associated with them. And so it is with Bethsaida and its connection with the encounters with Jesus. The narratives are certainly not verbatims and transcripts, but are reflections considerably removed on the time line from the initial events.

BETHSAIDA AND THE EASTER EXPERIENCE

What, then, is the significance of the Bethsaida references within this kind of a context? Here only two aspects will be addressed. First of all, it is instructive to see the long recognized fact that the accounts of Jesus' feeding the multitudes are all narrated from the standpoint of Easter faith and experience, and in particular, from the standpoint of the meal at the Lord's Table—the Eucharist. Hence, in all six pericopes with all of their differences and variations, the one standard formulaic sequence is repetitiously presented where Jesus takes the loaves, gives thanks or blesses them, breaks them (here John is the only exception in omitting this term), and gives them. The terms—*takes, blesses, breaks,* and *gives*—determine the overall character of these pericopes.

Secondly, consider how the tradition demands that these encounters tie into the variously described epiphany presentations of Jesus on the water—they read like transposed Easter appearances in which the reality of Jesus' presence overwhelms the disciples. These narratives, in other words, are retold from the perspective of the community's Easter faith. Where would these developments have taken place but in the hamlets and peasant villages where Jesus' ministry of free healing, subversive teaching, and meal fellowship created new relationships in the face of oppressive powers.

What does this have to do with Bethsaida? The Easter narratives in Matthew and Mark both include this directive "He is going ahead of you to Galilee; there you will see him." The Fourth Gospel also includes appearance encounters at the Sea of Galilee.[22] When these disciples leave Jerusalem, they return to Galilee and to those familiar places marked by their earlier experiences with Jesus, who never identified with one place but always kept on the move. Wouldn't the disciples, on the other hand, return precisely to those places with which they had attachments and identity? Didn't Paul, after his experience of spiritual upheaval, make it back to Tarsus to sort things out? If Philip, Andrew, and Peter, and perhaps James and John, had their homes in Bethsaida, where else would they go in Galilee but to those places where their formative years had been spent—

their homes? We may conclude that it certainly is not by chance that the later church would connect its beginnings with Bethsaida and the area around it and would tell the story of Jesus from the perspective of the Easter experiences with his continuing presence, however they may have been understood.

JOHN AND BETHSAIDA

Our final point deals with the Johannine references to Bethsaida as the home of Peter and Andrew (John 1:44) and of Philip (John 12:21). Within the Johannine community there seems to have been a special relationship with Bethsaida. It could well be that this has something to do with the yet unresolved problem of the development and transmission of the Johannine texts which some recent scholarship has identified with Jewish Christian communities in Gaulanitis, Batanea, and Trachonitis,[23] areas in the larger or extended vicinity of Bethsaida. Additionally, it needs to be noted that the Fourth Gospel is the preserve of many special geographic traditions which do not occur anywhere else in the Gospel accounts. Some of these traditions are associated with special baptismal movements, others are linked to the mission in Samaria, and some may have been remembered as the locale for early Christian congregations, house churches, or as the pilgrimage sites for different Christian groups that associated significant faith experiences with these places—locales such as Bethany on the other side of the Jordan, Cana of Galilee, Aenon by Salim, Jacob's well by Sychar (Mount Gerizim), Ephraim near the wilderness.[24] And then there is Bethsaida, mentioned twice, once in John 1:44 as the home of Philip, "the city of Peter and Andrew," and again in John 12:21 where again Philip is mentioned: "who was from Bethsaida in Galilee."[25]

What is striking here is the association of disciples of Jesus with particular geographical places. Normally, in the lists of the apostles (John never uses that term for the Twelve) the names commonly given are patronymics—James and John, sons of Zebedee; Bar[-]tholomew; James, son of Alphaeus; and Judas son of James. The one possible exception is Judas Iscariot. But in John at least four of the disciples are distinguished by their hometowns: Nathanael of Cana of Galilee, Peter and Andrew of Bethsaida, and Philip of Bethsaida. What is striking about Philip, Andrew, and Peter is that they are all Greek names. Since they come from Bethsaida, that should not be surprising, since, as has been noted, Philip Herod the Tetrarch had established the village as a *polis*. Some Greek must have been spoken in Bethsaida. It is reasonable to assume that Peter would have been in some sense bilingual[26] since otherwise he could not have so success-fully engaged in missionary work outside Judea from Antioch via Corinth to Rome. It is noteworthy that we are told in John 12:20 that "some Greeks" went up to Jerusalem and spoke to Philip, thereby affirming once again the Greek connection with Philip and, by extension, with Bethsaida.

Why would the tradition be so solid in identifying Philip with Bethsaida? Could it be that one of the early house churches there had been in the home of Philip? Were there still relatives and extended family and friends of Peter and Andrew in Bethsaida? Were there some who re-membered the ministry of Jesus and his mighty works? Were there still contacts with the Zebedee family? Was Bethsaida in the first three or more decades after the crucifixion of Jesus a place of intensive mission activity by early Jewish Christian disciples in a setting that was distinctly Jewish yet strongly shaped by Greek influence? The story of the texts we have considered underscores the probability of a resounding yes.

CHAPTER NOTES

1. Josephus, *Ant* 18.2.1.
2. See Kuhn and Arav 1991, 87–90. In this volume see especially the chapter of Frederick Strickert.
3. Pliny, *Natural History* 5.15.71.
4. Ahead of Bethsaida are Bethlehem (8 times), Bethany (12 times), Nazareth (12 times), Capernaum (16 times), and Jerusalem (65 times).
5. See most notably Fortna 1988. Although the *SQ* hypothesis has still not been universally accepted, its original proposal by Faure 1922, 99–121, and Bultmann 1941 (*Ev. d. Joh.*), and then the further critical development by successive scholars continue to offer the most viable explanations for the background of the Johannine narrative of Jesus' mighty works.
6. The assertion that Jesus would not have condemned the towns that did not accept him (so Funk et al. 1993, 320) is somewhat skewed by the unwarranted assumption that Jesus could not have reflected an apocalyptic view of history.
7. The area was inhabited mainly by Jews; see Safrai and Stern 1974, 1:103. Still it was not without marked Hellenistic influence; ibid., 2:1058. It would not have been possible for Philip to have founded Bethsaida as a Greek polis without the establishment of a Greek school there; Hengel 1991, 55. It is not unreasonable to assume that Greek remained a second language for the people at large.
8. In an effort to capture the color and force of the original term, the Scholars Version of the Jesus Seminar translates οὐαι σοι Βηθσαϊδα "Damn you, Bethsaida!" At the expense of trying to be current, the use of "damn" loses, not the sense of anger, but certainly the sense of the gravity and pain conveyed by the original οὐαι. As O. Betz notes (*Theologische Literaturzeitung* 119 [1994], no. 11, p. 989) such "vulgarizing" destroys the original thrust of Jesus' words.
9. Catchpole 1993, 172.
10. Mack 1993, 36. Here Mack summarizes current proposals in *Q* studies.
11. Koester 1992, 140.
12. Kloppenborg 1987, 195–196.
13. Theissen 1992, 37–59.
14. Hennecke 1965, 2:689–691.
15. Koester 1992, 286, argues that "some of these sources can be recognized with a high degree of certainty, because Mark was more of a collector than an author."
16. Schweizer 1968, 92: "Bethsaida ist eine Stadt (Luke 9:10) was zu v. 23.26 nicht paßt."
17. Lohmeyer, 1963, 158, "Die Erzählung, die Mk allein überliefert, ist ursprünglich ort = und zeitlos."
18. Cf. Meier 1991, 1:168. For more on the healing of the blind man in the context of the healing rituals of the ancient near east and these issues see John J. Rousseau's chapter in this volume.
19. P. Vielhauer (in Hennecke 1965, 1: 118): "The church fathers hand down the title of only one Jewish Christian Gospel, that of the Gospel according to the Hebrews. On the basis of their accounts it is possible to see in this Gospel of the Hebrews either with Jerome the Gospel of the Nazaraeans, or with Epiphanius that of the Ebionites, or with Eusebius an independent entity and so to distinguish it from each of these."
20. Hennecke 1965, 1:151.
21. The numbering references have been one of the most cogent reasons for suspecting an underlying source in John. While it has been suggested that this enumeration may be John's own (Conzelmann and Lindemann 1988, 249), it hardly seems likely that the

evangelist would start enumerating and then abruptly discontinue it. Cf. Appold 1976, 86–102.

22. Crossan 1994, 176ff., understands this cluster of texts as dramatic and symbolic narrative about power and authority in the earliest Christian communities. Recognizing the presence of these social dimensions, however, does not rule out the larger issue of a widespread emergence of individual and communal faith in response to the Risen One.

23. Wengst 1983.

24. Kundsin 1925.

25. The reason why John mentions Bethsaida as a part of Galilee is an interesting question, which will be dealt with more systematically in forthcoming volumes. At the end of the first century Bethsaida could easily have been thought of as part of Galilee when Gaulanitis and other territories to the east were politically connected under Agrippa II.

26. So Hengel 1989, 16.

Literature Cited

Appold, Mark. 1976. *The Oneness Motif in the Fourth Gospel.* Tübingen: J. C. B. Mohr.

Bultmann, Rudolf Karl. 1941. *Das Evangelium des Johannes.* Göttingen: Vandenhoeck und Ruprecht.

Catchpole, David A. 1993. *The Quest for Q.* Edinburgh, T. and T. Clark.

Conzelmann, Hans, and Andreas Lindemann. 1988. *Interpreting the New Testament.* Peabody, Mass.: Henrickson.

Crossan, John Dominic. 1994. *Jesus: A Revolutionary Biography.* San Francisco: Harper.

Josephus, Flavius. [*Works,* English & Greek, 1958–]. Loeb Classical Library. 9 vols. Cambridge, Mass.: Harvard University Press; London: W. Heinemann, 1958–1965.

Faure. A. 1922. "Die alttestamentliche Zitate im vierten Evangelium und die Quellenentsheidungshypothese," *ZNW* 21:99–121.21

Fortna, Robert. 1988. *The Fourth Gospel and Its Predecessor: From Narrative Source to Present Gospel.* Philadelphia: Fortress Press.

Funk, Robert, Roy Hoover, and the Jesus Seminar. 1993. *The Five Gospels.* New York: Macmillan.

Hengel, M. 1989. *The "Hellenization" of Judaea in the First Century after Christ.* Philadelphia: Trinity Press International.

_____. 1991. *The Pre-Christian Paul.* Philadelphia: Trinity Press International.

Hennecke, E. 1965. *New Testament Apocrypha.* London: Lutterworth Press.

Kloppenborg, John. 1987. *The Formation of Q,* vols. 1 and 2. Philadelphia: Fortress Press.

Koester, Helmut. 1992. *Ancient Christian Gospels.* Philadelphia: Trinity Press International.

Kuhn, H.-W., and Rami Arav. 1991. The Bethsaida Excavations: Historical and Archaeological Approaches. In T*he Future of Early Christianity.* Minneapolis: Fortress Press.

Kundsin, Karl. 1925. *Topologische Überlieferungsstoffe im Johannes Evangelium.* Göttingen: Vandenhoeck and Ruprecht.

Lohmeyer, Ernst. 1963. *Das Evangelium des Markus.* Göttingen: Vandenhoeck and Ruprecht.

Mack, Burton. 1993. *The Lost Gospel of Q.* San Francisco: Harper.

Meier, John P. 1991. *A Marginal Jew: Rethinking the Historical Jesus.* New York: Doubleday.

Safrai, S., and M. Stern, eds. 1974. *Compendia Rerum Judaicarum ad Novum Testamentum. The Jewish People in the First Century.* Philadelphia: Fortress.

Schweizer, Eduard. 1968. *Das Neue Testament Deutsch 1.* Göttingen: Vandenhoeck und Ruprecht.

Theissen, G. 1992. *Social Reality and the Early Christians.* Minneapolis: Fortress Press.

Wengst, K. 1983. *Bedrängte Gemeinde und verherrlichter Christus.* Neukirchen–Vluyn: Neukirchener.

Heinz-Wolfgang Kuhn

Bethsaida in the Gospels: The Feeding Story in Luke 9 and the Q Saying in Luke 10

HIS CHAPTER FOCUSES ON THE NEW TESTAMENT PERIOD as it relates
the Bethsaida Excavations Project with the Gospels, especially the
Gospel of Luke. I will first summarize the situation at the excavation site
as it appeared to me at et-Tell, in conversations with Dr. Rami Arav and
other researchers, as well as at the International Conference of the Society
of Biblical Literature in Münster, Germany, all in July 1993. The official excavation drawing made available to me by Dr. Arav in Autumn 1993 has
also been taken into account. The interdisciplinary seminar on Galilee,
Gaulanitis, and the excavations of et-Tell (Bethsaida) which was held
during the Winter term 1992–1993 at the Faculty of Protestant Theology
at the Ludwig Maximilian University, Munich, has proven important for
my evaluation. Also involved in conducting the seminar were Professor
Manfred Görg of the Institute for Biblical Exegesis, who holds the Chair
for Old Testament Theology of the Catholic Theological Faculty; Professor
Barthel Hrouda, who holds the Chair for Near Eastern Archaeology; Dr.
Stephan Kroll, also from the Institute for Near Eastern Archaeology; and
Professor Hatto H. Schmitt, who holds a Chair at the Institute for Ancient
History. Dr. Arav also participated in the last session. A summary of my re-
sults to the present now follows:[1]

1. By reason of Josephus' works, there is no doubt that et-Tell is identical to Julias.
2. Supporting the view that et-Tell and Bethsaida are identical, apart from Josephus, *Ant* 18.2.1§28, is the fact that Philip, son of Herod the Great, was not the first to make a town on the hill out of what seemed to be a place directly on Lake Gennesaret below (el-Araj or el-Mesadiyeh). This hypothesis (Julias as the Acropolis of Bethsaida built by Philip), once widespread, is ruled out by the excavations since et-Tell was a significant locality long before Philip (i.e., from the Early Bronze Age through the Iron Age and the Hellenistic period).
3. A smaller place on today's shore, which also bore the name Bethsaida, would be possible since el-Araj was at least settled during the Byzantine period. El-Araj and el-Mesadiyeh should certainly be investigated more closely. The trial excavation of 1987 provided no evidence, however.
4. It is conceivable that there was a direct water link from et-Tell to the lake through a kind of port at the southwestern spring at the foot of the Tell. We are awaiting the results of the geologists, Dr. John F. Shroder, Jr., of the University of Nebraska at Omaha, and Dr. Moshe Inbar of Haifa University, who began their investigations in 1992, some of which are included in this volume. Insofar as geological investigations do not provide convincing evidence, one could perhaps postulate no longer demonstrable fishermen's huts on the former shore.
5. Only if future excavations directly on the shore or near the lake were to uncover a place from Jesus' time, and if we had to assume that Josephus had erroneously equated Bethsaida with Julias, would we have to postulate a separate Bethsaida on the lake; then the excavation at et-Tell would have nothing to do with Bethsaida. There is, however, absolutely no evidence of this, not least of all because of the spongy soil of the region.
6. The New Testament or other literary sources (apart from Josephus) permit no decision to be made between et-Tell and a place directly on the water farther away.
7. Of the larger remains of buildings from the Hellenistic/Early Roman period in Area A, the oval structure in F-G 51–52, which was perhaps a granary, deserves mention. Clearly identified is the house with courtyard in the northern section of Area B, the so-called fisherman's house. Here and at other places of the excavation fishing utensils have

been found, especially anchor stones, lead weights for nets, and a 15-centimeter-long needle suitable for repairing nets. Moreover, Areas A and B demonstrate that the Iron Age buildings were used or built over during the Hellenistic/Early Roman period. In Area C, so far, architectural remains only from the Hellenistic/Early Roman period can be demonstrated with certainty. (Without doubt, the rectangular room in G–I 30–32 was not a synagogue). Two coins of Philip (4 BCE to 34 CE) from the time of Jesus have been found. Evidence of the Hellenistic/pagan influence on this place, presumably inhabited by Jews (including the disciples Philip, Andrew, and Peter) is given by the oil lamp with two cupids discovered in 1989 in Area A, dating from the last two centuries BCE,[2] and the *strigilis* from the Hellenistic/Early Roman period (with which athletes cleaned their bodies of oil and sand) found in Area C in 1993. That the place was not poor may perhaps be deduced from the two courtyard houses excavated in Areas B and C, both quite generous, along with the gold earring, probably dating from the Hellenistic/Early Roman period, found in Area C in 1993.

Scientific work on the New Testament achieved a breakthrough during the second half of the eighteenth century. Since then, numerous methods have been developed, from literary criticism and form criticism to the synchronic analysis of texts, and to the more recent research on local color and time contexts.[3] With the help of these methods, questions of historicity, dating, and localization of the sayings of Jesus and the narrative material presented in the Gospels often can be encountered with more certainty. These methods are applied in a highly specialized manner and can be understood only with difficulty by lay students of the New Testament. I shall attempt to apply modern critical exegesis to the various references to Bethsaida found in the four canonical Gospels. I concur with almost the entire critical research of the New Testament in the assumption that the Gospel of Mark is the oldest, dated at about 70 CE, and that the two Gospels of Matthew and Luke use the Gospel of Mark and the source Q, a collection of sayings of Jesus.

Let us first glance at the occurrences of Bethsaida in the oldest Christian literature. Apart from the mention of Chorazin and Bethsaida in the so-called Hebrew Gospel or possibly the Gospel of the Nazaraeans from the first half of the second century CE, which is said to have reported that Jesus worked very many miracles at these two places, namely 53,[4] the four canonical Gospels are the only Christian witnesses for Bethsaida up to approximately the middle of the second century CE. I have limited detailed discussion to only two references to Bethsaida which are particularly controversial. The remaining occurrences are discussed briefly at the conclusion.

THE FEEDING OF THE FIVE THOUSAND

I begin with a story found in all four Gospels which readily comes to mind when Bethsaida is mentioned, the Feeding of the Five Thousand in Mark 6 and parallels. In my opinion, there is no original connection between the story and the place-name. Only the Gospel of Luke places the Feeding of the Five Thousand in Bethsaida. It occurs immediately at the beginning of the story in Luke 9:10. This is particularly noticeable because the Gospel of Mark, at least the main source here, is, like Matthew, unaware of any such localization. On the contrary, after the Feeding of the Five Thousand in Mark, Jesus sends his disciples to Bethsaida on the "opposite" shore ("εἰς τὸ πέραν πρὸς Βηθσαϊδάν," Mark 6:45). The Gospel of John, which is independent, or almost independent, of the Synoptic Gospels, does not localize the Feeding of the Five Thousand in Bethsaida either, although Philip, who comes from Bethsaida, according to this Gospel, appears in the Feeding of the Five Thousand as one familiar with the area. Nevertheless this does not, as we shall see, justify the assumption that the Gospel of John is based here on a tradition which once contained the place-name Bethsaida.

Let us first examine in detail the version of John beginning at John 6:1. Insofar as the *Semeia* source, a collection of miracles of Jesus, is accepted, this story belongs to it. With reference to the question of localization in Bethsaida, three observations which could support such a localization must be pursued.

1. We have already mentioned the apparent local knowledge of Philip of Bethsaida. In addition to the Synoptic version, the Gospel of John names the two disciples Philip and Andrew in the Feeding story; both are from Bethsaida according to John 1:44 as well as information from the *Semeia* source.[5] On first reflection, the story could require from Philip local knowledge of his hometown, Bethsaida, when Jesus asks him in John 6:5: "Where are we to buy bread for these [the crowd] to eat?" But this question is more fitting for a remote area as expressly mentioned in the Synoptic Gospels for this Feeding miracle (Mark 6:31, 32, 35; Matt. 14:13, 15; Luke 9:12).

2. Less clear is the statement in John's version that Jesus goes up "the mountain" after his boat lands (v. 3) and that in the evening his disciples "descend," obviously from there to the lake (v. 16).[6] This would in fact describe Bethsaida (et-Tell), situated 25 meters above the surrounding area, since the article refers to a definite mountain, and the mountain in v. 3 belongs to the tradition of this story.[7] This is, however, even less convincing than the implied local knowledge of Philip, because the lakeshore rises to the hill at many places.

3. Finally, a further vague localization of the story in the Gospel of John does not yield greater clarity. In v. 1 Jesus travels by boat to the place of the feeding (neither the point of departure nor the destination is mentioned by name), and in vv. 16–17 the disciples depart from the still unnamed place of the feeding and arrive in Capernaum by boat. In both cases the respective destination is referred to as the opposite shore: "πέραν τῆς θαλάσσης." In v. 1, the story assumes that a large crowd can follow Jesus on foot,[8] so that "beyond the lake" cannot refer to a great distance. Here one could, for example, think of the distance from Capernaum to Bethsaida, but the text says nothing of this.

All three observations—the implied local knowledge of Philip, the nearness of "the" mountain to the lake, and the possibly short distance between Capernaum and the place of the feeding—certainly do not necessitate the interpretation that the story in the Gospel of John originally took place in Bethsaida.

The absence of Bethsaida from John as a place of Jesus' activity is of course noticeable because Philip of Bethsaida (John 1:44; 12:21), after Peter, is mentioned more often than any other disciple (twelve times, including seven times within the *Semeia* source). But obviously about 100 CE the tradition of Jesus' activity in Bethsaida, which was probably destroyed and/or deserted in 67 CE,[9] was available neither to the *Semeia* source nor to the writer of John's Gospel. An investigation of local color in the story in John does not allow the insertion of Bethsaida into this story any more than does the comparison of the two feeding stories in Luke 9 and John 6.

Conversely, in the version of Luke—and this ought to dispense for good with the interpretation that John 6 refers to Bethsaida—it can be shown that the story of Luke, the only version which mentions Bethsaida in connection with the feeding, does not have a tradition behind it. Luke inserted Bethsaida into his version of the feeding afterwards. The reason for this insertion is obvious if one does not overlook the fact that the Gospel of Luke omits a large segment of the Gospel of Mark here (Mark 6:45–8:26). The Gospel of Mark has the place-name Bethsaida at the beginning and end of this segment.[10] So far as I can see, the reason for this mention of Bethsaida in Luke 9:10 is not recognized clearly enough in the literature.[11] This, of course, fully undermines the view that the Gospel of Luke was written in ignorance of this large segment of the Gospel of Mark.[12]

Thus Luke patches the place-name Bethsaida as a kind of replacement into the last story before his omission of the Markan segment with the two stories of Bethsaida at the beginning and the end of the segment. The reference in the Gospel of Mark to Bethsaida as a κώμη in the context of the Healing of the Blind in Mark 8:23 is not a counterargument against the Gospel of Luke, which speaks of a πόλις. Luke inserted the place-name rather clumsily, however. The text calls the place where Jesus and his disciples are the city of Bethsaida; nevertheless the disciples express the thought that they will have to go from the "wilderness" to "villages [!] and farms" to seek food for the crowd (Luke 9:12).[13] This makes sense only in the Gospel of Mark and the parallel versions where the place of the feeding is not in fact Bethsaida, but rather a "wilderness," as expressly mentioned in all Feeding stories of the Synoptic Gospels (Mark 6:31, 32, 35 and parallels; also Mark 8:4, which parallels Matt. 15:33). At any rate, the inclusion of the place-name is to the point in the structure of the Gospel of Luke because it prepares the way for the woes on Bethsaida at the time of the Mission of the Seventy (Luke 10:13).[14] The connection to the verdict on Bethsaida which speaks of Jesus' miracles there is also indicated by the additional remark on Jesus' general healing activities immediately before the feeding (Luke 9:11; Matt. 14:14).

THE Q TRADITION

Although we reach a negative conclusion with respect to a historical localization of the Feeding story in Bethsaida, it may be otherwise with the woes on places in the Galilee and Gaulanitis, which were originally in Q. In their central statements, the versions of the saying in Luke 10:13—15 and Matt. 11:20–24 agree almost completely.[15] The saying has two parts. On the one hand, Chorazin and Bethsaida are addressed; on the other, Capernaum. The first two places are compared to the cities of Tyre and Sidon, while Capernaum, which is strongly emphasized in the saying, is expressly connected with Sodom only in the amended Matthew version.

Possibly the real reason for the allusion to the pair of cities, Tyre and Sidon, which were often mentioned together,[16] was that Bethsaida and the Phoenician Sidon bore similar names and were often confused (צידן and צידון)[17] as evidenced by the Rabbinical literature, so that the saying in question would appear to be a play on words.[18] If this is true, it would at least demonstrate a Semitic background of the saying which is attributed to Jesus. This saying is the only place in the canonical Gospels where the locality Bethsaida is granted a major role in the activities of Jesus. The question whether we can deduce from this a corresponding activity of Jesus for the historical Bethsaida around 30 CE is all the more important.

I now want to examine the exegetical arguments for and against the authenticity of the saying. I start with the arguments against it. The classical rejection of the authenticity can be found in Rudolf Bultmann's *History of the Synoptic Tradition*. Bultmann's formulation in the first German edition (1921) is identical to that of the second revised edition of 1931 (p. 112 in the English translation).[19] In discussing the saying, his three arguments against authenticity are: first, in this saying the community is looking back upon "Jesus' activity as something already completed"; second, "the failure of the Christian preaching in Capernaum" is assumed; finally, "it would have been difficult for Jesus to imagine that Capernaum could be exalted to heaven by his activity."[20] Moreover, Bultmann states in the second edition when discussing another saying on the Queen of the South and the people of Nineveh (Luke 11:31–32, which parallels Matt. 12:41–42) that this saying is so closely related to ours that one can concur with A. Fridrichsen in speaking of a scheme of early Christian polemic.[21] Bultmann's arguments are inconclusive. Let us restrict ourselves for the moment to these comments: of the last argument it can be said that the consciousness of Jesus in evidence here is quite typical of his preaching. The second argument, which assumes the failure of Christian preaching in Capernaum, directly contradicts Bultmann, for according to the Gospel of Mark, it can be assumed that the Christian community there was successful after Easter. The first argument, which states that the text looks back on the completed work of Jesus after his death is also incorrect. The saying would then not have mentioned only his healing in three rather insignificant localities in the Galilee and Gaulanitis, but should also have included his preaching.[22] The further argument used by Bultmann in the second edition, namely the similarity to another saying, fails to recognize the differences between our saying and the one compared to it.[23]

Let us now mention the arguments which support the authenticity of the saying or at least the formulation thereof not long after Jesus' death. I have already named some arguments in the Festschrift for Helmut Koester,[24] and here I wish to formulate them anew and incorporate the most important arguments from Gerd Theissen's book on local color and contemporary history in the Gospels.[25] In the version of Luke, the words of Jesus read:

> Woe to you, Chorazin! Woe to you, Bethsaida! For if the deeds of power done in you had taken place in Tyre and Sidon, they would have repented long ago, sitting in sackcloth and ashes. But for Tyre and Sidon it will be more tolerable at the judgment than for you. And you, Capernaum, will you be exalted to heaven? You will be brought down to Hades.

According to this saying, Chorazin and Bethsaida proved less penitent than the notorious Phoenician cities of Tyre and Sidon. Particularly Isaiah 23 and Ezekiel 26–28 are concerned with testimony against Tyre and Sidon. The saying on Capernaum does not mention any heathen cities expressly but attacks Capernaum with a near-quotation which is directed against the King of Babel in Isa. 14:11–15.[26] For the historical Jesus it must be said that the statement twists the words of the Hebrew Bible in a "provocative" manner,[27] taking a Biblical proclamation of judgment against great enemies of Israel and directing it against three small Jewish localities. This doubtless offensive way of using the Bible can most easily be attributed to Jesus himself.[28] The sentence on Capernaum represents the high point. The question may be left open as to whether Jesus, in alluding to Isa. 14:13–14, has taken up a sort of pride on the part of his followers in his work in this area. In any case the saying reflects a consciousness of his mission typical of Jesus. One must think only of the saying of Jesus about his miracles as proof of the presence of the Kingdom of God (Luke 11:20; which parallels Matt. 12:28). After all, it can be said historically that Capernaum was indeed one of the most important if not the most important place for Jesus' activities in the Galilee and Gaulanitis. When investigating the historical Jesus, various exegetic criteria can be helpful when judging a saying to be presumably authentic. In particular, when we are concerned with Jesus' consciousness of his mission, the criterion of convergence must be discussed; i.e. the question of whether a saying viewed as a word of Jesus in ancient tradition conforms to that which is special in the total character of the teaching and works of Jesus. With the provocative manner of speaking and the self-awareness of Jesus here, this is certainly the case.

The second argument, which certainly supports the authenticity of the saying, or at least places wandering charismatics in close proximity to the activity of Jesus, is that here the text looks back neither on the later community's preaching nor on Jesus' entire works, because the saying speaks "only" of Jesus' "deeds of power" in three small localities.[29] If the criterion of dissimilarity is applied here, the difference between this saying and later Christian preaching is clear. Applying the first argument of convergence, the saying would seem to originate not with wandering charismatics immediately after Easter, but rather only with Jesus himself.

Finally, as a third argument, I would like to mention that not very long after the crucifixion of Jesus in Jerusalem these three small localities in the Galilee and Gaulanitis, which form a geographically meaningful triangle, were no longer representative of the works of Jesus in the consciousness of the Christian communities. Chorazin does not occur at all in the subsequent canonical tradition.[30] Conversely, Capernaum would probably not have been spoken of so negatively, for (if one interprets Mark 1 in terms of redaction criticism, archaeology, and social history) this very place seems to have had a Christian community continuously up until the composition of the Gospel of Mark and presumably beyond this time. The saying certainly does not presuppose Christian communities in Tyre and Sidon, which in any case existed in the fifties at the latest.[31] Here again, therefore, the dissimilarity to the later Christian communities allows us to claim authenticity or at least, with this argument based on the three places named, the extreme temporal proximity to the activities of Jesus.

Conclusions

The saying of the "woes" discussed above, which is most probably authentic and cannot have been formulated long after Jesus' death, is, as we have already stated, the only text in the canonical Gospels which requires Jesus to have worked extensively in Bethsaida. As we shall see, the further occurrences of Bethsaida do not help us much more.

The further sayings in question are two places in the Gospel of Mark, since the two occurrences of Bethsaida in the Gospel of John (John 1:44; 12:21) merely mention that the three disciples Peter, Philip, and Andrew come from Bethsaida, and say nothing about activities of Jesus there (no more than the origin of a Mary from Magdala means that Jesus worked there). Regarding the localization of Bethsaida in the Galilee instead of in Gaulanitis in John 12:21, suffice it to say that, in my view, this statement justifies neither the assumption of a second Bethsaida lying to the west of the Lake Gennesaret nor the assumption that the course of the Jordan ran differently during Jesus' time.

Let us now briefly discuss the two occurrences in the Gospel of Mark. In the Healing of a Blind Man near the "village" of Bethsaida (Mark 8:22-26), the place-name appears only in the frame of the story in v. 22. Frames of Gospel narratives are often later redactional connections of older units, as the form critical research on the Gospels has demonstrated. In this case it must be considered whether Mark placed this Healing of the Blind Man close to Bethsaida for the first time by reason of a certain geographical interest (because Jesus was soon to move into the territory of Caesarea Philippi). The situation is different with the planned journey by ship to Bethsaida in Mark 6:45, where Jesus sends his disciples (immediately after the Feeding of the Five Thousand), and the actual arrival of the boat in Gennesaret in Mark 6:53. Here, at least, Bethsaida proves to be a place-name which the Evangelist had found in the story.

Let us conclude for Bethsaida in the four canonical Gospels that only the one saying of the Q source with the "woes" requires extensive activities of Jesus in Bethsaida. For the historian the situation is similar to the occurrences of Bethsaida and Julias in Josephus, which are equated there at only one place (*Ant* 18.28). The historian must rely repeatedly on the accidental nature of such singular statements. In this case a further consideration is of importance for Bethsaida. The canonical Gospels were not written until the time between 70 and approximately 110 CE. With respect to Bethsaida they no longer seem to reflect fully the activity of Jesus there. Despite the origin of the disciples Peter and Philip in Bethsaida, who are even preferred by the late Gospel of John, there is no knowledge of Jesus' activities in Bethsaida. In Luke, where Bethsaida appears twice, the connection of this place with the Feeding Story is a mere "writing desk construction." Matthew simply eliminates the name Bethsaida which he finds in Mark 6:45 and also omits the Healing of the Blind Man in Mark 8:22-26; the saying of the Q source is the only Bethsaida reference left. At least Mark still shows a certain interest in Bethsaida when he has Jesus pass through it in Mark 8:22 on his way to Caesarea Philippi.

What would we know about the activities of Jesus in Bethsaida without the saying of the Q source in the Gospels of Matthew and Luke? Through this saying of the woes it is also made clear how much tradition concerning Jesus' works has been lost, and that the canonical Gospels transmit only limited knowledge. In the case of Bethsaida we must assume on the basis of the saying of the Q source and a few scattered reports that this place was of much more importance for appearances of Jesus than the Gospels now reveal.

CHAPTER NOTES

1. With reference to Kuhn and Arav 1991, 77-91. My collaborator Monika Hesselt helped in the evaluation of the New Testament literature for this essay. For the translation of this paper from the German original I wish to thank James O'Meara, Munich.

2. See Israeli and Avida 1988, 17: "Fragments of this type of oil-lamp have been discovered at almost all the Hellenistic sites in Israel."

3. Theissen 1992, 2.

4. Cf. Schneemelcher 1990, 136, no. 27; Aland 1985, 153 (on Matt. 11:20-24), 260 (on Luke 10:13-15).

5. Cf. Becker 1991, 101. John 12:21 once again takes up this indication of Philip's origin.

6. According to v. 15, Jesus ascends the mountain again alone, although in v. 3 he has already climbed it with the disciples. The competition of v. 3, where only John mentions Jesus' ascending the mountain after his boat lands (the landing of the boat, but not the ascending of the mountain, at the beginning of the Feeding Story is found also in Mark 6:32 and Matt. 14:13), and v. 15, where Jesus climbs the mountain again before he walks on the water, was, if at all, seemingly understood by the Evangelist as Jesus having in fact left the mountain previously. In Mark 6:46 and Matt. 14:23 (as in John 6:15) Jesus ascends the mountain before his walking on the water.

7. Only here and in v. 15 does the Gospel of John speak of Jesus withdrawing to a mountain. Thus there is no theological motive of the Evangelist, at least not in v. 3.

8. Bultmann 1941, 156.

9. This assumption is supported by the results of excavations hitherto undertaken (with the one exception of a coin of Agrippa II minted during the reign of Domitian, which was found 1993 in Area B).

10. In Mark 6:45, in the first verse of the segment which is missing in Luke, and in Mark 8:22, in the last story of this part, which Luke leaves out.

11. It is, however, often asked whether the Gospel of Luke takes the place-name Bethsaida from Mark 6:45 and 8:22. See, e.g., the commentaries of Holtzmann 1901, Klostermann 1929, Schürmann 1988, Schneider 1984, Bovon 1989 (all on Luke 9:10).

12. This view, to which I cannot subscribe, is supported in detail by Koester 1990, 284-286.

13. There are two unsatisfying attempts to harmonize the geographical contradictions of the narration: (1) The claim that ὑποχωρεῖν in v. 10 merely means that Jesus withdrew "in the direction of a city," i.e., Bethsaida (which Bovon 1989, 1:466, 468, considers "probable"). This interpretation cannot explain the situation described, not only because Jesus and his disciples are in a wilderness (ἐν ἐρήμῳ) according to v. 12, but also because the people are expected to gather food in "villages and farms" despite the proximity of the "city" (v. 10). (2) The suggestion that a change of scene from the πόλις to the wilderness be assumed with v. 12 (Schürmann 1988, 1:514) is very artificial.

14. Schürmann 1988, 1:512.

15. The addition in Matthew, i.e., the extension of the verdict on Capernaum in 11:23b-24, was without doubt added subsequently. The formulation of 11:23b is based on v. 21b; v. 24 corresponds above all to the original conclusion of the Mission of the Seventy in Q, Matt. 10:15. The third Evangelist adds our saying to this conclusion (after 10:12). The original *logion* and the conclusion of the Mission of the Seventy are related by reason of the ἀνεκτότερον ἔσται ἤ.

16. Both cities and their inhabitants often were mentioned together in the Hebrew Bible (e.g., Jer. 47:4, Zech. 9:2, 1 Chr. 22:4, 1 Macc. 5:15). With this in mind, the disputed geography in Mark 7:31 is also understandable.

17. See Kuhn and Arav 1991, 82.

18. This was pointed out by Manfred Görg in the above-mentioned interdisciplinary seminar group on Galilee, the Gaulanitis, and the excavations of et-Tell (Bethsaida) at the Faculty of Protestant Theology of the University of Munich.
19. Bultmann 1921, 68; 1931, 117–118.
20. Bultmann 1921, 112.
21. Bultmann 1921, 113 (1931, 118).
22. Cf. also the discussion of Bultmann's three arguments in Theissen 1992, 53 n. 73.
23. Lührmann 1969, 64, on the other hand, agrees with this last argument of Bultmann.
24. Ibid., 78.
25. Ibid., 53–54.
26. Cf. Theissen 1992, 53.
27. Gnilka 1988, 1:430.
28. Hahn 1965, 27; see also Gnilka 1988, 1:430.
29. Cf. Theissen 1992, 53–54.
30. Concerning this argument, cf. Grundmann 1896, 313; Schweizer 1898, 173; Wiefel 1988, 199; Theissen 1992, 53–54.
31. According to Acts 21:3 ff., Paul visits the Christian community in Tyre; cf. Theissen 1992, 54.
32. Schmidt 1919.

LITERATURE CITED

Aland, K., ed. 1985. *Synopsis Quattuor Evangeliorum: Locis parallelis evangeliorum apocryphorum et patrum adhibitis*. 13th ed. Stuttgart: Deutsche Bibelgesellschaft.

Becker, J. 1991. *Das Evangelium des Johannes: Kapitel 1-10*. Ökumenischer Taschenbuchkommentar zum Neuen Testament 4/1. 3d ed. Gütersloh: Gerd Mohn; Würzburg: Echter Verlag.

Bovon, F. 1989. *Das Evangelium nach Lukas: Luke 1, 1-9, 50*. EKKNT 3/1. Zürich: Benziger Verlag; Neukirchen-Vluyn: Neukirchener Verlag.

Bultmann, R. 1921. *Die Geschichte der synoptischen Tradition*. FRLANT 29. Göttingen: Vandenhoeck and Ruprecht. 2d ed. 1931; reprinted 1972 (English trans., 1968. *The History of the Synoptic Tradition*. Rev. ed. Oxford: Blackwell).

_____. 1941. *Das Evangelium des Johannes*. MeyerK 2. 10th ed. Göttingen: Vandenhoeck and Ruprecht.

Gnilka, J. 1988. *Das Matthäusevangelium.*Vol. 1. HTKNT 1/1. 2d ed. Freiburg: Herder.

Grundmann, W. 1986. *Das Evangelium nach Matthäus*. THKNT 1. 6th ed. Berlin: Evangelische Verlagsanstalt.

Hahn, F. 1965. *Das Verständnis der Mission im Neuen Testament*. WMANT 13. 2d ed. Neukirchen-Vluyn: Neukirchener Verlag.

Holtzmann, H. J. 1901. *Die Synoptiker*. Hand-Commentar zum Neuen Testament, 1. 3d ed. Tübingen/Leipzig: J. C. B. Mohr (Paul Siebeck).

Israeli, Y., and U. Avida. 1988. *Oil-Lamps from Eretz Israel: The Lovis and Carmen Warschaw Collection at the Israel Museum, Jerusalem*. The Israel Museum.

Klostermann, E. 1929. *Das Lukasevangelium*. HNT 5. 2d ed. Tübingen: J. C. B. Mohr (Paul Siebeck).

Koester, Helmut. 1990. *Ancient Christian Gospels: Their History and Development*. London: SCM Press; Philadelphia: Trinity Press, Int.

Kuhn, H.-W., and R. Arav. 1991. The Bethsaida Excavations: Historical and Archaeological Approaches. In *The Future of Early Christianity: Essays in Honor of Helmut Koester*. Minneapolis: Fortress Press, 77–91 (Kuhn) and 91–106 (Arav).

Lührmann, D. 1969. *Die Redaktion der Logienquelle*. WMANT 33. Neukirchen-Vluyn: Neukirchener Verlag.

Schmidt, K. L. 1919. *Der Rahmen der Geschichte Jesu: Literarkritische Untersuchungen zur ältesten Jesusüberlieferung*. Reprinted 1964. Darmstadt: Wissenschaftliche Buchgesellschaft.

Schneemelcher, W. 1990. *Neutestamentliche Apokryphen in deutscher Übersetzung*. 1: *Evangelien*. 6th ed. Tübingen: J. C. B. Mohr (Paul Siebeck).

Schneider, G. 1984. *Das Evangelium nach Lukas: Kapitel 1-10*. Ökumenischer Taschenbuchkommentar zum Neuen Testament 3/1. 2d ed., Gütersloh: Gerd Mohn; Würzburg: Echter.

Schürmann, H. 1988. *Das Lukasevangelium*. Vol. 1, HTKNT 3.1. 3d ed., Freiburg: Herder.

Schweizer, E.1986. *Das Evangelium nach Matthäus*. NTD 2, 16th ed. Göttingen: Vandenhoeck and Ruprecht.

Theissen, G. 1992. *Lokalkolorit und Zeitgeschichte in den Evangelien: Ein Beitrag zur Geschichte der synoptischen Tradition*. 2d ed. Freiburg, Schweiz: Universitätsverlag; Göttingen: Vandenhoeck and Ruprecht.

Wiefel, W. 1988. *Das Evangelium nach Lukas*. THKNT 3. Berlin: Evangelische Verlagsanstalt.

John J. Rousseau

The Healing of a Blind Man at Bethsaida

THE MIGHTY WORKS OF JESUS in the Gospel tradition that are referred to in Matt. 11:20–24 and Luke 10:13–15 include only one specific instance of healing that took place in or near the city of Bethsaida. The purpose of this chapter is to discuss whether this particular healing can be seen as authentic. This is a formidable task since my colleagues of the Jesus Seminar in October 1990 gave a unanimous "black rating" to the sayings of Jesus in Mark 8:23 and 26, which means that these sayings, in their opinion, most likely are not authentic. I say the rating was unanimous because the one abstention, by me, was not counted. At the time, I thought I had not done enough research to express an opinion. In Mark 8:23, Jesus asks, "Do you see anything?" and in Mark 8:26, he says, "Do not even enter the village." The negative rating given by the Seminar is based on the fact that since Jesus and the blind man were in an isolated place, there was no independent witness to report the conversation. Another negative factor is single attestation (the story appears only in the Gospel of Mark)

I contend that multiple attestation does not mean much, since it is impossible to know for certain whether each attestation corresponds to only one source different from the others. New Testament scholars usually recognize three main independent sources: Mark; Q, which refers to material found in Matthew and Luke in common but not found in Mark; and the Gospel of Thomas, a list of Jesus' sayings found in the Nag Hammadi Library. Additional independent sources are *L* material found only in

257

Luke, and *M* material found only in Matthew. There is no assurance that the same storyteller was not the common originator of two or three stories or sayings found in different texts; travel and intellectual exchanges between Asia Minor, Palestine, and Egypt were common. I rely much more on the three criteria of embarrassment, coherence, and subversive character. If the saying or the fact was embarrassing for the writer or the early church, then there is a good chance that it was kept only because it was authentic. Coherence with Jesus' gestalt as it emerges from the general, common account of the Gospels is also an indicator of authenticity (although one may invoke the argument of circularity). Another strong indicator of authenticity resides in coherence with Jesus' sociohistorical environment. If the saying or action appeared as subversive or shocking to the righteous and the religious establishment, it probably was authentic.

The texts that came to us were written one or two generations after Jesus, they are not in their most probable original language (Aramaic), and each writer brought his own literary style and theology. Thus it is useless to argue about the exact wording of the Greek text and how the original language could have been translated. The futility of such exercises is evidenced by the diversity of opinions among New Testament scholars. Before proceeding further, it is necessary to describe briefly Jesus' gestalt as it emerges from the Synoptic Gospels. I think that most would agree at least on the following general image of Jesus. He was:

- A charismatic Jewish religious leader or prophet
- A wandering healer, exorcist, and miracle worker
- A teacher of new socioreligious ethics, and wisdom
- A friend of the poor and outcast
- A proclaimer of the Kingdom of God
- One who was spiritually close to God, whom he called Father

CRITICAL COMMENTARY ON THE PERICOPE

MARK 8:22–26

22. And they came to Bethsaida. And some people brought to him a blind man, and begged him to touch him. 23. And he took the blind man by the hand, and led him out of the village; and when he had spat on his eyes and laid his hands upon him, he asked him, "Do you see anything?" 24. And he looked up and said, "I see men; but they look like trees walking." 25. Then again he laid his

hands upon his eyes; and he looked intently and was restored, and saw everything clearly. 26. And he sent him away to his home, saying, "Do not even enter the village." (RSV)

MARK 8:22

And they came to Bethsaida. And some people brought to him a blind man, and begged him to touch him.

The location, Bethsaida, is plausible in consideration of other references to this place in Jesus' ministry. Jesus' reputation as a healer was well established and it was not unusual for the people to bring their relatives or friends to him so they could be healed by touching (imposition of the hands), which was common practice. Blindness was widespread in the Near East, especially as a result of latent trachoma, a chronic contagious conjunctivitis caused by chlamydia. Interestingly, a survey made in Bavaria and Prussia in 1880 showed that Jews, although they had left Palestine for eighteen centuries, were more prone to blindness then non-Jews.[1]

MARK 8:23

And he took the blind man by the hand, and led him out of the village; and when he had spat on his eyes and laid his hands upon him, he asked him, "Do you see anything?"

Jesus took the blind man by the hand. Since no one else was with them, Jesus had to guide the blind man, a detail which gives credibility to the story. He led him out of the village, says Mark. Gallons of ink have been spent on whether Bethsaida was a village (κομε), as in the Gospel of Mark, or a city (πολις), as in Josephus, Matthew, and Luke. Numismatic discoveries and studies tend to prove that the change from village to city was made in 30 CE.[2]

In a first attempt to cure the blind man, Jesus spat on the blind man's eyes and laid hands upon him. The spitting on the face of someone is shocking to the modern reader, and the NRSV edulcorates the Greek text into "put saliva on his eye"; it was not an unusual practice as will be seen below. As for the laying of hands, it commonly was done, as demonstrated by the Genesis Apocryphon found in Cave I at Qumran. The question, "Do you see anything?" was quite natural and it adds credibility to the story.

Mark 8:24

And he looked up and said, "I see men; but they look like trees walking."

The man was no longer blind, but his vision was blurred; the healing was accomplished only partly. This incident is the only occurrence where Jesus was not fully successful when he performed a healing—a most embarrassing situation for the early Christians, especially in consideration of statements such as those found in Luke 24:19 and Acts 2:22, which record the "mighty deeds" of Jesus. The fact that the story was kept as it is tends to prove that the event was authentic. The criterion of embarrassment is probably the most powerful in favor of authenticity.

Mark 8:25

Then again he laid his hands upon his eyes; and he looked intently and was restored, and saw everything clearly.

At the second attempt, Jesus does not spit on the eyes but imposes his hands one more time, and the man's vision is restored fully.

Mark 8:26

And he sent him away to his home, saying, "Do not even enter the village."

The healed man did not live in Bethsaida, which is not surprising since farms and houses were dispersed on the fertile plain around et-Tell, and the lake was rich in fish. Usually, according to Mark, Jesus did not want publicity about his miracles (the messianic secret). Here, he does not expressly formulate the command to remain silent, but he forbids the man to go back to the town to satisfy people's curiosity.

Coherence with the Synoptic Gestalt of Jesus

Here Jesus appears as an itinerant healer, which is in conformity with his gestalt. In this specific instance he used saliva, which is not exceptional for him. In the healing of the man born blind in John 9, he makes a plaster of earth and spittle to apply to the eyes of the blind beggar; in the healing of the deaf-mute in Mark 7:32–36, Jesus "spat (on his fingers) and touched his tongue." The story is somewhat parallel to that of the blind man of Bethsaida. In both cases, the sick man is brought to Jesus, who leads him apart, uses saliva, and imposes his hand. Both stories end with a command of silence or discretion.

Jesus' healing of the blind is well attested to in the Gospel tradition: the healings of Bartimaeus at Jericho (Mark 10:46–52), two blind men (Matt. 9:22–31), the blind and mute demoniac (Matt. 12:22), and the man born blind (John 9). Thus, the healing at Bethsaida is in line with Jesus' activity. Healing of the blind has a special significance in the ministry of Jesus; it was one of the great messianic signs given as an answer to the emissaries of the imprisoned Baptist, "the blind receive their sight" (Matt. 11:15; Luke 7:22; cf. Isa. 35:5–6).[3]

Despite its particularity of a two-step healing, the story is perfectly coherent with Jesus' gestalt, which is in favor of its authenticity. There is a proviso, however. As in all cases of exorcism and miraculous healing, it is very often difficult to explain the healing process in a totally rational and scientifically satisfying manner. The social scientist will simply conclude that the curing of a blind man was probably performed by Jesus at Bethsaida, according to the beliefs and practices of the time.

COHERENCE WITH THE SOCIOHISTORICAL CONTEXT OF JESUS

I shall now examine whether the story is in harmony with the sociohistorical context of the Palestine of Jesus' time. Consideration is given to the practitioners of healing, the disease that was cured, and the techniques that were used.

THE PRACTITIONERS OF HEALING

There were in Palestine, in the period of Jesus, several categories of individuals who claimed they could perform healings: physicians, traditional healers (folk medicine practitioners), miracle workers, magicians, and *goetes*. Paul makes a distinction between traditional healers and miracle workers (1 Cor. 12:28). Sometimes it was difficult to discern who was what and whether the claimant was a bona fide practitioner or a quack.

Roman Palestine was a cosmopolitan country; the "Galilee of the Gentiles" was surrounded by Phoenicia on the west, the Decapolis on the east, Seleucia on the north, and Scythopolis on the south. It included several Hellenized if not Hellenistic cities: Ptolemais, Sepphoris (three miles from Nazareth), Caesarea–Philippi (with a sanctuary and festivals to the god Pan), and Tiberias. Nobody lived more that twelve miles from a center of Greek influence. Hippocratic medicine was certainly practiced there, and the Gospels make reference to physicians (Jesus at Nazareth, the woman with a flow of blood; Luke himself is said to have been a physician). A physician was a craftsman who either resided in a city or was itinerant.[4] The itinerant physician worked in patients' homes or had a booth set up for a short time in a town marketplace. There were no restrictions to the medical craft, nor was there any required training or official examination. The difference between the physician and other types of healers was one of technique; the physician would make a diagnosis and prescribe remedies which he had learned from a master (e.g., potions, herbs, diets), and he could also perform surgery. But he would seldom evoke a god (except Asklepios perhaps) or use incantations or offer sacrifices for the healing of his patient.[5]

The traditional healers or practitioners of folk medicine applied techniques from ancient times that were akin to magical recipes. Besides using plants (a practice they had in common with physicians), they resorted to the use of flesh, milk, blood, hair, and urine as well as the dung of animals as diverse as camels, wolves, vultures, donkeys, hyenas, porcupines; they would crush scorpions or beetles to make plasters. They also used minerals such as clay, salt, sulfur, petroleum.[6]

On the other hand, the miracle worker performed healing through God's power, or so he claimed. But he could be accused of using satanic powers, as happened to Jesus himself (Matt. 12:24; John 8:48). The miracle worker would perform healing through prayer, touch, command, or simply with an affirmative statement as Jesus did in several cases. The miracle worker could also use some techniques that resembled those of the magician.[7]

During Jesus' time there was not much difference in the public eye between magicians (magi) and *goetes*. Magi originally were members of a famed priestly caste in Persia, but after magus Gaumata usurped power in Persia while King Cambyses was fighting in Egypt (522 BCE),[8] magi fell into disfavor. Most of them moved to Asia Minor, Egypt, Greece, or Italy to exercise their talents and serve as tutors and advisers of governors, kings, and even emperors like Nero. However, there is no indication that the Samaritan Simon Magus (Acts 8:9–24) was one of them; the word had been vulgarized and could be used to designate ordinary *goetes* or charlatans.

According to Josephus, the Jews were well versed in magic, and the greatest magician among them had been no less than King Solomon himself. Josephus also reports that the Essenes practiced the art of healing, and Philo makes an identical report concerning the Therapeutae of

Alexandria. Even Jesus would have learned magic in Egypt according to Celsus, whose work was destroyed but partly preserved in quotations by Eusebius in his "Contra Celsum." Thus, in the Hellenized Palestine of Jesus many individuals were involved in healing activities of one form or another. Miraculous healing was just one therapeutic method, and Jesus in his role as a healer or miracle worker fit perfectly in the sociohistorical context of the Palestine of his time.

THE DISEASE

As mentioned, blindness was a common condition in Palestine. Biblical tradition has perceived blindness as a curse or a punishment from either God or temporal rulers. It was a current belief, grounded in Exod. 20:5, that children would suffer from the sins of their parents and thus could be born blind. In many cases, congenital blindness was a result of physical or psychological disorders (similar to modern birth disorders in children of alcoholics, smokers, drug addicts, or those afflicted with sexually transmitted diseases). The rabbis were convinced that the position of the parents during sexual intercourse could cause birth defects. For example, in BT Nedarin we find, "R. Johanan B. Dabai said, 'people are born lame because their parents overturn their table (have intercourse from behind), dumb because they kiss 'that place,' deaf because they speak during intercourse, blind because they look at 'that place.'"[9] Another cause of blindness was gouging. Gouging the eyes of an enemy was a normal practice (the Philistines bored the eyes of Samson; the King of Babylon blinded Zedekiah). The blind, together with the lame and lepers were outcasts of society and were restricted outside the town limits. They became beggars and a threat to passersby. Under these conditions, the healing of the blind by Jesus made an impact on the witnesses far greater than one can image in modern society.

Classical writers provide several reports of blindness in antiquity. For example, Aristophanes describes, in *Plutus*, a healing by a priest impersonating the god Asklepios in his shrine at Piraeus. The priest came at night as an apothecary, with a mortar, pestle, and box; he prepared a plaster of hot spices and vinegar and put it on the eyes of the patient. Plutus himself was healed of an eye ailment by two snakes which came from a back room and liked his eyes.[10] In such a milieu, the act of healing a blind man by Jesus at Bethsaida is extremely plausible.

The Technique

In the Synoptic Gospels, Jesus heals the blind in three ways: (1) spitting on the eyes and laying his hands on the patient (Bethsaida), (2) touching the patients (the two blind men), and (3) simply affirming verbally that the healing was done (Bartimaeus). In John 9, the techniques are more complex, and involve (1) the use of saliva to make clay, (2) the use of clay as a plaster on the eyes, and (3) the subsequent washing with water.

Is the use of saliva plausible in the sociohistorical context? It was certainly believed that saliva had special powers. The Egyptian goddess Isis was revered in the Greco–Roman world in the time of Jesus. It is said of her that one day when the great but aging god Re was going for a stroll to survey his creation, he drooled saliva on the ground. Isis picked up the earth mixed with Re's saliva and fashioned a snake of clay, which came to life. On his way back, Re was bitten by the snake, became very ill, and was healed by Isis only after he revealed his true name to her as she had demanded.[11]

In his *Natural History* XXX, Pliny the Elder reports that saliva, among other bodily fluids, was a potent remedy: "The best of all safeguards against serpents is the saliva of a fasting human being." Other uses include spitting on epileptics during a seizure, spitting in one's hand to increase the force of a blow, and using saliva to treat boils, leprous sores, and eye diseases. In fact, the saliva of a fasting woman was seen as a powerful medication for the healing of watery eyes.[12] Tacitus depicts Vespasian moistening the eyes and cheeks of a blind and lame follower of Serapis whose eyesight was thus restored.[13] According to Morton Smith, "fluid could help make the contact closer; the readiest form of fluid was spittle, and both spittle and the act of spitting were commonly believed to have magical powers."[14] Thus it follows that the use of saliva by Jesus for healing the blind man at Bethsaida is highly plausible in the sociohistorical context of his time.

Conclusion

In summary, the story of the blind man cured at Bethsaida by Jesus meets all the criteria I have selected in order to detect its possible authenticity. Of course, three of these criteria may be criticized: embarrassment for the early church, coherence with Jesus' gestalt, and coherence with Jesus' sociohistorical environment. The criterion of subversive characteristic is not applicable in this case since healing by any method was common practice in the Palestine of Jesus. Thus, we may reasonably conclude that Jesus most probably healed a blind man at Bethsaida by using saliva and imposing his hands.

Archaeology can help to ascertain that a certain story is plausible in the time and setting in which it is placed. For instance, large stone jars with a capacity of seventeen gallons were discovered in the Herodian Quarter of Jerusalem, especially in the Burnt House. They correspond to the description given by the Fourth Gospel for the jars used at the marriage of Cana in Galilee: "six stone jars were standing there for the Jewish rite of purification, each holding twenty or thirty gallons" (John 2:6). At Bethsaida, we did not find the footprints of Jesus or the blind man walking away from the city nor the place where they stood during the healing, and I doubt we ever will. This is why I resort to abstract reasoning to find out whether the story is authentic or not. But it seems that someone knows more than I do. A Stone of Bethsaida, decorated with symbolic signs, had the honor of a photograph in *Biblical Archaeologist,* December 1985, with a detailed description but no information as to its origin. Now, visitors stop there and say, "This is the place where Jesus healed the blind man who saw men looking like trees."[15]

Chapter Notes

1. 13.8:10,000 for Jews, versus 8:10,000 for non-Jews; *Jewish Encyclopedia, s. v.* "Blindness."
2. This is one more reason to believe that the Julia after whom the city was renamed was the wife and not the daughter of Augustus, contrary to what Josephus wrote. See Rousseau and Arav 1995, s.v. "Coins as Historical Documents."
3. See also Luke 4:18.
4. Edelstein 1967, 87.
5. See Rousseau and Arav 1995, *s.v.* "Medicine, Physicians."
6. See Rousseau and Arav 1995, *s.v.* "Traditional Healing."
7. See Rousseau and Arav 1995, *s.v.* "Magic, Miracles."
8. Cambyses died soon after and Darius, a distant relative who served as his spear bearer, rushed back to Persia, murdered Gaumata and his clique, and became king.
9. BT Nedarin 20a; see also BT Pesahim 112b: if one has intercourse in the light of a lamp, epileptic children will be born.
10. Kee 1983, 81.
11. The name was "The Great of Magic"; see Kee 1983, 109.
12. Kee 1986, 104.
13. Ibid., 83.
14. Smith 1985, 128.
15. The stone was planted in 1981.

Literature Cited

Edelstein, Ludwig. 1967. *Ancient Medicine.* Ed. O. Temkin and C. L. Temkin. Trans. from the German by C. L. Temkin. Baltimore: The Johns Hopkins University Press.

Galipeau, Steven A. 1990. *Transforming Body and Soul.* New York: Paulist Press.

Grmek, Mirko D. 1989. Diseases in the Ancient Greek World. Trans. from the French by M. Muellner and L. Muellner. Baltimore: The Johns Hopkins University Press.

Kee, Howard C. 1983. *Miracles in the Early Christian World.* New Haven: Yale University Press.

_____. 1986. *Medicine, Miracle and Magic in the New Testament Times.* Cambridge: Cambridge University Press.

Latourelle, Rene. 1986. *The Miracles of Jesus and the Theology of Miracles.* New York: Paulist Press.

Majno, Guido. 1975. *The Healing Hand: Man and Wound in the Ancient World.* Cambridge, London: Harvard University Press.

Navich, Joseph, and Shaul Shaked. 1985. *Amulets and Magic Bowls: Aramaic Incantations of Late Antiquity.* Jerusalem: Magnes Press.

Rousseau, John. March 1993. *Background Information on Traditional Healing in the Time of Jesus: Investigating Ancient Healing Practices of the Bedouins.* Jesus Seminar Papers. Sonoma: Polebridge Press.

_____. 1993. Jesus: An Exorcist of a Kind. SBL Seminar Papers, Historical Jesus Section.

_____, and R. Arav. 1995. *Jesus and His World: An Archaeological and Cultural Dictionary.* Minneapolis: Fortress Press.

Smith, Morton. 1985. *Jesus the Magician.* Willingborough, Great Britain: The Aquarian Press.

Strassfeld, Michael. 1985. *The Jewish Holidays.* New York: Harper and Row.

Theissen, Gerd. 1983. *The Miracle Stories of the Early Christian Tradition.* Trans. from the German by Francis McDonald. Philadelphia: Fortress Press.

Vermes, Geza. 1973. *Jesus the Jew.* Philadelphia: Fortress Press.

Richard A. Freund

The Search for Bethsaida
in Rabbinic Literature

T HE NEED FOR A CHAPTER dealing with the search for Bethsaida in Rabbinic literature is not self-evident. The tell under excavation has a Roman Provincial occupation level in the 1 to 3 CE era. Bethsaida is known in both the writings of Josephus and the New Testament as a Jewish settlement, and its location is near other Jewish Rabbinic settlements in the Golan and Galilee. Even so, Bethsaida is not well known from classical Talmudic or Rabbinic literature,[1] and therein lies part of the difficulty for making a literary investigation of the site.

Despite rapid expansion of archaeology in Israel after World War II, little systematic attention has been paid to archaeological data from sites of the late Roman/Early-Byzantine or Diaspora periods which are associated with localities or artifacts mentioned in classical Talmudic or Rabbinic literature of that period. Some studies were made during the early twentieth century, but those generally lack critical literary methodology and may lead to problematic understandings. This chapter uses archaeological, geological, and geographic information from the Bethsaida excavations together with text-critical examinations of classical Rabbinic texts to restore important pieces of information about the excavations at et-Tell and about the texts.

BIBLICAL, RABBINIC, AND NEW TESTAMENT ARCHAEOLOGY

The discipline of Biblical archaeology together with the texts of the Old and New Testaments has provided significant insights for understanding

Israel's history, especially for the Old Testament era, but less so for the New Testament era. Unfortunately, studies in Biblical archaeology have taken little or no notice of the wealth of sources present in Rabbinic archaeology literature.

New Testament archaeologists have succeeded in establishing parameters for research and use of archaeological data to track the travels of Paul in the Roman world outside of first-century Palestine. But these kinds of parameters do not seem to exist for investigation of the named cities or towns in Palestine in which Jesus and the Apostles were active. Lack of interest in New Testament archaeology[2] inside Israel may result from the presence of medieval Christian Holy Land or relic shrines built on ancient sites, which prevent systematic excavation. Any suggestion to relocate such shrines is met with resistance by many who would view such a move as heretical or blasphemous. Fortunately, the Bethsaida site has no significant ideological issues to prevent New Testament archaeological research. Unfortunately, Rabbinic archaeology[3] carries its own ideological baggage, not the least of which is the connection between Rabbinic literature and certain towns and cities.

Both New Testament and Rabbinic archaeology pay much attention to the background of the non-Israelite or non-Jewish ancient Near East. Rabbinic geography—the study of the geography of the Land of Israel according to the texts of the rabbis—has antecedents in travel accounts from different periods, four examples of which are (1) an account preserved by Eldad the Danite in the Epistle of Hasdai bin Shaprut in the ninth century CE, (2) the twelfth-century CE journeys of Benjamin of Tudela, Petahia of Regensburg, and Jacob ben Nathaniel HaCohen, (3) the detailed studies of Estori HaParhi in the *Sefer Kaftor vaFerah* from the fourteenth century CE, and (4) the "Imrei Binah" section of Azariah dei Rossi's sixteenth-century *Meor Enayim,* among many others. Except for Dei Rossi's work, these studies do not employ a text-critical approach to the information, and they suffer from the same types of legends, conflations, exaggerations, and nonspecific information found in medieval Christian pilgrim or traveler literature from the same period. Despite their problems, these works cannot be dismissed; they preserve valuable insights and traditions not found elsewhere and should be seen as possible sources for reconstructing historically accurate Rabbinic archaeology and geography.

Modern Rabbinic archaeology began alongside modern Biblical studies and modern Biblical archaeology as well as with the *Wissenschaft des Judentums* literature of the nineteenth century. Eighteenth- and nineteenth-century travelers and explorers in Palestine, the Levant, and Egypt—such as Edward Robinson, Ernest Renan, and Charles Warren—attempted to link Rabbinic traditions with exact locations. Their reports sparked hopes in the late nineteenth century that these early site locations would provide direct links to Rabbinic narratives. Abraham Berliner, Joseph Derenbourg, and Adolf Neubauer laid the groundwork for later studies and comparisons. In the early part of the twentieth century, Samuel Krauss produced his two-volume work, and Samuel Klein and Jacob Obermeyer wrote about cities and towns in both Israel and Babylonia that are mentioned in the Talmud in an attempt to analyze critically some of the problems associated with identifications made in the previous century.[4] In these works one finds the problem of attempting to link the Talmudic stories to the places that nineteenth-century soldiers, explorers, and travelers had linked to locations mentioned in Rabbinic literature. This type of identificaton system proved inadequate or, in the case of the Masoretic Text and Old Testament, theologically weighted. The case of Talmudic information was even more problematic.

There is yet another problem associated with nineteenth- and even the twentieth-century Biblical archaeology which makes Talmudic archaeology problematic. In Old and New Testament archaeology the search parameters are determined by the two fixed canons. While these works are compared with ancient Near Eastern and Greco–Roman literature, and while text criticism is taken into account, the parameters of Biblical archaeology often begin with the Biblical version of an event, site description, or history that is fixed in the canon. Even though the archaeology of the New Testament goes beyond the scope of the twenty-seven-book canon, it is often directed only by the parameters of the canon. In much the same way, Talmudic archaeology parameters were thought by Krauss and others in the nineteenth and early twentieth centuries to be set by the canon of the Babylonian Talmud (BT) and Palestinian Talmud (PT). Over the past fifty years, however, this concept has been challenged. On one hand, determiniation of so-called Talmudic archaeology of Israel that is based on BT references only, for example, is suspect. Although the BT has ample information about the life and times of Israel during the Tannaitic and Amoraic periods (corresponding to the Roman and Early Byzantine periods), there remain textual and factual problems. The overwhelming size of the Talmudim and the unwieldy nature of Talmudic language and argumentation in both canons, coupled with the problematic state of Talmudic manuscripts, make it difficult to produce a single, unified "Talmudic archaeology." In short, Talmudic information about Israel can be used only after it is subjected to serious critical analysis.

In modern critical Talmudic studies, especially those following World War II, the Talmudim are seen as intelligible only as they are compared with other parts of classical Rabbinic (and non-Rabbinic) literature such as collections of halakhic and haggadic midrashim, Tosefta, Mishnah, and other Rabbinic collections (commentaries, responsa, etc.) which date from the early Middle Ages. Later medieval Rabbinic and especially post-Geonic works preserve some readings of worth to critical scholarship but are themselves subject to revisions based on medieval criteria which have little to do with their original late Roman/Early Byzantine worldview. In general, modern studies view the Talmudim and classical Rabbinic literature as intelligible only in relation to a much greater and fluid comparative study of various collections rather than as the study of one work. Text reconstruction and comparison is a necessary part of any Rabbinic literature research. The fact that the only surviving complete manuscripts of the BT (Munich 95) and the PT (Leiden Codex Scal. 3) date from the twelfth or thirteenth century CE is a crucial factor for understanding one part of the problematic nature of so-called Talmudic archaeology.[5] Serious text-criticism study of individual Talmudic manuscript texts should be done simultaneously with study of other classical Rabbinic works to establish datum in this branch of archaeology.[6] For this reason, the discipline should be called Rabbinic archaeology rather than Talmudic archaeology.

This chapter presents two types of Rabbinic archaeology. The first involves an analysis of the Rabbinic texts, and their traditional manuscripts, which mention specific sites (in this case Bethsaida). The other type involves comparing the information gleaned from the text-critical analysis with the knowledge gained from the present field excavations. All citations of classical Rabbinic literature used in this chapter are from text-critical editions (where available), first printings, or comparisons with manuscripts. In the case of the PT, for example, the Venice first printing is used, unless otherwise noted, and comparisions are made with the Leiden Codex Scal. 3 manuscript. In the case of the BT, citations are from the well-known Vilna printing, but comparisons are made with available manuscripts

Using Rabbinic Literature

Problems associated with the use of Rabbinic materials cannot be resolved fully, but scholars need to be aware of them. In the modern Rabbinic studies of the late nineteenth and early twentieth centuries, the historical authenticity of Rabbinic traditions was generally accepted as reliable for modern scholarly analysis. Critical textual methodology was used by such early scholars as Israel Frankel, Abraham Geiger, Heinrich Graetz, and Abraham Kochmal, and by contemporary writers such as Saul Lieberman, Efraim Urbach, and David Weiss Halivni, for example. Even so, these scholars fundamentally accept attributed and unattributed information from Rabbinic sources as genuine expressions of historical circumstances. In the past thirty years, this acceptance has been challenged by Jacob Neusner[7] and a host of other scholars in a variety of works. Neusner writes:

> The sources of Judaism of the dual Torah, oral and written, accurately and factually testify to particular moments in time. But how shall we identify the right time, the particular context to which the documents and their contents attest—and those to which they do not provide reliable testimony? Using the canonical sources of Judaism for historical purposes requires, first of all, a clear statement of why, in my view, these sources tell us about one period, rather than some other. The problem, specifically, is that the documents preserved by Judaism refer to authorities who, we generally suppose, flourished in the early centuries of the Common Era. But at the same time, we also know, these documents were brought to closure in the later centuries of late antiquity. . . . At the same time, we cannot show, and therefore do not know, that these sayings really were said by the sages to whom they are assigned, and we frequently can demonstrate that the sayings are attributed by diverse documents of the same canon to two or more figures. Along these same lines, stories that purport to tell us what really happened exhibit marks of stylization that show reworkings, and, more important, we rarely find independent evidence, e.g., corroboration by outside observers, of other views of what happened. Not only so, but where sages' stories about events can be compared to stories told by outside observers, we rarely can find any correlation at all, either as to causes, or as to circumstances, let alone as to actual events.[8]

As we will see, there are a number of questionable attributions in connection with the Bethsaida site and the sages associated with it. In this attempt to organize Rabbinic traditions that may be associated with the site, we will note these questionable attributions, but space does not allow fuller investigation of all of them. Only a small number will be analyzed fully: those whose attribution, history, and other stylistic features suggest that they are more authentic than others. This chapter should be considered as part of an ongoing study, a work-in-progress, of an archaeological site in a particular historical context in late antiquity where corroboration from outside observers, literatures, and material culture may eventually enlighten the information in the Rabbinic traditions. A driving force behind any decision to eliminate from consideration certain attributed materials has been the important work of Professor Neusner, as will be clear in the following analyses.

The Rabbinic Scribal Tradition

Medieval Jewish scribes and commentators were not always intimately acquainted with all the locations mentioned in the texts with which they dealt, and they sometimes unwittingly provided well-known names for lesser-known localities that had similar spellings. Such seems to be the case with Bethsaida. In a familiar Rabbinic text regarding the Land of Israel one finds:

> Maaseh Rabbi Elazar ben Shamoa and Rabbi Yohanan HaSandlar (both from Alexandria) were going to Netzivim/Nisibis (in Mesopotamia) to study Torah with Rabbi Yehudah ben Batayrah.[9] They arrived Tzaidan and remembered the Land of Israel. Their eyes opened and filled with tears and they ripped their clothes. . . . They returned to their original place [in the Land of Israel] and said that living in the Land of Israel outweighs all the commandments in the Torah.[10]

In this case, the scholars are going to Mesopotamia from Israel. Netzivim was a well-known city. The name Tz(a)idon/an (צידן) appears in some manuscripts, and Sidon (צידון) is found in others. Three major problems present themselves in the investigation of this tradition: (1) the logistical, (2) the literary, and (3) the textual.

THE LOGISTICAL PROBLEM

The city in question could be Sidon, which is located on the present coast of Lebanon. Sidon was not considered an integral part of the historical Land of Israel in many of the variant definitions, and it is possible that Sidon is the original reading here. It is assumed in this tradition that Rabbis Elazar ben Shamoa and Yohanan HaSandlar were in the Land of Israel at the time of this incident, and that they were considering going to Nisibis to study with the eminent scholar Rabbi Yehudah ben Batayrah. In this second-century-CE period, the center of Rabbinic Judaism had moved to the Galilee and it is more likely that the route they took to Mesopotamia was northeast along the traditional land route that passed directly by Bethsaida, rather than a northwest route from the Galilee to the coast and then east to Mesopotamia.

The textual problem is that the city or village ציידן was not a familiar name for medieval scribes and was not generally a spelling for Sidon (צידון was the most widely used Biblical spelling). While it is possible that the scribe erred and wrote ציידן for צידון, this would be unusual since the name ציידן was an unfamiliar one. It is more likely that the name of the city in this tradition was originally ציידן and other scribes corrected it to the more familiar צידון.

THE LITERARY PROBLEM

The drama of this Rabbinic narrative is dependent upon the close proximity of the transit city to the Land of Israel. Sidon is distant from the traditional northern border of the Land of Israel.[11] If the travelers were really at Sidon when they realized their dilemma, they would have been long past the borders of the Land. If they were at Bethsaida, which is directly over the Jordan River in the Golan, then they would have realized they were leaving the sanctity of the traditional Land (which some Rabbinic authorities considered improper) and immediately reconsidered their decision. The drama of the situation is heightened if the city in question is in the Golan. The city to which they referred probably was not Sidon, but one less familiar to most medieval scribes—Bethsaida.

Other examples from classical Rabbinic literature demonstrate the difficulty in identifying the city or village close to the border of the historical Land of Israel. In the Rabbinic account of a priest (*kohen*) who goes to study outside the Land of Israel, a Tannaitic source (Tosefta Avodah Zarah 1.8) mentions Tzaidan as an example of such a location. In general, Rabbinic tradition forbade a *kohen* who resided in Israel to leave the Land, even to perform other commandments. In this Tannaitic tradition, however, other commandments—study of the Torah and respect for teachers—are juxtaposed with the commandment to remain in the Land of Israel. A priest named Yosef HaKohen goes to Tzaidan (which is outside the Land) to demonstrate that in a case of these conflicting commandments, the study of Torah and respect for teachers might outweigh the commandment to remain in the Land. In the traditions of Tosefta Avodah Zarah 1.8, PT Nazir 56a, and BT Eruvin 47b, the incident is related as having occurred at ציידן.[12] The Tosefta Avodah Zarah tradition indicates that Tzaidan (probably Bethsaida) is a compromise location. It was close enough to the border of the Land of Israel for easy access and return. Other versions of this tradition, in the PT Brachot 6a and BT Avodah Zarah 13a, hold that the incident happened at צידן, another possible spelling for Sidon (but in this case it appears to be a corrupted version of ציידו. Rabbinic literature may use both Biblical spellings of Sidon: צידן and צידון,[13] but the latter spelling is certainly the most widely used in both Biblical and Rabbinic literature. In the Biblical text, Sidon is never spelled ציידו. Rabbinic literature has many variants of צידן. It is possible, of course that the ציידו spelling in some of these traditions resulted from the casual addition of a י (*yod*) by a scribe, with the result that ציידו refers to Sidon. More likely, however some of these צידו and בצידן traditions are the result of the contraction(or deletion) of the י (*yod*) to ציידו and בציידו traditions.

Unfortunately, since Bethsaida was not a well-known place-name to medieval commentators and scribes, traditions of Bethsaida may have been attributed to Sidon. Investigation of manuscript readings in the earliest levels of classical Rabbinic literature, that is to say, Tannaitic literature (e.g., Mishnah, Tosefta, and Midrashei Halachah) provide important insights on the question.

In the Mishnah Codex Kaufmann A50, the oldest surviving complete manuscript of the Mishnah, the place-name בציידו appears as Sidon in the four most regularly cited sources: Gittin 4.7, Gittin 7.5, Avodah Zarah 3.12 (in printed editions of the Mishnah chap. 3.7), and Ketubot 7.10. The Mishnah Codex Parma manuscript (De Rossi 138) also agrees with the spelling found in the Kaufmann manuscript for these three mishnayot: בציידו. In short, the oldest and some of the most reliable manuscript information from one of the oldest sources of Rabbinic literature, the Mishnah, indicate that these "Sidon" mishnayot are more likely Bethsaida traditions.

This is not the case with all major medieval manscript traditions. In the Mishnah Codex Parma C manuscript (De Rossi 984), Gittin 7.5 and Ketubot 7.10 read בצײדן, while Gittin 4.7 and Avodah Zarah 3.12 have בצידן. The so-called Lowe manuscript at Cambridge University for Gittin 7.5 reads בצײדן, while Ketubot 7.10, Gittin 4.7 and Avodah Zarah 3.12 read בצידן. The PT Leiden manuscript of the Mishnah reads בצײדן for Mishnah Avodah Zarah 3.12 and Gittin 7.5, but Gittin 4.7 and Ketubot 7.10 read בצידן.

Sometimes it is possible to find reasons for a change in spelling. In Tosefta Zevahim 1.5, for example, the Erfurt manuscript has ר׳ יוסי בר צײדן. The first printed edition and the Vienna manuscript reads: ר׳ יוסי ברבי בצידן, and it appears that the original may have read: רְבִּי יוסי בביצײדן, but was subsequently corrected to ר׳ יוסי בר צײדן by scribes.

Possible spellings of Bethsaida (or Sidon) found in the different manuscript traditions of various Rabbinic texts surveyed in the course of the research for this chapter were: צדן,[14] צײדן, צדון, צידן, צײדן, and צידן, usually prefixed with "to" (לצידן)[15] or "in" (בצידן) to make the combinations: בצידון, בצײדן, בצידן, or בצדון (even בצדן in one case[16]). Although no such reading is found in any manuscript, the preferred Rabbinic formulation may have been בײצידן prior to the editing and ordering of the texts. One reason why geographic references are not easily identifiable has to do with the textual history of Rabbinic manuscripts. In comparison with other ancient documents, such as the New Testament for example, the manuscripts of Rabbinic literature have a rather complex and often tragic textual history.[17] Even though the earliest Rabbinic texts were edited and ordered by the third and fourth centuries CE, the earliest complete surviving manuscript of the BT dates only to the thirteenth or fourteenth century CE.[18] Fragments of texts are extant, and reconstruction of textual history is always necessary when examining Rabbinic traditions. All of these factors contribute to the difficulty in establishing the corpus of stories relating to Bethsaida.

The problem of identifying צידן is apparent in recent secondary research. A few examples and their implications for research in Rabbinic literature will suffice. Aharon Oppenheimer, in his recent *The Galilee in the Period of the Mishna* (Hebrew), examines citations from Rabbinic texts that relate to Sidon in order to demonstrate the relationship between Sidon and the Galilee.[19] Unfortunately, he has chosen citations where the name Tzaidan (צידן) appears in the most ancient manuscript traditions and not Sidon (צידון). Oppenheimer admits that the ancient manuscripts read צײדן

and not צידן, but he is certain that the manuscripts are incorrect and that instead of צייד they should read צידן. It is difficult to follow the logic here since צידן was a well-known city and the possibility that an ancient scribe should confuse it with the less common (or relatively unknown) צייד is very slim. Rather, the ancient manuscript traditions probably preserve traditions regarding a city named צייד, and the traditions may reveal something about the relationship between the Galilee and Golan rather than between the Galilee and Sidon.

In B. Segal's *Geography in the Mishnah*, Rabban Shimon ben Gamiliel is identified with the scholars of Sidon in the article entitled "Sidon." In the very next article, "Bethsaida," Segal cites Mishnah Gittin 7.5 in which Rabban Shimon ben Gamiliel is involved in an incident at Bethsaida.[20] This leads to speculation as to whether Rabban Shimon ben Gamiliel should be associated with the far northern city of Sidon or with only Bethsaida.

The *Macmillan Bible Atlas* includes a map entitled "The Sages of Jabneh," which lists only Hananiah ben Hakhinai at Bethsaida. This listing apparently is based on the tradition of Tosefta Niddah 6.6 and BT Niddah 52b. This identification is important since Hananiah ben Hakhinai was also associated with the inner circle of rabbis in B'nai Brak, Jericho, Sogane, and Bethsaida. The spelling of the settlement in many of these traditions is בצידן. If Hananiah ben Hakhinai was at בצידן, it is reasonable to assume that other Rabbinic traditions which use בצידן might also be referring to Bethsaida and not to Sidon. Recent excavations demonstrate that there was an active presence of Jewish settlements in the Golan during the third through fifth centuries CE and one may assume that there were also settlements in the Golan (besides Gamla and Caesarea Philippi) in the first through the third centuries. Since Bethsaida was a well-known settlement in first-century Jewish sources such as Josephus and the New Testament it is reasonable to assume that it was known to the Galilean rabbis of this period. Therefore, the צידן[ב] traditions (in addition to צייד accounts) may be another source of references to the Golan village or city of Bethsaida and not to the far northern city of Sidon.

Before analyzing any of the traditions which can be attributed to Bethsaida in classical Rabbinic literature, serious textual criticism of the manuscript readings of these traditions must be made. The name בית צידה/א/ן (as found in Greek texts = Bethsaida or Bethsaidan) does not appear in Rabbinic texts for a variety of possible reasons.[21] Additional information about why Rabbinic texts may have used Tzaidan rather than Bethsaida can be summarized as follows:

1. In early Rabbinic tradition the name Bethsaida may have been contracted by local dialects (or scribal traditions) to ביציידן, which was further contracted to בצידן, צידן, and צידן.[22]

2. The final ן (nun) in צידן in Rabbinic texts of this period often indicates a profession.[23] Since the final ן (nun) (rather than צידה/א) is the equivalent of the בית in Beth-saida, the "Beth" is slightly redundant and may have been dropped in Rabbinic texts.

3. Rabbinic nomenclature for certain cities sometimes differed from the local Hellenistic custom. This may account for the differences in a city name as used by Josephus, the New Testament, or Rabbinic literature.[24]

4. The addition of a final ן (*nun*) in צידן (rather than צידה/א) and dropping of the "Beth" may be a result of the post-67-CE renaming of the city. Rabbinic traditions about the site are generally from the second and third centuries CE, after the site was damaged (or destroyed) in the war against the Romans. The fact that the rabbis do not use the full designation of Bethsaida (as it was known to Josephus and the New Testament) may indicate that the city was reinhabited in the second and third centuries and renamed simply צידן.

5. The Rabbinic name for the city, צידן, may preserve the name of the Josh. 19:35 city of צד (or הצדים). A Rabbinic traveler, Estori HaParhi, appears to have visited Bethsaida, according to his fourteenth-century chronicles of Galilee, and apparently called the site ציידן.[25]

Any of these reasons could account for the Rabbinic designation of the place as ב[י]צידן or simply צידן.

BETHSAIDA AND SIDON: THE BORDERS OF THE LAND OF ISRAEL ACCORDING TO THE RABBIS

After establishing by way of textual criticism the reading of a Rabbinic tradition, another factor for considering whether to associate a Rabbinic tradition with Bethsaida or Sidon is the content of that tradition. Classical Rabbinic sources would have considered Bethsaida to be within their sphere of influence (it was across the Jordan from the Galilee and on a major land route to Babylon). Making the same case for Sidon is not so simple. Although there was a Jewish community in Sidon during the period when classical Rabbinic literature was written (as evidenced from epigraphic data), the Rabbinic traditions found in the Mishnah–Tosefta, the earliest level of Rabbinic discourse, are concerned mainly with settlements in Judea, Samaria, and Galilee. The largest blocks of material in Rabbinic texts on the city of Sidon are either commentaries on Biblical references to Sidon or Rabbinic pairings of Tyre and Sidon, which were known in most ancient literatures.[26] Sidon is mentioned in the Bible, but it was not generally considered a part of the territory of ancient Israel (Judges 1:1). Although Sidon is mentioned in the NT,[27] it does not seem to be as significant to the NT Gospel writers as Bethsaida. In one instance, a Gospel writer (or manuscript tradition of the Gospels) may have confused Bethsaida with Sidon.[28] The status of Bethsaida in the writings of Josephus and in the NT demonstrate its importance to Jewish writers in the first century CE. Sidon may have been a well-known geographic location in the period, but the Gospel writers seem to indicate that the activity of Jesus and his Jewish supporters was centered in Galilee, the Golan, and Judea (or very close to its borders); their writings include Bethsaida, but not necessarily Sidon. This is crucial when considering the Rabbinic traditions of Bethsaida. Just as Josephus and the NT authors considered Bethsaida to be a place of significant Jewish activity in the first century CE, the city of Bethsaida, rather than the city of Sidon, also may have been the site of significant Rabbinic traditions.

Locating Bethsaida and/or Sidon on the borders of the Land of Israel is a complex problem. On the one hand, the Rabbinic borders of Israel for certain Rabbinic issues were different from the borders of the Land for other Rabbinic matters. On the other hand, Rabbinic sources (and their manuscript traditions) do not always agree about the names (and spellings) of the cities located on these borders. It seems that the farther, in time and space, the Rabbinic scribes were from the Land of Israel, the greater the errors in copying and interpreting. Most Rabbinic scribes of the medieval period lived in Babylon, North Africa, and Europe, and were unfamiliar with the historic geography (as we understand the discipline today) of the Land and were probably unable to detect (and correct) manuscript errors committed by an earlier generation of scribes. In addition, the question of the historical borders of Israel during the Biblical or Hellenistic periods according to non-Rabbinic materials is a complex one, since these sources had different audiences and addressed different issues than Rabbinic writings. These are only a few of the issues that affect modern investigation of the ancient city of Bethsaida.[29]

It is important to understand why Rabbinic texts might have developed confusion between the cities of Bethsaida and Sidon (or between any well-known Biblical cities) and about the historic borders of the Land of Israel. Although Bethsaida and Sidon were both fishing villages (and their names have a common Semitic root) their locations represent different assumptions about the borders of the Land of Israel. Divergent medieval Rabbinic interpretations of MT passages that concern the borders of the Land of Israel and the cities located within it may have been caused by scribal error, lack of knowledge about its historical geography, or by radically different assumptions about the historic borders of the Land of Israel.

While Greek, Roman, and early Christian literature contains information relevant to identifying the borders of ancient Israel, it must be recognized that its writing and preservation were subjective. Jewish Hellenistic (non-Rabbinic) literature as well as epigraphic data of the period is replete with references that complicate an understanding of the historic borders of the Land of Israel. In the Apocrypha, for example, there are a variety of possible borders for the Land of Israel. Citations from the books of the Testaments of the Twelve Patriarchs, Jubilees, Judith, and Maccabees, for example, would demonstrate that there was no agreement among Jewish Hellenistic writers over the historic borders of Israel; therefore, it is no surprise to discover that Rabbinic literature has a variety of designations. Unlike Jewish Hellenistic writers, however, Rabbinic writers established borders for the Land of Israel in relation to certain religious, economic, social, or political agendas which are logically consistent within classical Rabbinic literature but which are not particularly well known outside of the literature. Just as the rabbis seem to have had different reasons for categorizing time and the calendar year,[30] so too, they categorized the borders of the Land of Israel.

The Rabbinic classifications for the Land of Israel are significant when investigating a border town such as Bethsaida or Sidon. R. Sarason notes "that virtually every Mishnaic case involving the Land of Israel deals with issues of boundaries and confusion of boundaries, both spatial and social."[31] These borders were not necessarily intended to be politically defensible or representative of historical boundaries of any one kingdom or period, but rather represented issues which linked together Rabbinic communities of similar backgrounds and traditions. This literary and often mythic Rabbinic Land of Israel was a rallying point for Rabbinic decrees and a center for ethnic identification and fund-raising, and it seems to have preserved historical memories of a long and spiritually rich Biblical past. In short, it was a utopian vision of an optimal land. Despite the obvious problems, individual rabbis from the classical Rabbinic through the modern periods attempted to harmonize into one ideal view the borders of Israel and various geographic references cited in classical Rabbinic literature.

Three sources are generally employed for establishment of the Land of Israel according to the rabbis and are found in Sifrei Devarim, Par. Eqev, 51, Tosefta Shevi'it 4.7-11, and PT Shevi'it 36c. These sources and the manuscript versions of these accounts do not agree as to the exact borders and the names of the cities on the borders, and the differences likely represent more than just textual variants.[32] The latest of these sources, PT Shevi'it, is found with manuscript variants that suggest scribal unfamiliarity with the place names of Israel in later periods. The differences reflect the rabbis' approaches to various issues when discussing the borders of the Land of Israel. Some of the Rabbinic issues in which discussions of the borders of the Land of Israel are relevant include (a) the intercalculation of the calendar and the authority of the rabbis of Israel for informing the Diaspora (especially Babylonian Jewry) of the timing of various holidays, (b) the ritual purity laws in the Land of Israel versus those which continued in the Diaspora, (c) Biblically ordained agricultural laws with regard to the Seventh Year, tithing, etc.; many of these laws continued in effect inside, but not outside, the Land of Israel (even after the Destruction of the Temple), (d) Rabbinic divorce and marriage (especially Rabbinic divorces contracted outside the country which needed to be scrutinized by Israel's Rabbinical standards with regard to reliable witnesses), and (e) relations between non-Jews and non-Jewish laws and customs to Jews in the Land of Israel and in the Diaspora

Some Rabbinic Texts Relating to Bethsaida

After addressing difficulties of the Rabbinic traditions of Bethsaida it is necessary to categorize them. Of the Bethsaida references which I have been able to identify in classical Rabbinic literature up to the early medieval period, many are of a highly personal nature and relate to Rabbinic legal (halachic) observations made at Bethsaida. More than half of the halachic issues can be traced to some issue related to Bethsaida's location, while others can be generally traced to the issue of relations between Jews and non-Jews. Quite a few of the examples analyzed here begin with a descriptive setting linked to a historical example or precedent that uses the Hebrew word *maaseh*. Jacob Neusner describes this word as indicative of a form of narrative, as "What separates legal narratives from conventional, testimonial, and debate sayings is their historical focus, the reference in the past tense to a one-time action, ruling, setting, or event."[33] About this literary form, Gary Porton writes:

> Narratives are introduced by "it once happened [*maaseh*]." Often the narratives contain debates. The narrative seems to have been frequently used for transmitting sayings of the Patriarch Gamliel and his family and many of our narratives do discuss the Patriarchs.[34]

Some of the Bethsaida traditions are formulated as *maaseh* narratives. These *maaseh* narratives appear to be one-time, original statements of a historical fact, but it still does not mean that they can be relied upon for accurate historical information. Neusner remarks:

> It was the convention of Rabbinic historiography to invent dramatic "incidents" out of the evidence of conflict, and so to represent as a clash of personalities what was originally a difference, of some seriousness to be sure, in matters of law.[35]

It could be added that some of the most well-known *maaseh* narratives in Rabbinic literature involve historic figures from before the destruction of the Temple in Jerusalem in 70 CE.[36] Some of the Bethsaida materials are related to the famous Rabban Shimon ben Gamliel. Two rabbis called Rabban Shimon ben Gamliel appear in classical Rabbinic literature, one who lived in the first century CE and another who lived in the second. The dating of the sages mentioned in the Bethsaida traditions is significant because of possible correlations between datable archaeological information at the site and narratives about the site that are contained in Rabbinic literature. Systematic finds (coins, pottery, artifacts) at et-Tell that can be dated to the third century CE (Roman Provincial period), but not later, indicate some permanent occupation at the location during this period but not after. Both Rabban Shimon ben Gamliel I and II lived in the period before Bethsaida was finally abandoned, thus traditions concerning either one of these sages might be correlated with the datable archaeological finds.

Some of Rabban Shimon ben Gamliel's traditions are associated with the Galilee and the areas directly east and west of the Galilee so that the traditions regarding the far northern coastal city of Sidon are unusual in this context of Rabbinic historiography. Of course, many cases of tradition associated with Rabban Shimon ben Gamliel can be related to Sidon on the coast of modern Lebanon, but one wonders if they might not be exceptions to the norm. The traditions surveyed here are related in the language: בצידן (מעשה). The מעשה ב form for these traditions presents an opportunity for a critical study of the form: "It happened at a certain city." Athough a full study of this form is beyond the scope of the present work, some preliminary remarks about this *maaseh* form will help contextualize the מעשה בצידן traditions.

The *maaseh* form appears thousands of times in Rabbinic literature, but when the form is used with a named city and a named sage, it helps to define the scope of comparison. While even this specific city and sage *maaseh* form is found throughout Rabbinic literature, there are only a few groups which appear in the earliest and latest collections of Rabbinic literature. The appearance of *maaseh* traditions in the Mishnah is especially important since this is generally believed to have been redacted in Galilee. The מעשה בצידן traditions appear in the Mishnah, Tosefta, Midrashim, and both the PT and BT, and they provide independent and substantive traditions. Very few groups of specific city and sage *maaseh* form traditions appear in all of these collections. One such group of traditions is found in the form מעשה בצפורי, or "It happened at Sepphoris," traditions.[37] These traditions, similar to the "It happened at Bethsaida" traditions, involve the major Rabbinic figures of the period as well as precedents set at the city, but for different reasons. Most of the circumstances are not entirely unique but do involve legal precedents set because of an incident involving an often-unnamed individual or a group of individuals.

An example is a *maaseh* in Mishnah Baba Metzia 8.8 that involves Rabban Shimon ben Gamliel. An unnamed individual makes an agreement to pay twelve golden denar a year (at the rate of one denar a month) to rent a bathhouse; it turns out it is a leap year, with a thirteenth month (and thirteenth payment). The incident was resolved with the ruling that the tenant pay only half of a golden denar for the thirteenth month since the agreement was not clear about the leap year rent.

Another *maaseh* is described in BT Sukkah 16b in regard to Shabbat practice:

> . . . with regard to the incident which occurred at Sepphoris, on whose authority was it done? Not on the authority of R. Jose, but on that of R. Ishmael son of R. Jose. What was this incident? — [That concerning which] when R. Dimi came he related that on a certain occasion they forgot to bring a Scroll of the Law on the eve of the Sabbath. On the morrow, they stretched sheets over the pillars and brought the Scroll of the Law and read therein.

This incident juxtaposes two fundamental Jewish concerns: the sanctity of the Shabbat and the study of Torah. In this incident, a creative method for resolving the matter is implemented and both fundamental points are simultaneously maintained. Some of the precedents in these מעשה בצפורי involve unique circumstances (such as those mentioned above) coupled with the fact that the incident took place specifically in a city such as Sepphoris (with a large population of Jews and numerous Jewish dwellings and institutions in close proximity to one another). In short, the locale of the *maaseh* as well as the sages involved appears to have been relevant to the redactors.

While there are thousands of *maaseh* traditions in classical Rabbinic literature, very few can be classified as specific city and sage *maaseh* traditions which appear in all of these collections and provide independent and substantive references about a city. Of those *maaseh* traditions which fit all criteria, most involve cities in the historically defined Land of Israel (or in close proximity to Israel).[38] This is relevant to the investigation of the מעשה בצידן traditions. While it is true that the Talmudim contain traditions about some cities in Rome, Asia Minor, Babylonia, and Egypt,[39] it is difficult to find a group of independent and substantive *maaseh* traditions attested in Tannaitic literature and the Talmudim about these Diaspora cities. Although it is true that the presence of the מעשה בצידן and מעשה בצפורי traditions in Tannaitic literature does not guarantee their authenticity, the possibility of their being close to historic reality is greater when the traditions are attested in the major collections of classical Rabbinic literature. This brief analysis of the *maaseh* traditions reveals that it is more likely that the מעשה בצידן traditions relate to Bethsaida, a city located directly adjacent to the border of the historical Land of Israel, and not to Sidon, a city located far from the border of Israel.

Rabban Shimon Ben Gamliel and the Sages of Bethsaida

The Mishnah and Tosefta, or tractate, Gittin begins with the question of a man who brought a bill of divorce from outside the Land of Israel to be delivered to his wife in the Land of Israel. This section gives important information about the perceived borders of the Land of Israel in the time of the rabbis. There is a dispute among the rabbis as to the borders and places where a Get (Jewish divorce document) has been prepared. Some of these disputes involve the issue of reliable witnesses for the Get as well as "agent(s)" to deliver it to the woman. There are some questions involved in bringing a Get from the Diaspora to be delivered to someone in Israel because it usually necessitated the mediation of an acceptable and reliable agent who was sent to deliver it. The Tosefta has a number of other *maaseh* accounts that demonstrate legal precedents regarding questions of borders and jurisdictions.[40] In Tosefta Gittin, the Mishnah and Tosefta present the position of Rabbi Aqiva, who held that any writ is valid so long as it is drawn up in the registries of the Gentiles, even if it was signed by Gentiles. He includes in this ruling divorce and emancipation documents. The majority of the rabbis, however, did not hold this opinion. In defense of Rabbi Aqiva's position the Tosefta Gittin 1.4 states:

> Rabbi Eleazer the son of Rabbi Yosi said: Thus did R. Shimon ben Gamliel[41] say to them, *to the sages* בצידן : The sages did not disagree with Rabbi Aqiva on the issue of a writ drawn up in the registries of the Gentiles, that even though they were signed by Gentiles they were acceptable. Upon what they did they disagree? Or that they were prepared by an unauthorized person. Rabbi Aqiva declaring all such documents to be valid and the Sages declaring them all invalid, save only writs of divorce and of emancipation.

Tosefta Gittin 1.3 and 1.4 contain other legal precedents raised from cities in the Galilee (1.3, Kefar Sassai; 1.4, Kefar Othnai). This suggests first a question of precedents regarding locations but also suggests a question of the status of non-Jews in these cities.

The question of the relations between Jews and non-Jews appears to be the basis of some of the *maaseh* traditions from Bethsaida. In Mishnah Gittin 4.6, which deals with whether scrolls of the Torah, phylacteries, and mezuzot may be bought from non-Jews at more than their value, it is said to be possible "for the sake of amelioration of the world" (*Mipne Tiqqun Olam*). In the BT tractate commentary on this Mishnah in Gittin 45b, the tradition is quoted as having been made at בצידן, and that Rabban Shimon ben Gamliel permitted it. This BT section apparently quotes Tosefta Avodah Zarah 3.7:

> . . . *Maaseh B'Goy Echad.* . . . *BeTzaidan* בצידן—It happened that there was a non-Jew in Bethsaida who used to write scrolls of the Law (Sefarim) and the *Maaseh* (incident) came before the Sages and they said it was permitted to buy from him.

Another instance of specific policy set by Rabban Shimon ben Gamliel after an incident at Bethsaida is found in Mishnah Gittin 7.5:

[If a man says] this is your Get on condition that you give me two hundred Zuzim, she is divorced thereby and she has to give [him the money]. [If he says], on condition that you give [it] to me within thirty days from now, if she gives him within thirty days, she is divorced, but if not (not according to the thirty day stipulation) she is not divorced. Rabban Shimon ben Gamliel said: "*Maaseh BeTzaidan*—It happened BeTzaidan בצידן[42] that a man said to his wife, 'This is your Get on condition that you give me (back) my robe,' and his robe was lost, and the Sages said that she should give him its value in money."

A legal precedent concerning Jewish divorce was established by this *maaseh* at Bethsaida and related by Rabban Shimon ben Gamliel. The precedent established at Bethsaida and upheld by the sages allowed the issuing of a Get conditioned on the fulfillment of a certain exchange (of property), which could not ultimately be fulfilled (it was lost), and a replacement for the property was allowed (for the value of the item). The precedent itself is significant because Rabbinic literature frowned upon the introduction of conditional Jewish divorce agreements, and the condition in this case is even more problematic since it could not be fulfilled. This particular Bethsaida precedent became an issue among later redactors of the BT. All of the most ancient, complete manuscripts of the Mishnah examined agree that the incident took place at בצידן. Most of the locations mentioned in tractate Gittin of the Mishnah (especially regarding special stipulations of a Get) are directly adjacent to Bethsaida in the Galilee and not at a location so far away as Sidon. In the Amoraic commentary on this section in BT Gittin 75a a redactional statement is included which cancels this *maaseh* of Rabban Shimon ben Gamliel:

Rabbah bar Hanah said in the name of Rabbi Yohanan: Wherever Rabban Shimon ben Gamliel gives a ruling in our Mishnah, the Halachah follows him, save in the matters of Surety, and *Tzaidan* (וצידן), and of a later proof [evidence brought after the time allowed by the court]."

Redactional statements of this type are well known in the BT and are often transferred from an original context to another context. The original context of this statement is significant in this case since original manuscript readings of the Mishnah Gittin 7.5 established the place as Bethsaida (בצידן), and not Sidon. Unfortunately, this redactional statement appears in eight places in the printed versions of the BT[43] as וצידן (but in printed and manuscript versions of this tradition in PT Baba Batra 17d, it is (וציין); it could be translated (and understood) as "Sidon."[44] The later medieval commentaries of the BT[45] understood the וצין reference to mean that the mishnaic precedent of Rabban Shimon ben Gamliel found in Mishnah Gittin 7.5 was not to be accepted as Jewish law. Even though all the printed versions of medieval commentaries apparently cite Mishnah Gittin 7.5, it is cited as וצידן instead of בציין in the eight places in the BT where this redactional statement appears. This raises the question of when and how the text was corrupted from בציין to וצין, but such an investigation is beyond the scope of this chapter.[46] If one includes these eight references together with the other BT Bethsaida references collected during this research, Bethsaida (and not Sidon) emerges as a city of regular activity for traditions about or by Rabban Shimon ben Gamliel.

Now that it is possible to say that ציין was a place of regular activity for Rabban Shimon ben Gamliel, how does one establish that this is ציין by the Sea of Galilee? One tradition about Rabban Shimon ben Gamliel which establishes the location of ציין near the Sea of Galilee (and not on the Mediterranean coast) appears in PT Sheqalim, chapter 6.2, 50a, which presents information about the administration of the Temple in Jerusalem and about the types of ceremonies associated with it. In describing the Water Gate to the city of Jerusalem, discussion turns to the question of water sources in general and more specifically to the lakes and rivers of Israel. There are a few contextual indicators in this section as well as a Rabbinic play on words which alludes to Bethsaida as a place of swamps. The section begins with a citation from Ezek. 47:8ff. and a Rabbinic play on words. The same section is found in Tosefta Sukkah 3.9, to discuss the rivers and lakes of Israel, but without the Rabban Shimon ben Gamliel Bethsaida tradition. Thus, it may represent an ancient Tannaitic tradition and interpretation of Ezek. 47. Ezek. 47:8 is usually translated: "And he said to me, this water flows [אל גלילה קדמונה] towards the eastern region and goes down into the Arabah; and when it enters [footnote *i* in RSV: *into the sea, to the sea*] those that were made to issue forth, the water will become fresh." While Ezekiel was not necessarily giving a geographic but rather a nostalgic and symbolic look at the Land of Israel from his perspective in exile, Biblical citation in Rabbinic literature is a common vehicle used to express relevant information about the life and times of the rabbis. The rabbis in PT Sheqalim, however, use the verse to develop their understanding of the water resources of Israel. The opening words of Ezek. 47:8, גלילה קדמונה, are interpreted—through the use of Rabbinic wordplay on homonyms and synonyms—to mean "[to the] Galilee eastward," making the translation of this section: "And he said to me, this water [the Jordan] flows [אל גלילה קדמונה] towards the Galilee eastward and goes down into the Aravah." If so, the PT Sheqalim section (as well as the Tosefta Sukkah section) refers to the movement of the Jordan River from its northern sources southward towards the Dead Sea. The PT Sheqalim section continues:

a. "The water [the Jordan] flows towards the Galilee eastward"; this refers to the Sea of Semcho[Semechonitis: another name for Hulah Lake in antiquity]. "And it goes down into the Aravah"; this refers to the Sea of Tiberias. "And it enters the sea"; this refers to the Salt Sea. ". . . to the sea [whose waters] were made to issue forth"; this refers to the Great Sea. [47]

b. "There is no problem in understanding why the Great Sea and the Salt Sea should be included [in this verse] since it is to show [demonstrate] their waters are sweetened [by the river water], but as to the Sea of Tiberias and the Sea of Semcho [what is the reason to include them in this verse?]. It is included because of the many fish that are in them [the Sea of Tiberias and Lake Semechonitis as opposed to the river itself], concerning which it is written [referring to Ezek. 47:10], ". . . its fish will be of very many kinds. . . ."; very many kinds of fish [are found there].

c. It has been taught [in this regard]: Rabban Shimon ben Gamliel said, "*Maaseh Shehalachti LeTzaidan* [לציידן]." "It happened that I went to Tzaidan, and they put before me more than three hundred kinds of fish in a single dish."

d. [It is written in Ezek. 47:8] ". . . and its waters will be healed . . ." [and it is also written in Ezek. 47:11] "But its swamps[48] and marshes will not be healed; they are to be left for salt." It is written, "And its waters will be healed," and yet you have said, "And they will not be healed?" There is a place which is called, "And they will not be healed."

As we analyze the different part of this tradition, we see, first, that the interpretation of how the Jordan flows is paralleled elsewhere in Rabbinic literature[49] and in Josephus. In his description of the Lake of Gennesaret in *JW* 3.10, Josephus writes:

Now Jordan's visible stream arises from this cavern, and divides the marshes and fens of the Lake Semechonitis: when it has run another one hundred and twenty furlongs, it first passes by the city Julias, and *then passes through the middle of the Lake of Gennesaret. . . .*[50] [Emphasis mine.]

The second part of this section explains that the waters of the Sea of Galilee and the Hulah Lake are singled out by Ezekiel because, similar to the Jordan Rvier, they contain fresh water. The section then points out that these fresh water lakes were singled out in this verse because of the large number of fish in them.

The third part of this section brings a *maaseh* tradition from Rabban Shimon ben Gamliel to complement (and bolster) the reasoning established in the first two sections. In order for this tradition to be effective, Tzaidan must be located in the area of the Sea of Galilee and Hulah Lake. Rabban Shimon ben Gamliel's personal knowledge of many types of fish at Tzaidan is used here to prove that the observations made in the first two parts of the section are correct and that there is a place in this area of the Sea of Galilee and Hulah Lake which still contains "very many kinds." It is interesting that instead of noting the size or quality of the fish it states: "more than three hundred kinds of fish in a single dish." These would appear to be very small fish, which might fit the tradition which held that this place was shallow and perhaps swampy.[51]

The last part of this section, like the opening, contains an unattributed discussion in which no names of scholars are mentioned. It is the continuation of the interpretation begun in the first part of the section. This anonymous statement is about an apparent contradiction between the verses from Ezek. 47:8 and 47:11. This discussion is not a freestanding interpretation of the apparent contradiction between these verses, but an inquiry into whether the cited *maaseh* tradition of Rabban Shimon ben Gamliel at Tzaidan reconciles these verses or not. On the one hand, Ezek. 47:8 states that it is a place whose "waters will be healed," while the Ezek. 47:11 text holds that "its swamps and marshes will not be healed."

The "healed or not healed" question seems to allude to whether the water is fit for fishing or not. This may be the key to understanding other ancient literary information about Bethsaida and the connection to geographic and geological investigations at the site. A Rabbinic story (such as the Rabban Shimon ben Gamliel *maaseh* tradition) is often told to bolster the interpretation of Biblical texts. In this case, it is concluded that the tradition of Rabban Shimon ben Gamliel fulfills both contradictory parts of the verses from Ezekiel 47. Tzaidan is a place whose waters will be both "healed" and yet "not healed." It is full of fish and yet contains "swamps and marshes." The anonymous discussion makes use of an apparent Hebrew play on words between the words *BeTzaidan* (Bethsaida) and *Betzotav* (Hebrew for "its swamps") to demonstrate the connection between Tzaidan and the verse in Ezekiel. Wordplay is a common interpretive device in Rabbinic literature to draw connections between diverse elements.[52] This section of PT Sheqalim uses wordplay in both its opening and closing.

The Rabbinic information gleaned from this section about Bethsaida being a place of marshes and swamps is significant because of the geological investigations which confirm the presence of marshes and swamps north of the Beteiha plain (in front of et-Tell) some two thousand years ago.[53] Greco–Roman literary traditions of the period also confirm this information. Strabo specifies that the Jordan waters "a country that is fertile and all productive. It also contains a lake which produces the aromatic rush and reed; and likewise marshes. The lake is called Gennesaritis."[54] Josephus' *Life* refers to there being a marshy area in front of Bethsaida (where he was injured) and that it was possible to sail directly from Tericheae to Bethsaida.[55] One of the Greek terms used by Josephus to describe the area in front of Bethsaida in *Ant* 18.28 is προς λιμνη τη Γεννη–σαριτιδι; the word λιμνη, one way of referring to a small pond or lake, is also a well-known Hellenistic word for marshy lands or standing water.[56]

Fishing traditions relating to Bethsaida are well known from Tannaitic texts and it is often possible to locate the traditions based on the juxtaposition with Bethsaida of other named locations in a particular Rabbinic tradition. One finds, for example, in the Tannaitic Sifrei Devarim 4.39: "He taught that the fish which comes from Akko is as good a taste as the fish which comes up from Tzaidan (צידן) and that those fish are not as good as the fish which comes from Banias (Panyas)."

The dating of this and other fishing traditions with Bethsaida is important if we are to understand what may have happened to the water resources there and what may have contributed to their decrease. The description of Bethsaida as a place of "swamps and marshes" is confirmed by literature of the period and by geological investigations of the Beteiha plan and the et-Tell site. The fact that this discussion in the PT Sheqalim is portrayed as being anonymous may also tell us something about the way Bethsaida was seen in the period of the Rabbinic redactors of the PT in the early fifth century CE. Often, later sections of Rabbinic discussions which used earlier named traditions and discussions would appear as anonymous discussions,[57] which indicates that this PT Sheqalim discussion is

probably of an earlier date. Bethsaida was a place which in the time of
Rabban Shimon ben Gamliel (second century CE) still produced fish, but
the fact that these waters were "swamps and marshes [which] will not be
healed," may allude to the decline of the site during the period of the final
redaction of the PT (fifth century CE).

RABBI SHIMON BEN YOHAI

Another important second-century-CE teacher (and contemporary of
Rabban Shimon ben Gamliel), a student of Rabbi Aqiva, is Rabbi Shimon
bar (or ben) Yohai, who became a significant figure in later Rabbinic writings.[58] Works such as the Geonic (eighth to eleventh centuries) *Nistarot de
Rabbi Shimon bar Yohai* and the thirteenth-century mystical *Zohar*, were attributed to him because of the earlier corpus of Rabbinic stories and traditions about him. Earlier Rabbinic literature associates his life with some
nonconformist Rabbinic ideas and lifestyles. As a disciple of Rabbi Aqiva,
for example, Shimon bar Yohai was openly opposed to the Roman government and, according to some Rabbinic sources, after the failed Bar Kokhba
Revolt he practiced an ascetic lifestyle, living in a cave with his son for
thirteen years. It is this paradigm of asceticism and personal charisma
which, although not considered normative in Rabbinic tradition, set Rabbi
Shimon bar Yohai apart from other rabbis in classical Rabbinic literature.
Rabbi Shimon is also associated with Bethsaida. *Song of Songs Rabbah*
relates:[59]

> There we have learned on Tannaitic authority: If one has married
> a woman and lived with her for ten years and not produced off-
> spring, he has not got the right to stop trying. Said R. Idi, It hap-
> pened at Bethsaida [מעשה באשה אחת בצידן] that one who married a
> woman and stayed with her ten years and they did not produce
> offspring. They came before R. Shimon ben Yohai and wanted to
> be parted from one another. He said to them, "By your lives! Just
> as you were joined to one another with eating and drinking, so
> you will be separated from one another only with eating and
> drinking." They followed his counsel and made a festival and
> made a great banquet and drank too much. When his mind was at
> ease, he said to her, "My daughter, see anything good that I have
> in the house! Take it and go to your father's house." What did she
> do? After he fell asleep, she made gestures to her servants and
> serving women and said to them, "'Take him in the bed and pick
> him up and bring him to my father's house." Around midnight he
> woke up from his sleep. When the wine wore off, he said to her,

"My daughter, where am I now?" She said to him, "In my father's house." He said to her, "What am I doing in your father's house? But I have nothing in the world as good as you!" They went to R. Shimon ben Yohai and he stood and prayed for them and they were answered (and given offspring). This serves to teach you that just as the Holy One, blessed be He, answers the prayers of barren women, so righteous persons have the power to answer the prayers of barren women.

The tradition about this childless couple of Bethsaida and the miraculous intervention of Rabbi Shimon is interesting because of other miracle stories associated with the site in the NT. Procreation was valued highly in Rabbinic literature, and if a couple did not have children after ten years of marriage they were permitted to separate.[60] Although such a tradition is not universally accepted by the rabbis, this *Shir HaShirim* account uses the tradition to demonstrate the power of Rabbi Shimon ben Yohai in a particular case. Miracles performed by rabbis are not unusual, but the power to help childless couples procreate is generally reserved in Rabbinic tradition to direct Divine or angelic intervention, as witnessed by Rabbinic exegesis of Biblical narratives about childless couples that are found in Genesis and elsewhere. In the *Shir HaShirim* midrash, however, it is stated that Rabbi Shimon ben Yohai had the power (through prayer) to intercede on behalf of childless couples. While the use of prayer in this manner is not unique in Rabbinic literature, it may be a significant factor in this story. Perhaps it is important that the power of prayer by Rabbi Shimon ben Yohai is associated with Bethsaida.

Now that it can be said that צידן was a place of regular activity for Rabbi Shimon ben Yohai, how does one establish that this צידן is located in the Golan and not on the coast of the Mediterranean Sea? Although it is well known that Rabbi Shimon's main area of activity was in the Galilee, one tradition in particular reveals that he was also active in border towns of the Golan. As mentioned, the Diaspora was considered by some Rabbinic sources to be ritually impure. Since for some (but not all) Rabbinic issues the Jordan River was the line of demarcation between the Land of Israel and the Diaspora, many questions relating to borders were decided by individual precedents. The Mishnah of tractate Ohilot 18.7 relates:

If a man bought a field in Syria that lies close to the Land of Israel and he can enter it in ritual purity (there is a corridor of land which is just over the border and touches his land), it is ritually pure (and considered as if it were a part of the Land of Israel even though it is not), and it is subject to the laws of Tithes and Seventh Year produce; but if he cannot enter it in ritual purity it is deemed impure. . . ."

Tosefta Ohilot 18.2 contains supplementary and complementary data about the traditions mentioned in Mishnah Ohilot 18.7. In general, the role of the Tosefta is to provide a follow-up or additional information to the Mishnaic presentation of a topic they both discuss. While the language of the Mishnah and Tosefta will be similar, the Tosefta will usually employ its own style and choice of vocabulary for the topic. With regard to the Tosefta Ohilot 18.2 passage, the Tosefta relates its information in similar language but provides amplification:

> (a) 18.2: "The land of the Gentiles"—if one can enter it in ritual purity, it is ritually pure. And how near must it be so that one may be able to enter it in ritual purity? Rabban Shimon ben Gamliel says: "Even a single furrow intervenes."

> (b) Rabbi Shimon said, "I can make it possible for priests to be fed with ritually pure food [even] in the tannery [בצדון][61] and in the villages of Lebanon[62] because they are near the sea or the river."

> (c) They said to him: "The fish pools [פסנין)][63] intervene."

> (d) 18.3: The assumption concerning roads taken by immigrants from Babylonia, even though they are surrounded by the land of the Gentiles, is that they are ritually pure.

> (e) 18.4: Cities surrounded by the Land of Israel, for example Susita and the villages around it, Ashkelon and the villages around it, even though they are free of tithe and of the rule of the sabbatical year, are not subject to the law governing the land of the Gentiles.

The tannery mentioned in (b) must have been an important element in the historical memory of the city, since it appears in other places in Rabbinic literature. It is possible that in a large city such as Sidon a single tannery may have stood out for the rabbis, but it is more likely that this tannery was located in a much smaller village or city, such as Bethsaida in the Golan. It also appears because of logistical, contextual, and text-critical arguments found in Rabbinic literature.

In PT tractate Avodah Zarah 1.10, 40b, and in Mishnah Ketubot 7.10, traditions relating to tanners and a tannery of בצידן are found.[64] In major manuscripts of the Mishnah Ketubot 7.10 tradition it is בציידן. The

Rabbi Shimon tradition which is used by Tosefta Ohilot 18.2 is an example of a place near the border of Syria (mentioned in the Mishnah) where one could enter the Diaspora in a ritually pure state. This location appears to be near the Jordan River and close to where fish pools were found. The location of this Rabbi Shimon tradition, therefore, is probably Bethsaida, and not Sidon.

The other traditions found in (d) and (e) confirm that eastern land routes that bordered Galilee and the Jordan are meant, and not the northern border with Tyre and far northern Sidon. The land route to Babylonia passed north and east of Bethsaida, and Susita is one of the Decapolis cities around the Sea of Galilee. The logistical, contextual, and text-critical arguments found in these traditions demonstrate that the famous tannery of the rabbis was located in Bethsaida, and not in Sidon, and that Rabbi Shimon was acquainted with the city of Bethsaida.

The Mishnah Avodah Zarah 3.7 (3.12 in manuscripts) continues in a similar demonstration of the type of events which occurred at Bethsaida in which Rabbi Shimon was involved:

What is an Asherah? Any tree under which is located an idol. Rabbi Shimon [ben Yohai] says: "Any [tree] that people worship." *Maaseh BeTzaidan* [בצידן]—It happened at Bethsaida, there was a tree that people worshipped, and they found a pile of stones underneath it. Rabbi Shimon said to them, "Investigate the type of pile of stones." They did investigate it and found an image in it. He said to them, "Since they are worshipping the image [and not the tree], let us permit them to make use of the tree"'

This passage, similar to the *Shir HaShirim* midrash passage above, shows that some event occurred at Bethsaida and Rabbi Shimon was involved in the event. In this case, the question is whether a tree (or wooden object) which was worshipped by Jews at Bethsaida was considered to be a Biblical Asherah. In Rabbinic texts, the category of pagan worship was often defined by the interpretation of historical examples of paganism in the Hebrew Bible. Most of the Rabbinic examples of paganism are connected with the Land of Israel since it was impossible to impose rules upon foreign nations. In the Bible, for example, one historical example is the worship of Asherah, whose symbol was a tree. Asherah worship was one kind of pagan worship forbidden in Biblical times. By the Roman period, Asherah had long since been replaced by other symbols of pagan devotion. According to Rabbinic interpretation, however, paganism included both the ancient and recent symbols. If the tree was determined to be a focus of paganism, it was forbidden for use by Jews, and should be destroyed. In this case, Rabbi Shimon takes pains to ensure that the issue of this particular tree of Bethsaida was resolved without having to destroy it. The fact that the tree has stones at the bottom and an image in the pile of stones may indicate that the tradition here is not referring to a freestanding or planted tree, but to some wooden post with stones to keep it upright. The Hebrew word for tree could correspond to a wooden cross as well.[65] If so, this "tree" may not be a living tree but some early Jewish Christian devotional wooden object associated with the Cruxificion.

According to the letter of the law, worship of a freestanding or planted tree was forbidden, but here Rabbi Shimon allows the tree to be used as a devotional symbol (or cross). It is not clear what image was found in the pile of stones, but through clever interpretation the rabbi does not declare the tree to be forbidden. It is possible, of course, that this tradition alludes to early Jewish Christians at Bethsaida who used a wooden object as a symbol of devotion, but no distinction is made between these "people" (in the Mishnah) and Jews at Bethsaida. The religious practice of the Bethsaida residents seems to be an issue (here and elsewhere) for the rabbis, but Rabbi Shimon finds a way of not designating it as pagan or Asherah worship, and the issue is defused. A secondary issue not directly apparent in this passage is whether this possible *Avodah Zarah* (pagan worship) is taking place in an Israelite/Jewish city in the Land of Israel (or in close proximity to the Land) or in the Diaspora, where such practice was obviously expected. Again, Sidon was a non-Israelite, non-Jewish city that clearly stood outside the Land of Israel; therefore, the relevance of the tradition in connection with Sidon is questionable. In the case of Bethsaida, however, the possibility of paganism in a city with a Jewish population close to the borders of the Land of Israel would be of great importance and worthy of Rabbi Shimon's intervention.

OTHER MAASEH BETZAIDAN RABBINIC TRADITIONS

NON-JEWISH WITNESSES AND REMARRIAGE OF WIDOWS

Another *maaseh* tradition involving Tzaidan (and indirectly Rabban Shimon ben Gamliel) concerns the sage Abba Yehuda of Tzaidan, who may have met with other sages at Bethsaida. BT Yevamot 122a begins by citing Tosefta Yevamot 14.10:

(a) *Abba Yehudah Eesh Tzaidan* [צידן] related: *Maaseh*—It once happened that an Israelite and an idolater went on a journey together, and when the idolater returned he said, "Alas, for the Jew who was with me on the journey, for he died on the way and I buried him (along the way)." And (the Israelite's) wife (on this evidence) was allowed to marry again.

(b) Rabban Shimon Ben Gamliel said "*Maaseh*—It happened that a group of men were going to Antioch and a idolater came and stated, 'Alas for that group of men, for they died and I buried them,' and (based on this evidence) their wives were permitted to marry again."

(c) Moreover, it happened that sixty men were going to the camp of Bethar and an idolater came and stated, "Alas for sixty men who were on the way to Bethar, for they died and I buried them," and (based on this evidence) their wives were permitted to marry again.

These three traditions form a unit and are apparently used to bolster a more lenient policy toward the acceptance of non-Jewish witnesses in Jewish courts regarding the remarriage of widows, who according to Rabbinic law had to provide acceptable evidence that the first husband was dead before a second marriage could take place. The rabbis had developed the requirement, based on Biblical citations, that two witnesses were necessary for evidence to be acceptable in a Jewish court. Furthermore, acceptance of non-Jews as witnesses before a Jewish court was a difficult question among the rabbis. This question is problematic because it involves not only one non-Jewish witness, but also the important issue of personal status—remarriage—by a widow.

Case (a) involves one Jew and a lone non-Jew who went together on the unspecified journey. The case is resolved by the testimony of the non-Jew. The fact that the first tradition is associated with Abba Eesh Tzaidan—who is not a rabbi—may be significant. Perhaps the incident took place at a border location or was of interest to one who, like Abba Eesh Tzaidan, may have been giving advice in a frontier town.[66]

The first case connects well with the second tradition, which is more problematic. A non-Jew provides information about a group of Jews who are killed on their way out of the country, but had not yet reached the border (lending itself to a Bethsaida location). One needs to examine closely each element of this tradition. Although it involves the testimony of only one person, who is a non-Jew, and permission for widows to remarry, it differs from the first in several respects. There is one non-Jew reporting the deaths of an entire group of Jews; the group was still in the Land of Israel, having not yet reached the border; and no doubt Rabban Shimon ben Gamliel's name is associated in this tradition because of its importance.

The third unnamed tradition that involves leniency toward non-Jewish evidence is an event associated with the Bar Kokhba war. Most of the fighting during this war took place in Judea, and Bar Kokhba's last fortress was in Bethar. Again, one non-Jew is bearing witness to multiple deaths in order to allow widows to remarry. The journey in this tradition is apparently within the country, and mention of Bethar, the final seat of the second revolt against the Romans of 135 CE, seems to be noteworthy. The mention of Bethar is important since so many Jewish women were widowed in this war and because the relations between Jews and Romans were especially strained during this period. One of the amazing parts of this tradition, therefore, is that it is alluding to a non-Jew bearing witness in a Jewish court at a time when Jews had only recently been defeated in their war against the Romans. This *maaseh* highlights one attitude among the Rabbis which accepts non-Jewish evidence even under the most difficult of circumstances. Rabban Shimon's appearance here confirms his agreement with such a practice and may be linked to other Bethsaida traditions which also confirm this attitude.

Rabbinic standards for marriage and divorce continued to be a question at this location. In this case, in the Mishnah of tractate Gittin 4.7 a solution is proposed which resolves the difficult problem of remarriage after divorce:

> Rabbi Yose the son of Rabbi Yehudah said: "*Maaseh BeTzaidan* [בצייד]"[67]—A case happened *Betzaidan* of a man who said to his wife, "*Qonam* (a type of vow formula) if I do not divorce you," and he did divorce her. And the sages permitted him to remarry her—all this for the good order of the world (*Tiqqun Olam*).

The commentary on this section in the BT tractate Gittin 46a–b states:

> Gemara: . . . what has preceded this should be given as an illustration [the different vows of the wife are given and now an instance of a vow by the man]. There is a lacuna, and the Mishnah should say this: These rules apply only in the case where the wife vowed, but if he vowed he may remarry. And Rabbi Yose Ben Rabbi Yehudah adduced a *Maaseh BeTzaidan* [בצידן] (a case which happened

Betzaidan) of a man who said to his wife *"Qonam* (a type of vow formula) if I do not divorce you," and he did divorce her. And the sages permitted him to remarry her—all this for the good order of the world (*Tiqqun Olam*). What *Qonam* is there here? Rabbi Huna said: We suppose he said: "Every species of produce shall be forbidden to me if I do not divorce you."

Tiqqun Olam is a well-known Rabbinic device for resolving questions in which the social, political, or economic demands of a period required the radical reshaping of a tradition despite there being no extant textual precedent that might direct this change. If this is the case with Bethsaida, it could indicate that the demands of the social situation of the locale dictated such a change. This correlates with other information from the Rabbis regarding this city.

Relations between Jews and Non-Jews at Bethsaida
The unique social situation of Bethsaida might be revealed by the archaeology of the et-Tell site. The small finds such as a *strigilis* (Roman body scraper), stamped jar handles with Greek inscriptions, and pieces of imported Eastern Terra Sigillata pottery indicate that the population had ties to Greco–Roman culture and life and may also indicate the extent of the non-Jewish population. Although the common ware pottery is of the type associated with the Rabbinic settlement of Kefar Hananya and some Jewish coins point to the settlement having Jewish inhabitants, most finds indicate strong ties with non-Jewish life and customs. This physical data shows a mixture of Greco-Roman elements with some Jewish influences and is quite revealing, given the number of Rabbinic references to Bethsaida which are connected with the relations between Jews and non-Jews there. Some examples follow.

Rental of Houses. The relations between Jews and non-Jews at Bethsaida is alluded to in the PT tractate Avodah Zarah 1.10, 40b, which discusses rental practices of Jews to non-Jews. The Rabbis use the example of a situation in nearby Syria where Jews rent out land and spaces to Gentiles in or next to their own residences, despite the problems which may arise from such a close connection. The PT continues:

In a place in which it is customary to sell [houses to a Gentile], one sells him even a residence or rents him even a residence. Rabbi Aha, Rabbi Tanhum bar Hiyya in the name of Rabbi Eleazar

ben Rabbi Yose said, "and even a small stall, for example, like the
BeTzaidan [בצידן] Tannery.'"[68] It is therefore not the end of the
matter that one may rent out the entire house, but even a single
room [in a house].

The implication of this story is that Gentiles and Jews together live in the
same large house. This is a very different view of Jewish and Gentile relations than one finds in the rest of the tractate Avodah Zarah.

RITUAL IMPURITY AND FETUSES. Another *Maaseh BeTzaidan* Rabbinic tradition in the Tosefta Niddah 4.6 relates:

> *Maaseh BaEeshah Echat BeTzaidan* [בצידן][69]—It happened at Beth-
> saida—that three times a woman produced an aborted fetus
> shaped like a raven, and the matter came before the Sages, and
> they said, "Anything which does not bear human form is not
> deemed a fetus."

The issue of an aborted fetus was raised by the rabbis for a number of reasons. On one level this question relates to ritual impurities, and that is the
reason why it appears in tractate Niddah. Jewish laws regarding the birth
of children (and the status of an aborted fetus) and the ritual impurity of
the mother after birth had to be considered. If a women bore a fetus
which did not have human form it was not a human being; therefore, the
woman's period of impurity was shorter than if the fetus was considered
a human being. On another level, however, this relates to a fundamental
definition of life, a matter of some importance to the rabbis which may
tell us something about the views held by the rabbis and the residents of
Bethsaida. It seems that the rabbis divided the life of the fetus into three
stages. According to some Rabbinic texts, in the first stage (for the first
forty days) a fetus was not considered human. In the second stage, as the
fetus gained some resemblance to human form in the womb it gained
some status, but was still not considered to be human. Finally, in the birth
process the fetus achieved human status. The definition of a second-stage
fetus, which did not bear human form nor have any "human" rights, was
developed by some Jewish Greco-Roman and Rabbinic sources. Most Rabbinic traditions, however, held that a fetus did not possess full rights until
it had emerged from the birth canal.[70]

The question is complex for a number of reasons related to Jewish
ritual purity laws. First, there is the issue of impurities incurred by priests
and others who come in contact with a dead body (if an aborted fetus is

considered a human being). Laws concerning contact with women who were impure by virtue of birth were different from laws concerning women who were impure by virtue of a miscarriage. According to some Rabbinic traditions, if all aborted fetuses were considered to be human dead bodies then the homes of Jews and non-Jews would be constant sources of ritual impurity. The determination of the status of a fetus is therefore connected, indirectly, to Jewish–Gentile relations. This matter is discussed at considerable length in the Mishnah of Ohilot 18. The ruling of the Tosefta Niddah 4.6 regarding the raven-shaped fetus seems to indicate that the sages attempted to create a precedent at Bethsaida that would allow Jews and Gentiles to come in contact with one another without constant fear of ritual defilement.[71]

SCRIBAL ARTS. Another major issue in some Bethsaida traditions in classical Rabbinic literature concerns the scribal arts. Again, as in the case of the Avodah Zarah references above, the behavior of some Bethsaida residents (perhaps Jews or even Jewish Christians) came under suspicion. In this case, it was the writing of certain benedictions that contained the Divine name. BT Shabbat 115b states:

> Our Rabbis taught: Benedictions and amulets, though they contain letters of the [Divine] name and many passages of the Torah, must not be rescued from a fire [on the Sabbath] but must be burnt where they lie, they together with their [Divine] names. Hence it was said: they who write down benedictions are as though they burnt the Torah. *Maaseh Beachad shehayah kotev BeTzaidan* [בצידן]—It once happened that someone was writing [professionally for amulets and such, the Divine name] at Betzaidan. Rabbi Yishmael was informed thereof, and he went to question him. As he was ascending the ladder, he [the writer] became aware of him; he took a sheaf of benedictions and plunged them into a bowl of water. In these words did Rabbi Yishmael speak to him. "The punishment for the latter (diluting in water the benedictions) is greater than the former (writing down the benedictions in general)."

This account may correspond to a similar text mentioned above in the Tosefta Avodah Zarah 3.7.

Apparently, both Jewish and non-Jewish scribes were involved in the writing of texts used by the Jews. In the Tosefta cited above, we have unusual language in that it just says "someone" and does not indicate whether the writer was a Jew or non-Jew. The implication here is that this "someone" who was engaged in the scribal arts was writing something suspicious in the texts and therefore Rabbi Yishmael was checking his work. The final dictum of Rabbi Yishmael would be relevant only if the scribe was a Jew, since erasing the Divine name in benedictions was a violation of Rabbinic law.

Conclusions

Bethsaida was a well-known settlement in northern Israel during the Hellenistic–Roman periods as witnessed by the number of references to it in ancient literature. It is surprising that little has been written about this settlement in Rabbinic sources. In most recent Rabbinic literature, one or two names are mentioned which represent Bethsaida. It is clear from this investigation that sages were acquainted with traditions from this site in the Golan, and this raises an even larger issue. The history of the Jews of the Golan has yet to be written, especially with regard to the early first- and second-century settlements such as Bethsaida. Recent surveys of the ancient Roman road system in the eastern Galilee indicate that a Roman road led almost directly from the clearly Rabbinic sites such as Kefar Hananya[72] through Chorazin to Bethsaida. This road no doubt carried trade between Kefar Hananya and Bethsaida during the Greco-Roman period.[73] The relationship between the Galilee and Golan needs to be fully investigated in order to fully understand the history of Rabbinic Judaism in this period. Twenty-five archaeological sites in the Golan have produced Mishnaic and Talmudic evidence—Rabbinic names, inscriptions, and so forth[74]—but most of these sites have only third- and fourth-century-CE remains associated with them. Investigations into the material culture of first- and second-century Golan Jewry, similar to investigations into the material culture of Galilean Jewish society of the same period, may reveal differences and similarities between the literature of the rabbis and the material culture of the area.

Rabbinic and NT archaeological studies of the region should include as many sites from this period in the Golan as possible and not disregard a site simply because it does not have clearly identifiable Rabbinic remains.[75] The Rabbinic passages which relate to Bethsaida are illustrative of problems involved in tracing Golan Jewish life in general; the names and nature of the settlements were not well known to early medieval and premodern writers. Despite the fact that so little is known about Bethsaida in the Roman period, some preliminary observations regarding Bethsaida in Rabbinic literature can be made.

1. Sidon and Bethsaida Rabbinic traditions have been connected by medieval scribes. This is certainly the case with the teachings of Rabban Shimon ben Gamliel and others of the first and second centuries CE. One must be careful in using manuscripts, however, since Bethsaida was not a familiar city to the rabbis after approximately the third century CE. The fact that both Sidon and Bethsaida were located near large bodies of water with potential for fishing was perhaps confusing for later Babylonian teachers and scribes. It is possible, however, to separate some independent Bethsaida passages on the basis of proximity to other geographical Galilean cities, and to identify Bethsaida in contextual and substantive questions in the different traditions.

2. Bethsaida does not appear to have been a major Rabbinic settlement but was the site of some Rabbinic precedents of the first and second centuries CE. Perhaps because of its proximity to the borders of the Land of Israel and its easy access by traffic to and from Babylonia and Palestine, Bethsaida seems to have gained some notoriety among the rabbis. Bethsaida would have had significance for the rabbis even without its fishing industry because of Rabbinic concerns about the borders for certain halachic issues such as tithing, divorce, ritual purity, and the sanctity of the Land of Israel.

3. Rabbinic traditions associated with Bethsaida were in general agreement with Rabbinic standards of the period concerning ritual purity, marriage, and divorce. Precedents cited in these traditions vary only in degrees of observance but indicate circumstances which necessitated individual rulings. In some of these rulings, relations between Jews and non-Jews seem to play an important role.[76]

4. On the question of why there was no continued Rabbinic settlement at Bethsaida in the fourth and fifth centuries, when other areas of the Golan flourished, the history of the region as well as the geology and archaeology of Bethsaida may provide certain answers. In the second-century, the region of Jezreel and the Golan where our site is located was leased to Patriarch Rabbi Judah I by imperial decree. This arrangement seems to have continued through the mid–third century.[77] By the latter part of the third century, however, there appears to have been a shift in power from the patriarch to a wider circle of rabbis in Caesarea and with it perhaps a change in the fortunes of those areas under the patriarch's control. Politically, a shift in the fortunes of the area occurred when in

260 CE the Palmyrene leader Odenathus was put in charge of the Roman Orient, including Palestine, and ruled there until 266 CE. Only in 273 CE did the Roman Emperor Aurelian take back this region for Rome. It appears that early on the rabbis saw the Palmyrene leaders as more sympathetic to them than the Roman leaders,[79] and when the Roman leaders came back into power in 273 CE a shift may have occurred away from the former leadership of the area to a new group in Caesarea. In any case, as Michael Avi-Yonah notes in *The Jews Under Roman and Byzantine Rule*, "In the first generation of the crisis (200–230) the numbers of Jewish villages in the Golan and Bashan fell below the number of city communities. In the second generation (230–260) the same process appears among the Jewish communities in the coastal plain. . . . In Galilee itself a decline can be observed only in the last stages of the crisis (260-290)." Included in this political and demographical change might be the border town of Bethsaida whose fortunes may have declined after the death of the Patriarch Judah I in the third century CE.

5. Bethsaida's decline in importance seems to have been slow. The archaeological strata of Bethsaida are rich in the Hellenistic and early Roman period. Finds from the second century CE are smaller in number, and the last systematic archaeological finds come from the third century CE. The decline of the site appears to coincide somewhat with a decline in Rabbinic literature. The largest number of Rabbinic traditions are from the first and second century CE, with only a few from third century CE sources. The existence of Bethsaida, a site known to the rabbis of the Roman Provincial period (and the period of early classical Rabbinic literature), which was close to Galilee and which contained a mixed Jewish and non-Jewish population, seems to be present in both the historical literature and the physical data.

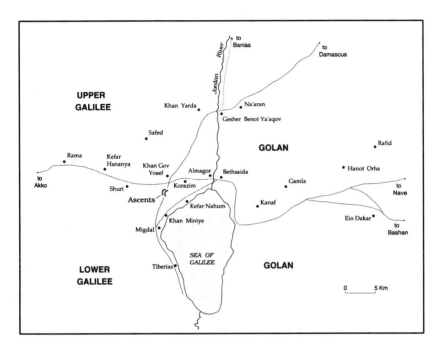

Cities of the Rabbinic Period

CHAPTER NOTES

1. The classical period of Rabbinic literature usually covers the first through third centuries CE.

2. New Testament archaeology, as defined in this book, deals not only with the fixed canon of the New Testament but also includes evidence from first-century Judaism and the rise of early Christian traditions. The writings of Flavius Josephus and Philo Judaeus about Israel's cities and peoples in the Greco–Roman period might also be included. I was introduced to New Testament archaeology and Talmudic archaeology in graduate school with the now classic 1981 paperback book by Meyers and Strange 1981.

3. Rabbinic archaeology (sometimes called Talmudic archaeology) is concerned primarily with the towns and cities, individuals and events that are mentioned in Rabbinic literature, which was redacted between the third and tenth centuries CE.

4. See under Literature Cited, for this chapter.

5. At present, no complete critical edition of the Babylonian Talmud exists. Because of its widespread use during the Middle Ages throughout Jewish communities, many hundreds of thousands of variant readings could be established from the comparison of the extant manuscripts. Rabbinovicz 1867–1886 collected some of the variants in fifteen volumes (a sixteenth volume was completed later). This work contains only a part of the entire Babylonian Talmud, and while certainly a groundbreaking labor at the time it contains serious methodological problems by current standards.

    Many of the manuscript fragments predate the complete manuscripts, and their deciphering and recording are only recently underway. Although critical editions of the Hebrew Bible and New Testament exist, only partial attempts have been made, in individual tractates, to create a critical edition of the Babylonian and Palestinian Talmudim. Extensive research and comparison is needed to determine if the text has been corrected, censored, or "updated," or if is simply difficult to understand. Hundreds of thousands of medieval manuscript fragments (eighth to fifteenth centuries) have been found, in various parts of the world, which preserve readings that differ from the standard printed editons.

    The Palestinian Talmud (so-called Talmud HaYerushalmi or Jerusalem Talmud, although not written in Jerusalem) exists in one almost complete manuscript, Codex Scal. no. 3 from Leiden. It is medieval in origin even though internal evidence in the Palestinian Talmud assumes completion in the fifth century CE. Although completed before the Babylonian Talmud, the Palestinian Talmud is shorter and historically was not viewed to be as authoritative as the Babylonian Talmud. sometimes its Aramaic dialect is obscure; sometimes it is unintelligible. It, too, contains many problemantic elements of redaction and language, and it is missing many books of commentary for unexplained reasons. For details, see Strack 1980, 65–66. Presently, the Palestinian Talmud has complete discussions (*gemara*) on only thirty-nine tractates. The Babylonian Talmud has *gemara* for only thirty-six-and-a-half tractates, but the scope of the Babylonian Talmud's discussions is much greater that that of the Palentinian Talmud.

6. A definition of the type of critical analysis of Rabbinic texts being suggested here is presented in Halivni 1963: "Source criticism seeks to differentiate between the original statements as they were enunciated by their authors and the forms they took as a consequence of being orally transmitted; that is, between the sources and their later traditions.... Source criticism claims that the transmission of the Talmud was not, and perhaps could not have been, verbatim, and that the text became altered in transmission, with the result that many statements in the Talmud have not come down in their original form. Instead, what survives is the form assumed in the last phase of transmissional

development. While such a study is pertinent to most ancient texts, it is particularly relevant to the Talmud, which primarily consists of quotations and their interpretations."

7. Three works (Neusner 1962, 1970, 1984) from different periods of the vast library of Neusner's writings on this subject will suffice.

8. Neusner 1987, 2:143–144.

9. There were perhaps two scholars of this name, the first one of the early Tannaitic sources in the pre-70 CE era, and the other a contemporary of Rabbi Aqiva in the 2d century CE. The sources are found in BT Shabbat 96b; Sifrei Devarim, 12.29.

10. Tannaitic Sifrei Devarim, Reeh 80:4.80, p. 146, in Finkelstein 1969; see Finkelstein, Sifrei commentary and notes there for the other citations of this tradition.

11. In some Rabbinic definitions of the Land of Israel, Akko was its northernmost border; e.g., the tradition in BT Ketubot 112a records that R. Abba would kiss the stones of Akko when he arrived there from the Diaspora.

12. In the printed editions צידן, but the Munich manuscript has צ״ידן; see Rabbinovicz 1976, 1,Tractate Eruvin 37a note 3.

13. In the MT, Sidon appears fourteen times as צידון with full vowels in the books of Joshua, Judges, II Samuel, Isaiah, Jeremiah, Ezekiel, and I Chronicles, and as צידן twice in Genesis. It is found as צידון in much of the Aggadic Midrashim and in Tannaitic works, such as Tosefta Demai 1.10, Mechilta Parsh. Bo, chap. 18 (beginning) and Sifrei Numbers Parsh. Naso, chap. 42 (end).

14. Printed editions of Mishnah Kiddushin 4.14.

15. Even more complicated is the designation "to Bethsaida," which should be: לבצײדן but may have been further contracted or corrected simply to לצײדן.

16. Tosefta Tohorot 8.11 (Erfurt manuscript).

17. Stack, 79, writes: "...in consequence of the repeated confiscations and foolish destructions of Jewish manuscripts by fire only a very small number of ancient Talmud copies are extant."

18. Ibid., 77 ff.

19. Oppenheimer 1991, 148, 154.

20. Segal 1979, 160–161.

21. Although in PT Yevamot 10a, 12c, and PT Nazir 56c there is a Rabbi Yosi Tzaidania (צײדנייה), and in PT Brachot a (צײדנײא) and also perhaps (Rabbi Yosef) in the BT Ketubot 46a in the Munich manuscript. The full reading of Bethsaida with בית was either contracted to בי (perhaps just ב) or was entirely disposed of by later Rabbinic tradition. This was a common Rabbinic technique. The town of בית זיהא is rendered in Rabbinic texts as ביזיהא, and sometimes as just בזיהא. See Jastrow 1976, 160. For some of the most common words, such as Beth Kenesset, בית כנסה (synagogue), for example, some Rabbinic manuscripts (and printed versions) have only בכנסה (Mishnah Eruvin 10.10). See also Aharoni 1979, 98, which notes that when the Septuagint translators transliterated certain Biblical city names to the Greek, they omitted the בית.

22. The addition of a final ן (nun) in Tzaidan may also be the result of local dialect changes or a scribal aid. The town of Sepphoris is written in most texts as צפורי, but is sometimes found in the PT as צפורין. Weak letters such as the א/ה/י seem to have attracted the final nun for a variety of reasons. The city of Caesarea (קיסריא) is found in many Rabbinic texts as קיסרין.

23. The addition of the final *nun* indicates a profession. Hence, rabbi is rabban; thus Rabban Gamliel and Rabban Shimon ben Gamliel. The Hebrew word *gan* (garden) can be made into *ganan* (gardener; see Yoma 5.6); *seder* (order) became *sandran* (collector; see BT Pesahim 105b), *pilpulan* (dialectic) can be made into נאלפּלפּ (dialectician; see PT Horayot

48c). The addition of the word בית during the Second Temple period may indicate certain professional activities that took place at the location as well.

24. Some city names were prefixed with בית and used universally during the entire Greco–Roman period by the entire Jewish population, while in some cases the בית was dropped at some point during the period or was not used by all segments of the Jewish population. Since it was only in the Second Temple period that the designation בית was added to some city names (which formerly did not have the designation בית before their names). For example: Gilgal (Deut. 11:30, Josh. 4:19, 5:9–10, etc.) and Beth-Gilgal (Neh. 12:29); Succoth (Gen. 33:17, Josh. 13:27, and other references) and Beth Socoth (Hieronymus, *Quaest.* in Gen. 53:8); see Avi-Yonah 1984, 167. It is possible that the Rabbinic custom differed from Hellenistic custom in this case. It is also possible that the designation בית was not always maintained by all Rabbinic traditions. The Biblical city of בית עמק (Josh. 19:27), for example, apparently became Kefar Amiko in Talmudic tradition; see BT Taanit 21a. The Rabbinic place name Beit Harodo (or, Harodan) in the Mishnah Yoma is referred to as simply Haradana in the Muba'arat documents of second century CE; ibid., Avi-Yonah 1984, 104, 226.

25. *Estori HaParhi* 1897, 286, states that in the 14th century CE, he visited a place near Tanhum (Capernaum), north of Ginnosar and south of a place he called Achbara, which he called צידין.

26. *Anchor Bible Dictionary, s.v.* Sidon; Rabbinic pairings such as BT Shabbat 19a and Pesahim 50b.

27. Matt. 11:21-22, 15:21; Mark 3:8, 7:24, 7:31; Luke 4:26, 6:17, 10:13-14. The pairing of Tyre and Sidon in most of these references apparently is literary. Mark 3:8; Luke 6:17, 10:13-1;, and Matt. 11:21–22; 15:21 do not provide any substantive information on Sidon. The other Mark references are suspect, as is the Luke 4:26 reference because of the context of Galilee there. See also the next footnote.

28. Mark 7:31 states: "Then he returned from the region of Tyre, and went through Sidon to the Sea of Galilee, through the region of the Decapolis." The reading of Sidon does not appear to be correct (and is not maintained by all NT manuscripts). Sidon is north of Tyre, and a route from Tyre to Sidon to the Sea of Galilee which would reach the region of the Decapolis is quite convoluted. The addition of "Sidon" above this in Mark 7.24 was probably based on its common pairing with Tyre and may have caused the confusion here. Some NT manuscripts omit Sidon there as well.

29. Other issues are raised by the use and interpretation of Biblical passages by medieval Rabbinic sources. To their credit, it should be noted that these interpretations sometimes preserve ancient traditions which need to be considered in modern investigations of the historical geography of the area. Unfortunately, these medieval interpretations contain much extraneous information which has little bearing on the historical geography of the ancient Land of Israel. In the MT, for example, there are cities which have the same name in different regions of the country. If one is unfamiliar with the regions of the country (as were most medieval interpreters) the interpretations of some MT episodes will be affected. In the MT there are cities such as Beth Shemesh, Qadesh, Hazor, Achziv, and Bethlehem in different regions of the country. In the MT, a city called Beer Sheva is located in the north and in the south of the country, and there are a number of cities called Hamat. Some similarity in city names is perhaps related to their similar roles (fortress, oasis, holy site, etc.) in antiquity, but their significance is often obscure. Some city names were changed totally, or new names ascribed to them based on episodes described in the MT. This last category also touches on the question of the redactional time periods present in the MT which is reflected in the naming and renaming of these places. The various borders of ancient Israel indirectly or directly referenced in the MT books of

Genesis, Numbers, Deuteronomy, Joshua, Judges, Samuel, Kings, Psalms, Ezekiel, Chronicles (and elsewhere) are not easily harmonized. Attempts at harmonization were made by Rabbinic interpreters throughout the Middle Ages, often with uneven results. Some Rabbinic interpreters in the Middle Ages limited the borders of the Land of Israel to a small area (similar to present day borders), while other interpreters extended the borders of the Land of Israel (some, north to parts of modern Turkey and east to the Persian Gulf). The names of border towns in antiquity and the understanding (and reconciling) of various approaches to the question of borders of the ancient Land of Israel are not the major thrust of this chapter.

30. Mishnah Rosh HaShanah 1.1.
31. Sarason 1986, 112.
32. See Feliks 1976, 812: 31-50, for discussion of this, and Klein 1965. Lieberman 1973 2:533 ff., in his discussion of Tosefta Shevi'it 4.11, also investigates the changing names in Rabbinic literature.
33. Neusner 1973, 3:23–24..
34. Porton 1988, 130.
35. Tosefta Nez. 4.7 and BT Sotah 33a concerning Simon the Just, Shemaiah, and Abtalion in Mishnah Eduyot 5.6, Yohanan the High Priest in PT Sotah 9.13, Hillel the Elder in Tosefta Sotah 13.3, Hillel and Shammai in Tosefta Hagigah 2.11, and Rabban Gamliel I in Tosefta Shabbat 13.2, Tosefta Sanhedrin 2.6.
36. Neusner 1984a, 91.
37. Mishnah Baba Metzia 8.8; Tosefta Shabbat 16.8; Tosefta Megillah 2.4; Tosefta Sheviit 4.13; Tannaitic Sifrei Devarim, Haazinu; Finkelstein 1969, 358. PT Peah 20b; PT Sheviit 39d; PT Terumot 45c; PT Yoma 43c; BT Yoma 12b; BT Sukkah 16b; BT Moed Qatan 21a; BT Eruvin 86b; BT Yevamot 64b; BT Baba Metzia 102a-b; BT Baba Batra 105a and 171a; Bereshit Raba 14.7; Vayiqra Raba 5.6.
38. Other examples are Lod בלוד מעשה in Mishnah Taanit 3.9; Tosefta Taanit 2.13, Tosefta Hagigah 2.13; Tosefta Sukkah 1.1; PT Sukkah 51d and 53a, PT Taanit 66a and 70d; BT Rosh Hashanah 18b; BT Sukkah 2b; BT Taanit 19a and 25b; BT Hagigah 18a and with Beth Shean בבית שאן מעשה-in Mishnah Avodah Zarah 1.4 and 4.12; Tosefta Avodah Zarah 8.3; PT Avodah Zarah 39d; BT Avodah Zarah 12b and 60b, for example.
39. Levine 1989, 66
40. BT Gittin 6b on Tosefta 1.3: "Maaseh Beahad Mekephar Sassai" (or Sasi/Sami manuscript readings of Tosefta and Yerushalmi Gittin 1.5). According to Lieberman 1973, pt. 8, p. 784, n. 34, *Maaseh* is *Pesaq* or halachic ruling.
41. Erfurt manuscript. In the Babylonian Talmud Gittin, 11a, just Rabbi Shimon. Y. Epstein, in Epstein 1977, pt. 2, p. 1199, who writes that there are cases where the Rabbi Simon who is mentioned in the Mishnah is Rabban Shimon ben Gamliel, and cites our case as an example of the BT. Lieberman 1973, 786, establishes it as Rabbi Shimon (ben Yohai); Rabbi Eleazar was a part of Rabbi Shimon's group, ibid., n. 38.
42. In the Mishnacodex Kaufmann A50, the oldest surviving complete manuscript of the Mishnah, the Mishnah Codex Parma manuscript (De Rossi 138), Codex Parma C manuscript (De Rossi 984), the so-called Lowe manuscript at Cambridge University, and the PT Leiden manuscript of the Mishnah 7.5 all read: בצידן.
43. This is an editorial statement and is repeated verbatim in eight locations in the BT: (1) BT Ketubot 77a, (2) BT Gittin 38a, (3) BT Gittin 75a, (4) BT Baba Qamma 69a, (5) BT Baba Metzia 38b, (6) BT Baba Batra 174a, (7) BT Sanhedrin 31b, and (8) BT Bekhorot 24a. In these verbatim statements, the almost superfluous conjunction ו in וצידן is suggestive of a possible oral transmission problem between an undotted ב and the conjunction ו (בצידן). The statement itself seems to indicate an editorial familiarity with a corpus of

decisions issued by Rabban Shimon ben Gamliel at "ציד" which are unusual in that they are not accepted as representative enough of the traditions of the time to be deemed normative, although they were seen as being worthy of preservation.

44. Both the Soncino English translation of the Babylonian Talmud (1930s) and the recent *Talmud of Babylonia: An American Translation* translate this as "Sidon."

45. Eleventh and twelfth centuries; see for example, the Rashi and Tosefot on BT Ketubot 77a, Baba Metzia 38b, and Baba Batra 174a, l.c. וצידן.

46. Since the most ancient complete (surviving) Mishnah manuscripts cited above are also from the 10th and 11th centuries, it is possible that the reading וצידן may itself be medieval or the product of later printing errors. An in-depth investigation of medieval commentary manuscripts might reveal this, but it outside the scope of the present work. See also Rabbinovicz 1976, 1: reference to Tractate Eruvin 37a, n. 3, which demonstrates that the manuscript reading of this BT tradition (as well as Rashi and other medieval commentators) was צידן.

47. Although generally the Rabbinic use of "the Great Sea" usually means the Mediterranean Sea, in some contexts it appears to be a more generic Rabbinic name for large bodies of salt water. In this case, the proximity between the Salt Sea and the Great Sea as well as the link between them and the Jordan River (which is not linked to the Mediterranean) indicate that perhaps the Gulf of Eilat (directly south of the Dead Sea) is meant here; see, e.g., BT Baba Batra 74b.

48. The Tosefta Sukkah 3.9, according to S. Lieberman 1973, 268, has the following manuscript readings for "its swamps," בצאתיו בצותיו ביצותיו. In the Leiden manuscript it has been emended to read בצ‎אתיו. This word for "its swamps," however, pronounced in Hebrew "Betzotav," is perhaps a play on words for the name of the place: Betzaidan. In BT Sanhedrin 5b , this same type of "error" or wordplay occurs: It says, "Upon inquiry, they told him that a certain scholar on a visit taught them: Water of *bize'im* [swamps]."

49. BT Baba Batra 74b; BT Bekorot 55a. The rabbis identified Gennesaret as a place where small dwellings were built seasonally, but not as a place of permanent residence (perhaps because of the rising water table?); see Mishnah Maaserot 3.7

50. Elsewhere in Josephus, *JW* 3.57, 4.456, "Sea of Tiberias." Pliny, *Natural History,* 5.71, calls it the Lake of Gennesaret and [Lake of] Tarichaeae.

51. Although not an exact parallel to this account, the NT miracle of the Feeding of the Multitudes (which is said in Luke 9 to have occurred at Bethsaida) demonstrates that large numbers of fish traditionally were associated with the site.

52. For an analysis of this technique see Eilberg-Schwartz 1987, 765–790.

53. See the chapter by J. F. Shroder and M. Inbar in this volume.

54. Strabo in Stern 1976, 288.

55. Josephus, *Life,* secs. 71–73.

56. *S.v.* λιμνη Liddel-Scott 1977.

57. On the question of anonymous Talmudic discussions see Halivni 1986, 66–92.

58. Other citations include Rabbi Shimon ben Yohai: Tosefta Parah 4.9 and (BT Niddah 52b) Tosefta Niddah 6.6

59. *Song of Songs Rabbah* 1.4:89 ff.; *Pesikta De Rav Kahana,* 1:327 cites this event as well: מעשה בצידן.

60. BT Yevamot 64a and BT Ketubot 77a.

61. This is the reading of the Erfurt manuscript according to the Zuckermandel 1970 edition of the *Tosephta,* which does not list any other variants for this reading.

62. The reading is supposed to be: שבלבנון, "which is in Lebanon." The reading "Lebanon" is a possible reconstruction but is not actually found in the manuscripts of the Tosefta. The Erfurt codex reads שבלבוב, and the Vienna codex, שבלבנו.

63. The Tosefta reads פסנין, a word with no apparent parallel which appears to be in need of some reconstruction. It should perhaps read פסקין, which could be the naturally occurring pools mentioned by commentators of Alfasi on BT Moed Qatan 4b. See Jastrow 1976, *s.v.* פיסקינות, which points to the Latin *piscina* (reservoir, swimming bath or fish tank).

64. The mention of the tannery at Bethsaida may be linked with the comments in NT Actgs 9:43 and 10:6 since in the latter citation Peter is lodging with Simon, a tanner, whose house is by the seaside.

65. Mishnah Sanhedrin 6.4 and in BT Sanhedrin 43a and 67a (with regards to Jesus HaNotzri and Ben Stada) found only in *Diqduqei Soferim* reconstructions from manuscripts.

66. As discussed above, *Maaseh* is used in Rabbinic literature to describe a whole host of individuals and situations from the earliest levels of Rabbinic literature. One finds, for example, in Mishnah of Sheqalim 5.1 a number of different traditions from the time of Second Temple in Jerusalem that use the *maaseh* designation. *Maaseh U'badaq Ben Zakkai*, or *Maaseh U'badaq ben Azzai BeUqtzei Tannaim* demonstrate early traditions when perhaps the designation of rabbi was not yet current in the first century. A sage such as Abba Eesh Tzaidan or another designation, Abba Gurion of Tzaidan (Tzaidan is spelled in printed versions as ציד) also without the title rabbi might indicate its antiquity or the nature of the source (not an official Rabbinic figure). A Mishnah in Kiddushin 4.14 relates: "Abba Gurion of Tzaidan said on the authority of Abba Guria: One should not teach his son [to be] an ass- driver, camel driver, waggon-driver, sailor, shepherd, or shopkeeper, because their profession is the profession of robbers."

     Another tradition involving this scholar is found in a late midrashic source. In Midrash Abba Gurien on Esther: "Abba Gurien related 5 things in the name of Rabban Gamliel (the whole section is in Palestinian Aramaic; Rabban Gamliel is probably the 2nd Rabban Gamliel from 90–130, who was the son of Rabban Shimon ben Gamliel): "From the time that the false judges became many, the false witnesses became many"; "From the time that many different traditions became many, the wealth of violent/cruel people has multiplied"; From the time that insolent people has increased, glory was taken from God's creatures"; "From the time that a younger person says to an older person: 'I am greater than you,'the life of human beings has been cut short."; "From the time that beloved children angered their Father who is in Heaven, there has been placed upon them a wicked king."

67. See above for discussion of this Mishnah.

68. This tannery is interesting since another Sidon reference in the Mishnah of Ketubot 7.10 includes a *maaseh* regarding the ability of a woman to refuse a Levirate marriage with a tanner, despite the fact that her husband had been a tanner: "It once happened [בצידן] that a tanner died and had a brother who was a tanner. The Sages said . . . She may say: Your brother I could endure; but you I cannot endure."

69. Although the reading here is written: בצידן, in Tosefta Niddah 6.6, Hananiah ben Hakhinai is found at בציידן Betzaidan.

70. The issue of whether or not the fetus possessed human form seems to be a category developed from Greco–Roman standards which was adapted by some Jews. The Samaritans, the early Christian Didache, and the Karaites developed this view while the rabbis generally did not. Philo, *The Special Laws*, 7:545, clearly holds this standard when he writes: "If a man comes to blows with a pregnant woma,; and strikes her on the belly and she miscarries, then, if the result of the miscarriage is unshaped and undeveloped, he must be fined both for the outrage and for obstructing the artist Nature in her creative work of bringing into life the fairest of living creatures, man. But, if the offspring is already shaped and all the limbs have their proper qualities and places in the system, he

must die..."; but this law was not maintained by most Rabbinic sources. See Mishnah Ohilot 7.6; BT Sanhedrin 72b (and especially the 11th-century commentator Rashi), and Maimonides, a 12th-century codifier of Jewish law, in his *Mishneh Torah;* "Laws on Murder" 1.9. For an extensive investigation of this question, see Freund 1990.

71. Another tradition related to this question from Abba Yehudah Eesh Tzaidan ציד in Tosefta Ohilot 18.7 seems to indicate that scholars from Bethsaida were particularly concerned about how to deal with this issue.

72. Recent studies reveal that there were centers of Jewish pottery making in the Galilee, such as Kefar Soganeh, Kefar Hananya, and Kefar Shihin. See the groundbreaking study of Adan-Bayewitz 1993, which contains many of the Rabbinic materials regarding these cities.

73. See Zvi Ilan 1993, 14–16, and fig. 1 of this chap.

74. See the map in Levine 1989, 100. Bethsaida is not included on the map!

75. Ibid., 98.

76. For example, Tosefta Parah 2.1 has a tradition where a non-Jew (named Duma; בצידן) possessed the famous "Red Cow" (whose ashes were used in purification rituals), and the rabbis allowed his animal to be used .

77. BT Berachot 43a; Rabbi Jeremiah in PT Avodah Zarah 41c.

78. Avi Yonah 1984b, 122.

79. Ibid., 126.

Literature Cited

Adan-Bayewitz, D. 1993, *Common Pottery in Roman Galilee.* Tel Aviv: Bar-Ilan Press.

Avi-Yonah, Michael. 1984a. Historical Geography of Palestine. Jerusalem (in Hebrew).

————. 1984b. *The Jews under Roman and Byzantine rule : A Political History of Palestine from the Bar Kokhba War to the Arab Conquest.* New York: Schocken; Jerusalem: Mangus.

The Babylonian Talmud. 1935–1948. 35 vols. Ed. I. Epstein. London: Soncino Press.

Berliner, Abraham. 1884. *Beiträge zur Geographie und Ethnographie Babyloniens im Talmud und Midrasch.* Berlin: Gorzelanczyk.

Derenbourg, Joseph. 1986. *Essai sur l'Histoire et la Géographie de la Palestine d'après les Thalmuds et les autres sources Rabbiniques.* Paris: Imprimie Imperiale.

Eilberg-Schwartz, Howard. 1987. Who's Kidding Whom? A Serious Reading of Rabbinic Word Plays. *Journal of the American Academy of Religion* 55.4: 765–790.

Epstein, Shimon. Y. 1977. Mavo LeNusah HaMishnah, pt. 2. Tel Aviv: Dvir.

Estori HaParhi in the Sefer Kaftor vaFerah. 1897. A. M. Luncz, ed. Jerusalem, 1897.

Feliks, Y. 1976–1981. *PT Tractate Shevi'it* (Hebrew). (Jerusalem: Magnes. Vol. 2.

Finkelstein, L. 1969. *Sifrei-Deuteronomy.* New York: Jewish Theological School of America.

Freund, Richard. 1990. The Ethics of Abortion in Hellenistic Judaism, chap. 14 of *Understanding Jewish Ethics,* vol. 1. New York: Mellen.

Halivni, David Weiss. 1963. *S.v.* Talmud: Source Criticism, in *Encyclopedia Britannica* 31.

————. 1986. *Midrash, Mishnah, and Gemara: The Jewish Predilection for Justified Law.* Cambridge, Mass.: Harvard University Press.

Ilan, Ziv. 1993. Eastern Galilee, Survey of Roman Roads, in *Excavations and Surveys in Israel,* vol. 9. Jerusalem: The Israel Antiquities Authority.

Jastrow, Marcus. 1903. *A Dictionary of the Targumim, The Talmud Babli and Yerushalmi, and the Midrashic Literature.* Reprinted: Jerusalem, 1976.

Klein, Samuel. 1909. *Beiträge zur Geographie and Geschichte Galiläas.* Leipzig.

Klein, S. 1965. "The Boundaries of Eretz Israel According to the Tannaim," in *Studies in the Geography of Eretz Israel.* Jerusalem: Magnes.

Kraus, Samuel. 1910–1911. *Talmudische Archaeologie.* Leipzig: G. Fock.

_____. 1922. *Synagogue Altertümer.* Berlin: B. Harz.

Levine, L. I. 1989, 66. *The Rabbinic Class of Roman Palestine in Late Antiquity.* New York: JTSA.

Liddel, Henry George, and Robert Scott. 1977. *A Greek-English Lexicon.* Oxford: Clarendon Press.

Lieberman, Saul. 1973. *Order Zeraim,* vol. 2 of *Tosefta Ki-fshuta: A Comprehensive Commentary on the Tosefta,* 7 vols.. New York: Jewish Theological Seminary of America, 1955-1982.

Macmillan Bible Atlas, 3d ed. 1993. Ed. Y. Aharoni, M. Avi-Yonah, A. F. Rainey, Z. Safrai. New York: Macmillan.

Mandelbaum, Bernard. 1962. *Pesikta de-Rav Kahana: Al pi ketav yad Oksford, ve-shinuye nushaot....* Ed. Bernard Mandelbaum. New York: Jewish Theological Seminary of America. Bet ha-midrash le-rabanim sheba-Amerikah.

Meyers, Eric M., and James F. Strange. 1981. *Archaeology, the Rabbis, and Early Christianity.* Nashville: Abingdon.

Neubauer, Adolf. 1868. *La Géographie du Talmud.* Paris: Michel Levy frères.

Neusner, Jacob 1962. *A Life of Yohanan ben Zakkai.* Leiden: Brill.

_____. 1970. *Development of a Legend: Studies on the Traditions Concerning Yohanan ben Zakkai.* Leiden: Brill.

_____. 1971. *The Rabbinic Traditions about the Pharisees before 70,* 3 vols. Leiden: Brill.

_____. 1984a. *In Search of Talmudic Biography.* Chico, Calif.: Scholars Press.

_____. 1984b. *The Talmud of Babylonia: An American Translation.* 1984-. Brown Judaic Studies. Trans. Jacob Neusner. Chico, Calif.: Scholars Press.

_____. 1987. *Understanding Seeking Faith,* vol. 2. Atlanta: Scholars Press.

_____. 1989. *Song of Songs Rabbah: An Analytical Translation.* Brown Judaic Studies 197-198. Atlanta: Scholars Press.

Obermeyer, Jacob. 1929. *Die Landschaft Babylonien im Zeitalter des Talmuds und des Gaonats.* Frankfurt am Main.

Oppenheimer, Aharon. 1991. *ha-Galil bi-tekufat ha-Mishnah Yerushalayim [Galilee in the Mishnaic Period].* Merkaz Zalman Shazar le-toldot Yisrael.

Pesikta de-Rav Kahana: al pi ketav yad Oksford, ve-shinuye nushaot... / im perush u-mavo me-et Dov Mandelboym. 1962. Ed. Bernard Mandelbaum. New York : Bet ha-midrash le-rabanim sheba-Amerikah.

Porton, Gary. 1988. *Goyim: Gentiles and Israelites in Mishnah-Tosefta.* Atlanta: Scholars Press.

Rabbinowitz, Raphael Nathan. 1867-1886. *Sefer dikduke sofrim: Im hagahot nikraot divre sofrim* [Variae lectiones in Mischnam et in Talmud Babykonicum ...]. 15 vols. in 8. Manachii: H. Roesl, E. Huber.

_____. 1976. *Sefer Diqduqei Soferim.* Reprinted New York: M.P. Press.

Sarason, R. 1986. The Significance of the Land of Israel in the Mishnah, in *The Land of Israel: Jewish Perspectives,* ed. L. Hofmann. Notre Dame: Notre Dame Press.

Segal, B. 1979. *Geography in the Mishnah* (Hebrew). Jerusalem, Machon Marot HaMishnah.

Song of Songs Rabbah: An Analytical Translation. 1989. Jacob Neusner. Brown Judaic Studies 197-198. Atlanta: Scholars Press.

Stern, M. *Greek and Latin Authors on Jews and Judaism,* vol. 1. Jerusalem: Monson Press.

Strack, H. L. 1980. *Introduction to the Talmud and Midrash.* New York: Atheneum.

Philo, *The Special Laws.* 1958. Trans. H. St. J. Thackeray. London: Heinemann, 1958.

The Talmud of Babylonia: An American Translation. 1984-. Brown Judaic Studies. Trans. Jacob Neusner. Chico, Calif.: Scholars Press.

Zuckermandel, M. S.. 1970 [730]. *Tosefta: al pi kitve yad Erfurt u-Vinah : im mareh mekomot ve -hilufe girsaot u-maftehot.* Jerusalem: Sifre Vahrman.

Contributors

MARK APPOLD, TH.D.
Professor of Religion and History
Truman State University

RAMI ARAV, PH.D.
Director of Excavations
Bethsaida Excavations Project
University of Nebraska, Omaha

BARUCH BRANDL, M.A.
Curator of the State Collection
Israel Antiquities Authority

SANDRA FORTNER, M.A.
Ph.D. Candidate
University of Munich, Germany

RICHARD A. FREUND, PH.D.
Professor of Religion
University of Nebraska at Omaha

JOHN T. GREENE, PH.D.
Professor of Religious Studies
Michigan State University

MOSHE INBAR, PH.D.
Professor of Geography
Haifa University

HEINZ-WOLFGANG KUHN, TH.D.
Professor of New Testament
University of Munich

JOHN J. ROUSSEAU, PH.D.
Research Associate
University of California, Berkeley

JOHN F. SHRODER, JR., PH.D.
Professor of Geology
University of Nebraska at Omaha

FRED STRICKERT, PH.D.
Professor of Religion
Wartburg College

TONI TESSARO, M.A.
Ph.D. Candidate
University of Tennessee, Knoxville

Bibliography

Bethsaida in Greek and Roman Literature

Josephus, Flavius. *Works*, English & Greek, 1958–. Loeb Classical Library. 9 vols. Cambridge, Mass.: Harvard University Press; London: W. Heineman, 1958–1965. See: *Ant.* XVIII.28; XVIII.2:1, 4:6; *Wars* II.9:1; III.3:5, 10:7; IV.8:2; *Life* 71.

Pliny. *Natural History*, V.15:15.

Ptolemy. *Geographia*. [*Claudii Ptolemaei geographia*]. Ed. Carolus Fridericus Augustus Nobbe. Editio stereotypa. Lipsiae: Sumptibus et typis Caroli Tauchnitii, 1843-1845.

Bethsaida in Pilgrims' Accounts

Abbas, Daniel [Naqshabandi, Usamah Nasir; Abbas, Zamya Muhammad], ca. 1106. *Khitrowo*. x

Bonifacius de Stephanis (1551–1564). *Liber de Perenni cultu Terra Sancta*.

Burchardus de Monte Sion [13th cent.] *Burchard of Mount Sion: A.D. 1280*. Tr. from the original Latin by Aubrey Stewart ; with geographical notes by C. R. Conder. New York: AMS Press, 1971 Palestine Pilgrims' Text Society. Library, vol. 12, [no. 1]. Reprinted from the London edition, 1896.

Cotovicus, Joannes. *Itinerarium Hierosolymitanum et Syriacum; in quo variarum gentium mores et instituta, insularum, regionum, urbium situs, una ex prisci recentiorisque saeculi usu, una cum eventis, quae auctori terra marique acciderunt, dilucide recensentur. Accessit Synopsis reipublicae Venete*. Antverpiae, apud H. Verdussium, 1619.

Descriptiones Terrae Sanctae ex saeculo VIII., IX., XII. et XV. nach Hand- und Druckschriften. Ed. Titus Tobler. Leipzig: J.C. Hinrichs, 1874. (Contains: S. Willibaldus, *Commemoratorium de casis Dei*; Bernardus Monachus, *Innominatus VII*; Johannes Wirziburgensis, *Innominatus VIII*; Johannes Poloner, *La citez de Iherusalem*.)

Eusebius of Caesarea, ca. 260–ca. 340. *Eusebius schrift [Peri ton Topikon onomaton ton en te Theia Graphe* (romanized form)]. Ed. Erich Klostermann 1870-1963. Leipzig: [J. C. Hinrichs], 1902.

———. *Chronicle*, Armenian & Latin. [*Eusebi Chronicorum libri duo*]. Ed. Alfred Schoene. Berolini, Weidmannos, 1875-76.

Laurent, J. C. M., tr. *Peregrinatores medii aevi quatuor; Burchardus de Monte Sion, Ricoldus de Monte Crucis, Odoricus de Foro Julii, Wilbrandus de Oldenborg, quorum duos nunc primum ed., duos ad fidem librorum manuscriptorum recensuit J.C.M. Laurent*. Lipsiae, J.C. Hinrichs, 1864. (*See esp.* Ricoldus de Monte Crucis and Odoricus de Foro Julii)

Niccolo, da Poggibonsi (fl. 1345-1350). [*Libro d'Oltramare*] *Viazo da Venesia al sancto Iherusalem, et al monte Sinai, sepulchro de Sancta Chaterina*. Bologna: Giustiniano da Rubiera, 6 Mar. 1500].

Quaresmio, Francesco (1583-1650 or 1656). *Elucidatio terrae sanctae, by Francisci Quaresmii*; brani scelti e tradotti da Sabino De Sandoli. Studium Biblicum Franciscanum. Collectio maior, no. 32. Jerusalem: Franciscan Print. Press, 1989. (Latin and Italian.)

314

Seawulfus, ca. 1102. *Peregrinatio ad Hierosolyman*. Ed. T. S. d'Avezac. (p. 38).

Situ urbis Jerusalem, De. [ca. 1130], in *Les eglises de la Terre Sainte*. Ed. Melchior, Marquis de Vogue et supplement bibliographique par Joshua Prawer. Toronto: Presses de l'Universite de Toronto, 1973. [Reprint of the 1860 ed. published by V. Didron, Paris]. [p. 422]

Suriano, Francesco [1450-ca. 1529]. *Treatise on the Holy Land*. Tr. from the Italian by Theophilus Bellorini and Eugene Hoade. Preface and notes by Bellarmino Bagatti. Publication of the Studium Biblicum Franciscanum, no. 8. Jerusalem, Printed by Franciscan Press, 1949.

Theodericus, of Wurzburg [fl. 1172]. *Libellus de locis sanctis*. Editiones Heidelbergensis ; Heft 18. Ed. von M. L. u. W. Bulst. Heidelberg: Winter, 1976 [p. 101].

Theodosius. *De Situ Terrae Sanctae* in: *Itinera Hierosolymitana saeculi IIII-VIII. Recensuit et commentario critico instruxit Paulus Geyer*. Corpus scriptorum ecclesiasticorum Latinorum, vol. 39. Vindobonae, F. Tempsky, 1898.

Thetmarus, Magister [ca. 1217]. *Iter ad Terram Sanctam*.

Torsello, Marino Sanuto. *Liber secretorvm fidelivm crvcis super Terrae Sanctae recvperatione et conservatione. quo et Terrae Sanctae historia ab origine. & eiusdem vicinarumque prouinciarum geographica descriptio continetur. Cuius auctor Marinvs Sanvtvs dictus Torsellvs patricius venetus. Nunc primum, cum libello eiusdem argumenti, sine auctoris nomine, ex mss. veteribus editus*. Orientalis historiae tomus secundus. Hanoviae: Typis Wechelianis, apud heredes I. Aubrii, 1611. (Vol. 2 of *Gesta Dei per Francos, siue Orientalivm expeditionvm...*, ed. Jacques Bongars.)

Verona, Jacopo da (fl. 1335). *Liber peregrinationis. A cura di Ugo Monneret de Villard*. Il Nuovo Ramusio; raccolta di viaggi, testi e documenti relativi ai rapporti fra l'Europa e l'Oriente, 1. Roma: La Libreria dello Stato, 1950.

Willibaldus, ca. 723. *Itinerarium S. Willibaldi*, vol. 1. Tobler–Molinier.

HEBREW LITERATURE

ירושלמי : שקלים ו'ב'.

קוהלת רבה : ב', יא'.

משנה, עבוה זררה : ג'ז'.

ש'ר חש'ר'ס רבה : א'.

MODERN RESEARCH

Abel, F. M. *Geographie de la Palestine*. Vol. 2. Paris: Librarie Lecoffre, 1933-1938.

Abel, F.-M. (Felix-Marie), 1878-1953.

Arav, Rami. "Et-Tell and el-Araj" " *IEJ* 38 (1988): 187–188.

_____. "Et-Tell and el-Araj" " IEJ 39 (1989): 99–100.

_____. "Bethsaida 1989," *IEJ* 41 (1991): 184–186.

_____. "Bethsaida 1992," *IEJ* 42 (1992): 252–254.

_____. "A Mamluk Drum from Bethsaida," *IEJ* 43 (1993): 241–245.

_____. "Et-Tell (Bethsaida) 1989)," *Excavations and Surveys in Israel* 9, no. 2 (1989–1990): 98–99.

_____, and J. J. Rousseau. "Elusive Bethsaida Recovered," *The Fourth R* 4, no. 1 (January 1991): 1–4.

_____, and J. J. Rousseau. "Bethsaida, Ville Perdue et Retrouvee," *Revue Biblique* (1993): 415–428.

Avi-Yonah, M. *Gazetteer of Roman Palestine*. QEDEM 5. Jerusalem, 1976.

Baldi, P. Donatus. *Enchiridion Locum Sanctorum*. Jerusalem, 1982.

Dalman, Gustaf Hermann. *Sacred Sites and Ways: Studies in the Topography of the Gospels.* New York: Macmillan. 1935.

Kochavi, M., S. Gutman, and C. Epstein. *Judea, Samaria and the Golan: Archaeological Survey, 1967–1968.* [Hebrew]. Jerusalem, 1972.

Kuhn, Heinz-Wolfgang, and Rami Arav. "Bethsaida Excavations: Historical and Archaeological Approaches," in: *The Future of Early Christianity: Essays in Honor of Helmut Koester.* Ed. Birger A. Pearson et al. Minneapolis: Fortress Press, 1991, pp. 77–107.

McCown, Ch. "The Problem of the Site of Bethsaida," *JPOS* 10 (1930): 32–58.

Meistermann, P. *Capharnaum et Bethsaida.* Paris: 1930.

Pixner, Bargil. "The Search for the Lot City of Bethsaida," *Biblical Archaeologist* (December 1985).

Robinson, Edward *Biblical researches in Palestine, and in the Adjacent Regions: A Journal of Travels in the Year 1838, drawn up from the original diaries, with historical illustrations, by Edward Robinson.* Vol. 2. Boston: Crocker and Brewster, 1856; 2d ed., London: Murray, 1856.

Rousseau, J. J., and Rami Arav. *Jesus and His World.* Minneapolis: Fortress Press, 1995.

Schumacher, Gottlieb. *The Jaulan surveyed for the German Society for the Exploration of the Holy Land,* tr. from the Transactions of the German Society. London: R. Bentley, 1888

Smith, George Adam. *Historical Atlas of the Holy Land.* 2d ed. London: Hodder and Stoughton, 1936.

TEXTUAL CRITICISM AND THE CANON OF THE HEBREW BIBLE

Aejmelaeus, A. "What Can We Know about the Hebrew *Vorlage* of the Septuagint?" *Zeitschrift für die Alttestamentliche Wissenschaft* 99 (1987): 58–90.

Ap-Thomas, D. R. *A Primer of Old Testament Text Criticism.* Philadelphia: Fortress Press, 1966.

Barthélemy, D. *Les Devanciers d'Aquila.* Leiden: Brill, 1963.

Bikerman, E. *Studies in Jewish and Christian History,* vol. 1. Leiden: Brill, 1976.

Brown, J. W. *The Rise of Biblical Criticism in America, 1800–1870.* Connecticut: Wesleyan University Press, 1969.

Cross, F. M. *The Ancient Library of Qumran,* chap. 4. New York: Anchor Books, 1961.

_____, and S. Talmon, *Qumran and the History of the Biblical Text.* London and Cambridge: Harvard University Press, 1975.

Engnell, I. *A Rigid Scrutiny: Critical Essays on the Old Testament.* Nashville: Vanderbilt University Press, 1969.

Fishbane, Michael. *Biblical Interpretation in Ancient Israel.* Oxford: Clarendon, 1985.

_____. "Biblical Colophons, Textual Criticism, and Legal Analogies," *The Catholic Biblical Quarterly* 42 (1980): 438–449.

Frerichs, E. S. "The Torah; Canon of Judaism and the Interpretation of Hebrew Scripture," *Horizons in Biblical Theology* 9 (1987): 13–25.

Ginsberg, C. D. *Introduction to the Massoretico–Critical Edition of the Hebrew Bible.* London, 1897.

Goshen–Gottstein, M. H. *The Book of Isaiah: Sample Edition with Introduction.* Jerusalem. 1965.

_____. *The Bible in the Syro–Palestinian Version.* Jerusalem, 1973.

_____. "The Textual Criticism of the Old Testament: Rise, Decline, Rebirth," *Journal of Biblical Literature* 102 (1983): 365–399.

Hayes, J. H., ed. *Old Testament Form Criticism.* San Antonio: Trinity University Press, 1974.

Jellicoe, S. *The Septuagint; and Modern Study.* Oxford: Clarendon, 1968.

Kahle, P. E. *The Cairo Geniza.* London, 1959.

_____. "Untersuchungen zur Geschichte des Pentateuchtextes," *Opera Minora*. Leiden: Brill, 1956, 3–37.

Kenyon, F. M. *The Text of the Greek Bible*. London, 1937.

_____. *Our Bible and the Ancient Manuscript*. New York, 1958.

Klein, R. *Text Criticism of the Old Testament: The Septuagint after Qumran*. Philadelphia: Fortress Press, 1974.

Koch, K. *The Growth of the Biblical Tradition: The Form-Critical Method*. New York: Charles Scribner's Sons, 1969; paperback, 1971.

Kraft, R. A., ed. "Symposium on the Methodology of Textual Criticism in Jewish Greek Scriptures with Special Attention to the Problems in Samuel, Kings," *Septuagint, and Cognate Studies* 2: 2–108.

Noth, M. *The Old Testament World*, chapter 4. Philadelphia: Fortress Press, 1966.

Orlinsky, H. M. "The Septuagint as Holy Writ and the Philosophy of the Translators," *Hebrew Union College Annual* 46 (1975): 74–93.

Soulen, R. N. *Handbook of Biblical Criticism*. Atlanta: John Knox Press, 1981.

Tigay, J. H. *Empirical Models for Bible Criticism*. Philadelphia: Fortress Press, 1985.

Tov, E. "Dimensions of Septuagint; Words," *Revue biblique* 83 (1976): 529–554.

_____. "On 'Pseudo-Variants' in the Septuagint," *Journal of Semitic Studies* 20 (1975):165–177.

Tucker, G. M. *Form-Criticism of the Old Testament*. Philadelphia: Fortress Press, 1971.

Wellhausen, J. *Prolegomena to the History of Ancient Israel*. Edinburgh, 1885; also in paperback.

Wevers, J. M. "The Earliest Witness to the LXX:Deuteronomy," *The Catholic Biblical Quarterly* 39 (1977): 240–244.

Archaeology and the Text of the Hebrew Bible

Freedman, D. N., and J. C. Greenfield, eds. *New Directions in Biblical Archaeology*. New York: Doubleday Anchor, 1971.

Kenyon, K. *Archaeology in the Holy Land*. New York: Praeger, 1960.

McCown, C. C. *The Ladder of Progress in Palestine*. New York, 1943.

Noth, M. *The Old Testament World*. Philadelphia: Fortress 1966.

Pritchard, J. B., ed. *The Ancient Near East in Pictures Relating to the Old Testament*. Princeton: University Press, 1969.

_____, ed. *Ancient Near Eastern Texts Relating to the Old Testament*. Princeton: Princeton University Press, 1969.

_____, ed. *The Ancient Near East: An Anthology of Texts and Pictures*, 2 vols. Princeton: Princeton University Press, 1965, 1976.

Sanders, J. A., ed. *Near Eastern Archaeology in the Twentieth Century* [Glueck Volume.] New York: Doubleday, 1970.

Thomas, D. W. *Archaeology and Old Testament Study*. Oxford: Clarendon, 1967.

Wright, G. E. *Biblical Archaeology*. Philadelphia: Westminster Press, 1962.

_____, ed. *The Bible and the Ancient Near East: Essays in Honor of W. F. Albright*. New York: Doubleday, 1961; Doubleday paperback edition, 1965.

History and Religion in the Biblical Period

Ackroyd, P. *Exile and Restoration*. Philadelphia: Westminster Press, 1968.

Albright, W. F. *The Biblical Period from Abraham to Ezra*. New York: Harper and Row, 1963.

Alt, A. *Essays on Old Testament History and Religion*. Garden City: Anchor, 1968.

Bickerman, E. *From Ezra to the Last of the Maccabees*, New York: Schocken, 1962.

Bright, J. *A History of Israel*. Philadelphia: Westminster Press, 1972.

Buber, M. *The Prophetic Faith*. New York: Macmillan, 1949; paperback: Harper Torchbook, 1960.

Cross, F. M. *Canaanite Myth and Hebrew Epic*. Cambridge: Harvard University Press, 1972.

De Vaux, R. *The Bible and the Ancient Near East*. Garden City: Doubleday, 1971.

Gaster, T. H. *Thespis: Ritual, Myth, and Drama in the Ancient Near East*. New York: Henry Schuman, 1950.

Hanson, P. D. *The Dawn of Apocalyptic*. Philadelphia: Fortress Press, 1975.

Heidel, A. *The Babylonian Genesis*. Chicago: University of Chicago Press, 1951; paperback: Phoenix Books, 1963.

Herrmann, S. *A History of Israel in Old Testament Times*. Philadelphia: Fortress Press, 1975.

Heschel, A. J. *The Prophets*. New York: Harper and Row, 1963.

Kaufmann, Y. *The Religion of Israel*. Chicago: University of Chicago Press, 1960; paperback: New York: Schocken, 1972.

Kraus, H. J. *Worship in Israel*. Richmond,Va.: John Knox Press, 1965.

Mazar, B. *The World History of the Jewish People:* vol. 2, *Patriarchs;* vol. 3, *Judges*. Rutgers: University Press, 1970–71.

Miller, J. M. *The Old Testament and the Historian*. Philadelphia: Fortress Press, 1976.

Noth, M. *The Laws in the Pentateuch and Other Essays*. Philadelphia: Fortress Press, 1967.

Orlinsky, H., ed. *Interpreting the Prophetic Tradition*. Cincinnati: Hebrew Union College Press, 1961.

Patai, R. *The Hebrew Goddess*. New York: Avon, 1978.

Pedersen, J. *Israel*. Oxford: Oxford University Press, 1926.

Ringgren, H. *Israelite Religion*. Philadelphia: Fortress Press, 1966.

Swidler, L. *Biblical Affirmations of Woman*. Philadelphia: Westminster Press, 1979.

Reference Works on the Bible

Black, M., ed., and H. H. Rowley. *Peake's Commentary on the Bible*. London: Nelson, 1962.

Brown, R. E., et al. *The Jerome Biblical Commentary*. Englewood Cliffs: Prentice Hall, 1968.

Buttrick, G. A., et al. *The Interpreter's Dictionary of the Bible*. Nashville: Abingdon, 1963; Supplement, 1976.

Oxford Annotated Bible, ed. Herbert G. May and Bruce M. Metzger. New York: Oxford University Press, 1962.

Judaism in the Hellenistic, Greco–Roman, Second Temple Period

The Apocrypha and Pseudepigrapha of the Old Testament, 2 vols. Ed. and trans. R. H. Charles et al. Oxford: Clarendon, 1913.

Jewish Apocryphal Literature, 7 vols.. Ed. S. Zeitlin. Philadelphia: Dropsie University, Harper and Brothers, and E. J. Brill, 1950–1972.

Avi-Yonah, M., ed. *The Herodian Period: World History of the Jewish People*, vol. 7. New Brunswick, N.J.: Rutgers University Press, 1975.

Baron, S. W. *A Social and Religious History of the Jews*, vols. 1 and 2. New York: Columbia University Press, 1952.

Charlesworth, J. H. *The Pseudepigrapha and Modern Research*. Missoula, Mt.: Scholars Press, 1976.

Cross, F. M. *The Ancient Library of Qumran and Modern Biblical Studies*. New York: Doubleday, 1961.

Driver, G. R. *The Judean Scrolls: The Problem and a Solution*. Oxford: Blackwell, 1965.

Dodd, C. H. *The Bible and the Greeks*. London: Hodder and Stoughton, 1935.

Feldman, L. H., ed. *Scholarship on Philo and Josephus, 1937-62*. New York: Yeshiva University, 1963.

Frey, J. *Corpus Inscriptionum Judaicarum*, vol. 1. Reprinted, New York: Ktav, 1975.

Freyne, S. *Galilee from Alexander the Great to Hadrian: 323 BCE to 135 CE*. Notre Dame, Ind.: Michael Glazier and University of Notre Dame Press, 1980.

Goodenough, E. R. *An Introduction to Philo Judaeus*. Oxford: Basil Blackwood, 1962.

_____. *The Politics of Philo Judaeus*. New Haven: Yale University Press, 1938.

_____. *Jewish Symbols in the Greco-Roman Period*, 12 vols. New York: Pantheon, 1953-65.

Hadas, M. *Hellenistic Culture: Fusion and Diffusion*. New York: Columbia University Press, 1959.

Hengel, M. *Judaism and Hellenism: Studies in Their Encounter in Palestine during the Early Hellenistic Period*, 2 vols. Trans. J. Bowden. Philadelphia: Fortress Press, 1974.

Josephus, Flavius. [*Works*, English & Greek, 1958- .] Loeb Classical Library. 9 vols. Cambridge, Mass.: Harvard University Press; London: W. Heineman, 1958-1965.

Leon, H. J. *The Jews of Ancient Rome*. Philadelphia: Jewish Publication Society of America, 1960.

Mantel, H. *Studies in the History of the Sanhedrin*. Cambridge, Mass.: Harvard University Press, 1965.

Meshorer, Y. *Jewish Coins of the Second Temple Period*. Tel Aviv: Am Hassefer, 1967.

Pagels, E. *The Gnostic Gospels*. New York: Random House, 1979.

Philo of Alexandria. [*Works*. English & Greek] Loeb Classical Library. 12 vols. Cambridge, Mass.: Harvard University Press; London: W. Heineman.

Rabin, C. *Qumran Studies*. New York: Schocken, 1957, 1975.

Rhoads, D. M. *Israel in Revolution, 6-74 CE: A Political History Based on the Writings of Josephus*. Philadelphia: Fortress Press, 1976.

Rostovtzeff, Michael. *The Social and Economic History of the Hellenistic World*. Oxford: Clarendon, 1941.

_____. *The Social and Economic History of the Roman Empire*, revised by P. M. Fraser. Oxford: Clarendon: 1957.

Russell, D. S. *The Method and Message of Jewish Apocalyptic, 200 BC-AD 100*. Philadelphia: Westminster Press, 1964.

Safrai, S., and M. Stern. *The Jewish People in the First Century: Historical Geography, Political History, Social, Cultural, and Religious Life and Institutions*, 2 vols. Philadelphia: Fortress Press, 1974-1976.

Sandmel, S. *Judaism and Christian Beginnings*. New York: Oxford University Press, 1978.

Schürer, E. *The History of the Jewish People in the Age of Jesus Chris, 175 BC-AD 135*, rev. ed. Ed. Geza Vermes and Fergus Millar. Edinburgh: T. and T. Clark, 1973—.

Smallwood, E. M. *The Jews under Roman Rule from Pompey to Diocletian*. Studies in Judaism in Late Antiquity 20. Leiden: E. J. Brill, 1981.

Stern, M., ed. and trans. *Greek and Latin Authors on Jews and Judaism*, 3 vols. Jerusalem: Israel Academy of Sciences and Humanities, 1974-1984.

Tcherikover, V. *Hellenistic Civilization and the Jews*. Translated from the Hebrew by S. Appelbaum. Philadelphia: Jewish Publication Society of America, 1959.

Tcherikover, V., A. Fuks, and M. Stern, eds. *Corpus Papyrorum Judaicarum*, 3 vols. Cambridge, Mass.: Harvard University Press, 1957-1964.

Vermes, G., ed. and trans. *The Dead Sea Scrolls in English*, 2d ed. Baltimore, Md.: Penguin Books, 1975.

_____. *The Dead Sea Scrolls: Qumran in Perspective*. London: Collins, 1977.

Wolfson, H. A. *Philo: Foundations of Religious Philosophy in Judaism, Christianity, and Islam*, 2 vols. Cambridge, Mass.: Harvard University Press, 1947.

Yadin, Yigael. *Masada: Herod's Fortress and the Zealots' Last Stand.* New York: Random House, 1966.

_____. *Bar Kokhba.* New York: Random House, 1971.

Zeitlin, Solomon. *The Rise and Fall of the Judean State,* vol. 1: *332-37 BCE*, vol. 2: *37 BCE-66 CE.* vol. 3: *66 CE-120 CE*. Philadelphia: Jewish Publication Society of America, 1962–1978.

_____. *The Dead Sea Scrolls and Modern Scholarship,* Philadelphia: Dropsie College, 1956.

CLASSICAL RABBINIC JUDAISM

Alon, G. *The Jews in Their Land in the Talmudic Age.* Cambridge, Mass.: Harvard University Press, 1989.

Avi-Yonah, M. *The Jews of Palestine: A Political History from the Bar Kokhba War to the Arab Conquest.* Jerusalem: Magnes Press, 1984.

Baron, S. W. *A Social and Religious History of the Jews,* vols. 2-5. New York: Columbia University Press, 1952.

Cohen, B. *Jewish and Roman Law,* 2 vols. New York: United Synagogue Books, 1966.

Finkelstein, L. *Akiba: Scholar, Saint, and Martyr.* Cleveland: William Collins and World Publishing, 1962.

Ginzberg, L. *The Legends of the Jews,* 7 vols. Philadelphia: Jewish Publication Society of America, 1909–1938.

_____. *On Jewish Law and Lore.* New York: Meridian Books, 1962.

Guttmann, A. *Rabbinic Judaism in the Making: The Halakhah from Ezra to Judah I.* Detroit: Wayne State University Press, 1970.

Halivni, D. Weiss, *Midrash, Mishnah, and Gemara.* Cambridge, Mass.: Harvard University, 1986.

Lauterbach, J. Z. *Rabbinic Essays.* Cincinnati: Hebrew Union College Press, 1951.

Lieberman, S. *Greek in Jewish Palestine.* New York: Feldheim, 1956.

_____. *Hellenism in Jewish Palestine.* New York: Ktav, 1962.

Mechilta on Exodus. Ed. and trans. J. Neusner. Atlanta: Scholars Press, 1988.

MIDRASH, MISHNAH, TALMUD

Midrash Rabbah, translated into English with notes, glossary, and indices, 10 vols. ed. H. Freedman and M. Simon. London: Soncino Press, 1939.

The Mishnah. Ed. and trans. H. Danby. Oxford: Clarendon, 1933.

Neusner, J. *Early Rabbinic Judaism: Historical Studies in Religion, Literature, and Art,* Studies in Judaism in Late Antiquity, 13. Leiden: E. J. Brill, 1975.

_____. *First-Century Judaism in Crisis: Yohanan ben Zakkai and the Renaissance of Torah* . Nashville: Abingdon Press, 1975.

_____. *From Politics to Piety: The Emergence of Pharisaic Judaism.* Englewood Cliffs, N.J.: Prentice-Hall, 1973.

_____. *Invitation to the Talmud: A Teaching Book.* New York: Harper and Row, 1973.

_____ *Talmudic Judaism in Sasanian Babylonia: Essays and Studies,* Studies in Judaism in Late Antiquity, 14. Leiden: E. J. Brill, 1976.

_____. *There We Sat Down: Talmudic Judaism in the Making.* Nashville: Abingdon Press, 1972.

Rivkin, E. *A Hidden Revolution: The Pharisees' Search for the Kingdom Within.* Nashville: Abingdon Press, 1978.

Safrai, S. "The Era of the Mishna and the Talmud 70-640" in *A History of the Jewish People.* Ed. H. H. Ben-Sasson. London: Weidenfeld and Nicolson, 1976, pp. 307-382.

Sifra on Leviticus. Ed. and trans., J. Neusner. Atlanta: Scholars Press, 1988.

Sifrei on Deuteronomy. Ed. and trans., J. Neusner. Atlanta: Scholars Press, 1987.

Sifrei on Numbers. Ed. and trans., J. Neusner. Altanta: Scholars Press, 1986.

Strack, H. L. *Introduction to the Talmud and Midrash,* trans. from the 5th German edition. Philadelphia: Jewish Publication Society of America, 1931.

Swidler, L. *Women in Judaism: The Status of Women in Formative Judaism.* Metuchen, N.J.: Scarecrow Press, 1976.

The Babylonian Talmud, 35 vols. Ed. I. Epstein. London: Soncino Press, 1935–1948.

The Talmud of the Land of Israel. Ed. J. Neusner. 35 vols. projected. Chicago: University of Chicago, 1982—.

The Tosefta, Translated from the Hebrew. Ed. J. Neusner, 5 vols. New York: Ktav, 1977–80.

Tosefta and Tosefta Ki-fshutah [Hebrew], 13 vols. critical edition. Ed. S. Lieberman. New York: Jewish Theological Seminary, 1955–1982.

Urbach, E. E. *The Sages: Their Concepts and Beliefs,* 2 vols. trans. from the Hebrew by Israel Abrahams. Jerusalem: Magnes Press, 1975.

BETHSAIDA IN THE GOSPELS

Matthew 11:21.
Mark 6:45; 8:22.
Luke 9:10; 10:13.
John 1:44; 12:21.

EARLY CHRISTIANITY AND JUDAISM

Brandon, S. G. F. *Jesus and the Zealots: A Study of the Political Factor in Primitive Christianity.* New York: Charles Scribner's Sons, 1967.

Frend, W. H. C. *The Rise of Christianity.* London: Darton, Longman and Todd, 1984.

Sanders, E. P. *Paul; and Palestinian Judaism: A Comparison of Patterns of Religion.* Philadelphia: Fortress Press, 1977.

Sandmel, S. A. *Jewish Understanding of the New Testament.* New York: Ktav 1974.

_____. *We Jews and Jesus.* New York: Oxford University Press, 1965.

Stendahl, K. *Paul among Jews and Gentiles.* Philadelphia: Fortress Press, 1976.

Vermes, G. *Jesus the Jew: A Historian's Reading of the Gospels.* London: Collins, 1973.

Index of Scripture References

Index of Rabbinical Writings

Index of Ancient Writings

Index

Composed at
Thomas Jefferson University Press
Kirksville, Missouri 63501

Book design, cover, and title page, Tim Rolands
Composition, Paula Presley
Manufactured by Edwards Brothers, Ann Arbor, Michigan

Text is set in ITC Stone Serif 10/13
with SuperGreek and SuperHebrew from Linguist's Software
Display in Monotype Centaur

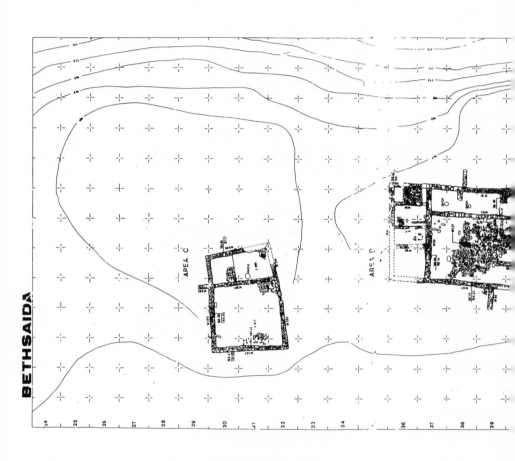

BETHSAIDA

AREA C

AREA D